MONROE COLLEGE LIBRARY
3 7340 0107
WITHDRAWN
D0627499
THE
TIN
NS
UNDERSTANDING THEIR LEGACY

THE LATIN AMERICANS

UNDERSTANDING THEIR LEGACY

Randall Hansis
North Adams State College

Boston, Massachusetts Burr Ridge, Illinois Dubuque, Iowa
Madison, Wisconsin New York, New York San Francisco, California
St. Louis, Missouri

McGraw-Hill

A Division of The ***McGraw·Hill*** *Companies*

This book was set in Times Roman by ComCom, Inc.
The editors were Nancy Blaine and Jill Gordon;
the production supervisor was Paula Keller;
the design manager was Chuck Carson.
The cover was designed by Lisa Cicchetti.
The photo editor was Anne Manning.
Project supervision was done by Editorial Services of New England, Inc.
R.R. Donnelly & Sons Company was printer and binder.

Cover photograph by Sr. Reynaldo Zabe Michel, part of the Museo
Regional de Antropología, Villahermosa, Tabasco., Mexico.

THE LATIN AMERICANS

Understanding Their Legacy

This book is printed on acid-free paper.

3 4 5 6 7 8 9 0 DOC DOC 9 0 9 8

ISBN 0-07-026081-8

Library of Congress Cataloging-in-Publication Data

Hansis, Randall.
The Latin Americans : understanding their legacy / Randall Hansis.
p. cm.
Includes bibliographical references and index.
ISBN 0-07-026081-8
1. Latin America—Civilization. 2. Ethnicity—Latin America.
I. Title.
F1408.3.H325 1997
980—dc20 96-21487

CHAPTER-OPENING PHOTOS

Chapter 1: Nik Wheeler/Corbis Media. Chapter 2: From *A Description of the Kingdom of New Spain* by Sr. Don Pedro Alonso O'Crouley, 1774. Chapter 3: Geo. G. Bain, Library of Congress/Corbis Media. Chapter 4: Macduff Everton/Corbis Media. Chapter 5: Jeremy Horner/Corbis Media. Chapter 6: Nik Wheeler/Corbis Media. Chapter 7: Sergio Dorantes/Corbis Media. Chapter 8: UPI/Corbis-Bettmann. Chapter 9: Reuters/Corbis-Bettmann. Chapter 10: Spencer Grant/Photo Researchers.

ABOUT THE AUTHOR

RANDALL HANSIS has been teaching Latin American Civilization introductory freshman courses at North Adams State College, Massachusetts, for a quarter century. This book results from experiments with effectively teaching Latin America as well as research and writing. Professor Hansis came to North Adams State with a Ph.D. in History from the University of New Mexico (1970), where he studied with Edwin Lieuwen, Martin C. Needler, Troy S. Floyd, and Foster Rhea Dulles. He earlier obtained a masters degree from Claremont Graduate School after receiving a B.S. from California State Polytechnic University in Pomona. In 1979, a National Endowment for the Humanities summer seminar allowed him to study with Stanley R. Ross at the University of Texas in Austin. In 1996, he attended a National Endowment for the Humanities seminar, "America and the Sea," with Benjamin Labaree at Mystic Seaport in Mystic, Connecticut.

To Teachers,
Mine, and Now Yours,
Especially
Werner Marti, Virginia Hamilton
Adair, Douglass Adair, Jr.,
Edwin Lieuwen,
and, Through His Students,
Herbert Eugene Bolton.

CONTENTS

PREFACE

This book addresses a question: What do North Americans need to know to understand Latin Americans and their region? Answering this query necessitates much information and significant comprehension. Any quality response must not only instruct, but correct a host of misconceptions. It must also engage many disciplines.

A comprehensive explanation of Latin America and Latin Americans must transcend the normal boundaries of academic scholarship and engage bits and pieces of history, anthropology, economics, philosophy, and literature. If past events best explain an important aspect of Latin America, history should be used. When ethnology or archaeology provide more appropriate insights, anthropology should be discussed. The same holds for economics, government, sociology, or literary studies. Even personal anecdotes provide pieces of the puzzle, sometimes filling a gap with colorful illustration. Since the region is large and Latin American identity complex, a singular academic domain cannot explain the region or its people. Tools from many scholarly fields are needed. Thus, this book is neither history, nor anthropology, nor economics, but parts of all used as they are needed. It is multidisciplinary as it seeks to explain Latin America and Latin Americans to a North American audience.

Learning about another society entails much more than a factual base. When new information about another society is presented without discussing a cultural context, it can be unconsciously misunderstood as the already familiar. Students seriously learning about Latin America for the first time often rely on personal references to conceptualize our hemispheric neighbors, paralleling apparently similar events in Latin America with supposed equivalents in the United States. Timeworn (and often erroneous) ideas about English colonization, relations with aboriginal peoples, U.S. frontier settlement, and national expansion preempt a novel perception of how similar challenges were met differently in Latin America. When contrasts are made, ethnocentrism emerges. Deeply held judgments about supposedly superior North American intent and achievement derive from Hollywood, television, advertising, and the unconscious lessons of earlier schooling. Self-righteousness becomes an extra burden that hinders clear understanding. Because additional data are processed alongside what is already known, assumed, or felt, new information can reinforce misunderstanding rather than generate more accurate perception.

Understanding Latin Americans requires familiarity with themes and concepts as well as facts and data. To comprehend the region's history, one must know events, statistics, chronologies, and biographies but also must fully appreciate the importance of machismo, the family, spirituality, and what it means to be mestizo. To understand Latin American ethnology, one must consider the historic themes of elitism and servitude, how changing international markets first brought Africans to grow sugar, then European peasants to plant wheat. To know why the region endures significant poverty, students must explore the long-term relationships among ecology, technology, and imperial exploitation. And no understanding of Latin American identity is complete without exploring how artistic expression has shaped its consciousness. To comprehend Latin America one must see designs as well as data. And major themes are the central structure of this book.

Perspective is also important, and learning new vision is sometimes disconcerting. A hierarchical Eurocentric view of the world—a "top-down" accounting of who supposedly matters most—has long been common and comfortable. The early explorers searched for both natural resources and *civilis* (civil authority): the political base of power. The "discoverers" wanted to know who had the authority to transfer sovereignty over the land to them. Too often, subsequent scholarly interpretation of Latin America unconsciously assumed this European perspective: tracing the twisting thread of political authority from Indigen empires to individual conquerors, to colonial regimes, to independence leaders, to national governments, to revolutionary regimes, to elected officials, and so on. What mattered most was who had power, or at least who claimed sovereignty. But a Eurocentric accounting of legitimacy is not fully appropriate for understanding all of Latin America. Daily life—for poor and rich, illiterate and learned alike—was the real cauldron for both preserving tradition and creating change. What populations ate and sang, how multitudes worked and prayed, and the mixing of races and cultures matter more than singular chiefs, kings, viceroys, generals, or presidents. And circumscribing the decisions of all—crown and citizen, owner and slave—were powerful parameters such as markets, technologies, ideologies, and the very contours of Latin America's terrain. Even important people and watershed events were molded by contexts of culture, time, and place.

Explanations of ecology and technology need particular attention. Political leadership and military encounters may occasionally alter the flow of human behavior, but they appear incidental compared with the underlying currents of changing materials, methodologies, and relationships. For these reasons, we should better understand the stuff of daily life: everyday tools and techniques and how humans repeatedly manipulate natural environments to achieve values. More important than Moctezuma were his corn-fed armies. More important than Cortés were his dogs, horses, steel weapons, and European disease. Too often, texts have presented historical actors with great emphasis on individual will. Yet powerful systemic factors limit, allow, or encourage all human action. More important than an individual are the technologies, techniques, and values that allow one group to exploit natural environments and dominate other societies. Those who control technologies command both resources and the course of human events.

Other perspectives also need vision. Although feminism is now widely acknowledged as legitimate, it is too often an artifice of interpretation, an "add-on" to the story of male power. What needs to change is the attitude that "women were also there." Since half the agents of human tradition and change have been female, stories must be told that acknowledge women as central players. Women selected seeds for planting as settled agriculture moved humankind from barbarism to civilization. Indigenous values of a feminine earth still imbue Latin American philosophy. White women in the Americas determined the race, ethnicity, legitimacy, and status of the conquering caste. Grandmothers helped overthrow military tyrants in modern Argentina. And in Latin America, where family is the central institution, women are the center of family. This narration values the mothering of slave women, the idealism and political realism of Queen Isabella, the symbolism of the Virgin of Guadalupe, and the managerial skills of modern Latin American women. Understanding Latin America entails comprehending the profound role of the region's women.

In addition to advancing themes and perspectives, this book encourages readers to pursue different avenues of learning. It seeks a cognition born of inductive observation, description, and sensual experience as well as deductive scholarship, reading, and intellectual reflection. What one reads, or is told, or sees on a screen has meaning only as it mixes in the mind and heart with direct personal experience. Since knowing begins in sensory perceptions—sight, sound, taste, touch, and smell—then the purpose of deductive learning from lectures, discussion, and the written word should be to enhance the primary experiences of life itself. By reading and thinking with greater knowledge and understanding, one should shop, travel, eat, work, and play with greater awareness. After reading this book, bananas and store-bought strawberries should be considered differently. If one truly learns from these pages, then heating a home, driving one's car, and playing baseball will be cause for reflection. Likewise, if a person travels to Latin America or has Latin American neighbors, reading this book should add meaning to the experience and relationship.

Hopefully, this work combines the best of scholarly study and my own direct observation, balancing the information and insights of others with personal learning. It derives from much reading, research, and graduate study. It has been nurtured through travel and living in Mexico, Spain, and Central America, as well as southern California, New Mexico, and Texas. Twenty-five years of teaching and a lifetime of associating with Latin Americans also fill its pages.

This book has been difficult to compose because it straddles a balance between generalization and specialization, pattern and particulars, overview and case study. Because it surveys half a billion contemporary Latin Americans (and U.S. Latinos) and their ancestors, scattered over two continents and dozens of centuries, it may at times appear contradictory. With such varied conditions, contrasts exist. At other times it may seem too generalized, without detail and specifics. This arises from trying to create a framework, from supplying a skeletal structure serving readers who will later augment and alter the design of their personal understanding with even greater knowledge.

As a piece of literature, this book seeks to be a story, a series of stories. It uses nomenclature when such terms convey a particular meaning or insight. Part of understanding another people is "walking in their shoes," adopting their vision, framing consciousness with their vocabulary. This work also visits museums and markets, and introduces shamans and saints. It seeks to engage a contemporary readership with strong imagery, mixing concept with description, statistics with symbols. This narration also relates accounts as an elder presents lessons to succeeding generations. It uses metaphors and depiction, seeking to illustrate as a means to understand life.

This book is designed for multidisciplinary courses introducing Latin America to college or college preparatory persons seriously studying Latin America for the first time. It is also helpful for individuals grounded in particular academic disciplines who want a cultural context, conceptual framework, or broader overview of Latin America and its people. It can also help explain the region or local Latin American populations to those desiring better understanding of the news, traveling the region, or getting to know an acquaintance. It should certainly further the comprehension of persons who read Latin American novels and poems, or those who view its films and art. It is not meant to supplement standard histories, anthropology texts, or academic approaches but to complement them, to add cultural, historical, and economic perspective to chronologies, surveys, or monographs.

In answering the question of what do North Americans need to know to understand Latin Americans and their region, this book often alludes to North America itself. Frequent comparisons to events or places in the United States or Canada are intended to give North American readers a basis of personal comparison, a bridge between their known world and new knowledge concerning Latin America. North Americans need to understand their own world better as they better understand Latin Americans.

Finally, this work hopes to serve Americans throughout the hemisphere, from Canada to Chile, Alaska to Argentina. Increasingly, in economics, culture, travel, and through migration, the regions are mixing. Latin Americans deserve a better appreciation by their North American neighbors. They have suffered from neglect, bias, and myopia. And North Americans, for their own sake, need to understand Latin Americans more accurately and completely. Old relationships are ending and new associations have begun. Latin Americans migrate to the United States, and North Americans retire to Mexico and Costa Rica. NAFTA and peacekeeping are replacing commercial exploitation and military domination. For the betterment of all, future relationships should be based on quality knowledge and more honest understanding.

ACKNOWLEDGMENTS

No person is an island. As author, I am the medium, the facilitator, the creator. But bits and pieces of others are here. Creation is as much collective gathering as individual expression. Most contributors remain anonymous, having engaged in conversations and discussions that quietly formed perspective and understanding. Particularly important are many Latin Americans met during travel, and as colleagues and students. Other contributors are identifiable.

Family comes first. My wife, Roma, and sons, Ryan and Evan, have endured almost a decade of dad doing "his thing." They are the principle witnesses—and victims—of a long and difficult process. Good friend Cindy Jones was also always supportive.

North Adams State College is only one of many small public schools that struggle to achieve excellence in the face of limited resources. It succeeds due to the endless dedication of its staff: hardworking professors, but equally dedicated service personnel. While preparing students, these many individuals also challenge each other to achieve excellence. I sincerely thank the following colleagues: Bob Bence, Dan Connerton, Matt Silliman, Tim Jay, David Langston, Mike Sabol, and Dan Daniels. Tom Aceto as President and Ray Rodrigues as Academic Vice President have been encouraging and supportive. But the most eager to see this book published are college service personnel who have witnessed its evolution over a decade. Among them are Carol Robare, Bettina Nadeau, Karen Lillie, and Lisa Milanesi. The greatest resource of North Adams State College is its students, and many have road tested and helped reengineer this book. The most helpful have been Sandra Mullan-Oliva, Marjorie Belizaire, María Magdelena Agosto González (talented Maggie), Lisette Ramos, Nancy Edgren, Chris Nolan, Kevin McInnis, Jennifer Hickey, Ann Mottarella, and Jennifer Harrington. I also wish to thank Brother Paul Beaudin of St. Lucy's Academy in Spanish Harlem for both his critical reading and so many years of helping me learn about a special community. *Gracias* also to former students Claire Dignan and Lori Lovezzola for helping teach their former teacher when I visited them in Guatemala. Special gratitude goes to Leon Peters, an artist in his own right, who occasionally crunches numbers into shapes. He contructed the maps and figures for this book.

Latin Americanist colleagues have been invaluable during my writing of this work. I am appreciative of Tulane University's Karen Bracken and Matt Wirzberger, the latter a former North Adams State student and immensely important as this book materialized. As an academic reviewer, Tulane's Alex Coles has been a genius with his sympathetic and substantive suggestions for every chapter. Another Costa Rican to whom I am profoundly indebted is Marcía Watson. Her year of teaching at North Adams State College as a Fulbright scholar has had an impact on this project far greater than either of us initially realized. At Northern Arizona University, Miguel Vásquez offered important encouragement. I also wish to thank the following academic reviewers chosen by McGraw-Hill: Virginia Garrard-Burnett, University of Texas; Roberto Márquez, Mount Holyoke College; Louis A. Pérez, Jr., University of North Carolina at Chapel Hill; Randy Stoecker, University of Toledo; and Charles Wood, University of Texas at Austin.

The staff at McGraw-Hill has been wonderful. I am deeply thankful for the discerning judgment of Jill Gordon, Nancy Blaine, and Phil Butcher. Together with Amy Smeltzley, they have been supportive and patient. Special thanks goes to Brian McKean, an early guardian angel, and Steve Boillot, who began the process when he challenged me to write something people would want to read.

Finally, particular appreciation goes to Louis A. Pérez, Jr. As an exemplary scholar and *buen amigo,* Lou helped make this book happen—more than he realizes.

1

PANORAMAS OF PLACE AND TIME: PORTRAIT OF A REGION

In the past I have written . . . about my return from those new regions which . . . can be called a new world . . . . I have discovered a continent in those southern regions . . . .

Amerigo Vespucci, chronicler, 1503[1]

Today, Mexico City is the largest metropolitan area in the world, with a projected population of thirty million by the year 2000.

Peter Winn, scholar, 1992[2]

Latin American legacies encompass an area almost three times grander than the United States. They derive from 30,000 years of human history. And they characterize a diverse population twice larger than the population of Anglo-America.

Place and time have formed Latin America's legacies. Geology, geography, and climate interact like factors in mathematical equations, affecting all human activity. But time—and the technologies and thinking particular to centuries ago or yesterday—has also created unique outcomes of power, profit, and prestige. The cumulative result of such natural and human interaction is modern Latin America—and the complex legacies of its diverse peoples.

Latin American space encompasses breadth, height, and enveloping atmosphere, all of which influence human behavior. The region is two-thirds of a hemisphere, spanning half the globe's latitudes and one-quarter its longitudes. Where continental plates collide—along the Pacific Rim and under the Caribbean Sea—huge mountains surge to great heights. Lowland rain forests—the earth's largest—feed the world's broadest river, the Amazon. Regional deserts include the Atacama of northern Chile, with no recorded rainfall. More than extremes, Latin America is also fertile plains: the pampas of southern South America and the central valley of Chile are among the most productive farm regions on earth. Agriculture also thrives on rich volcanic soils scattered across the region. Joining mountains and rain forests are vast expanses of undulating hills. This massive and varied space forms a stage for the region's human drama.

Latin America's human story unfolds as historical tides. The broadest are three: native civilizations, European colonialism, and almost two centuries of national autonomy. Together these three eras form 1500 generations of succeeding aspirations and accomplishments, with each sequential society reworking and bequeathing inherited legacies to its successors. Past behaviors and precedents continually mold later human actions as surely as do the region's distinctive patterns of rock, distance, height, and heat.

From place and past, modern Latin America emerges into popular consciousness as a complex of mythical image and factual reality. Posters and postcards portray lush tropical islands and snowcapped mountains, boulevards curving around luxury hotels and paths twisting among hillside shanties. Images of exotic jungle fauna somehow mix in the human mind with those of parched desert flora. Spacious estates seem to coexist with congested cities. Portraits from time fill a jumbled album: of naked natives greeting Columbus, of armored conquistadores astride their mounts, of friars in Spanish missions, of decorated dictators and scruffy revolutionaries, of noisy village markets and boat people fleeing Haiti and Cuba. Cultural sights and sounds intermingle: the music of carnival and fiestas, the taste of tacos and margaritas, the color of piñatas and ponchos, the movement of matadors and tango dancers.

But Latin America's realities exceed even its profuse images. Here economic resources are among the world's richest: from early silver and sugar to present petroleum and productivity. Industrious people once dug mines and tended plantations. Today they build automobiles in some of the world's largest factories and manage four of the earth's ten largest cities, including mammoth Mexico City. The wealth produced is shared unevenly among small groups of fantastically rich families, the many poor, and foreign societies, particularly the United States. Understanding Latin America has always involved contrasts: joining image to information, fact to fantasy, data to description, bridging extremes. A better understanding begins by reviewing the region's physical environment.

PHYSICAL SPACE: SIZE AND SHAPE

Despite occasional excellence, no map or globe projects the earth's real size. And modern metaphors claiming that the earth is shrinking belie the planet's undiminished magnitude. The size of the western hemisphere alone becomes evident in comparing new world dimensions.

In size, proportions, and population, Latin America dwarfs the already large United States. Just shy of 9 million square miles, the area of Latin America is about two-and-one-half times larger than the United States, which measures about 3.6 million square miles. Latin America's largest nation, Portuguese-speaking Brazil, is 3.2 million square miles, an area equivalent to the United States minus Alaska. Spanish America, composed of eighteen nations, fills more than 5.5 million square miles. The combined size of Argentina and Bolivia equals half that of the American "lower forty-eight." Latin America is very large, and this great size fosters diversity.

Table 1-1 lists Latin American nations by area, from the largest to the smallest. Comparisons with North America illustrate dimensions.[3] Table 1-1 reveals size and similarities rather than differences and diversities. Brazil is half of South America, the largest nation in Latin America, but is Portuguese rather than Spanish in language and legacy. Shapes contrast. While Cuba compares to Tennessee in area, it spans the distance between New York City and St. Louis. Not apparent on this chart are the effects of topography and climate. For example, although Guatemala's size is comparable to that of Ohio, the midwestern U.S. state has a rather uniform topography and climate, while Guatemala is highly complex. Also lacking from such a table are contrasts with neighbors. Guatemala is much more distinct from Honduras, Mexico, Belize, or El Salvador than is Ohio from Kentucky, Indiana, or Michigan. This table measures area but only as a mathematical quotient.

In Latin America, linear distances are also great. Corner to corner the contiguous United States is about 2700 miles, measured from Seattle to Miami or San Diego to Eastport, Maine. Expanses in Latin America double that, from Tijuana, Mexico, to Rio de Janeiro, or Cuba to Chile's southern tip, straight lines trace one-fifth the earth's circumference. And the ridge of mountains winding from northern Mexico to southern South America—outlining the "backbone" of Latin America—is 8000 miles long: a length equaling one-third the earth's circumference. The Caribbean islands—if superimposed on the United States—would arc from Salt Lake City to Washington, D.C. In Latin America, elongated nations like Mexico and Chile extend lesser area into greater distance. Although Mexico is one-fifth the size of the United States in area, crossing Mexico from Tijuana to Cancún nonetheless approximates traveling from Philadelphia to Los Angeles. But Chile presents the world's greatest contrast: less than one-tenth the size of the United States, Chile would reach from northern Labrador, Canada, into the Caribbean Sea if located in North America. Of course,

TABLE 1-1
LATIN AMERICAN NATIONS BY AREA

Nation	Area, 1000 sq mi	Approximately
Brazil	3286	1/5 western hemisphere
Argentina	1100	1/3 United States
Mexico	764	1/5 United States
Peru	496	Twice the Midwest
Colombia	440	Southeastern U.S.
Bolivia	424	Texas and California
Venezuela	352	British Columbia
Chile	292	California, Oregon, and Washington
Paraguay	157	California
Ecuador	107	Colorado
Guyana	83	Kansas
Uruguay	68	Oklahoma
Suriname	63	New England
Nicaragua	57	Florida
Cuba	44	Tennessee
Honduras	42	Maine and New Hampshire
Guatemala	42	Ohio
Panama	29	South Carolina
Costa Rica	20	Twice Maryland
Dominican Republic	19	1/3 Florida
Haiti	11	Twice Hawaii
Belize	9	Vermont
El Salvador	8	New Jersey
Jamaica	4	Connecticut
Puerto Rico	3	Twice Long Island
Canada	3852	1/4 new world
United States	3617	2/5 Latin America

such elongation through many latitudes further enhances diversity of wet and dry, high and low, hot and cold.

Length and breadth are important aspects of Latin American space. But in this massive region another dimension looms critical. In conceptualizing Latin America's physical space, one must join altitude to area. And colors on maps only suggest magnitude.

Mountains do not exist everywhere in Latin America. With half of South America's territory, Brazil has few mountains and they are low. Where mountains exist, they profoundly influence human affairs. More than majestic, the Andes Mountains of South America are a geologic wall, the world's longest. As impediments to human commerce, only the Himalayas are higher. Mexico, Central America, and the Caribbean islands are also mountainous. And low mountains exist in eastern South America.

Comparisons with North America provide contrasts with Latin American mountains. The Andes and the Appalachians were both critical to early European colonists as mountains forged patterns of human behavior. The Andes extend about 6000 miles, four times farther than the Appalachians of eastern North America. Along the South American range, thirty-two peaks exceed 20,000 feet. If located along the eastern United States, the Andes would create a barrier six times higher than most Appalachian ridges, imposing a dense line of Mount McKinley–like pinnacles from far beyond Florida well into northern Quebec. Such escarpments assist as well as obstruct human activity. Because of their immense height, the Andes often raise deeply buried minerals to the earth's surface, and arriving Spaniards found gold and especially silver in huge amounts. By contrast, the low Appalachians hold few precious minerals. However, their coal and petroleum fueled an industrial transformation. Meanwhile, both the height and the steepness of the Andes still impede eastward and westward movement across South America. But once atop the Andean plateau, colonial Spaniards followed linking mountain valleys north and south, creating a chain of empire. While the Appalachians did temporarily contain Europeans along the eastern seaboard, much of this concentration was by decision rather than destiny: the English were a seafaring people and chose not to venture far inland. (In contrast, the French during colonial times followed their native allies along rivers and lakes across North America from Montreal south to New Orleans and westward to the Rocky Mountains.) Eventually, the Appalachians were but a minor obstacle. When a transportation transformation occurred in the early nineteenth century, canals, turnpikes, and railroads made New York and Baltimore major ports for midwestern commerce. Similar links across or through the massive Andes have not yet happened.

The Rocky Mountains also contrast with the Andes. Both are long chains, but the Andes are relatively narrow and high while the Rockies (in the United States) are broader and lower. Only two U.S. peaks (both in Alaska) are as high as the dozens of Andean mountains that surpass 20,000 feet. High mountains in the American west are relatively low, about 14,000 feet. And because these peaks rise from a 5000-foot plateau, valley floors and mountain heights are less dramatic in Colorado and Utah than in Ecuador or Chile, which border sea level. With broad valleys and high basins—and more numerous mountain passes—travel among the Rockies is much easier than through the Andes.

Elsewhere in Latin America mountains are spectacular, although not as high as the Andes. At an altitude of about 7000 feet, Mexico City is surrounded by peaks reaching 16,000 feet. Traveling from Mexico City to the Gulf coast, one climbs a mountain pass to about 11,000 feet and emerges on the eastern escarpment. At one side is the majestic 18,000-foot Citlaltepetl volcano. Ahead, the road descends steeply to the sea. From a high lookout the traveler sees low foothills and even lower valleys with roads appearing as mere threads. Even flying aircraft—lower than the observer—appear to be gnats. Similar trips in Central America are also dramatic: one seems raised to the heavens on a sometimes narrow ridge of earth separating the Atlantic and Pacific basins. On Caribbean islands, peaks are not as high (about 10,000 feet in Cuba and the Dominican Republic), yet these are three times greater than most Appalachian elevations. And Latin American heights become surreal when one measures waterfalls. The 182-foot drop of popular Niagara Fall is tiny compared with that of Venezuela's Angel Falls: 3200 feet.

The profiles in Figure 1-1 illustrate contrasting geographies. Each is a cross sec-

FIGURE 1-1

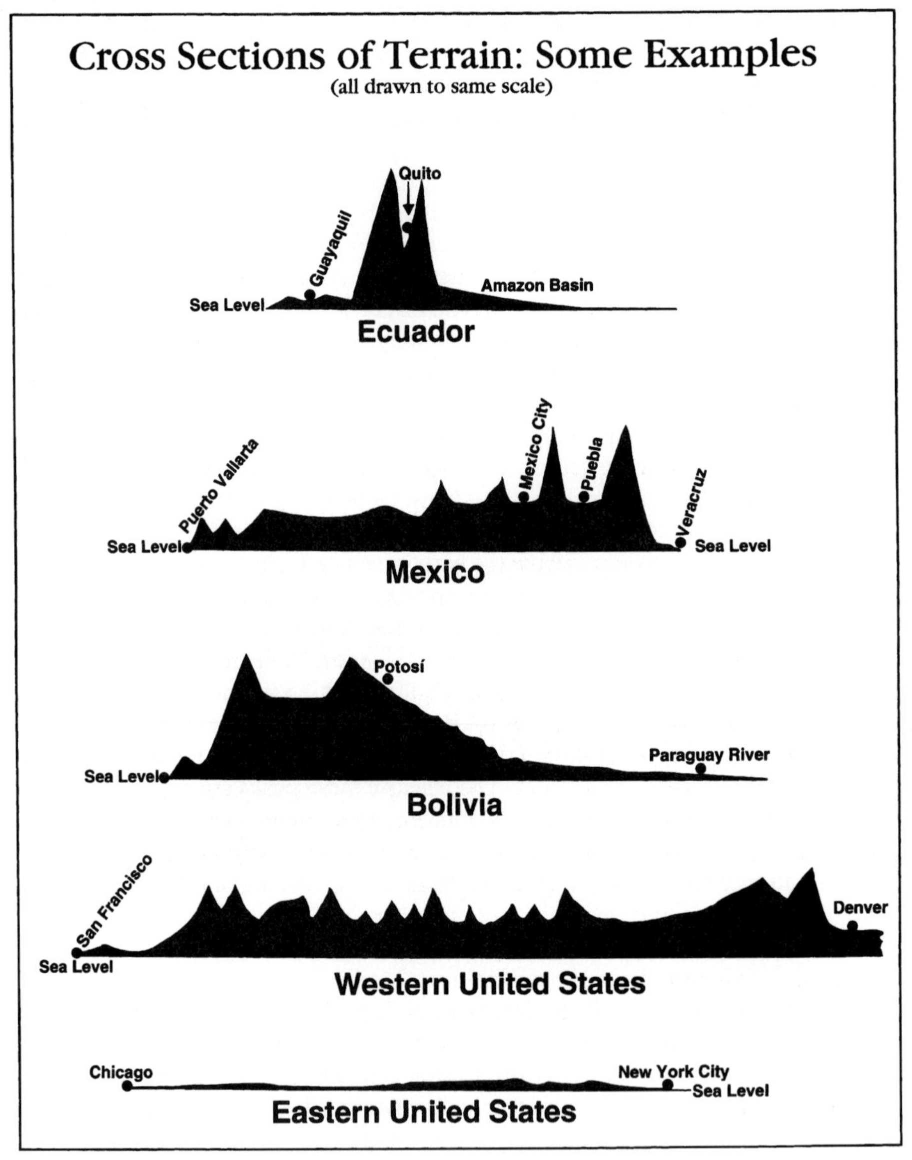
Cross Sections of Terrain: Some Examples
(all drawn to same scale)
Quito
Guayaquil
Amazon Basin
Sea Level
Ecuador
Puerto Vallarta
Mexico City
Puebla
Veracruz
Sea Level
Sea Level
Mexico
Potosí
Paraguay River
Sea Level
Bolivia
San Francisco
Denver
Sea Level
Western United States
Chicago
New York City
Sea Level
Eastern United States

tion of topography. Andean profiles show Ecuador and Bolivia. North American profiles trace topography from San Francisco to Denver, and Chicago to New York City. A profile of Mexico is also included. They are all the same scale.

More than awesome, Latin American size and space create complexity and diversity. How complex and diverse becomes evident when climate joins the equation of length, breadth, and height.[4]

A GEOGRAPHY OF ATMOSPHERE

Ancient peoples worshiped the sun. Tourists in Cancún and Aruba still do. But the effect of sunshine on Latin America's climate has long been misunderstood. European explorers initially feared humans would broil in the tropics. Many outsiders still associate "tropics" with unbearable heat and home "temperate zones" with mildness. However, from Nevada to New Jersey seasonal baking and freezing belie the label "temperate." Likewise, tropical is not always torrid, since the zone is not defined by temperatures but by the northern and southern limits of the sun's vertical position: the tropic of Cancer (23°30′ north latitude, just south of Florida) and the tropic of Capricorn (23°30′ south latitude at Rio de Janeiro). Those North Americans curious about the "feel" of equatorial conditions receive a taste of the tropics each year, during the weeks surrounding June 21. On summer solstice the tropic of Cancer becomes (in effect) the earth's temporary climatic equator as tropical weather surges far north, even into Canada. Checking world weather statistics during late June and July, one often finds Dallas, Chicago, or New York hotter than Havana, Caracas, or other Latin American cities. However, for a true simulation of tropical life, North Americans would need to forgo winter and return again to summer after September 23, the autumn equinox.[5]

Viewing a map (Figure 1-2), one sees the great bulk of Latin America located within the tropics. Whereas North America expands dramatically as its coasts widen from tropical to polar zones, South America does the reverse: borders narrow as distant equatorial shores converge farther south. Between the two tropical lines are found all or portions of all Latin American nations except Uruguay (although Chile and Argentina are mostly temperate). Since the predominant atmosphere of Latin America is tropical, we need to understand it.

Labeled tropical and generally warm or hot (near sea level), weather in the tropics varies greatly according to altitude and atmospheric conditions. Where prevailing sea winds come ashore, tropical coasts are pleasant. Local temperatures are also determined more by local conditions: barometric pressure, cloud cover, rainfall, evaporation, and so on. And when the sun's zenith moves far north, temperate conditions move toward the equator from the south, giving a touch of spring or fall (or winter at high altitudes) to northern South America. At such times, southern South America experiences true winters with cold rains, arctic blasts, and blizzards. For this reason European and U.S. ski buffs vacation in the southern Andes in July and August. And Chile supports a winter Olympics team that leaves home during its summer to compete in Japan, Norway, or Canada. However, these many conditions in the tropics are reversed when the sun moves south in December and January. Then the Caribbean and Central America experience springlike temperatures.[6]

FIGURE 1-2

Source: Cathryn L. Lombardi and John V. Lombardi, with K. Lynn Stoner, *Latin American History: A Teaching Atlas*. Copyright ©1983. Madison: University of Wisconsin Press. Reprinted by permission of the University of Wisconsin Press.

The most important geographic factor affecting tropical atmosphere is altitude, and high Latin American mountains produce dramatic weather patterns. Since rising air cools, a mountain provides natural refrigeration and freezing: 5°F for every 1000 feet of height. Thus, while sea level Guayaquil, Ecuador, steams at 90° F, nearby Quito at 7000 feet of altitude may be 55°F and the heights of neighboring 20,000-foot Mount Chimborazo are about 30° below freezing. Each 4000-foot ascent recreates climates typical of equivalent altitudes located another 1000 miles farther from the equator. Thus, Quito has a climate similar to that of southern California and Mount Chimborazo recreates conditions of Canada's arctic.

A corollary to cooling is precipitation. Warm air can hold vast amounts of water vapor, and lowland tropical air is typically very humid. But cold air holds relatively little moisture. Thus, tropical air rising and cooling is like a sponge being squeezed as it condenses to cross a high ridge, dropping torrential rain or heavy snow on windward slopes. Descending the far side, the same air—now arid—expands and warms, acting as a wrung-out sponge seeking moisture. Thus, mountain ranges in tropical Latin America typically have one side that is wet and cool, and the other hot and dry.

These many factors create immensely different local climates. Resulting ecologies are diverse, often within small areas, as complex patterns characterize the Andes, Central America and Mexico, and high Caribbean islands. Traveling short distances, it is common to encounter a pleasant coastline, then hot and humid coastal plains, and a sequence of foothill rain forests, grass-covered upland prairies, cool forests resembling those in Canada, valleys and plateaus with Mediterranean climates, subarctic tundra, polar snow fields, hot deserts, and much else between. North Americans viewing maps have little sense that Latin Americans who are almost neighbors to each other are either irrigating parched fields from artesian wells or paddling swollen rivers; that residents of temperate towns using binoculars can alternately view alpacas on cold Andean meadows or survey steamy banana plantations.

So important is climate that Latin Americans have historically defined place by weather. In tropical Latin America, low land is called *tierra caliente:* "hot land." *Tierra caliente* is usually a rain forest–like ecology of intense solar heating, heavy rainfall, and truly tropical flora and fauna. As an example, the wet *tierra caliente* of Panama receives about 11 feet of rainfall annually (the eastern United States receives about 3.5 feet). Wet *tierra caliente* in the Amazon has snakes as long as house trailers, ants that march in armies, and two ecologies: one on the ground and another in the thick forest canopy, about 200 feet overhead. Meanwhile, dry *tierra caliente* in Chile's Atacama Desert has had *no recorded rainfall* since European explorers first noticed almost 500 years ago. Here plants and animals are rarely encountered as the land is mere rock, sand, and dust: thorny plants draw moisture from Pacific Ocean fogs, and human activity is limited either to tiny streams fed by distant melting snow or to scattered mines and quarries in lunar landscapes.

Latin Americans use the term *tierra fría* (cold land) to designate areas where tropical mountains rise above 10,000 or 14,000 feet (depending on proximity to the equator). *Tierra fría* is more than sweater weather as communities from New Mexico to the Straits of Magellan live with layers of woolens and Gore-Tex. In highland Guatemala or Peru, vacation cabins year-round are equipped with heavy blankets and a night's supply of firewood. Of course, *tierra fría* broadens to all altitudes and becomes seasonal in southern South America. In Argentina's far south, early European sailors ironically called the local cold land Tierra del Fuego (land of fire) when they saw numerous campfires warming natives.

Also scattered throughout Latin America is *tierra templada* (mild land), found at intermediate altitudes, where sea breezes come ashore and as South America reaches beyond the tropics. Again, Ecuador provides an illustration. Its capital, Quito, is located at the equator, in a mountain valley of perpetual springtime. The Spaniards founded many such temperate cities in the tropics: Mexico City, San José, Bogotá, and hundreds more. In some regions *tierra templada* is connected by interlocking mountain valleys or is found on plateaus, as in Mexico, Central America, and the Andes. Other areas of *tierra templada* are mere pockets, as on Caribbean islands or isolated highlands surrounded by *tierra caliente.*[7]

Adding to regional and national complexities are local microecologies. Since sunlight is intense in the tropics, its angle has an immediate affect. Interacting with high and steep mountains, the slant of sunlight hitting deep valleys often leaves one slope shadowed and moist while the other bakes with intensity. Likewise, a sharp hill with uniform rainfall may have thorny brush and cactus on one side and lush vegetation on the other. In Latin America, extremes come naturally. They begin with geography, which has deeply influenced human behavior.

THE PSYCHOLOGY OF ECONOMICS AND PLACE

Geography channels humans into patterns of behavior. This human response to spatial realities may or may not be deterministic, depending on other factors. For example, the geography of North America fosters unity, which has become both a popular value and an assumed norm. Unity even precedes ethical authority as an enumerated description in the United States Pledge of Allegiance: "*One* nation, under God. . . . " But geography has been a blessing, as the broad interior plain reaching from the subarctic to the Gulf of Mexico facilitates movement. Integration is enhanced by moving people and things on the extensive Great Lakes–St. Lawrence–Mississippi waterways. Mountains on either side of this temperate lowland are generally passable, allowing interchange with either the eastern coast or broad western valleys. And evolving transportation technologies—canals, telegraphs, rails, roads, and air service—have overcome the physical obstacles that do exist. The geography of the United States encourages economic integration, which, in turn, fosters political and social unity. Geographic cohesion and economic integration also link Canada and the United States.

The combination of difficult geography and localized but extreme climates creates different historic patterns in Latin America. Here, diversity and disunity are more characteristic; they are accepted and assumed as normal. Such values begin with a more broken pattern of settlement. *Tierra templada, tierra fría,* and *tierra caliente* have made economic and political integration difficult. A brief tour shows how. In the Caribbean, dozens of islands are divided by language and culture as well as distance. In this fractured geography, colonial rivalry among the French, Spanish, English, and Dutch enhanced geographic disunity. In Mexico, colliding continental plates created large and tortured geologic faults, resulting in a topsy-turvy geography of high mountains and deep valleys. Modern civil engineering and public works better unify Mexicans, but ancient legacies respect localism and parochial identities.

Such patterns continue in Central America, which is broken into seven different nations. Most countries are highland enclaves of *tierra templada* scattered along a narrow belt of *tierra caliente.* Each Central American nation also demonstrates dramatic internal contrasts, including tiny Costa Rica, no larger than West Virginia. On any given day in Costa Rica torrential rains intermittently bathe coastal Caribbean banana plantations, springtime weather of warm days and cool nights characterize central highland farms of coffee and corn, and dry, hot winds on the western coast help tourists enjoy the surf and sun. Day trips in Costa Rica become lessons in economics as well as geography and climate.

South American patterns are similar, but the scale is larger. As in North America, the central section of the continent is a broad plain. But this low land along the equator is far different from the temperate savanna of Illinois or Oklahoma. The Amazon basin is a region of tropical rain forest, which despite much recent devastation is still the world's largest. And while Amazon jungle contrasts with Mississippi farmland, the Andes differ markedly from North American mountains. For example, lowland Peruvians in the east commonly trade not with the nation's Pacific or highland cities but with Brazilian communities on the distant Atlantic Ocean via the long Amazon River. Only southeastern South America—Argentina, Uruguay, and southern Brazil—enjoys a geography and a climate that foster integration. But here political rivalries—involving England as well as Portugal and Spain—have historically divided the region.

In general, the physical space of Latin America does not encourage unity. Human activity often concentrates around pockets of dense population separated by immense zones of relatively few people. The net effect is evident on any map of South America, where large cities surround a sparsely settled interior. In the Andes and Central America, cities in high valleys are typically isolated from one another by barriers of mountains or expanses of *tierra caliente.* By contrast, North American cities from Edmonton, Alberta, to Miami, Florida, and San Antonio, Texas, to Halifax, Nova Scotia, are more evenly dispersed, and also more connected, like the population itself. In the United States, geography encouraged historical boasting about "manifest destiny": a supposedly God-ordained continental expansion. Such claims in South America would have echoed against Andean granite or been muffled in dense undergrowth.

Despite its significance, geography is not normally deterministic. Other factors like technology and changing markets greatly affect the strategic importance of place. Petroleum illustrates how changing markets enhance the value of unlikely real estate. The Maracaibo marshes in Venezuela and tar springs of eastern Mexico were once normally avoided. Their importance emerged when newly invented internal combustion engines thirsted for industrial fuels. Often the fortunes of a place decline. Cane sugar was once sovereign in the Caribbean, whether islands were English, French, Spanish, or Dutch. When rum and molasses held court, French diplomats traded all Canada for small Guadeloupe. But today the world's sweet tooth and taste for booze are more generally satisfied by beet and corn sweeteners, wine and beer. In the Caribbean, descendants of enslaved cane cutters try to attract foreign jet-setters by remodeling former sugar plantations into luxury resorts. They also serve saccharine with tea and coffee and provide artificially sweetened desserts.

While changing economic conditions add to or detract from the worth of local real estate, geographic place—wealthy or poor—often promotes certain human values. Because silver and steers created wealth in Latin America, the Spanish mastered the technologies and techniques of mining and ranching. In the process they developed a landed empire. By contrast, the New England region offered little more than rocky coasts, big trees, and fish. However, these stimulated shipbuilding and a seafaring empire.

Geography and patterns of human activity create dynamics. In Latin America the lack of regional integration—and proximity to the sea—allowed outsiders to dominate the region. Whether on Caribbean islands, the isthmus of Middle America, or ports surrounding South America's interior, trade has been easier with distant nations than with nearby neighbors. More could be moved cheaply in the holds of ships than on the backs of mules. A geography of rugged land and access to the sea fostered a tendency to look outward for leadership and to view neighbors as competitors. Of course, those who command the seas also control the avenues of commerce and communication. Like pawns in chess, isolated Latin American colonies become strategic pieces of global colonial empires. And this is how Latin Americans entered the modern world, not as unified nations but as former enclaves of empire: localities having little to do with each other and much to do with foreign markets.

In Latin America, patterns of time overlay patterns of space. *What happened when* becomes significant as events reveal how technologies and techniques allow societies to either persist or change their relationship with physical environments. Without wheels and sails, native Americans could create only so much empire. Without railroads and dynamite, Spanish colonists could mine only so much mineral wealth. The particulars of time react with physical space; knowledge of both provides keys to understanding Latin America.

CONCEPTUALIZING HISTORY

Certainly individuals and events matter. The world would be different without Christ and Mao Zedong or the fall of Rome and the U.S. Declaration of Independence. Yet individuals and events often represent rather than determine history. After all, a person is formed by his or her society. And would-be leaders remain anonymous failures if they do not generate a collective response. Likewise, a great event occurs in an evolving context, as a keystone rather than an arch. Our example of a person and event revealing a tide of history is Christopher Columbus, hailed for "discovering" America.

Let's imagine that while crossing the Atlantic during the hurricane season of 1492 (which he did), Columbus was not so lucky and lost his ships with all hands on board.

How would history have changed? While such questions are ultimately hypothetical, our response is fairly certain: very little would have changed. Here's why.

Europe was prepared intellectually, economically, militarily, politically, and technologically to expand, and going south and west was inevitable since the east was controlled by rival Islamic forces and the north was already familiar and forbidding. Even without Columbus, his contemporaries would have reached the Americas. In fact, they did. The Portuguese captain Vasco da Gama just missed discovering Brazil in 1497 as he swung far to the west on South Atlantic winds during his historic voyage to India. On the next Portuguese expedition, Pedro Cabral circled a little farther west and encountered Brazil in 1500. Without Columbus, we would be celebrating Cabral Day. They do in Brazil.

With Cabral rather than Columbus as "discoverer," would Portugal instead of Spain have been the major European nation in the Americas? Probably not. At that time, the Portuguese were little interested in Brazil. Determined to reach the known riches of India and the east, they were not about to abandon the efforts of a century—trying to round Africa—by spending scarce resources on some speculative encounter in the western Atlantic. Other than Portugal, the only other European nation immediately prepared—politically, economically, and militarily—to undertake overseas expeditions was Spain. Even before Columbus appeared, the Spanish had ventured far into the Atlantic by conquering the Canary Islands. Blocked from the South Atlantic by their Iberian rivals, Spanish captains like Bastidas, Ojeda, La Cosa, Pinzón, and Solís most likely would have flocked to the Americas, just as they did following Columbus. The achievement of Columbus was important, but neither he nor his actions were singular reasons for Europe's encounter with America.

The example of Columbus illustrates that individuals often ride rather than create the tides of history. The European conquest of the Americas derived from a timely convergence of many factors: ship design, chart making, new navigational instruments, the unified authority of a Christian nation, colonizing precedents set by Italian city-states, the fervor of crusades, new armaments, and much more. And the expeditions of Portugal and Spain (later joined by England, France, and Holland) were really team projects, as each nation created bureaucratic and logistic infrastructures using past discoveries to support further explorations. Each nation organized exploration centers—little NASA-like command posts like Portuguese Prince Henry's Sagres—where captains' logs were filed, charts updated, sailing plans prepared, pilots trained, ship design improved, and so on. And national initiatives were really broadly European: Germans drew charts, Dutch craftsmen made instruments, Jews financed ventures, and Italians served as pilots. Columbus never would have boarded a Spanish ship financed by Jews without the logistic support of many other Europeans.

Of course, Columbus was not the first old world sailor to cross the Atlantic. Viking settlements have been excavated in Newfoundland. Brendan was an Irish monk who led followers in leather boats to the west. Accounts from Arab historians tell of massive expeditions from west Africa to the new world during the 1300s. Fishermen from Portugal and northern Spain visited Canada's Grand Bank repeatedly after 1450. But unlike these visits, Columbus's voyage profited from evolving technologies that made his journey a precedent for continuing and expanding contact.[8]

The deeds of Columbus were part of Europe's progression from the Dark Ages into the Renaissance. Only after the mid-1400s was Europe prepared for oceanic exploration and continental colonization. Its readiness resulted from direct and indirect contact with the cultures of Arabs, Indians, and the Chinese, where innovations such as lateen sails, sextants, charts, and experience with winds and currents allowed ever longer oceanic voyages. By the fifteenth century, the time was right for someone from the Eurasian land mass to cross a great ocean (the Pacific or the Atlantic), accidentally encounter the Americas, return, and make the connection permanent. After the expeditions of Chinese Admiral Cheng Ho were curtailed for political reasons, it was merely a matter of time until some Arab or European navigator succeeded.

This is not to say that individuals are incidental to history. The values and actions of Columbus gave a particular character to inescapable events, establishing in the Caribbean a tone and tradition of European domination different from others in similar roles: for example, Spain's compassionate Alvar Nuñez Cabeza de Vaca in the American southwest or France's realistic Samuel de Champlain in Canada. A European encounter with the Americas was inevitable; the way Columbus did it was not. Individuals matter, but within the broad flow of collective experience, that is, historical tides.

Since comprehension derives from concepts as well as facts, let's consider some other perceptions of history, such as what matters most and whose view is assumed. Because humans rather than moments are the true measure of history, try conceptualizing Latin American time as lives instead of dates or years. Considered as generations rather than accumulating solar orbits, history in the Americas comprises about 1500 generations (for those still counting years, that's about 30,000). But only twenty-five generations have existed since the European encounter. Such an elementary perspective on the past looks like the following:

Simple Chronology of the Americas

Era before Europeans arrived: 1475 generations (est.)
Era after European encounter: 25 generations

The longer period of hemispheric history is clearly native. Yet some persons still cling to a perception that history (or "meaningful" history) in the Americas commenced when Europeans arrived. If history attempts to understand human antecedents, much is missed with such a myopic attitude. And since Europeans in the Americas "piggybacked" on native civilizations—incorporating rather than eliminating earlier populations and progress—we need to understand that one history did not end and another begin in 1492. Native time is not some romanticized nostalgia about extinct Incas and Aztecs. As demonstrated by news from Chiapas, Mexico, in 1994, native peoples in the Americas—the Mayans in this case—still make history. And just as the "European era" did not erase the "native era," the "national era"—

commencing with Latin American independence movements after 1800—did not end European influence. History is process, a blending of past and present. Like tides on the seashore, much of what preceded remains to mix with the next flood.

THE TIDES OF LATIN AMERICAN HISTORY

With hindsight and insight, Latin American time can be organized according to themes. Legacies from the past can be delineated into three eras: native peoples, European empires, and modern nations. Such categorization provides divisions useful for both immediate understanding and subsequent discussion. Just remember, such parting of historical waters and the measuring of lives by chronological time are merely tools for comprehending. Real history remains in lives once led.

A chronology of events surrounding the experience of native Americans begins early and continues to the present. Such a listing is malleable as more is discovered about the pre-Columbian past and more is acknowledged about native history since 1492. Due to both greater scientific inquiry and growing interest, today's archaeologists and anthropologists can solve questions that have long baffled scholars. Using "before the common era" (B.C.E.) as a designation, the broad tides of native time are as follows:[9]

The Tides of Native Time

30,000 B.C.E.: Arrival of migratory peoples
5000 B.C.E.–200 A.D.: Formation of sedentary communities
1000 B.C.E.–1500 A.D.: Rise of major civilizations
1492–1550: Encounter and initial European conquest
1500–present: Persistence and resistance

This chronology is a broad overview. Greater specifics will accompany discussion of ethnic groups, religion, economics, and other topics. Understanding native time is integral to comprehending modern Latin America, as well as our own lives.

The second major delineation of Latin American time is the story of Europeans in the Americas. Although this era recounts the rise and fall of empires, the overall logic and values imposed by European rule still dominate modern thinking. Spain and Portugal were the first European nations to venture far into the Atlantic, building on imperial precedents as ancient as the Greeks and Phoenicians and as immediate as the Holy Crusades and commerce by Italian city-states. Being first was the only unique aspect of Iberian imperialism, for when other Europeans exploited the Americas—from Dutch, French, and English "pirates" in the Caribbean to Russian and Danish explorers in Alaska—European empires could be seen as more similar than different. Searching for gold, glory, and God, the Europeans found the first two: the main motivations were wealth and prestige.

A time line of major events measuring European rule in the Americas actually begins long before Columbus boarded the *Santa María.* European conquests in the new world perpetuated both the Christian reconquest of Iberia from Islamic Moors—who had invaded and occupied the peninsula after 711—and the Crusades for the Holy Land: they all expanded European dominance. In the Americas, the flood and ebb of European colonialism contain the following:[10]

European Tides in the Americas

Around 1500: Arrival of Iberians in the new world
Mid-1600s: Arrival of northern Europeans in the Caribbean
1810–1823: Independence movements among mainland colonies
1898: Spanish American empire finally ends
1960s: Independence for Caribbean colonies

By accident, Europeans created a world system of commerce and empire. That accident was the Americas. Existing in a cultural and commercial backwater following the fall of Rome, former European barbarians learned from Asian and African teachers: knowledge and technologies ranging from geography and agriculture to making gunpowder and sailing ships. Eventually, scientific inquiry and commercial expansion generated a materialistic realism. Europeans surpassed their mentors and achieved technological, military, and commercial superiority. Meanwhile, the vast resources of the new world—minerals, naval stores, plants, farmland, and native labor—enhanced Europe's strategic advantage. The wealth of the Americas combined with emerging science and secularism to confirm Europe's role: uniting the world through conquest and commerce.

European colonialism impacted Latin America longer and more firmly than any other global region. Consider the following. The future United States had a brief colonial era lasting from 1607 to 1776, about 160 years. European control in Africa and Asia was even shorter: except for ports and islands it lasted about five decades before and after 1900. In Australia, New Zealand, and a few other places, European colonization was thorough but relatively recent. European domination of Latin America was longer. It characterized three centuries, from the early 1500s to the 1820s on the mainland, and almost four centuries, from 1508 to 1898, in Cuba and Puerto Rico, and a half century longer for northern European colonies seized from earlier Spanish rulers. Measuring time alone, the European era was two or three times more significant in Latin America than anywhere else on earth.

But European empires eventually faltered. The Napoleonic Wars, the decline of monarchical power, the rise of industrialism and democracy, the growing maturity of new world elites, and expanding free trade all undercut European colonialism—at least direct imperialism—in the Americas. Most Latin American nations were independent even before Europeans finally controlled Africa and Asia. The wars for independence were violent, bloody, and internally divisive. Subsequent decades witnessed repeated cycles of progress, compromise, and regression. But for two centuries Latin Americans have been masters—or at least managers—of their own destinies. A political map of Latin America in 1830 appears as Figure 1-3.

When the dust of disappearing empires finally settled—only in recent times—the map of Latin America contained thirty-three nations. Organized as subregions, Latin America nations can be grouped as follows:

FIGURE 1-3

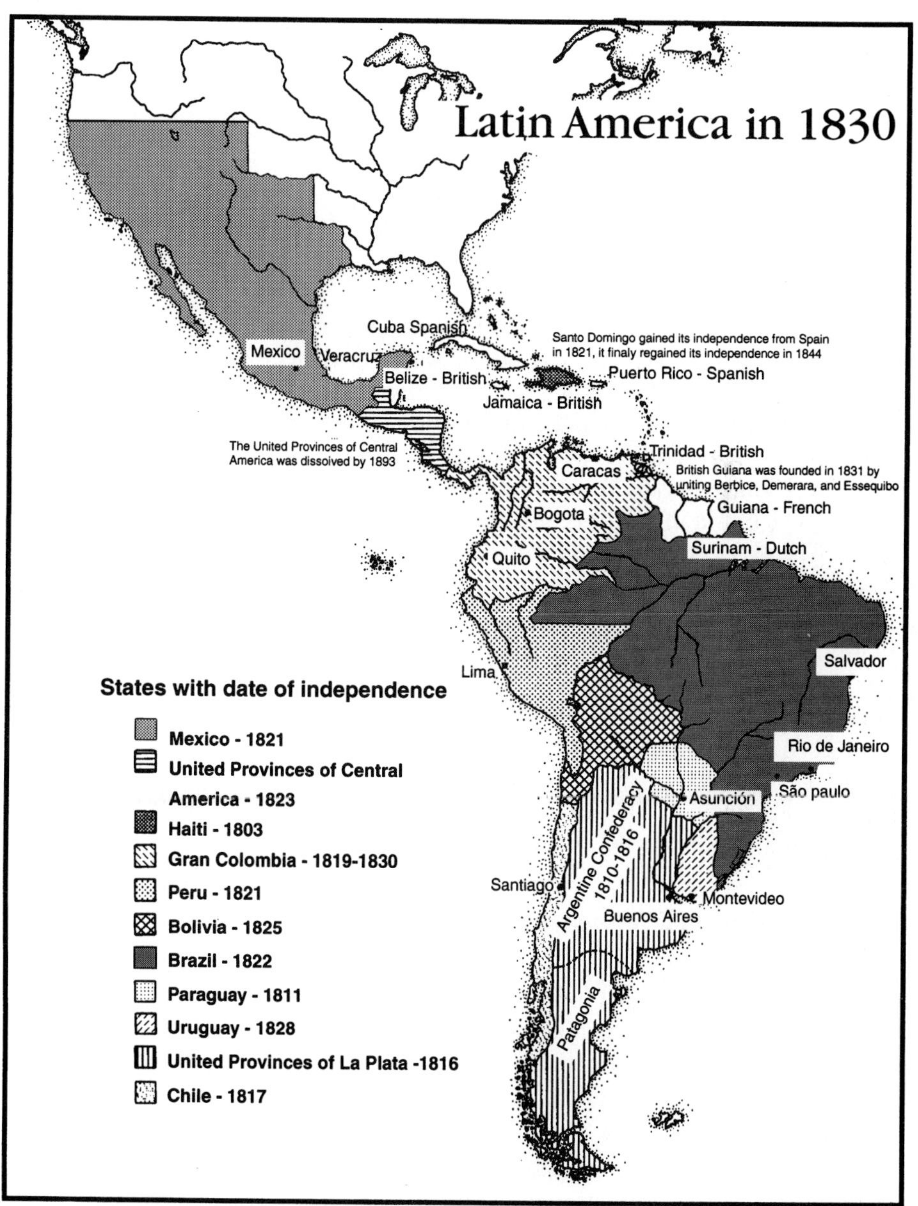

Source: Cathryn L. Lombardi and John V. Lombardi, with K. Lynn Stoner, *Latin American History: A Teaching Atlas*. Copyright ©1983. Madison: University of Wisconsin Press. Reprinted by permission of the University of Wisconsin Press.

- *North America:* Mexico
- *Central America:* Belize, Guatemala, Honduras, El Salvador, Nicaragua, Costa Rica, Panama
- *South America:* Colombia, Venezuela, Guyana, Suriname, Ecuador, Peru, Bolivia, Paraguay, Chile, Argentina, Uruguay, Brazil
- *Large Caribbean nations:* Cuba, Jamaica, Haiti, the Dominican Republic, (Puerto Rico)
- *Small Caribbean nations:* Antigua and Barbuda, the Bahamas, Barbados, Dominica, St. Vincent and the Grenadines, Grenada, St. Kitts–Nevis, St. Lucia, Trinidad and Tobago

Some Latin American territories are not sovereign. French Guiana on the mainland of South America and the Caribbean islands of Guadeloupe and Martinique are "departments" of France, sending representatives to the National Assembly in Paris. Aruba, Curaçao, and a few small Caribbean islands are administered as "autonomous provinces" of Holland. The United Kingdom still administers many small islands: Anguilla, Montserrat, the Turks and Caicos, the British Virgin Islands, and the Cayman Islands (all in the Caribbean), and the Falklands (Malvinas) in the South Atlantic. The U.S. Virgin Islands are a Caribbean dependency, and Puerto Rico is a commonwealth: a status somewhere between that of a state and a colony. Puerto Rico may eventually choose—and be accepted for—U.S. statehood. All other political authorities, as well as boundaries, have long been generally stable. Latin America has few and minor territorial disputes. Even the Malvinas war of the 1980s, when Argentina fought Great Britain for the South Atlantic islands, did not change Latin America's map. A map of modern Latin America appears as Figure 1-4.

During almost two centuries Latin Americans have gained great experience governing independent nation-states. A chronology of major events during the national era looks like the following:[11]

The Tides of Time in Modern Latin America

1820s–1850s: Era of caudillos
1850s–1930s: Order and progress
1930s–1960s: Era of populism
1960s–1980s: Cold war national security regimes
1980s–present: "Free market" democratization

The national era in Latin America has witnessed many contradictions. Independence introduced a period of both anarchy and authoritarianism known as the era of caudillos (caudillos are military chiefs, like warlords). Antonio de Santa Anna of Mexico was a classic *caudillo.* He and other personalist autocrats replaced the stability of imperial rule with intense competition for local power. From this emerged elitist centralism in the guise of constitutional government. Around the 1850s, new leaders reflecting industrial values established political order and almost a century of material progress. But economic depression in the 1930s brought popular demands for strong government planning. The result was a wave of charismatic leaders—

FIGURE 1-4

Source: Cathryn L. Lombardi and John V. Lombardi, with K. Lynn Stoner, *Latin American History: A Teaching Atlas*. Copyright ©1983. Madison: University of Wisconsin Press. Reprinted by permission of the University of Wisconsin Press.

socialists or fascists (at times a little of both), from Sandino or Somoza in Nicaragua to the Peróns in Argentina and Fidel Castro in Cuba—who nationalized economies, planned industrial development, and sometimes involved the poor in progressive programs. Many of these leaders were genuine, some charlatans, but their politics were always intense. The era of populism culminated with the Cuban Revolution of 1959. After that, U.S. policy planners, regional elites, and local militaries forged powerful conservative alliances under a philosophy called the "national security doctrine." Reacting to the fear of supposed communism, armed regimes aided by the United States seized power almost everywhere. For a while economies prospered even as citizens were repressed, but during the 1980s, excessive national debts caused regional economic collapse. The positive result of economic failure joining political oppression was that authoritarian regimes everywhere fell before a wave of citizen anger. By the 1990s, and largely through grassroots efforts, a movement toward democracy strengthened and economies improved. These democracies are far from perfect (none—anywhere—ever are), but they represent valiant efforts of citizens to achieve pluralism, toleration, and responsive governmental behavior. However, even these modest democratic achievements are threatened by authoritarian and violent political legacies.

LATIN AMERICA IN THE GREAT TIDES OF HISTORY

World history has seen much progress. From inventing mathematics and the printing press to forming democracies and launching space probes, innovations in thought and technology are often amazing. However, hindsight places such changes within broader patterns: global tides of history. During human time, the truly momentous achievements have been few but comprehensive. They are agriculture, commerce, and industry. These profound transformations sculpted the history of Latin America.[12]

The agricultural transformation developed as hunters and gatherers sought better diets. Planting rather than immediately eating seeds profoundly impacted both local tribes and human history; so did breeding animals rather than hunting them. Horticulture and animal husbandry created human civilizations. Farming necessitated settled communities that developed written languages, complex mathematics, sophisticated arts, greater crafts, elaborate architecture, ingenious engineering, and other human achievements. Knowing the seasons and planning cultivation fostered science; this all allowed for regular and enlarged food supplies. Better-fed populations grew in size and complexity, becoming urban, stratified, and often militarized. The resulting cities evolved into commercial empires.

The commercial transformation was a subsequent and equally decisive human achievement. Like the agricultural transformation, it did not suddenly emerge one day, since hunters and farmers had long bartered with their neighbors. But at some point commerce became both a priority and a philosophy as societies developed regular, intricate, and ever larger patterns of exchange, including the use of money and credit. Empires in various world regions discovered the magic of creating wealth through specialization and comparative advantage, through managing supply and meeting demand, and through applying technologies to transportation. Commerce transformed farms into plantations producing marketable commodities rather than subsistence crops. The commercial transformation also enlisted religion and science to justify and strengthen expansion. With larger and better ships, and sometimes continental caravan routes, entrepreneurs pushed ever farther, seeking new resources, more commodities, larger markets, cheaper labor, and more appropriate ecologies for growing specialty products. When the world's regions had been explored, exploited, and interlaced with commercial empires, another transformation occurred.

The industrial transformation had precursors but became pervasive only as a result of earlier transformations. Ancient peoples manufactured everything from needles to oxcarts but usually as home crafts or cottage industries. And during the commercial transformation, slaves mass-produced agricultural commodities such as sugar and wine, or raw materials such as lumber and leather. But the industrial transformation was more than making things. It was also a way of thinking differently, of establishing new priorities and means of manufacturing. The industrial transformation was a concept that land, labor, and capital could be combined with energy, technology, and markets to mass-produce everything, eventually even factories and machines to make machines. The core motivation of industrialism has been to reduce costs through ever greater efficiency, constantly adjusting inputs to reduce overhead and multiply profits.

Like societies worldwide, Latin America reflects these three great tides of history. Appropriately, the development of agriculture, commerce, and industry parallels the three divisions of Latin American time: the native era, the era of European empires, and the national era.

Native American civilizations achieved a wondrous version of the agricultural transformation as early hunters and gatherers evolved into very successful gardeners. Few animals were domesticated in the Americas, but the cornucopia of nurtured plants astounded arriving Europeans. Not only were potatoes, corn, and tomatoes different from old world wheat, oats, and rice, but the methods of farming were ecologically sound. And new world peoples cultivated extensive inventories of natural products like rubber, sisal, and medicines.

Latin America's commercial transformation began with native societies but closely corresponds to the era of European empires. Certainly Columbus and his contemporaries were propelled by Europe's commercial transformation. Later agents of European commerce covered the Americas wearing labels such as conquistador, explorer, colonist, prospector, planter, and merchant. They all sought marketable commodities, whether in the guise of saint or sinner. During 300 years of colonialism, the quest for salable products remade the Americas. Africans were enslaved to grow commodities on American plantations; natives were forced into the mines of Peru and Mexico; forests and grasslands became raw materials for dyed cloth, sturdy ships, and European armies. Commerce transformed the Americas: their economies, ecologies, ethnicity, religions, and very identity. And Latin America's commercial transformation has not ended.

Meanwhile, the industrial transformation has been shaping Latin American destinies for eight generations. Industrialism converted petroleum from a gooey curiosity to a treasured resource, and also remade the politics of Mexico and Venezuela. Copper, lead, and zinc did the same for Chile and Bolivia. Throughout Latin America, emerging elites initially exported raw resources but soon built refineries, factories, cities, and eventually institutions like public schools, national health systems, and economic development agencies. Railways, steamships, air transports, pipelines, wires, radio waves, and satellite transmissions linked Latin American hinterlands with mushrooming cities like Buenos Aires and São Paulo. New technologies also moved vast quantities of raw materials, commodities, finished goods, people, energy, and information from Latin America to Europe, the United States, Japan, and now Africa, Asia, and Arab lands. Industrialism has transformed Latin American society: it brought immigration, new roles for women, labor activism, a large professional middle class, mass consumption, and new materialistic values. Whether as native civilizations, European empires, or nation-states, Latin America has been remade by the historical transformations of agriculture, commerce, and industry.

MODERN LATIN AMERICA

Space and time have shaped Latin America. But outsiders often misunderstand the modern results. Too often, popular knowledge of Latin America derives from Hollywood fantasies or a myopic North American media. Specific aspects of this large and complex region will later be explored through such topics as ethnicity, family, religion, and economics. But for background and a "reality check," our immediate survey presents information as objectively and comprehensively as possible: using statistics rather than descriptions. With comparative categories and data derived mostly from United Nations and World Bank sources, readers may construct their own realistic understanding of modern Latin America.

Profiling the region begins with trying to define what constitutes "Latin America." The term originated in the French Caribbean and quickly came to mean any area where European Romance (i.e., Latin) heritage blended with new world cultures. Geographically, Latin America encompasses South America, the Caribbean, Central America, and Mexico. But, historically, Latin America also reached well into North America: Spaniards explored the Pacific northwest, Kansas, and the Carolinas; held sovereignty over what became the Louisiana Purchase; and settled a vast arc reaching from northern California, through Colorado to Florida. Culturally, Latin America is about a half billion people of diverse identities, including (by 2050) perhaps 70 million Latinos in the United States, about one-fourth of its population. However the area is delineated, definitions of Latin America are difficult. Since parts of the Caribbean were colonized by the British and the Dutch, one often hears the more culturally correct term "*Latin* America and the Caribbean." And many who live in Latin America are racially neither Latin nor "American": they descend from early arriving Africans and later immigrants from India, China, or Syria. However, whether living in British Jamaica or Dutch Suriname, descended from German, Japanese, or Arabic ancestors, all who live in the region participate in a broad culture, a long history, and an extensive geography that encompasses Latin America.

While lacking precise delineation, Latin America nonetheless exists. And as thirty-three modern nations (and various dependencies), its people and their lives can be profiled variously. To understand the lives of modern Latin Americans, we shall review data on income, education, health, and other indexes. Such information constitutes building blocks of accurate understanding, but all such information is merely a snapshot in time, since Latin America is evolving quickly, perhaps faster than at any time except when Europeans first conquered the region. The following tables list sizable Latin American nations. (Information on "micro" Caribbean nations is found in chapter notes.) The tables also include Canada and the United States to allow comparisons among new world societies. Table 1-7 suggests Latin America's middle ranking according to global indexes by comparing a few regional nations with others in Asia and Europe.

Review these data to design your own patterns of understanding, but remember that statistical profiles can be both enlightening and misleading. They provide generalized measurements of education, consumer consumption, health, and so on.

TABLE 1-2
LATIN AMERICA: POPULATION, DENSITY, AND PROJECTED GROWTH

Nation	1994, millions	Density, persons/sq mi	Projected 2020, millions
Brazil	158.7	48	197.5
Mexico	92.2	121	136.0
Colombia	35.6	81	49.3
Argentina	33.9	31	43.2
Peru	23.7	48	34.3
Venezuela	20.6	58	31.3
Chile	14.0	48	19.2
Cuba	11.1	251	12.8
Ecuador	10.7	100	15.9
Guatemala	10.7	255	18.1
Dominican Republic	7.8	412	11.2
Bolivia	7.7	18	12.5
Haiti	6.5	590	9.5
El Salvador	5.8	719	8.8
Honduras	5.3	126	9.0
Paraguay	5.2	33	9.5
Nicaragua	4.1	72	6.9
Puerto Rico	3.5	1018	—
Costa Rica	3.3	167	5.2
Uruguay	3.2	47	3.8
Jamaica	2.6	638	3.5
Panama	2.6	91	3.9
Guyana	0.7	9	0.8
Suriname	0.4	7	0.6
Belize	0.2	23	0.4
Canada	28.1	7	34.3
United States	260.7	72	323.1
Latin America	474.2	—	652.4

But each statistic is an average, a middle estimate between sometimes great extremes—combining the marginally literate and highly educated professionals, rattling buses and chauffeured limousines. Later we shall explore contrasts in greater detail. But the following is a general overview, the broad proportions.

With almost 500 million people, Latin American nations demonstrate various population sizes and densities. These countries are profiled by population in Table 1-2.[13]

Latin Americans outnumber the U.S. population almost two to one. And with about as many Latinos in the United States as Canadians in Canada (about 28 million), persons of Latin American origin constitute about two-thirds the western hemisphere. Mexico has the most Spanish speakers on earth: three times more than Spain. Colombia and Argentina are also more populous than the mother country. Throughout Latin America population densities vary. The Caribbean, Mexico, and Central America generally face tremendous pressures on land and resources. Other nations, from large Brazil to small Belize, have sparsely settled expanses.

Latin America is highly urbanized. About three-quarters of Latin Americans live in cities, many of them huge. Great metropolises have characterized the region since before Europeans arrived. In 1500, Tenochtitlán surpassed any European community, and as today's Mexico City it ranks just below Tokyo as the world's largest megalopolis. Latin American cities like Bogotá and Lima register 5 and 6 million inhabitants. And four of the world's ten largest cities are found in Latin America (see Table 1-3), a region where citizens are far more urban than rural.[14]

Latin American cities grew after about 1850. So did favorable standards of health. But the region's health statistics vary greatly. In Table 1-4, infant mortality is per 1000 live births, longevity is life expectancy at birth, and diet is the percentage of the United Nations recommended caloric consumption. These and many other factors including sanitation, water quality, and equity of access to education, employment, education, and health care constitute the human development index (HDI), a 1990 United Nations listing of 130 world nations and measuring quality of life.[15]

Viewing Table 1-4, one sees that, despite a high level of personal income, the

TABLE 1-3
WORLD'S LARGEST CITIES IN THE YEAR 2000, MILLIONS

City	Population
Tokyo	30.0
Mexico City	27.9
Sao Paulo	25.4
Seoul	22.0
Bombay	15.4
New York City	14.6
Osaka	14.3
Rio de Janeiro	14.2
Calcutta	14.1
Buenos Aires	12.9

TABLE 1-4
WELL-BEING

Nation	1990 HDI ranking	Diet, % minimum	Longevity, in years	Infant death per 1000 persons
Chile	24 (high)	114	72	17
Costa Rica	28 (high)	118	76	14
Uruguay	29 (high)	110	72	20
Argentina	32 (high)	125	71	29
Trinidad and Tobago	37 (high)	121	71	15
Panama	38 (high)	103	73	21
Cuba	39 (high)	121	76	10
Mexico	40 (high)	114	72	40
Venezuela	42 (high)	107	70	33
Jamaica	44 (high)	119	74	14
Colombia	45 (high)	108	69	21
Brazil	51 (mid)	114	72	40
Paraguay	52 (mid)	126	67	36
Ecuador	56 (mid)	97	67	45
Peru	57 (mid)	98	65	52
Nicaragua	60 (mid)	99	67	56
Dominican Republic	68 (mid)	106	68	41
El Salvador	72 (mid)	94	66	40
Guatemala	76 (mid)	93	65	62
Honduras	80 (mid)	96	66	49
Bolivia	82 (mid)	91	59	82
Haiti	102 (low)	96	55	93
Canada	5 (high)	130	78	7
United States	19 (high)	137	77	9

United States ranks nineteenth among world nations in providing quality well-being for all citizens. Japan, Holland, Finland, Canada, and more than a dozen other nations rank better than the United States. The 130 nations on the United Nations list are broken into categories of "high," "mid," and "low." Of Latin American nations, only Haiti is listed among the almost four dozen poor countries of the world; a sizable proportion of Latin American nations are listed in the high category. Statistically, Latin Americans are relatively well fed, healthy, and long-lived. By world standards they occupy middle to high positions of well-being, yet health varies by country and often dramatically within nations. Countries high on the list, from Chile and Argentina to Costa Rica and Cuba, have quality standards and also fairly equitable access. Meanwhile, only elites in Haiti and Bolivia experience a full table, fine health, and long lives.

Rates of consumption in Latin America both reveal and mislead. As we shall see later, Latin America demonstrates the world's greatest gap between rich and poor, and statistical averages mask this chasm. Table 1-5 ranks nations by average personal income, measured by the gross national product (the value of a nation's total goods and services) per person in equivalent U.S. dollars. Other categories include televisions and radios (per thousand population), and energy consumption (annual

TABLE 1-5
RATES OF INCOME AND CONSUMPTION

Nation	GNP per person, U.S.$	TV sets per 1000 persons	Energy per person, kg oil/year	Radios, per 1000 persons
Argentina	7,290	220	1,351	682
Uruguay	3,910	231	642	607
Mexico	3,750	148	1,525	255
Trinidad and Tobago	3,730	315	4,910	492
Chile	3,070	209	837	344
Brazil	3,020	207	681	386
Venezuela	2,840	162	2,296	477
Panama	2,580	166	520	224
Belize	2,440	165	436	577
Costa Rica	2,160	140	566	257
Cuba	—	163	978	345
Paraguay	1,500	50	209	171
Peru	1,490	98	330	253
Colombia	1,400	116	670	177
Jamaica	1,390	131	1,075	420
El Salvador	1,320	92	225	412
Suriname	1,210	130	1,903	637
Ecuador	1,170	84	524	317
Guatemala	1,110	52	161	66
Dominican Republic	1,080	84	347	171
Bolivia	770	103	255	625
Honduras	580	73	175	386
Nicaragua	460	65	253	266
Guyana	350	39	350	489
Haiti	—	5	48	47
Canada	20,670	639	7,912	1,029
United States	24,750	814	7,662	2,118

kilograms of petroleum per person). From energy use we can surmise the degree of mobility via auto, bus, plane, or train. Much of this oil also generates electricity used in domestic life as well as commerce (in powering stores, shops, and malls) and industry (machines, assembly lines, processing crops, etc.). Consumption in Latin America is obviously less than in Canada or the United States, but this fact obscures as much as it reveals. With 5 percent of the world's population, North America consumes about 40 percent of the world's resources. And no nation uses more energy per person than Canada. It is North America, not Latin American, that is unusual. Latin American consumption rates more closely resemble world averages.[16]

Contrasts in consumption become ironies within Latin America. Residents of Argentina and Haiti, for example, lead very different lives even without considering topography and climate. In Haiti, people crowd 590 to the square mile. Argentina is 100 times larger with 30 persons to the square mile, although much of the nation is virtually empty since more than a third of the population lives in Buenos Aries. With a $7290 per capita annual income, the "average" Argentine is about twenty-five times richer than the typical Haitian. Argentines have one television per 4 persons, while (statistically) 200 Haitians share one set. An Argentine typically consumes twenty-seven times more energy than a Haitian.

Individual nations often contain extreme polarities within their own borders. Recent political unrest in Chiapas, Mexico, derives from huge disparities in material wealth that divide social classes, ethnic groups, and geographic regions. Living standards in some suburbs of Mexico City and rural Chiapas approximate the differences between Argentina and Haiti within the borders of one nation. Again, statistical averages are instructive but also potentially misleading.

Education in Latin America has long been a priority. Nations like Argentina and Trinidad not only sustain high rates of literacy but produce as many professionals per population as do Europe and North America. Table 1-6 displays adult literacy rates and newspaper circulation per thousand citizens.[17]

TABLE 1-6
LITERACY AND NEWSPAPER CIRCULATION

Nation	Adult literacy rate	Newspapers, per 1000 persons
Uruguay	96	233
Trinidad and Tobago	95	—
Argentina	95	124
Suriname	95	95
Guyana	95	101
Cuba	94	172
Costa Rica	93	101
Chile	93	455
Belize	91	—
Paraguay	90	39
Panama	88	70
Venezuela	88	145
Mexico	87	133
Colombia	87	62
Ecuador	86	87
Peru	85	—
Dominican Republic	83	32
Jamaica	82	64
Brazil	81	54
Bolivia	78	56
Honduras	73	39
El Salvador	73	88
Nicaragua	57	68
Guatemala	55	21
Haiti	53	7
Canada	98	—
United States	98	—

Overall, Latin Americans are literate. About one-third of the region's nations educate more than 90 percent of their citizens. Another third of the region's countries achieve literacy rates in the 80 percent range. Even the 75 percent rate for poor Bolivia and the 50 percent range for Nicaragua are testimony to dedicated efforts at overcoming huge educational obstacles. Latin America is generally an area of well-informed citizens.

Contrasting Latin America with the United States and Canada provides comparisons for North American readers, but the extreme affluence of North America is atypical, particularly by world averages. Latin American lifestyles emerge in a more balanced perspective when one compares regional consumers with their counterparts around the world. Table 1-7 profiles relative purchasing power of individuals in seven world nations, based on local wages and prices. One hundred equals the consumption ability of an average citizen in the U.S. economy.[18]

By global rather than hemispheric standards, Latin Americans generally occupy middle levels of consumption. We shall see later that some Latin Americans are among the richest families on earth. But nations like Haiti and Nicaragua struggle with pervasive poverty. Overall, regional economic indexes compare favorably with those of Africa, eastern Europe, and central Asia. Of course, western Europe, North America, and eastern Asia have generally greater levels of personal wealth. Had Latin America not suffered social repression and economic depression during the 1980s, its overall position would be higher.

PORTRAIT OF A REGION

Latin America is a region of grand scale and immediate detail. It is large and filled with contrasts. Sometimes great extremes and local variations form contradictions. This is true whether discussing modern society, history, or place. The region is both rich and poor, demonstrates legacies of democracy and despotism, and is ethnically diverse just as it is hot and cold, high and low, wet and dry. And it is often poorly perceived by outsiders who understand the region through a mist of misconception.

TABLE 1-7
CONSUMER STRENGTH: SOME WORLD COMPARISONS

Nation	Personal purchasing power (US = 100)
China	7.6
Poland	20.3
Iran	21.1
Brazil	23.7
Chile	31.9
Mexico	32.4
Portugal	42.7

It is hoped that this panorama of Latin American space, time, and society has provided a substantive introduction.

But an overview of geography, history, and modern life merely begins our quest for understanding. To comprehend Latin America more deeply one must know its legacies: both those that live and others that threaten—or promise—to return. The precedents of the past bequeath patterns of human behavior that either endure or are overcome. The legacies involve ethnicity, family, religion, economics, diplomacy, politics, and culture. As should already be evident, the region holds many surprises for those who do not know it. The region is also a constant wonder for longtime students. And the biggest surprise about Latin America is always what happens next.

SUGGESTED READINGS

Blakemore, Harold, Simon Collier, and Thomas Skidmore, general editors. *The Cambridge Encyclopedia of Latin America and the Caribbean.* Cambridge: Cambridge University Press, 1992.

Blakewell, Peter J., John J. Johnson, and Meredith D. Dodge. *Readings in Latin American History.* 2 vols. Durham, N.C: Duke University Press, 1985.

Burns, E. Bradford, ed. *Latin America: Conflict and Creation: A Historical Reader.* Upper Saddle River, N.J.: Prentice Hall, 1993.

Fuentes, Carlos. *The Buried Mirror: Reflections on Spain and the New World.* Boston: Houghton Mifflin, 1992.

Galeano, Eduardo. *Memory of Fire.* 3 vols. New York: Pantheon Books, 1985–88.

González Casanova, Pablo, ed. *Latin America Today.* Tokyo-New York-Paris: The United Nations University Press, 1993.

Goodwin, Paul. *Global Studies: Latin America.* 6th ed. Guilford, Conn.: Dushkin Publishing Group, 1994.

Hauchler, Ingomar, and Paul M. Kennedy, eds. *Global Trends: The World Almanac of Development and Peace.* New York: Continuum, 1994.

Keen, Benjamin. *A History of Latin America.* 2 vols. Boston: Houghton Mifflin, 1992.

Preston, David, ed. *Latin American Development: Geographic Perspectives.* Essex, England: Longman Scientific & Technical, 1987.

Rosenberg, Mark B., A. Douglas Kincaid, and Kathleen Logan, eds. *Americas: An Anthology.* New York: Oxford University Press, 1992.

Sánchez-Albornoz, Nicolás (trans. W.A.R. Richardson). *The Population of Latin America: A History.* Berkeley: University of California Press, 1974.

Skidmore, Thomas E., and Peter H. Smith. *Modern Latin America.* 3d ed. New York: Oxford University Press, 1992.

Tenenbaum, Barbara A., editor in chief. *Encyclopedia of Latin American History and Culture.* 5 vols. New York: Scribner, 1996.

Wilkie, James W., ed. *Statistical Abstract of Latin America.* Vol. 31. Los Angeles: UCLA Latin American Center Publications, 1995.

2

WEAVING AN ETHNIC TAPESTRY: EARLY PATTERNS

The behavior of most Latin Americans are mainly patterns of behavior and institutional forms that derive from the Iberian Peninsula of the sixteenth and seventeenth centuries but that have been modified in their New World setting.

Charles Wagley, scholar[1]

I always questioned authority. I wanted to make sure that the rules in my game were wide open—new, clean, fresh, redefined every time so I could keep growing. I was always ambitious. I had a sense of possibility.

Edward James Olmos, mestizo actor[2]

Latin America is a region of great ethnic diversity and dynamism. Native American societies still exist in various sizes from Mexico to Argentina. They concentrate where Maya, Inca, and Aztec empires once reigned: Guatemala, the Andes, and Mexico. Conquest of the Americas created the criollos (kree-O-yos): whites descended from colonial-era colonists. Never numerous, criollos still created a dominant culture. The sexual encounter of Europeans and native Americans created the mestizos, a people genetically mixed but culturally distinct. Today, mestizos are numerous. Latin America is also a region of massive immigration. The first importation was forced: for almost four centuries Africans from scattered cultures adapted to the demands of forced labor and new neighbors. European ships also brought Asians—from China, India, Indonesia, and eventually Japan—and both Arabs and Jews from eastern Mediterranean regions. And millions of poor immigrants from Europe streamed into Latin America during the nineteenth and twentieth centuries.

Latin America's diverse ethnicity resembles a huge tapestry, grand yet detailed. Old ethnic identities persist in many places. But from aboriginal peoples to recent immigrants, no group remains unchanged after meeting the others. The ethnic tapestry of Latin America continues to enlarge.

Called a "new world" by amazed Europeans, the western hemisphere was already old to those who lived here. However, following Europe's invasion, the twin continents were transformed. And after 500 years, the changes continue. The new world is ever newer.

"INDIANS"

The European domination of two continents was long justified with subtlety. Rationalizations for rule begin with the term "discovery," a standard label that seems innocent or merely descriptive yet holds powerfully possessive implications. Like invention, "discovery" implies insight, license, and even patent. This was true for Spanish, English, or French captains as they cruised new world coastlines. With great arrogance, each asserted national sovereignty over what they claimed was a first-time sighting of supposedly "new" or "wild" lands. Ritual acts such as planting a sword, erecting a cross, drawing a chart, and filing affidavits quickly turned observation into ownership.

But others already possessed the hemisphere, at least by right of residency. In truth, the "new" world was old, and "wilderness" was often densely settled. Five hundred nations held sovereignty over an area discovered 30,000 or 40,000 years before Europeans first arrived. Thus, the encounter of 1492 was less a discovery than a surprise, for both sides. Most surprised, even eventually disappointed, was Columbus, who anticipated reaching east Asia. But human events are filled with unforeseen events—and more amazing explanations.

Stories of new world domination are told separately, yet the plots and consequences of new world conquest by the Spanish, Portuguese, French, English, Dutch, and Russians are more like serial chapters of a continuous narrative. The repeated drama has used assorted actors, but only rarely did the scripts differ: intruders arrive from afar, native inhabitants are "pacified" (displaced or dominated), and the land is "settled" (colonized or developed). And from center stage, the victors loudly proclaimed the drama's redeeming themes: the march of progress, the advance of civilization. Projected as inevitable and definitive, it seemed that voiceless victims merely vanished. Such is not the case. Because natives remain—and remain natives—their story is far from complete. New chapters remain to be told: by those once conquered.

Before Columbus arrived, the natives of the new world had many identities. They were the Taino, Maya, Mexica, Arawak, Algonquian, Tupi, Quechua, Aymara, Apache, and many hundreds more. They existed within urbanized civilizations and as pastoral hunters. Once invaded, the "People" (as many called themselves) were dispossessed of lands, resources, labor, often their lives, and always their dignity. The first theft was their names. For the Europeans, naming was a godly power to create—or at least designate—an unfolding world. And they defined the "discovered" as "Indians."

The term "American Indian" is either a blunder or a lie. When Columbus encountered dark-skinned Tainos, he was confused. East Asia was his destination, and legitimizing previously contracted privileges necessitated his reaching "Cathay" or "Cipango": China or Japan. He had accurate descriptions of the flora, fauna, and civilizations of south and east Asia, even an interpreter who claimed familiarity with Asian languages. So Columbus knew something was terribly wrong when he found no horses, goats, or sheep, no written languages, and no gold-roofed temples as described by Marco Polo and others. Yet, consulting conjectural charts, fixing latitude, and estimating longitude, he *imagined* where he was, arrogantly dismissed doubters, and declared the natives to be *los indios,* the people of south Asia. (He later answered persistent doubters by claiming to have reached the earthly paradise of Adam and Eve, which he also located in east Asia.) Through imperious name-calling, endlessly distinct new world peoples entered history (and eventually literature and Hollywood movies) as generic "Indians." When the error was eventually realized, habit had been established: the terms "Indian" and "Indies" were common parlance among Europeans.[3]

In 1503, another Italian unwittingly compounded the early naming problems. Amerigo Vespucci realized the western hemisphere was previously unknown territory (at least to Europeans). For calling it a "new world," Amerigo was rewarded by a German geographer who labeled the region "America." Henceforth, all new world natives wore an Italian label: "American Indian."[4]

Those who study history seek to accurately know the past to better understand the present. Current terms like "Indian" or "American Indian" perpetuate ignorance—and injustice—even if commonplace. A more accurate term for new world natives initially seems odd but becomes reasonable with use (particularly when we later discuss Indians from India). Many scholars use "Amerindian"—a hybrid that eliminates confusion between south Asian and new world peoples but still uses Columbus's error or arrogance. Fortunately, a little-used English noun works nicely. "Indigen" simply means a native person. And since contemporary Latin Americans commonly use the Spanish equivalent, *indígenas,* we shall use "Indigen" instead of "Indian" when discussing natives of the new world. Whether we can rectify centuries of ignorance, arrogance, and confusion is doubtful. But we shall try.[5]

INDIGEN WORLDS

All Americans had immigrant ancestors. Historians have long referred to a supposed land bridge between Alaska and Siberia as the first immigrant highway to the Americas. However, since humans and not horses (or any other Asian animals too large to fit in a small boat) made the crossing, it is unlikely that a "land" bridge ever existed. Ancestors of Indigens probably used dugout canoes to catch fish and hunt coastal mammals along the shores of a temporary marshland between Siberia and Alaska during various ice ages reaching back perhaps 40,000 years. Advancing with each generation, these frontiersmen followed new world game into Central and South America. Sporadic wayfarers later arrived by sea from Scandinavia, Ireland, Polynesia, Japan, Korea, and Africa. More important than origins, however, are Indigen achievements.[6]

Indigen societies were both varied yet similar. By 1500, over 350 major tribal groups occupied what is now Latin America. Rather than written languages, pictorial systems recorded and communicated information, and in Mesoamerica alone (central Mexico through Guatemala) 260 different Indigen languages have been studied. Most are still used. In technology, Indigens lacked wheels on land and sails on water. Domestic animals were few: only dogs and (in the Andes and Argentina) cameloid alpacas, llamas, and guanacos. No Indigens used iron until Europeans arrived, but they often excelled in working copper, silver, and gold.[7]

Indigen populations were at their height when Europeans invaded. Between 60 and 80 million Indigens inhabited the Americas in 1492. Conservative estimates are shown in Table 2-1.[8] By all accounts Tenochtitlán (the Mexica capital) ranked among the world's major cities, as modern Mexico City, it rivals Tokyo for the designation of largest. Outside highland Mexico, Indigen numbers were not so dense, and everywhere they were reduced by European conquest and disease. Only in the twentieth century have native numbers again equaled those of the year 1500.

To catalog numerous evolving, distinct, and dynamic Indigen societies is difficult. The most studied are the Aztecs, Incas, and Mayas, but this reflects a European

TABLE 2-1
INDIGEN POPULATION ESTIMATES FOR WESTERN HEMISPHERE, 1492

Region	Population, millions
North of Mexico	5
Mesoamerica	27
Caribbean	6
Andes	12
Lowland South America	9

emphasis. The patriarchal and metropolitan bias of Europeans was displayed repeatedly, beginning with the first letter of Columbus: "I sent two men inland to learn if there were a king or great cities. They travelled three days' journey and found an infinity of small hamlets and people without number, but nothing of importance." European explorers sought male authority and urban wealth. Yet Indigen societies—and their significance—came in many forms.[9]

Although many levels of sophistication characterized hundreds of native cultures in 1492, it is conceptually useful to employ three categories. The simplest Indigen societies were semisedentary, occupying regions rather than fixed communities. More complex sedentary societies developed towns with settled agriculture, crafts, and trade. The most sophisticated Indigen cultures developed major civilizations. Figure 2-1 shows the locations of semisedentary, sedentary, and highly civilized societies in what is now Latin America.

Vast lowlands throughout the Americas were home to semisedentary societies. These people often built temporary homesteads of rudimentary materials as they practiced slash-and-burn farming or transhumance, migrating seasonally among a number of locations to hunt, fish, and gather. Semisedentary peoples used plants and animals for an amazing array of foods, medicines, materials, and tools, and transmitted specialized lore to succeeding generations. Through managed teamwork—as exemplified by modern studies of South American Yanomami—many semisedentary Indigens employed refined techniques of observation, comparison, planning, and action. Often dismissed as "primitive," semisedentary Indigens actually displayed sophisticated adaptations to nature.

Sedentary societies were common throughout the Americas. The pueblos of the American southwest exemplify these town dwellers. Living in sometimes ancient sites, sedentary Indigens practiced diversified agriculture—often with highly engineered irrigation systems—and developed commerce based on signature artistry and skill in making pottery, textiles, and other crafts. Settled towns traded both with one another and with highly evolved civilizations in either Middle America or the Andes. To do this, they developed extensive regional trade networks. Columbus repeatedly saw large and well-manned merchant canoes throughout the Caribbean, while Indigen trails linked sedentary towns along the Mississippi River with pueblos in northern Mexico. The social structures of these communities were often hierarchical, with nobility, commoners and slaves, merchants, warriors, and farmers.[10]

Indigens also created major world civilizations, all located in the Andes or Mesoamerica. The Incas and Aztecs of 1500 were the most famous, but both built on the cumulative achievements of sequential civilizations reaching back to the Chavín and Olmecs of 800 B.C. Together with once great Mayan city-states, the legacy of Indigen empires is large and growing, as modern archaeologists add greater data and detail. Both modern scholars and early European explorers have expressed awe when describing these massive cultures. The Spaniard Bernal Díaz del Castillo conveyed amazement when he beheld the lakeside Aztec civilization in 1519: "We saw so many cities and villages built in the water and the great towns on dry land . . . , we were amazed. . . . And some of our soldiers even asked whether the things that we saw were not a dream. . . ."[11] Similar esteem inspires modern students and

FIGURE 2-1

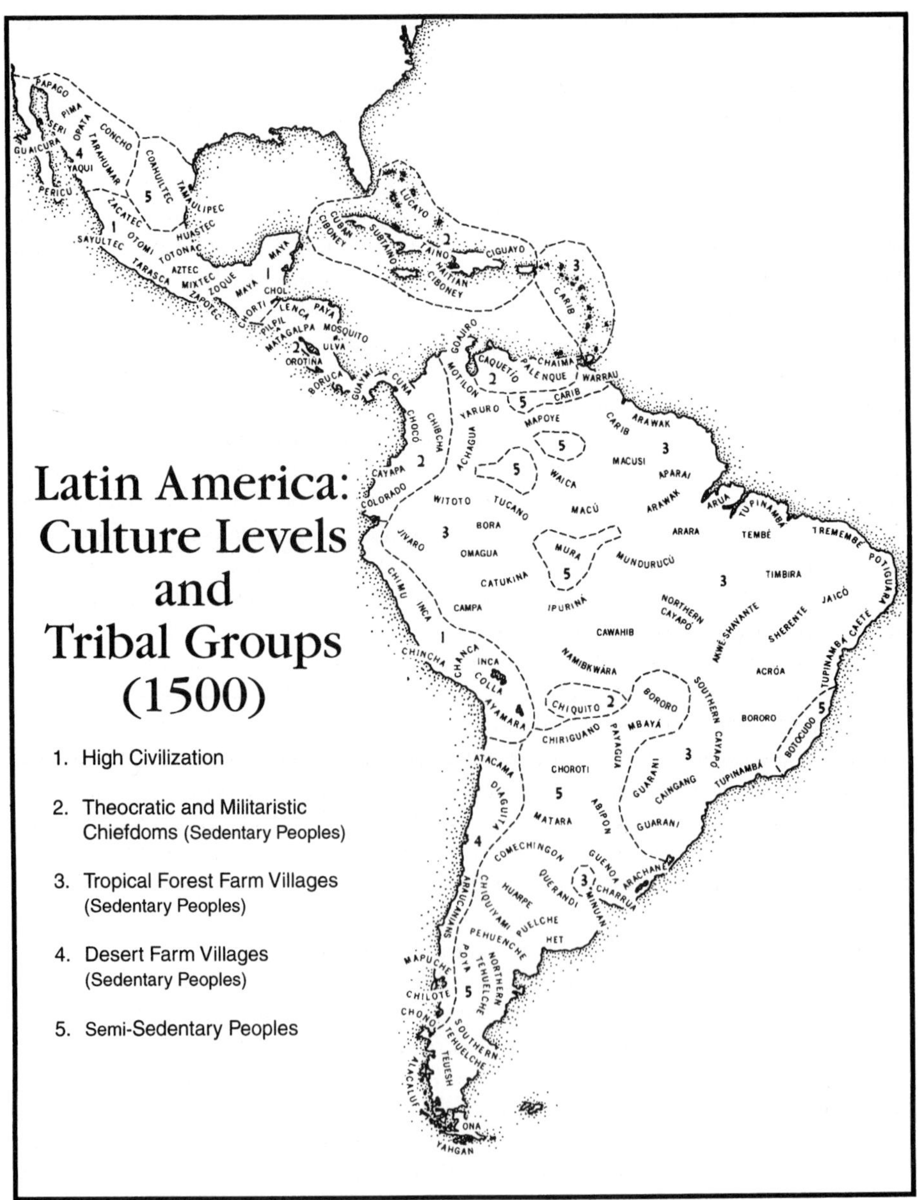

Source: Cathryn L. Lombardi and John V. Lombardi, with K. Lynn Stoner, *Latin American History: A Teaching Atlas*. Copyright ©1983. Madison: University of Wisconsin Press. Reprinted by permission of the University of Wisconsin Press.

tourists upon first seeing Cuzco, Chan Chan, Machu Picchu, Tikal, Palenque, Chichén Itzá, Monte Albán, Teotihuacán, and Tula. Like growing maize or weaving beautiful textiles, achieving urban grandeur was an oft-repeated Indigen art.

Indigens maintained their empires in varied ways. The Inca state was authoritarian yet provident, linked by administrative detail and a famous road system. Newly dominated peoples were moved to older areas of empire and mixed with other peoples to lessen their autonomy. Quechua (the state language) was taught to the children of defeated elites as a prelude to their intermarriage with Incas. Religion fostered Inca sovereignty as under the guise of honoring local deities—and with great pomp—Inca priests held hostage in Cuzco the religious icons of the conquered. The Inca economy was productive but exploitative: two-thirds of what Andean peasants produced went to the state. Cuzco, the Inca capital, probably held more gold than any other city in 1500. While the capital glittered, regional warehouses throughout the realm provided basic supplies to local inhabitants in times of need.[12]

Aztec imperialism was different. Rather than highly unified, like the Inca state, the Aztec empire was actually a confederation in the Valley of Anáhuac. The Mexica (May-SHE-ka) of Tenochtitlán were most prominent. The Aztec empire was based on extortion. Leaders of neighboring tribes were invited to staged battles called "flower wars" and witnessed mass executions of sacrificial victims. Duly intimidated, these "guests" usually paid tribute rather than face conquest. Some neighbors—like the Tlaxcalans and Tarascans—resisted Aztec domination. The empire flourished anyway, with requisitioned goods, services, and human life itself flowing into the Aztec capital. On the high temple of Huitzilopochtli, smoke from burning hearts solemnized the sovereignty of the Aztec god.[13]

Mystery surrounds Mayan cities. When Spaniards reached Yucatán shores and Guatemalan highlands, sites like Tikal, Copán, and Uxmal had already vanished beneath the jungle. Only in the nineteenth century did archaeologists begin unraveling Mayan mysteries. And more is learned each decade about the urban splendor and ecological overuse, the enlightened learning and political tyranny, the great prosperity and eventual decline of Mayan civilization.

Although Indigen civilizations varied widely, a composite model of the pre-Columbian city emerges. A typical Indigen metropolis had highly decorated buildings with fine masonry, and often boldly colored plasterwork and intricately carved stone. Temples were everywhere, dominating other structures and adorned with precious metals and jewels. Ruling elites lived in spacious palaces with many servants. Huge markets daily teemed with buyers and sellers, and arenas held popular sporting events. Monasteries and schools, observatories and libraries, barracks and arsenals, warehouses and artisan shops were each located in specific urban districts. Vast plazas linked public buildings, while neighborhood commons were scattered among blocks of one- and two-story residences. Gardens were everywhere, ornamental horticulture was highly prized, and both house plants and freshly cut flowers adorned windows, doorways, and streets. Canals often replaced streets; filled with canoes, barges, and rafts, they channeled traffic throughout the city. Fresh water was supplied to neighborhood fountains via springs, wells, aqueducts, and piping. Sanitation included both storm sewers and daily collection of "night soil." These Indigen cities were vortices of commerce, meccas for pilgrimages, forums for politics, and centers of art, science, and learning. They were grand places.

Whether living in great cities or simple homesteads, Indigens shared—and still share—a worldview. Time marked the Indigen cosmos and formed a circle, actually small cycles constituting larger cycles: always changing slowly but changeless overall. The most immediate and simple cycle was the day, with sunrise, daily routines, afternoon winds, sunset, and night. Slowly changing days made up the seasons, and seasons a year. And rather than yardsticks of progress, years linked greater circular chains: lifetimes, dynasties, civilizations, or gods who ascend and decline. Time was marked by the passing of human generations, a lengthy list of ancestors. In the native view, time creates time, and the present is permeated by the past.

Spiritual belief demonstrates circular time. Mexican mythology recounts how the Toltec god Quetzalcoatl fled in shame and his people disappeared. Mexicas later incorporated Toltec ideas, including a fear that their god, Huitzilopochtli, would abandon his people. Mystifying the past and dreading the future, Mexicas conceived time as a sequence of "Suns" (the First Sun, Second Sun, etc.): each a "human existence" or civilization that rose and fell. The Aztecs were children of the Fifth Sun, and their calendar—the great stone disk familiar to tourists in Mexico—resembled a roulette wheel wired to destruction. On it, fifty-two solar years—a cycle called a "reed year"—formed benchmarks of destiny. As each reed year approached, the Aztecs expected cataclysm. When reed years passed peacefully, governing regimes felt their sovereignty renewed. However, 1519 marked a reed year, and in that year Cortés arrived with a Spanish army. The prophecy was fulfilled. The empire of the Fifth Sun ended.[14]

Indigen cosmologies emphasized differing values, but all tended to link past and present time. In the Andes, natives derived the meaning of existence from individual and communal ancestry. These "ancestors" were both specific and immediate—a particular great-grandfather—but also general and remote: the uncounted ancestors who together created communal traditions. All ancestors became venerated spirits.

Other pillars of Indigen philosophy are nature and the supernatural, perceived as one since spirits govern both. If the natural world is mysterious, often benevolent, occasionally violent, and usually unpredictable, so then are spirits. Life is difficult to understand and even more difficult to control. The best hope is to achieve harmony and balance, both with natural and supernatural forces and with each other. For example, hunters not only take game but venerate the animals that are hunted. Likewise, rival tribes were not eliminated as much as incorporated into relationships of dominance and submission. Harmony extended to the gods of one's enemy, who were acknowledged as either significant spirits or lesser deities. Fearing possible reprisals—from nature, enemies, or rival gods—and hedging bets against a capricious destiny, Indigens still see life as revolving cycles and evolving relationships, not as absolutes.[15]

The search for harmony and balance governs relations between individuals and society. Indigen life centers on kin, community, and custom. One's family, village, and tribal tradition impart identity by creating familiarity, place, and shared rules.

Thus, outsiders are viewed with apprehension until ritually accepted. One must have membership to be whole. In Mexico, the Aztec unit of group identity was the *calpulli.* In the Andes, the central unit of social order has been the *ayllu* (EYE-you), and members descended from the same great-great-grandfather are called brothers and sisters. *Ayllu* shrines and rituals mark spiritual bonds with nature, one's ancestors, and fellow members. Private property is rare, and is limited to personal objects. Annual group decisions in the *ayllu* recognize persons through households and allocate the use of village land, division of labor, and use of common facilities. Traditions and elders provide judicial guidance. Reciprocity is expected: in families, work, sustenance, and communal celebrations.[16]

When realistically assessed, pre-Columbian America was neither a peaceful Eden nor a barbaric wilderness. Indigen life was brutal and humane, capricious and prudent, cooperative and competitive, elegant and crude—just like elsewhere. Indigen civilizations did not evolve as fast and far as old world societies for numerous reasons. For one, they lacked domesticated animals, particularly the horse and ox, which were engines of progress. Isolation also slowed cultural evolution. What Indigen cultures lacked—and old world civilizations had in abundance—was the stimuli of significantly diverse cultures conquering and trading with one another, cross-fertilizing minds and habits with endlessly new ideas and techniques whether they originated in Peking, Calcutta, Alexandria, Athens, or Córdoba. Nothing so broad and complex existed in the Americas. The natives of Mesoamerica had virtually no commerce with the high cultures of the Andes. Indigens experienced fewer cross-cultural stimuli. When old world cultures finally arrived, the encounter resembled a flood.

DUAL CONQUESTS: DEFEAT AND DISEASE

That Indigens still exist is remarkable. The twin calamities of conquest and contagion precipitated a long decline of Indigen populations. Studies of central Mexico show a population of around 21 million in the year 1500. Those numbers diminished to about 1 million within a century. At the end of the colonial era (around 1800), the native population of the Americas stood at 6 percent of its 1492 figure.[17]

From an Indigen perspective, invaders from across the eastern sea were awesome and fearsome. Carried in "towers floating on the waves," they were almost everywhere viewed as gods—unless preceded by rumors of their devilish behavior. Indigen curiosity surrounded these aliens: most had opaque skin; some had eyes the color of the sky and hair like fire; a few resembled charcoal; others appeared as beasts—half man, half deer—standing high as a house and clad in blinding armor. The charging beasts shook the earth with thunder. The strange invaders also used powerful wolflike dogs that mauled on command: they were enormous and fierce, with burning yellow eyes. The aliens wielded swords so hard and sharp that native weapons splintered and previously invincible war clans were slaughtered. The strangers also used barking sticks and roaring logs that spoke with volcanic breath, spreading terror with their resonance and their smell of rotting mud. The humble shamans of the invaders carried images—of a queen and child, and a tortured captive—and commanded powerful spirits that brought disease only to Indigens. Such was a native view of the conquest.[18]

Victories by hundreds of Spaniards against tens of thousands of Indigens have long been touted as evidence of European superiority. But this superiority was military rather than moral or racial. And contrary to popular belief, sixteenth-century firearms and cannons provided only marginal benefit, except in long sieges and as instruments of terror. The much more devastating European arms were the finely honed swords of Toledo steel, the long lances, and winch-cocked crossbows, quickly reloaded to fire volleys of powerful projectiles. Also more valuable than guns or cannon were attack dogs and cavalry. With animal allies, the Spaniards were usually invincible. Important defensive equipment included iron and—more commonly—tightly woven cotton armaments, which allowed greater mobility in battle.

On the native side, the ritualistic strategies of Indigen warriors hampered their effectiveness. Native Americans typically sought to capture rather than kill their opponents, and this strategy compromised their deadliness. And whenever an Indigen officer died in battle, his troops withdrew in shame; thus, Spanish troops quickly drove toward native leaders. Native armaments were also ineffective against European warriors. Rather than bows and arrows, the basic Indigen weapon was a wooden club laced with sharp obsidian chips. Warriors also carried shields of fibers, hides, and feathers. These worked nicely against rival Indigen warriors but not against the Spanish.[19]

While histories typically chronicle a series of European victories, most Indigens never fought the invaders. Instead, arriving Spaniards (or French or English) were typically welcomed as new allies in ancient rivalries of native against native. In Mexico, first the Cempoalans, then the Tlaxcalans, gained European assistance in long-standing struggles against Aztec oppressors. Indigen allies almost always formed the vast bulk of invading "European" armies. Following a major battle, subsequent "conquests" more resembled victory parades. After Tenochtitlán's defeat, Cortés was hailed throughout former Aztec domains as a liberator. Rather than battles, Indigens and Europeans more commonly met in bouts of gifting.

If the conquest of highly civilized Indigens was relatively easy, the domination of sedentary and semisedentary "primitive" natives was often impossible. In northern Mexico, on the Yucatán Peninsula, in southern Argentina and Chile, and throughout rain forests from Central through South America, European technical and strategic methods proved useless. The Apaches in Sonora, the Araucanians in Patagonia, and many other semisedentary Indigens utilized local habitats as a home court advantage against often naive and arrogant Europeans accustomed to victory. From poison darts to guerrilla hit-and-run tactics, these Indigens quickly adopted horses and firearms as they neutralized European power on the fringe of empire. Long successful opposing Indigen imperial troops, they likewise resisted would-be European masters.

In hindsight, the commander of European fleets was neither king, queen, admiral, nor captain but death itself with microscopic agents more potent than any army. Unknown at the time (since the germ theory was yet unrealized), microbes invaded virgin environments to easily accomplish what soldiers struggled to do. The arsenal of European disease included smallpox, measles, mumps, bubonic plague, influenza, typhus, scarlet fever, whooping cough, and others. African blood and intestines carried malaria, yellow fever, and dysentery. (The only Indigen revenge on transatlantic invaders was syphilis.) In the old world, disease took a deadly toll among infants and children, but high birthrates and resistance among survivors balanced the population ledgers. After 1492, Europeans and Africans reinfecting each other on crowded ships repeatedly brought living cultures to the hot and humid tropics. These plagues were not delivered at once but in debilitating waves over generations. Massive depopulating triggered social chaos. In the Andes, a smallpox epidemic killed multitudes, instilled deep fatalism, and spawned civil war after the ruling Inca died: all this even before the first Spaniards arrived. When transmitted directly by Europeans, germs contaminated victims while negotiating, in battle, at baptisms and banquet, and during sexual intercourse.[20]

The epidemics that swept away Indigens during the 1500s may have been the greatest holocaust in human history. In densely populated areas such as central Mexico the wind itself carried pathogens. Infestations were so quick and intense that within days of exposure native communities lay immobilized. Courtyards and plazas became open graveyards. The stricken suffered from oozing sores, bloody vomiting, and diarrhea as the dying far outnumbered survivors. Those who lived remained deeply scarred: physically, psychologically, and spiritually.[21]

ANOTHER CONQUEST: INSTITUTIONAL DOMINATION

Even before European epidemics began sweeping the Caribbean a generation after Columbus arrived, native populations declined from millions to perhaps thousands due to enslavement and brutality. And psychological defeat followed physical conquest, in 1492 and for many centuries. Meanwhile, Europeans in the Americas evolved many methods to dominate the conquered.

In 1500 arriving Europeans wanted a number of things: precious metals, souls for Christ, land (that grand measure of prestige in agrarian societies), and Indigens for all the above. Unlike the English, who eventually displaced natives to work the land themselves or with African slaves, the Spanish and Portuguese incorporated indigenous workers into Iberian institutions. As during the reconquest of Iberia, Spanish and Portuguese soldiers thought that losers should work to enrich the winners. Instead of driving natives away, the conquerors gathered them: wanting to coexist with natives, albeit as masters. In the Americas, land without labor was considered worthless. Preserving Indigens, exploiting their labor and land, became the foundation of empire. Tribute was the first domination.

Tribute is ancient, simple, and effective. It subsidized Roman grandeur and characterized Iberia, where Moors collected tribute from defeated Christians, and then vice versa. Indigen empires also levied tribute on conquered neighbors. Colonial tribute began with Columbus, who four times a year demanded either a hawk's bell of gold (more than a thimbleful) or twenty-five pounds of spun cotton; Indigens who did not comply had their hands severed. In Mexico and Peru, Spaniards built onto local tribute systems, with peasants supplying Iberian rather than Indigen masters.

This included the Catholic church, which collected the tithe—a tenth of peasant production.

Bygone institutions often imprint modern societies. In the United States, family farms influenced law, Jeffersonian values, deforestation, urban sprawl, and modern devotion to suburban lawn care. In Latin America, an equivalent institution involved labor, not land. The *encomienda* (en-koh-mee-END-ah) was a grant of Indigens "entrusted" (*encomendar* means "entrust") to a colonist (the *encomendero*) who agreed to Hispanicize and Christianize natives in exchange for tribute or personal service. *Encomenderos* were chosen for honor and dedication. However, such respect was military rather than ethical. Most *encomenderos* were conquistadores.

One example of *encomienda* is a document executed by the conquistador Francisco Pizarro addressed to a lieutenant in Peru. It says:

> In as much as you, Tomás Vásquez, have served His Majesty in the conquest, pacified the population of these Kingdoms and the great city of Cuzco, at your cost and trouble, with your horse and arms, in which you have had much expense and work and necessities to maintain dignity as you have maintained it considering your personal ability and that you are a *hidalgo,* to make some amends and satisfaction for service to His Majesty, for the time being, in the name of His Majesty, so long as it is his wish, and mine, in his Royal name, I deposit in [your care] the *cacique* [chief] Guanama, lord of the town of Campara, with all his Indians, which is in the province of Andesuyo, . . . that you may serve yourself of them in your household chores and farm lands and mines and cattle, and that you have and take charge of them, . . . and they will give you your will [fulfill your commands], provided that you are obliged to indoctrinate them and instruct them in the things of our holy catholic faith, and that you treat them well, and comply with them that which his Majesty has ordered and will order from now on.[22]

Rarely have high ideals and low cynicism touched so closely. Quickly *encomiendas* became feudal-like relationships of lord and vassal, nobleman and peasant. Religious instruction was usually superficial, often unintelligible to Indigens. Daily life for native populations changed little. Preconquest languages, dress, music, food, and philosophy largely endured. So did pre-Columbian tribute payments, now paid to Spanish rather than Inca or Aztec lords.[23]

Even patterns of city and countryside endured. Like Indigen elites, *encomenderos* preferred urban life. One affidavit from early Peru inventories the supplies sent to one city-dwelling *encomendero:*

> 2,500 pesos a year in gold and silver, 1,500 in wheat, corn, barley and potatoes, 15 sheep every six months, 75 pounds of tallow, 30 pigs, 300 birds, 45 partridges, 20 eggs every Friday fish day, 25 loads of salt, 101 parts and objects of wood, 184 sandals, 25 Indian shepherds, 12 Indians for ordinary service; . . . skilled workmen, potters, or carpenters, plus fifteen for ordinary service.

Indigens also supplied *encomienda* priests (often friends or relatives of the *encomendero*). The following tribute was typical:

> 1.58 bushels of corn each week, a load of potatoes, ten birds, a sheep each month, 1.58 bushels of wheat each month, a pig every two months, 12 eggs each fish day, a jugful of

chicha [local alcoholic beverage] every day and firewood for his house, herbs and salary in money if it is needed.[24]

But *encomiendas* faced problems. Changing demography was one. Since tribute was determined for *communities* and populations were diminishing, individuals labored ever harder to meet quotas set when villages had more people. A more explicit challenge came from clerics. The Spanish crown was committed to Christianizing natives, and priests' lobbying against *encomienda* abuses culminated in *The New Laws of the Indies for the Good Treatment and Preservation of the Indians,* issued by the king in 1542. *The New Laws* reveal a complex debate over public policy: conquistadores wanted personal service and tribute, the church sought native souls, and the crown wanted control of its empire. To avert a powerful aristocracy living on tribute, *The New Laws* decreed that Indigens were citizens subject to religious and civil authority: *encomiendas* would expire upon the death of holders. Angered by the loss of hereditary privilege, *encomenderos* resisted, even rebelled in Peru. So intense was the colonial reaction that *New Law* reforms were temporarily suspended. When eventually implemented, they were subverted according to Spanish custom: *"Obedece, pero no cumple"* (Obey, but do not comply).[25]

The early growth of colonial mining—together with dividing fewer workers among more bosses—led to replacing the *encomienda* with the *repartimiento* (from *repartir,* "to apportion"). Under the *repartimiento,* government bureaucrats (supposedly) mediated between colonists and the conquered. Crown officials determined work quotas, schedules, and wages, as well as market prices for Indigen crafts and produce as Indigens, hopefully, became wage laborers in a capitalist economy. But reality was different. For one, *repartimientos* evolved in a semifeudal environment of domination and duty, privilege and peonage. Another reality was past practice: even before the Spaniards arrived, Indigen elites enslaved those they conquered. In Peru, the Inca *mita* system was incorporated into the *repartimiento.* Another reality was bribery: crown bureaucrats often were friends or relatives of former *encomenderos* or themselves persons who bought their governmental office expecting a hefty return. Also—unlike labor in a truly free market—*repartimiento* Indigens could not quit their jobs, no matter how bad. Overall, the *repartimiento* was semislavery: typically six months of forced labor in Spanish mines, shops, plantations, and construction projects, followed by six months of life in native villages. Unlike African slaves, who were costly but permanent, Indigen workers were cheap but temporary. For this reason, many *repartimiento* Indigens were worked to death.

The need for a reliable workforce eventually led to formation of the hacienda, both a landed and a social institution. Under the *encomienda* and *repartimiento,* labor supplies were variable, even disruptive. The need for reliability led estate owners to lure Indigens with the promise of freedom from either *encomienda* tributes or *repartimiento* drafts. Haciendas offered loans and sharecropping: credit and use of one's own plot were powerful incentives. But haciendas became highly paternalistic. An *hacendado* (and his male relatives) were not only godfathers but often genetic fathers to local populations as racial mixing was common. However, all this must have been preferable to *encomiendas,* which became extinct, and *repartimientos,* which declined. Haciendas became Latin America's dominant institution by the end of the colonial era.[26]

While Indigen slavery was legally banned in Spain's colonies, it persisted officially or otherwise in Portuguese Brazil. Here natives were enslaved by *bandeirantes* (ban-dey-RHAN-cheez; flag-wavers), so named because expeditions carried colorful banners. Once described as "pathfinders" and "frontiersmen," *bandeirantes* were actually prospectors and bounty hunters from São Paulo who raided the interior: locating gold and diamond mines, expanding Brazil's borders, and depopulating native communities. During the colonial era probably 350,000 Indigens were herded along narrow forest paths, enduring *bandeirante* whips and shackled in chain gangs with sometimes thirty neck collars. One-third of Brazil's slaves may have been Indigens, whose genes fused with European and African genes to create a new race, called *mamelucos. Bandeirantes* were *mamelucos.*[27]

Religion was another European domination. In the sixteenth century, faith was the ultimate sovereignty and one's prayers demonstrated both spiritual belief and political loyalty This held for Catholicism, Protestantism, Islam, and Indigen faiths. Indigen conversions to Christianity saved souls but also made natives into Spanish citizens. To complete the conquest of Mexico, Hernán Cortés requested missionaries and soon twelve—an apostolic number—arrived. Eventually, from California to Chile, thousands of men in sandals labored to complete what booted soldiers began. Native shrines were destroyed and Catholic churches built. Indigen manuscripts were burned and the gospel preached. Drama was the most effective tool as priests wrote and Indigens reenacted pageants of Easter, Christmas, and the Spanish *reconquista.* And during a time when witches and heretics were hanged and burned throughout Europe, Indigens were flogged and held in stockades for remembering the spirits of an ancestral faith.

Spain's Catholic missions were institutions of irony. They ranged from benevolent to dictatorial and were often both. The official term— *reducciones*—introduces the many contradictions of mission history, for *reducción* (ray-duke-see-OWN) derives from *reducir* (to reduce) and means "reducing [to lowest common denominator]; mutation, alteration, exchange for an equivalent; reduction [submission] of a place or country by force of arms; conversion of infidels to the true religion; solution liquefaction."[28] *Reducciones* were Indigen resettlements where clerics indoctrinated natives in the faith and habits of Spanish peasants. Operated by religious fraternal orders such as Franciscans, Dominicans, Augustinians, and Jesuits, reductions became semiautonomous domains. Their concept emerged from debates over Spanish policy conducted by theologians, scholars, and lawyers at the University of Salamanca. The greatest proponent of reductions was Bartolomé de Las Casas, an *encomendero* turned priest. Arguing that Indigens were neophytes needing protection, Las Casas and his associates created missions, in effect, the church holding *encomiendas.* But reduction history was uneven during three centuries and across a realm measured in continents. Protected from colonists, Indigens were often exploited by priests who wanted churches built, fields tended, crafts produced, and personal service. Yet where reductions existed, so did Indigens albeit under a Catholic paternalism.[29]

Reductions were a frontier institution existing on the periphery of empire. The more common relationship between Indigen and cleric occurred in colonized areas where priests—scarce in rural areas—visited Indigen parishes to officiate on holy days or at festivals for patron saints.[30]

A final European domination was Indigen and cultural. Within a generation of conquest—and lasting until today—a class of Indigens adopting European values exploited fellow natives. At first this nexus was filled by chiefs, shamans, or anyone designated as an Indigen leader. Called caciques (a Caribbean Taino term applied by Spaniards throughout the Americas), native leaders initially handled European demands while protecting their own people. But quickly caciques felt new power and often orchestrated relationships for personal gain. They became operatives in a system that mixed idealism and duty with selfishness and privilege.

The cacique's role of power broker was replicated within a generation by intermediaries called ladinos. Ladinos were genetic Indigens raised in an environment where whites held privilege and natives either submitted or prospered by wit. Ladinos deferred to Spaniards while bossing Indigens. They served as translators, "gofers," petty entrepreneurs, and foremen who bridged the gap between policy and performance: helping Spaniards arrange *repartimientos,* arbitrate Indigen disputes, organize harvests, monitor tribute, deliver sermons, and even translate Indigen confessions. Like Spaniards, ladinos dominated Indigens for personal benefit.[31]

A FINAL CONQUEST: DESPAIR

With their lands invaded, populations declining, sovereignty destroyed, and gods exiled, Indigens fell into melancholy. The loss of self-esteem was evident in alcoholism and alienation, use of drugs and suicide. The greatest measure of despair was not just death but lack of births: a declining fertility rate. One friar in early Santo Domingo wrote:

> The women, worn out with work, avoid conception and childbearing. . . . The situation is so bad that many pregnant women seek and induce abortion, others have killed their children with their own hands so that they shall not have to endure the same hardships. . . . Christians . . . have caused these poor people to lose all desire to procreate.[32]

Indigens considered conquest and epidemics as signs of spiritual abandonment. An Aztec song records the profound sense of loss:

Nothing but flowers and songs of sorrow
are left in Mexico and Tlatelolco,
where once we saw warriors and wise men.
We wander here and there
in our desolate poverty.
We are mortal men.
We have seen bloodshed and pain
where once we saw beauty and valor.
We are crushed to the ground;
we lie in ruins.

Have you grown weary of your servants?
Are you angry with your servants,
O Giver of Life?[33]

The repercussions of conquest were profound. The shattering of native societies by defeat, disease, and domination forced Indigens to ponder life itself. And the loss was all the greater because Indigens had initially gifted the arriving strangers.

INDIGEN GIFTS

History is cumulative. Rather than disappear, things of the past layer upon one another. And seemingly abrupt changes transmit rather than terminate. The Spanish conquest seemed swift and complete, but the encounter involved long-term cultural absorption as many Indigen achievements became part of daily life in Latin America and around the world. First meetings reveal Indigen attitudes. And stereotypes of violent encounters malign history. More common were Indigen curiosity, cooperation, and generosity. Columbus recorded a common European experience: "They invite you to share anything they possess, and show as much love as if their hearts went with it."[34]

People worldwide eventually benefited from the Indigen trait of gifting strangers. More than generosity, gifting created mutual respect, even deference, since recipients were indebted and donors gained esteem. Europeans also employed ritual exchange, but their purpose was often contractual: to "buy" land or *accept sovereignty,* as in receiving tribute. In the Americas, the invaders came to possess and dominate, not give. Yet, Indigens "gifted" them: from Columbus receiving parrots and cotton to Cortés accepting maidens and silver icons.[35]

The greatest Indigen gift was food. Nurtured by native botanists, wild plants were developed into corn, potatoes, sweet potatoes, papayas, squash, beans, avocados, tomatoes, pineapples, pumpkins, cacao (chocolate), chilies, and manioc (cassava). The impact of this cornucopia has been global and historic. Potatoes and corn first fed the armies of Incas and Aztecs, and later those of France, Germany, and Russia. Better-fed Germans, Irish, and Poles multiplied, from eating not only potatoes but corn-fed pork. Many moved to the Americas when periodic famines struck: ironically replacing Indigens on native lands. Meanwhile, Indigen spices—chili, allspice, vanilla, and others—became mainstays of such national dishes as curry and chutney in India, and apple pie and ice cream in the United States. And today Indigen foods appear as French fries, potato salad, chocolate shakes, popcorn, spaghetti, pizza, and ketchup.[36]

Indigen gifts also supply modern pharmacies and laboratories. Native shamans in the Andes first developed quinine—now used globally for malaria—while ipecac, curare, copaiba, and other Indigen compounds are daily prescribed for birth control, colds, poisoning, headaches, and heart disease. Natives discovered fungicides that are commonly used today and rotenone (a biodegradable organic pesticide). Native chemists also elaborated compounds used in varnishes and paints, shampoos, soaps, and much more.[37]

Indigen commodities fostered worldwide commercial and industrial transformations. Their long-staple cotton allowed technicians to develop textile machinery in England and New England. Their dyes colored history: brazilwood's purple adorned royalty, priests, and popes; the bright red of Mexican cochineal was used for the capes of Catholic cardinals and the scarlet tunics of British troops, both "redcoats" and Canadian "Mounties"; and indigo dyed the denim of farm and factory coveralls and blue jeans. Indigens also developed sisal for strings, twine, and ropes, which eventually rigged ships, bailed hay, hanged prisoners, and pulled teeth. Rubber was an Indigen discovery first used as bouncing balls in native sports. Indigen tars and pitches, which first sealed rain forest homes and canoes, were adapted to make European fleets watertight. In the early twentieth century, oil prospectors followed Indigen guides to natural pools in the forests of Mexico and swamps of Venezuela. As with Columbus, such innocent assistance bore drastic consequences.[38]

One Indigen gift was subtle and profound. International capitalism—the development of world finance from 1500 to 1800—is indebted to generations of *repartimiento* Indigens who mined silver. During the era of Spanish rule Indigens produced $2 billion worth of silver coins in Mexico. Annually, Peru sent about 200 mules laden with silver to waiting Spanish ships. While American silver adorned European churches, dinner tables, and tombs, Spanish dollars fostered economic change and social revolution: everywhere bankers and merchants rose in status while landed aristocrats declined. Pieces of eight from Latin America first enriched Spain, then Spain's trading partners, and eventually shopkeepers in Shanghai, Calcutta, Cairo, and Philadelphia. Changing status changed politics. For example, as dollars from Caribbean commerce replaced British pound sterling, both the economy and attitudes in English North America grew independent. The United States eventually retained the English language and British measurements, but it adopted Latin American coinage. In the United States, the dollar is an indirect Indigen legacy.[39]

A final Indigen contribution to humankind was an idea: concern for nature. During the late eighteenth century, Enlightenment respect for human reasoning eventually led to seismic changes in philosophy. First came idealization of the "natural man," then nineteenth-century romanticism's fixation with nature, and eventually concern for ecological balance. In Europe, the early prophet of naturalness was Jean-Jacques Rousseau, while in the United States Henry David Thoreau eventually pioneered similar values. These and other naturalist thinkers interpreted Indigen philosophies. Rousseau discussed the "noble savage," Thoreau went to Walden Pond, and utopian communities on the frontiers of civilization experimented with natural goodness. Environmentalism was slow in coming, but it is the latest Indigen gift.

INDIGENS UNDER EUROPEAN RULE: CHILDREN OF THE SIXTH SUN

When the Aztecs were defeated, the empire of the Fifth Sun ended. Across the Americas, Europeans introduced new regimes based on foreign spiritualism and alien materialism. And when national governments formed in the early nineteenth century, European values remained. From a native perspective, foreign gods still rule.

Indigens are numerous in Latin America today, constituting approximately one-tenth of Latin America's almost 500 million people. Small groups totaling about 1.5 million are scattered throughout the lowland rain forests of central South America. The locations of major native populations are shown in Table 2-2.[40]

Characterizing modern Indigens is complex. During 500 years, Indigen culture changed endlessly as adaptation joined tradition. In the sixteenth century Indigens began using burros, raising chickens, weaving with sheep's wool, cooking with animal fats, and praying to Jesus and Mary. Today, Indigens in colorful native dress ride buses, eat junk food, buy cassettes, and watch televangelists. Plastic is pervasive. Thin sheets used as rain gear replace traditional layered palm fronds, plastic jugs in three standard colors supplant heavy clay urns for carrying water, and synthetic thongs often displace native sandals. More subtle adaptations include Maoist Marxism in Peru and using the Internet to gain allies for popular demands in Chiapas. Indigens are not locked in time.

What most determines Indigen identity is the logic and loyalty of language. As long as Cakchiquel or Quechua is spoken at home, both primary associations and world perspective are determined by ancient associations: to local groups, customs, and such concepts as nature. Speaking Spanish in public indicates adaptation, but only when Spanish becomes standard at home has the threshold between Indigen and ladino been crossed.

The end of European empires in the Americas exposed Indigens to the full force of market capitalism. During the colonial era, Indigens had reached a comfortable accommodation with Spanish rulers: they still retained land, customs, and significant autonomy. Few Indigens favored independence as instinctive caution warned that change was threatening. When independence came, conditions deteriorated. Again, Indigens were exploited as cheap labor, their lands seized for speculation. In Mexico, the Yaqui of Sonora lost territory during late-nineteenth-century "Indian wars," and were enslaved and shipped across Mexico to work tropical plantations. Everywhere national governments raised revenues by selling Indigen lands as public property. Nineteenth-century pseudoscience added another censure: Indigens were viewed as evolutionary anachronisms destined for extinction in a genetic struggle where only the fittest survive. National policies oscillated between annihilation and assimilation.

TABLE 2-2
NATIONS WITH LARGE INDIGEN POPULATIONS

Nation	Indigens	Percent of nation
Mexico	25 million	30
Guatemala	3+ million	40
Ecuador	2.5 million	25
Peru	10 million	50
Bolivia	3+ million	50+

Possible extermination had threatened Indigens since 1492. The generation of Columbus hung Tainos thirteen at a time to honor Christ and the twelve apostles. The ravages of disease and Brazilian *bandeirantes* took their toll. And in the nineteenth century, Argentine and Mexican cavalry practiced genocide against "wild people" in the name of order and progress. In the twentieth century anticommunism justified other aggressions: military search-and-destroy missions against Indigen villages suspected of communism in Guatemala and Peru.

But the most incessant assault against Indigens has been the systematic denial of resources, the plundering of production. The colonial era witnessed impoverishment through loss of water rights, *encomiendas, repartimientos,* and debt peonage. After independence, expropriation of native lands induced greater poverty. The results are evident in present panoramas of rural landscapes that show valley floors filled with prosperous estates raising cattle or growing crops for export. Some commercial plantations occupy surrounding hills, but the lower slopes generally hold small, struggling farms raising corn, beans, potatoes, and other vegetables for local markets. And on almost celestial heights campesinos on puny and rocky plots toil for mere subsistence. Such vistas reveal land use and relative wealth but also social and racial stratification: affluent whites hold the valleys, marginal mestizos and ladinos occupy hills, and impoverished Indigens exist on high slopes. Such landscapes reverse pecking orders: Indigens are on top.

Oppression and impoverishment have created a heritage of resistance. Colonial Spaniards witnessed a long list of major Indigen insurrections: the Mixton wars, the Taki Onqoy uprising, the revolt of Tupac Amarú, and many more. Indigens also rebelled quietly, alone or in small groups, escaping to hidden communities in mountains or jungles called *palenques,* where they were sometimes joined by fugitive slaves. Indigens repeatedly rebelled in the twentieth century. Among the first salvos of the Mexican Revolution was gunfire by Emiliano Zapata and poor Indigen and mestizo followers in Morelos. Indigen campesinos and miners also pushed for reform and revolution in Guatemala and Bolivia during the 1950s. In Peru, endless agitation has occurred since the 1930s, when the intellectual José Carlos Mariátequi began a major political movement based on creating agrarian communism using Inca traditions. During the 1960s the *mestizo* Hugo Blanco and other militants fomented Indigen consciousness while protesting abuses. To forestall unrest, a reform government from 1968 to 1975 expropriated ancient haciendas and distributed land to Indigen peasants. But the desperately poor remained so. During the late twentieth century, a movement called Sendero Luminoso (Shining Path), while not Indigen in origin or leadership, combined Maoist Marxism and ancient Quechua traditions. And in Chiapas, Mexico, the Mayan rebellion of January 1994 protested political fraud, the loss of land, systematic impoverishment, and the North American Free Trade Agreement (NAFTA) treaty. As long as Indigens and repression coexist, there will be native rebellion.[41]

Stereotypes regarding Indigens have obscured awareness of their public presence. However, leadership by Indigens themselves is often problematic. During the national era, shrewd, intelligent, and able Indigens repeatedly emerged as leaders, even presidents, in Mexico, but they were often unfriendly to native interests. The national hero Benito Juárez and some of his generals were Indigens, but this assimilative president pushed policies making Indigen communal villages into yeoman farm towns. And the Machiavellian autocrat Porfirio Díaz—he with a Napoleonic pose and powdered face—annihilated Indigens, although he was originally a Zapotec from Oaxaca. During the 1930s, President Lázaro Cárdenas restituted communal lands through the *ejido* program; he was part Tarascan.

Today, Latin American Indigens receive international recognition. The first Indigen to win the Nobel Peace Prize is the Guatemalan Rigoberta Menchú, who represents a movement of native leadership reaching from Alaska to Argentina. The Mayan protest in Chiapas is a sign of the times. So are native environmentalists in the Amazon. The simple message of many Indigen groups can be summarized in a computer-printed petition distributed in Mexico City's central plaza, the Zócalo, in March 1995. Standing before the nation's presidential palace, Indigens from Puebla merely requested the common standards of modern life: "public systems for clean drinking water, electrification, health clinics, roads and schools." Speaking for Indigens throughout the hemisphere, they could have added former farmlands, fair wages, and human dignity.

Recognition of Indigens is not new but rather newly realistic. For almost a century artists and intellectuals have extolled native themes. By the 1920s, the movement had a name, *indianismo (indigenismo),* and many criollo and mestizo adherents. Mexican artists like Diego Rivera, David Alfaro Siqueiros, and José Clemente Orozco painted public murals lauding the ancient achievements and contemporary struggles of Indigens. Archaeologists and anthropologists published impressive studies documenting both ancient and contemporary Indigen cultures. Writers across the Americas drew attention to Indigens with novels like *El Indio* by the Mexican Gregorio López y Fuentes, *Men of Maize* by Guatemalan Miguel Angel Asturias, stories by the Peruvian Ciro Alegría, and *Huasipungo* by Ecuadoran Jorge Icaza. *Indigenismo* in the performing arts helped create Mexico's Ballet Folklórico, a prototype for Latin American national dance companies. And composers Heitor Villa-Lobos (from Brazil) and Carlos Chávez (from Mexico) incorporated native themes into classical compositions. These impressive artistic initiatives demonstrated deepening appreciation of Indigen culture. However, such respect was highly idealized: designed for foreign or elite audiences. Few Indigens read novels, attended concerts, or viewed paintings. *Indigenismo* bypassed the daily lives of real Indigens.

Today, Indigen crafts enjoy great popularity. One sees Mayan jackets, Cuna wall hangings, Aymara caps, and ubiquitous string bracelets in North American malls. However, apparent commercial success masks historic frustrations and continuing exploitation. Mass-produced crafts turn personal expression into material objects, as Rigoberta Menchú noticed with her own clothing: "Our costumes are considered beautiful, but it's as if the person wearing it didn't exist." The alienation of crafts from craftsmen is evident when street vendors earn little, local tourist shops add 100 percent markups, and foreign outlets increase profit margins tenfold. Lucrative tourist industries have not enriched many Indigens.[42]

Traveling by launch on breathtaking Lake Atitlán in Rigoberta Menchú's Guatemala, I conversed with a Mayan peasant on a summer day in 1994. This man's beaming eyes and gentle smile contrasted with his worn and rugged hands. He was a hardworking farmer. We had just left Santiago, where hundreds of native women loaded with crafts undercut each other's prices, shoved rivals, and fought for attention from arriving boatloads of international tourists. It was market day. And because trade was brisk, this farmer was returning to his own lakeside village for another load of produce.

As we traveled, our conversation eventually turned from pleasantries to economics. We discussed the women selling their crafts, the hours needed to make various items, and the small profit earned from each sale. We also talked about the marginal profits of farming and eventually contrasted our very different occupations. When we both discovered that I probably earn as much in a week as he did in a year, the campesino lost his smile and grew quiet. Breaking his meditation, he touched my arm, looked into my eyes, and earnestly asked: "How can this be? Can you explain how this happens?" He really wanted to know. But my reasons sounded pathetic. Meanwhile, wealthy Guatemalans from the capital sported nearby with power boats, water skis, and aqua jets. In the distance another ferry loaded with eager tourists plied toward Santiago. And my Indigen acquaintance pondered his life.[43]

The greatest challenge to Indigens is modernity. Reduced to poverty by unrelenting political, social, and economic oppression, Indigens either struggle in the countryside or migrate to city slums. In the city—and increasingly in rural areas—they discover television, discount stores, evangelical preachers, and sometimes the ideas of Mao Zedong. Modern life sometimes invades with the force of dynamite and earthmovers. In the rain forests of Brazil the material wants of distant people—for lumber, oil, and minerals—drive Indigens from ancestral lands, often by killing them.[44]

CRIOLLOS

The victors in the contest for the Americas were Europeans who bequeathed wealth and status to their descendants. For centuries, the winner's circle was limited by restricted immigration and the arrival of relatively few white women. Since Iberian men mated with native women, producing many mestizos—who were quickly denied inheritance rights—white mothers bequeathed legitimacy. By the end of the colonial era, wealth and power were concentrated within a small caste of mostly whites: the criollos.

Today, whites are the second-largest group in Latin America. But like other immigrant societies, the present white population resulted mainly from European migration after 1860. Because Latin America's European descendants derived from distinct historic experiences, the region has two different white identities: one poor and recent, the other privileged and ancestral. Today, they sometimes blend.

The colonial white class is called "criollo," another imprecise but important term. The problem is partly criollo's English translation, "creole," meaning a person, a language, even a cuisine. A creole can be a person of pure European ancestry, or a person of mixed French-Indigen, Spanish-Indigen, African-Indigen, French-African, Spanish-African background, or a native Caribbean person of any race—but *born in the new world.* The English word also refers to new world blacks, such as those in Louisiana. For all this confusion, we shall avoid the term "creole."

In Spanish, "criollo" means someone born in the new world but of foreign ancestry and demonstrating a lifestyle derived from European culture. In Caribbean areas, "criollo" alludes to persons of African ancestry living by European values. Almost everywhere else in Latin America the foreign ancestors of criollos are assumed to originate in Europe, particularly Iberia, sometimes precisely Castile. Where European immigrants arrived in modern times, the term "criollo" usually distinguishes between descendants of early colonists and later-day immigrants: arrivals from Italy, Germany, Great Britain, Yugoslavia, Spain, and Portugal. Descendants of early and later migrations share race, but rarely class: immigrants are low and criollos high in the social hierarchy. But distinctions dissolve as children and grandchildren of immigrants assume higher status through education, marriage, and sometimes sizable wealth. Latin Americans have long witnessed the concept of *el dinero blanquea* (money whitens): people with dark skin (or low status) are considered "whiter" (or of higher status) if they are bankers, investors, prosperous businessmen, landowners, and so on. "Money whitens," particularly when it adopts criollo behaviors: the replication of supposedly superior European values and lifestyles.

Considering the primary definition of criollo—*born in the new world*—we see that European arrivals were *not* criollos. Persons born on the Iberian Peninsula were called *peninsulares* (pay-nin-so-LAH-rays). The distinction is neither esoteric nor unimportant. Colonial slang for *peninsulares* refers to them as "the spurred ones," meaning either horsemen or arrogant superiors who jab those who support them. Colonial peoples intuitively understood deep differences between *peninsulares* and criollos, well, between haughty *peninsulares* and everyone below them on the social pecking order. To comprehend criollo attitudes of superiority, we must first understand *peninsulares.*

PENINSULAR PRETENSIONS

Peninsulares parented criollos, but as social castes the two were distinct. Those born in Europe typically remained European until death. A new world child—legitimately born of both Iberian mother and father—was by birth American, not European. A parent may not have seen distinctions, but *peninsulares* arriving later thought their criollo cousins a little odd, often similar yet not as good. Such distinctions were ironic. Although *peninsulares* prided themselves on *limpieza de sangre* (lim-PAY-za day SAN-grey: purity of blood), its sanctity was doubtful as for centuries Iberia had been crisscrossed by conquerors, barbarians, merchants, or outcasts: the Carthaginians, Celts, Franks, Greeks, Gypsies, Jews, Moors, Phoenicians, Romans, Vandals, Vikings, and Visigoths.[45]

Few *peninsulares* were aristocratic; instead, they were often poor illiterates scrambling for wealth and prestige. Conquistadores were roughnecks, and the peasants of hardscrabble Estremadura—swine herders like the Pizarro brothers—made the toughest soldiers. And officers may have called themselves hidalgos (important somebodies), but most were sons of petty landlords in dusty Spanish villages. Most *peninsulares* had little to do with conquest or governance. Generations of poor Iberians—mesmerized by dreams of American wealth and status—left for the Americas as either stowaways or *engages* (indentured servants).

Peninsular pretensions were fueled by *Castilian* restrictions. Since Castile had united Spain (mainly by conquest), it feared that "other Spaniards" (such as Catalans and Galicians) and "non-Spaniards" (Jews, Moors, and Gypsies) were potential traitors, certainly competitors. Even when Jews and Moors converted to Catholicism—the required test of loyalty—they were denigrated as *conversos* (New Christians). Thus, *limpieza de sangre—old* Christian faith and *Castilian* status—became a litmus test as rigorous inquiry tried to assure that only *gente decente* (good people) reached the colonies. Probably 600,000 Spaniards migrated to the Americas during 300 years of colonial rule. Scattered across half a hemisphere, that is a sparse number. By contrast, about 11 million Africans were imported during almost four centuries, and 11 million poor European immigrants arrived in the century after 1860. The *peninsular* caste was small.[46]

Yet *peninsulares* dominated colonial life. With political and business connections in the motherland, they occupied prominent positions. Despite previous low status in Spain, many *peninsulares* claimed ancient exemptions and benefits called *fueros* (FWAY-rows). *Fuero* means "right" or "privilege," and these were bestowed by the crown on individuals and groups (and their heirs) for service to the kingdom. *Fueros* took many forms: exemption from taxes, trial by "peers" (often friends), patronage, grants (of land, or *encomiendas*), titles, and other benefits. For his discoveries, Columbus wanted *fueros.* For conquering the Americas, conquistadores claimed *fueros.* For administering colonies, officials received *fueros* (especially since they were paid little). For saving souls in the Americas, churchmen enjoyed *fueros. Peninsulares* demanded privileges for conquering, converting, and commanding: Indigens, mestizos, blacks—but also criollos. The superior attitude of *peninsulares* touched everything: Europe's lace was better, its silverware more splendid, its marble purer, its candies daintier, its perfumes finer. New world residency was considered vulgar and temporary, akin to civilized Romans enduring barbarians on the fringes of empire.[47]

The most desirable *fuero* was escaping physical work. Iberian tradition associated toil with travail, and *peninsulares* typically sought servants to perform every chore imaginable. Spaniards were so ashamed of work that early colonists—from Hispaniola to Buenos Aires—often died of starvation rather than till the land. Such was the pride of caste. And such values were taught by *peninsulares* to their *criollo* children. For three centuries schooling in superiority continued. On the eve of Latin American independence, centuries of colonial haughtiness revealed itself in a petition to the crown by *peninsulares* in Mexico City. They wrote:

> The condition of [Spaniards] as conquerors of a conquered land, makes them the first inhabitants, the preferred and the privileged of all America; and woe to us, woe to the peninsula, and woe to the Indies [Spanish colonies] the day we lose our ascendancy, source and sole shield of obedience and subordination.[48]

Following the independence movements of the 1820s, *peninsulares* no longer dominated mainland Latin America, although they governed Cuba and Puerto Rico until 1898. Here and elsewhere, *peninsulares* arrived as humble peasants. But the offspring of earlier *peninsulares* remained. So did their legacy.

DOMINANT MOTHERS

The conquest was tumultuous.[49] Conquistadores fought natives, each other, and crown officials. Once resolved, the scramble for power acceded to centuries of stability. As achievement yielded to ascription, inheritance was the surest way to wealth. Since European men produced many mixed-race children, the question arose: Which children of white fathers would inherit property? Spanish society answered: the white children. And being white meant having a white mother.[50]

The population of whites, particularly white women, was small during the colonial era. Cortés began the conquest of Mexico with 633 men, Francisco Pizarro counted about 500 warriors in his Peruvian army, and Jiménez de Quesada triumphed in Colombia with only 170 soldiers. None were women. And only about 10 percent of early *peninsulares* were female. The percentage of women among arriving *peninsulares* rarely reached one-third. Other factors—death during childbirth, proliferation of convents, early widowhood, and more—further reduced Iberian motherhood.[51]

The hand that rocks the cradle moves the world. Only in colonial Latin America, those gentle *peninsular* and criolla hands were trained to move little. Education of criollas was both a high priority and very conservative. *Peninsular* priests and monks usually drilled criolla girls in both Catholic doctrine and Iberian tradition during long sessions of memorization and repetitious prayer. Early religious schooling held some appeal, for many women chose convents rather than marriage. Convents were pleasant places, as nuns were freed from often-domineering fathers and the prospect of unfaithful husbands. Nuns administered their own affairs, created cuisine, composed, wrote, sang, played instruments, taught, or served their communities. Some religious orders were highly disciplined, others so lax as to allow personal servants, slaves, and even smoking. But convents withdrew many criollas from motherhood.[52]

The dearth of marriageable criollas reinforced *peninsular* values as criollo families often imported Iberian brides for their sons. Transatlantic marriages preserved class identity, concentrated family property, and were little concerned with romance. An Iberian girl was typically betrothed to an American man at age seven, instructed rigorously by Spanish or Portuguese clerics, and married at age twelve. These matches helped link the Americas with Europe. And as younger women typically outlived more elderly husbands, *peninsular* widows inherited vast estates, *encomiendas,* and mines. Some women married two or three times, accumulating vast inheritances. In Brazil, deceased males customarily left estates not to the oldest male offspring but to a widow, daughter, or niece. The reason? Male offspring might irresponsibly transmit a family inheritance to the illegitimate child of a mulatta, Indigen, or *mameluca* lover. White women, normally as widows, negotiated commerce, made investments, and bequeathed orphanages, hospitals, schools, and convents. The

Catholic church eventually acquired about half the wealth of Spanish America, a consequence of being named beneficiary when wealthy and religious widows died. Iberian women were the executors of conquest.[53]

THE CRIOLLO LEGACY

For all their wealth and privilege, criollos displayed uncertainties. They knew and valued Europe but only from parents and relatives, conversations, and reading. They self-consciously thought and acted European, but when visiting across the Atlantic they behaved unconsciously American: using new world speech and mannerisms, or repeatedly explaining places and foods unknown to transatlantic hosts. And criollos were introduced not as Spaniards or Portuguese but as *mexicanos, limeños* (from Lima), or *paulistas* (from São Paulo). Thus, criollos were painfully aware that identity was formed at birth: Spaniards really were from Spain.[54]

Meanwhile, criollo wealth and pride grew immensely. From *peninsulares* they acquired expensive tastes for things European, and inheriting the Americas provided high incomes to satisfy their wants. During the late colonial era criollos were the major consumers of imported luxury goods. One example illustrates many extravagances. At Lima, Peru, in 1788, criollas rioted when silk stockings were withheld from sale by customs officials unsure of whether the imports were contraband. Eventually, the 816 pairs of stockings were sold for almost their weight in gold.[55]

Copying European haughtiness, criollos grew resentful of haughty Europeans. *Peninsulares* rarely entrusted criollos with rule or responsibility. Excluded from governance, criollos longed for the esteem of equity, maybe superiority. Yearnings for legitimacy and prestige eventually fostered antagonisms—not against Europe so much as against Europeans insensitive to new world whites. By 1810, criollo resentments against *peninsulares* culminated in independence. Joined by mestizos and African Latins, the wars for independence began as a grudge match between criollos and *peninsulares*.[56]

Latin American independence reveals criollo dilemmas. They led the independence movement although many feared that their own power and privilege might disappear if social structures also changed. Hence, rebellion was ambivalent. In Venezuela, criollo liberal Simón Bolívar revolted against *peninsular* conservatives by advocating European Enlightenment values: liberty, equality, and fraternity. In Mexico, criollo conservative Agustín de Iturbide opposed a brief liberal government in Spain by declaring loyalty to old Iberian values: monarchy, church, and aristocracy. Criollos were clearly torn: they wanted old world prestige and new world power.

With *peninsulares* gone, criollos ascended, but life at the top was difficult. *Peninsulares* had enjoyed supreme authority: the legacy of conquest, the legitimacy of a monarch, the military resources of empire, and the endorsement of God, or at least his Catholic spokesmen. After 1820, rebellion replaced conquest, caudillos (strongmen) displaced the king, localism filled the void of empire, and church fathers condemned secular liberal philosophies. And nonwhites viewed criollos as the new "spurred ones."

Criollos began a long search for legitimacy. Democracy was rejected: Indigens, mestizos, and blacks were too numerous and the concept of human equality seemed patently false. The "great man" approach was tried, but such criollo "Napoleons" as Agustín de Iturbide and Simón Bolívar lasted only briefly. Nationalism occasionally worked, but pride in being Argentine, Brazilian, or Mexican was infectious: often mestizos and African Latins waxed emotional about *la patria.* For half a century—amid great political chaos—new justifications were sought for criollo rule.

Legitimacy for criollos was eventually achieved in the philosophy of positivism. Positivism in Latin America entailed a twisting of Charles Darwin's evolutionary thought into the belief that white elites were both genetically superior and obligated to lead others toward an emerging world of scientific achievement, material plenty, and political stability. In Argentina, criollo President Domingo Faustino Sarmiento contrasted modern urban civilization with traditional rural barbarism. Criollo elites in Mexico took the name *científicos* (scientists), as they micromanaged national finances, economic development, education, and politics. In Brazil, criollo positivists coined the term *Ordem e Progreso* (Order and Progress) as a national slogan. But order and progress were real. Between the 1850s and the 1930s Latin America's criollo elite (and "creolized" leaders like Juárez and Díaz in Mexico) achieved progressive despotisms: positivist plenty underwrote the criollo right to rule.

Today, criollo means more than "old white" lineage. The once-small class has been enlarged by others—mainly descendants of later European immigrants—who use education, marriage, and business as calling cards. Not thoroughly aristocratic, criollo is no longer racially unique. A small class of Haitian mulattoes thinks and acts criollo. Grandchildren of recent and successful Middle Eastern and Asian immigrants in Argentina and Brazil think and act criollo. In Mexico wealthy mestizo entrepreneurs think and act criollo. Colonial ancestry is not a requirement for holding European values.

So what is criollo?

The criollo legacy derives from a legacy of European superiority, of conquering and ruling the Americas. In the nineteenth century one critic claimed criollos knew only Europe: "*Spain,* the land of their origin; *Rome,* where the Pope reigns; and *Paris,* where they buy their clothes."[57] Today they also know modern Miami malls, prestigious U.S. schools, imposing New York banks, stylish European resorts, and efficient Japanese corporations. The criollo passion for things foreign began with *peninsular* forebears who introduced cattle, sheep, hogs, and horses as well as guns, steel, the wheel, and the written word. Later criollo leaders like Miguel Hidalgo and Simón Bolívar struggled to achieve emerging European ideals like nationalism and equality. The nineteenth century saw criollo businessmen, statesmen, educators, and inventors bring public schools, electricity, civil divorce, European literature, and public newspapers. More recently, criollo leaders have imported Mussolini's fascism, Lenin's communism, and U.S. capitalism. Much has reached Latin American shores in the suitcases, briefcases, books, magazines, memories, satellite transmissions, and E-mail correspondence of criollo trendsetters.

Criollos also seek to command, and they play democratic politics well. In mestizo Nicaragua, black Jamaica, Indigen Guatemala, immigrant Argentina, and elsewhere, criollos are a minority—often minuscule—but they win elections through persuading others to support their legacy of legitimacy, their prophecy of progress. Modern Mexico is an example. In a nation that is 60 percent mestizo and 30 percent Indigen, criollos set national policy. They turned the country away from a protectionist economic program and initiated the North American Free Trade Agreement. Criollo credentials—wealth, heritage, connections with powerful foreigners, and broad vision—are imposing. So is their legacy.

MESTIZOS: THE NEW WORLD'S NEW PEOPLE

The greatest surprise in the Americas was neither new land, new plants, nor new animals but the unforeseen creation of a new people. Mestizos (from the Spanish *mestizar,* "to crossbreed animals") resulted from the genetic mixing of European men and Indigen women. But culturally mestizos are distinct, for they were officially rejected by *peninsulares* and criollos while choosing to reject their native patrimony. What mestizos do accept is themselves—and a new culture marked by incessant imagination and ingenuity. Without a place in the culture of others, mestizos often reject other cultural rules. Doing things differently has allowed them to survive and even thrive. Creativity marks not only their behavior but their very being: they are the new world's new people.

The mestizo population commenced with that first birth of mixed parentage, probably in July 1493, and grew larger by year, by decade, by century. Today, mestizos constitute the largest group in Latin America's ethnic tapestry. Nine of ten persons are mestizo in Paraguay, Chile, Honduras, and El Salavador. Mestizos constitute from half to two-thirds the inhabitants of Ecuador, Venezuela, Colombia, Panama, Nicaragua, Guatemala, and Mexico. Nations with sizable mestizo minorities are Peru, Bolivia, and Brazil (where they are called *mamelucos*). Elsewhere mestizos mixed with African Latins, as in Cuba, Puerto Rico, and the Dominican Republic. There are few mestizos in predominantly white Uruguay, Argentina, and Costa Rica, and they are absent on black Caribbean islands.[58]

Mestizo psychology is complex, their relations with others complicated and emotional. What feelings would mestizo children have toward a European father, a native mother, and half brothers and half sisters: some criollos, others Indigens? Should mestizos claim a paternal inheritance of dominance? Would prestigious Iberian fathers share such a legacy? Did poor Iberian fathers—such as indentured *engages*—achieve enough status to bequeath esteem to their mestizo children? Would a mestizo sulk in humility or rage in anger against social injustice? How did an Indigen mother feel toward a mestizo child? Would the mother's people welcome mestizo offspring? Living an existence born of conquest, how did mestizos feel about each cultural legacy? Such questions fathom the complex well of mestizo psychology. Answers emerged slowly as mestizo identity incubated during the colonial era. Even today, answers are forthcoming.

THE MAKING OF MESTIZOS: LUST AND LEGITIMACY

The origins of mestizos indicate their dilemma. Initially, indigenous women were often gathered by macho Europeans who commanded sexual gratification as easily as they gave orders for something to eat. Native women were taken by force, purchased from other men, traded for tobacco, and wagered in games of chance. Early *encomenderos* audaciously petitioned the crown for authority to hold Indigen women as legal concubines—a request that was rejected—but the practice continued. So pervasive was concubinage following the conquest that places like Paraguay were dubbed "the Paradise of Muhammad" as probably twenty to thirty women were held by each male colonist. Sex became promotional, as seen in the letter of one conquistador who claimed that native women were "very handsome and great lovers, affectionate and with ardent bodies." Even priests and friars often kept Indigen and mestizo concubines. One cleric claimed that "the service rendered to God in producing mestizos is greater than the sin committed by the same act." Exploited Indigen women were fatalistic. The defeat, death, or servitude of Indigen men left native women defenseless. But resignation was not the only option, particularly early.[59]

The conquest viewed from a native viewpoint shows how mestizos were intended to bridge cultures. Indigens could only envision the conquest through the filter of their own cultural perspective, employing their customs to understand, accept, and—hopefully—control the European invasion. Patterns emerged. First, Indigens normally welcomed the invaders, "gifting" them with banquets and presents. These rituals sought recognition of indigenous status, to awe invaders into either accepting Indigens as equals or, as in the case of Moctezuma in Mexico, obey polite requests to get out. When Europeans bullied forward, a second tactic was used: fierce resistance. Often resistance was the first strategy, particularly when rumors of European behavior preceded their arrival. When resistance also failed, Indigens employed a third approach (sometimes also used during initial gifting): using sex, marriage, and childbirth to blend victor and vanquish. Thus, the birth of mestizos was initially seen by Indigens as accommodation, of melding conqueror and conquered, conveying rights from both cultures through joint offspring. Similar procedures characterized previous Indigen invasions: when Aztecs conquered Texcoco or Inca armies dominated frontier societies. Conquest was accepted when winners and losers shared children. Sex was a means to legitimacy.

Seeking a political and cultural "marriage," Indigens offered sisters, daughters, and even wives of ruling families to the soldiers of Spain. Many conquistadores quickly understood that baptism and nuptials transferred native tribute and labor systems into Spanish *encomiendas*. However, the consequence of easy "legal" conquests was that all rights joined in marriage were inherited by mestizo children. Martín Cortés, son of conquistador Hernán Cortés and native Malinche, was a first-generation mestizo who sought privilege and leadership in both cultures. The conquistador Bernal Díaz del Castillo litigated in Spanish courts to gain inheritance rights for his mestizo daughter. Early Indigen and mestiza wives also inherited lands and *encomiendas* by outliving more elderly *peninsular* husbands. Without warfare, mestizo children of the conquered were attaining ownership and control of the Americas.[60]

However, Iberian authorities recoiled at the prospect of "mixed-blood" rulers of Spain's new empire. In the view of Spanish aristocrats, rude conquistadores climbing the prestige ladder were bad enough, but allowing mestizos to gain high rank was unacceptable. Pressures increased to assure that those who ruled were truly Iberian. Spanish laws discriminating against mestizos commenced in 1549. Some mixed-race individuals "passed" to become criollos, but most faced painful restrictions. Colonists as well as mestizos protested. When told to remove mestizos from his army, the *peninsular* governor of Chile fumed to crown officials: "I should pray to God that there were as many good people among those sent to us from Spain as there are among the *mestizos.*" Feeling the sting of abandonment, the great mestizo writer Garcilaso de la Vega lamented: "In Peru, there have been few [Spaniards] who have married in order to legitimize their natural offspring." In the Americas, mestizos were rejected: legally, socially, politically, and often personally.[61]

Early apprehensions about mestizos may have derived from their rapid increase. Concubinage and restricted female emigration caused the mestizo caste to mushroom relative to slowly growing criollo populations and declining numbers of Indigens. A census of Santo Domingo in 1514 reveals the demographic patterns of empire. Of 689 European men, 107 married Spanish women, 64 took native wives, and 518 were "unmarried." That is, only 16 percent of the Iberian men could sire criollos and about 9 percent legitimized mestizos. Three-quarters of the male *peninsulares* probably held *casta* (nonwhite) concubines, each man producing dozens of illegitimate mestizo offspring. And given historic machismo, probably the 25 percent of married Spanish men were also begetting illegitimate mestizos on the side. Reasonable speculations from these statistics indicate that Santo Domingo saw the annual birth of about thirty criollos, twenty legitimate mestizos, and at least a thousand illegitimate mestizos.[62]

Expanding mestizo numbers accompanied the decline of Indigen populations. As an early Caribbean observer explained:

> Many Indian women are childless and completely sterile . . . ; in those same places and areas, Indian women married to Europeans and to *mestizos, cuaterones,* zambos [mixed races, including Africans], and Negroes are so fertile and produce so many children. . . . The difference is that the Indian woman with an Indian husband produces humble Indian children . . . .[63]

In the Caribbean, African slaves replaced natives. Elsewhere, mestizo populations filled the void. Mexico has seen the greatest *mestizaje:* creation of mestizos. There mestizos surpassed once-dense Indigen numbers by independence. Today, Mexico's population is 30 percent Indigen, 9 percent criollo, and 60 percent mestizo. Mexico is the world's largest mestizo nation.[64]

Mestizaje continued for centuries. Haciendas witnessed *el derecho de pernada,* the medieval "privilege of the first night" in which peasant brides went from the altar to the *hacendado*'s bedroom. Male relatives and the *hacendado* himself needed no formal recourse to institutionalized rape as they merely took lower-class women at will. The coexistence of poor women and rich men also perpetuated prostitution. Its extent is evident in a century of Brazilian baptism records. Between the 1740s and the 1840s, São Paulo annually listed one-quarter to one-half of its children with no identified father. Similar rates characterized Spanish America. And since many poor mothers could not afford baptismal fees, it is likely that most mestizo births were never recorded.[65]

People without legitimacy are typically people without property. Lacking much inheritance—and the legal status to litigate—mestizos typically lived and died with little to their name. While Indigens long retained village lands and criollos acquired vast estates, mestizos without property commonly became vagrants, squatters, and sharecroppers. Even now they face evictions after having farmed family plots for generations. Without legal titles, mestizos are still illegitimate.

From the beginning mestizos were viewed with apprehension by Iberians and Indigens alike. Fearing possible insurrection, Spanish officials often described mestizos using terms like "vicious," referring to the supposed "harm caused by their increase and bad ways." Defenders acknowledged that mestizos were "very astute, sagacious, active." Iberians and Indigens knew that mestizos, like ladinos, saw personal advancement through European rather than Indigen values. Iberian culture was dominant and more individualistic: one could maneuver more successfully by manipulating European rules. Choosing sides in the conquest, mestizos became (like ladinos) assistants and intermediaries helping Iberians exploit Indigens. In the early years, they served as military officers in campaigns against natives and occasionally inherited *encomiendas.* Later mestizos formed *bandeirante* raiding parties in Brazil and became foremen on haciendas throughout Latin America. Mestizos exploited natives, but their supple opportunism disturbed Iberians. They were used but not trusted by the white masters of the Americas.[66]

Culture and personality, rather than race, define mestizo identity. Ladino ("Hispanicized" Indigen) and mestizo (mixed race) remained precise definitions for only a generation or two: since the two groups acted similarly, the terms became interchangeable. In some places, like modern Guatemala, one commonly hears the term "ladino" and almost never "mestizo." Elsewhere, the reverse is true. But for either, behavior defines mestizo/ladino identity. For them, Spanish is the primary language, dress emulates changing European styles, economic relations are monetary rather than customary, individualism is strong, competition displaces communal cooperation, and accumulating wealth becomes a clear goal.[67]

Today, becoming mestizo is procedurally easy, however personally painful. Indigens drafted into the military usually become mestizos (ladinos, to be precise) during basic training: they speak Spanish, wear boots and uniforms, eat army chow, and learn aggressive behavior. "Passing" from Indigen to mestizo similarly occurs when a young woman migrates from a native village to the city, buys modern-style dresses and cosmetics, listens to pop music, and communicates in Spanish.

The story of the mestizo is one of individual struggle. Indigens held to their group customs, and criollos used corporate institutions. Indigens could escape to heritage and spiritualism: their villages, shrines, traditions, and nature. The criollo could turn to the army, the church, the university, and foreign friends. The mestizos' only asset was themselves.

THE WARP AND WEAVE OF THE EARLY ENCOUNTER

The encounter of Columbus and the Arawaks began Latin America's modern ethnic tapestry. Certainly native Americans were already complex. But arriving Iberians with their Latin cultures compounded the diversity. Neither natives nor Iberians in the new world remained unchanged after meeting one another, and an entirely new people emerged with a distinct culture and identity. With each generation, the ethnic consequences of Latins meeting Americans became greater. Native Americans declined but did not disappear. Iberians eventually departed, but remaining criollos continued ruling. And mestizos grew populous.

As the Indigen-Iberian encounter resonated worldwide, people from around the globe began emigrating to Latin America. Africans were enslaved and shipped to new world plantations. Chinese and Indians (from India) came as construction workers and indentured farm laborers. Arabs and Jews from the eastern Mediterranean and many more Europeans arrived seeking freedom and opportunity. The shaping of Latin America's ethnic tapestry is also their legacy.

SUGGESTED READINGS

Brading, D. A. *The First America: The Spanish Monarchy, Creole Patriots, and the Liberal State 1492–1867.* Cambridge: Cambridge University Press, 1991.

Burkholder, Mark A., and Lyman L. Johnson. *Colonial Latin America.* New York: Oxford University Press, 1990.

Crosby, Alfred W., Jr. *The Columbian Exchange: Biological and Cultural Consequences of 1492.* Westport, Conn.: Greenwood Press, 1972.

Díaz del Castillo, Bernal. *The Discovery and Conquest of Mexico, 1517–1521,* trans. A. P. Maudslay. New York: Grove Press, 1956.

Hobhouse, Henry. *Seeds of Change: Five Plants That Transformed Mankind.* New York: Harper and Row, 1985.

Jennings, Francis. *The Founders of America: How Indians Discovered the Land, Pioneered It, and Created Great Classical Civilizations.* New York: Norton, 1993.

Kicza, John E., ed. *The Indian in Latin American History: Resistance, Resilience, and Acculturation.* Wilmington, Del.: Scholarly Resources, 1993.

Klein, Herbert S. *Haciendas and Ayllus: Rural Society in the Bolivian Andes in the Eighteenth and Nineteenth Centuries.* Stanford, Calif.: Stanford University Press, 1993.

León-Portilla, Miguel. *The Broken Spears: An Aztec Account of the Conquest of Mexico.* Boston: Beacon Press, 1962.

Menchú, Rigoberta. *I, Rigoberta Menchú: An Indian Woman in Guatemala,* edited by Elizabeth Burgos-Debray, translated by Ann Wright. London: Verso, 1984.

Reck, Gregory G. *In the Shadow of Tlaloc: Life in a Mexican Village.* Prospect Heights, Ill.: Waveland Press, 1978.

Stern, Steve J. *Peru's Indian Peoples and the Challenge of Spanish Conquest: Huamanga to 1640.* Madison: University of Wisconsin Press, 1982.

Wachtel, Nathan. *The Vision of the Vanquished: The Spanish Conquest of Peru through Indian Eyes.* New York: Harper and Row, 1977.

Weatherford, Jack. *Indian Givers: How the Indians of the Americas Transformed the World.* New York: Fawcett Columbine, 1988.

3

WEAVING AN ETHNIC TAPESTRY: IMMIGRANT PATTERNS

Anglo-America and Latin America represent distinctive adaptions of man to the New World. Within the boundaries of each of them, the American Indian, the African Negro, East Indians, Chinese, Japanese, Italians, Polish, Germans, and other peoples have been incorporated and have made important cultural contributions . . . .

Charles Wagley, scholar[1]

The weaving of Latin America's ethnic tapestry intensified as local demographics were augmented by immigrations from around the world. The first to come—forced to come—were the Africans. From an area as large and diverse as Europe, many different Africans arrived on ships of the Atlantic slave trade. The children of these black immigrants did not remain African, for like criollos they were born in the new world. And persons of African ancestry mixed with whites, Indigens, mestizos, and Africans of different cultures. But a continuous stream—lasting 400 years—repeatedly renewed African awareness. Today, Africanness permeates the Americas: when not directly by race, then indirectly through taste, cadence, expression, and manners. And descendants of Africans are numerous in particular areas.

During the nineteenth century, heavy immigration from other continents replaced the stream of arriving Africans. Peasants from Europe flooded southern South America. Most came from Spain, Italy, and Portugal, but sizable numbers also departed from Ireland, Germany, and other northern and eastern European nations. Asians came too. In colonial times, Asians crewed Spanish ships leaving the Philippines for new world ports. During the national era, large numbers of Chinese were brought to Mexico and Peru, while smaller groups arrived in Central America and the Caribbean. The British and Dutch brought indentured workers from India and Indonesia to Caribbean estates. Japanese farmers settled in Brazil. And Jews and Arabs from the eastern Mediterranean traveled in the holds of European freighters to Buenos Aires, Santos, and wherever bulk commodities were exported from Latin America. These immigrants from many lands helped weave Latin America's ethnic tapestry.

The African Latin legacy blends a transatlantic heritage with new world demands. Held hostage for lifetimes, Africans arriving as slaves adapted by tapping the twin wellsprings of cultures remembered and creative pragmatism. They developed distinctive cuisine, craftsmanship, dance, music, spirituality, and language. Those regions steeped in African Latin heritage demonstrate a vibrancy of life that today attracts social scientists, tourists, and entertainers for whom modern life has been comfortable, predictable, and perhaps boring.[2]

THE SLAVE TRADE

The origins of the Atlantic slave trade are both ancient and Mediterranean, and had little to do with race and much to do with military power and commercial expansion. With greater military force, Greeks conquered and enslaved weaker neighbors. Romans eventually did the same to Greeks, making them teachers, artisans, and artists as well as household servants. Cycles of slavery continued during the Crusades as Christian and Muslim soldiers took each other hostage: captives with rich relatives or patrons were ransomed, while the poor dug fields on estates or manned oars for imperial fleets. During the late Middle Ages merchants from Genoa and Venice gathered Slavs (which meant slaves) from areas of modern Russia and Ukraine. Slavery also existed in Africa before Europeans arrived. Considered children rather than property, slaves were neither sold nor traded but educated, given responsibilities, and made members of a master's family.[3]

Although modern European slavery had religious origins, it quickly became capitalistic. In Iberia during the *reconquista,* victors (Moors or Christians) took prisoners *en buena guerra* (in a good war), that is, a religious, and hence "justified," attack. Following battles, it seemed compassionate to spare the defeated, despite their future enslavement. Besides, many of the "defeated" were not warriors at all, just peasants who already farmed the conquered lands. In the early 1400s, Christians completed Portugal's reconquest and immediately ventured into the Atlantic. On the Azores and Madeiras, and along the shores of north and western Africa *en buena guerra* justified overseas assault, occupation, and enslavement. When European forces were militarily superior, they raided coastal communities to pillage and remove marketable wealth, including inhabitants. If coastal towns were strongly defended, the Europeans traded instead.[4]

But greed rather than creed came to motivate enslavement as Iberians—both Spaniards and Portuguese—discovered the sweet profits of sugar. The Atlantic slave trade developed around expanding cane production in Iberia and the Atlantic islands of Medeira and the Canaries. When larger plantations demanded more workers, Portuguese captains created *feitorias* ("factories") on Africa's west coast. *Feitorias* were fortified sites where enslaved Africans were penned, inventoried, and shipped (along with gold and ivory) to European ports or possessions.[5]

Between 1500 and 1870, about 11 million African slaves reached Latin America. Probably 1 million Iberians emigrated during the same period. The flow of slaves to Latin America was twenty times greater than that to the future United States. Since smuggling and false documentation were common, the best estimates regarding the Atlantic slave trade are those shown in Table 3-1.[6] Such numbers show that Latin America experienced a massive African presence. By 1550, African Latins already outnumbered both *peninsulares* and criollos in Peru, just as they did in Mexico a few decades later. More slaves arrived at the Brazilian goldfields of Minas Gerais during the 1700s than were imported into the future United States during the entire era of slavery. Lima, Peru, was almost half African Latin at the end of the colonial era. By 1850, Africans or their descendants accounted for 60 percent of Cubans and about 75 percent of Brazilians. While later immigration, mainly from Europe, lessened these ratios, African culture remained strong.[7]

TABLE 3-1
ESTIMATED AFRICAN SLAVES EXPORTED, 1500–1870

Destination	Numbers	Percent
Old World	300,000	2
Dutch Caribbean	500,000	5
British North America	500,000	5
French Caribbean	1,700,000	15
Spanish America	1,700,000	15
British Caribbean	2,500,000	21
Brazil	4,200,000	37
Total	11,400,000	

Profits from African flesh and labor became the bedrock of European empires. By papal decrees and treaties with Portugal, Spain was excluded from tropical Africa and therefore from the Atlantic slave trade, so Portuguese ships first delivered Africans to the Spanish Main. Holland and France later competed for this lucrative contract, but eventually Great Britain gained the *asiento,* the monopoly of transporting slaves to Spanish colonies. As part of the British Empire, New England participated in the *asiento* as nascent U.S. industrialism was stimulated by slave trade merchants ordering ships, chains, shackles, and branding irons. Whips, salted cod, guns, ropes, and rum augmented slave trade inventories. The trade in slaves also stimulated New England's insurance industry.

As often happens, the flag followed trade as slaving and slave plantations led to colonies for northern European nations. During the 1600s, the English seized Jamaica, Guiana, Trinidad, Barbados, and other Caribbean islands. Pirates and plantations produced France's empire of Haiti, Martinique, other islands, and mainland French Guiana. For a time tropical estates were so lucrative that French diplomats ceded all Canada and the Mississippi Valley to retain small Guadeloupe in the Caribbean. The potent mixture of Africans and agriculture, of slavery and sugar also brought the Dutch to Aruba, Curaçao, Suriname, and Brazil, the last of which was seized from the Portuguese and held for a generation. European competition for slaves and slave colonies explains why many Caribbeans today speak French, Dutch, and English rather than only Spanish.[8]

For centuries financial balance sheets determined a slave's living conditions—and the need for constant imports. Mortality rates were high, not necessarily from hard work but from poor working conditions. On Brazilian plantations, slaves were typically issued two shirts and two pairs of trousers per year. Foreign travelers invariably noted that stevedores and field laborers were dressed in rags, if clothed at all, despite sometimes harsh weather. Slaves in the mines and sugar estates also slept on filthy straw cots infested with vermin. Bronchitis, diphtheria, and pneumonia, as well as poor water, consistently decimated slave populations. Poor diet particularly affected children, who also did the work of adults by about age eight. In Brazil, the life expectancy for a male slave was only twenty-three years.[9]

Since plantation owners wanted a labor force of strong young males, African women constituted less than a third of total imports. Hence, slave populations in Latin America did not naturally replenish, particularly since female mortality rates were high. Slave masters considered child rearing a burden: nurturing mothers worked less, growing children consumed profits, and family life distracted workers. Child rearing was a particular burden for slave mothers, as one observer noted:

> I was particularly astonished to see some women far gone in their pregnancy, toiling in the field; and others, whose naked infants lay exposed to the weather, sprawling on a goatskin or in a wooden tray. I have heard, with indignation, drivers curse both them and their squalling brats, when they were suckling them.[10]

Slave women frequently miscarried, mostly from exertion, poor diet, and wretched health caused by contaminated drinking water and miserable sanitation. Many died giving birth. Thus, slave "breeding" in Latin America never supplanted imports.[11]

Almost 400 years of importation rather than natural growth held profound consequences for Latin America as endless replenishing renewed cultural ties with Africa. Statistics for Brazil reveal that cultural contact grew with time. In the sixteenth century a quarter-million African slaves reached Brazil. Imports increased to almost 2 million in the eighteenth century and to about 1.5 million between 1800 and 1875.[12]

The black diaspora—the forced migration of Africans to the Americas—brought diverse peoples to different places. The patterns of commerce—where slave ships began and ended their journeys—left a crazy-quilt pattern of previously alien or hostile Africans jumbled together at various new world ports. The human stream of Africans originated from a region as large and differentiated as Europe, stretching from Senegal in the north through Angola in the south, and marked by deserts, jungles, savannas, forests, mountains, valleys, and plains. And many came during the last decades of the slave trade from east Africa. These immigrants were differentiated in appearance, culture, and social status. Slave ships plying African waters collected these mixed peoples from dozens of ports fed by hundreds of paths into distant African hinterlands. After enduring the trauma of capture and a hellish "middle passage," slaves on these ships were unloaded in American ports, usually those currently paying high prices. Seeking familiarity, African immigrants sought out persons with similar language and customs in new world ports and plantations. Somehow patterns emerged, as over decades and generations particular captains and shipping companies returned to familiar ports on both Atlantic shores. From present Nigeria, large numbers of Yoruba arrived in Cuba, Trinidad, and the southern hump of Brazil. Immigrants from Dahomey gathered in Haiti, and many from Angola journeyed to the hump of Brazil. Kromanti origins are today evident in Jamaica and other English Caribbean islands. Slave ships deposited Fanti-Ashanti ancestors in the Dutch and French Antilles. Ibo, Guinea, and Bantu peoples and even Sudanese from east Africa still form cultural clusters in the new world. The black diaspora known as the Atlantic slave trade began with diversity. It created complexity.[13]

The Atlantic slave trade changed the demographics of three continents—Africa and both Americas. It affected the fortunes of a fourth—Europe. In the process, hapless victims of demand and supply were subjected to terror, torture, and endless challenge. Racially and culturally, Africans blended with each other, Europeans, and—more often than acknowledged—Indigens and mestizos. The keys to survival were adaptation and assimilation.

SLAVERY

Not all blacks in the Americas were slaves. But slavery was so pervasive that slaves, indentured and free blacks, masters, and people far removed from slave regions (like New Englanders) felt its impact. A labor system, slavery also conveyed culture. Over twenty generations, the institution strengthened and waned, evolving as it encountered diverse environments and melding with other institutions. Variety was the only constant. And although slavery ended a century ago, its legacy endures.

The first blacks in the new world were Iberians of African descent. Called *moros,* their ancestors were Moors enslaved during *la reconquista.* Many came to the Americas after 1492 as trusted family members, arriving as personal servants, mechanics, carpenters, shipwrights, and even soldiers. Thoroughly Hispanicized and often indistinguishable from their masters, they occasionally slipped from servitude to arrive in another port as just another Spaniard. Like Estevanico in the American southwest, some were explorers. And some *moros* became *encomenderos.*

Many free blacks lived in Latin America during the era of slavery. Unlike in the United States, Latin American slaves often purchased their freedom. They used savings from odd jobs, profits from selling produce or handicrafts, or personal fees earned for services like herbal curing or repelling ants. In the Brazilian pits at Minas Gerais, slave miners fulfilled their quotas and often accumulated enough extra to buy liberty. In an environment of servitude, many former slaves purchased slaves—and they were just as demanding or benevolent as any white master. However, many blacks were never slaves, having arrived in the Americas under short-term work contracts such as crewing Spanish ships. And the population of freed blacks grew when masters granted manumission.[14]

The work of Latin Americans varied tremendously. Joining enslaved Indigens in Brazil, blacks supplied the endless toil on plantations. They sowed, harvested, and processed sugar, cotton, indigo, tobacco, and other tropical commodities. And slaves were domestics: cooks, nannies, coachmen, servants, household repairmen, barbers, musicians, and groundskeepers. But slaves also dove for pearls, fished the sea, harvested salt, mined the earth, sorted precious stones, drove cattle, and tanned hides. The more respected workers were the many skilled artisans—the blacksmiths, cobblers, sailors, mechanics, carpenters, masons, and shipwrights—who both built the infrastructure of tropical America and made it function. Slaves also held specialty professions such as town criers, harbor pilots, and public executioners. In Brazil, illiterate white masters allowed educated Muslim slaves both to keep plantation accounts and to correspond with other secretaries in Arabic. White masters also fostered and exploited vices such as hustling: in cities, slave women worked as prostitutes and pickpockets. Both freed blacks—and slaves earning their freedom—enlisted in colonial militias. Living accommodations for slaves varied greatly. Some resided in the plantation "big house"; many more occupied dirty and often windowless barracks. In urban areas, artisans usually enjoyed their own town houses and domestics lived in modest but comfortable servant quarters. Vaqueros (cowboys) led a natural existence, living as they liked on the open range or ranches. In hindsight, blacks during the era of slavery did many things under many conditions. They were adaptive and talented.[15]

From a captive's perspective, the major objective of slavery was escape, and flight was more common than rebellion. When slaves did revolt, they typically opposed immediate abuses rather than the entire slave regime. Those who fled were called *cimarróns* in Spanish or "Maroons" in English. These runaways left Caribbean islands by dugout or slipped from plantations, seeking remote hideaways in "the bush" or the *monte*—swamps, bayous, forests, or hills—where they established isolated homesteads and villages. For centuries Maroons and their descendants (typically moved freely between their isolated communities—called *quilombos* in Brazil, *palenques* in Spanish America—and the society from which they escaped, seeking in each what they lacked in the other. When Maroon genes and cultures blended with those of equally reclusive Indigens, the resulting societies were termed *zambos.* And fears of *casta* (nonwhite) unity caused imperial nightmares: prohibiting Africans from associating with Indigens prompted lengthy regulations and endless military preparations. However, *zambos* did not seek rebellion so much as autonomy. They formed isolated societies along swampy Caribbean shores from western Venezuela, through Colombia and Central America, and as far north as Mexico. Spanish Florida also had *zambo* communities: the Seminoles were a mixture of Cherokees and slaves, escaping both English and American domination. *Zambo* towns also dotted the Pacific coast islands of Colombia and Ecuador. In Latin America, many of these Maroon and *zambo* communities evolved into modern times as isolated rural people: for them, the more isolated, the better.[16]

Confrontations between Maroons and former masters usually fared badly for slaves. The process began early, in 1545, when an African "kingdom" in Peru was suppressed. But the most famous *quilombo* in the Americas was Palmares, a kingdom of villages and towns in Brazil's interior. Palmares existed for decades with its own farms and commerce, its own militia. The grand *quilombo* attracted growing numbers of Maroons until a Portuguese army subdued it following a long campaign. Maroon communities also existed in Jamaica before the English arrived. Relations between the Maroons and English planters oscillated between antagonism and accommodation: treaties even recognized Maroon autonomy in return for gathering new runaways. Like Palmares, Jamaica's Maroons were eventually conquered; many escaped to mainland Central America, others were deported to Nova Scotia.[17]

Economic transformations, particularly industrialism, eventually ended slavery. The economics of slavery limited not only rewards but incentives. Lack of inducements discouraged accumulation, innovation, and diversification. Industrialism—including workers with wages—promoted more efficient use of resources, including labor. Efficiency made for greater profits. As industrialism developed in the nineteenth century, slave economies declined.[18]

Economically inefficient, slavery was also socially dysfunctional. Slave families were rare as marriage and monogamy were sometimes prohibited and usually discouraged. Promiscuity, rape, and temporary cohabitation were common. A mother and her children often constituted a family. Race mixing occurred since masters usually kept concubines or mistresses, and miscegenation characterized Portuguese, English, French, and Spanish estates. Among the exploited women, mulattas fared best, if racial proverbs can be trusted. One claimed: "Brazil is hell for blacks, purgatory for whites and heaven for *mulatas*!" For some mulatta mistresses it must have been heaven, for they were adorned in silks and jewels, and were paraded publicly to symbolize both the master's wealth and their own privileged status.[19]

AFRICAN LATIN CULTURE

Born in the twin regimes of the slave trade and slavery, the resourcefulness of African Latin culture is evident everywhere. Black culture is neither singularly

African nor similar throughout the Americas. It blends things African, European, Indigen, and immigrant in endless diversity. Blacks in the Americas have adapted Spanish guitars, English parliaments, Dutch sloops, French cuisine, Portuguese architecture, and Indigen spirituality. Learning to adapt or perish, blacks persevere by modifying: combining strengths of their own cultures with what was needed from others. In music and dance, food and fashion, language and religion, African Latin culture is still creative five centuries after black cargoes first arrived.[20]

Probably no domain of culture is more important than food. While we only occasionally visit art museums or notice architecture, we eat every day. While we might endure unpleasant music, only rarely do we dine on the distasteful. From haute cuisine to fast food and ethnic dishes, what we eat says much about who we are. The realm of food reveals the subtle but central position of women in both daily life and cultural change. In African Latin societies—as virtually everywhere—cooking has been predominantly a female task. Slave cooks combined African customs with European and new world foods to feed families, masses of workers, and white masters. The challenge was formidable and innovation endless. In kitchens, gardens, markets, and homes, through street vending or at field workstations, generations of African Latin women experimented, adapted, and improvised. Through their efforts American palates became accustomed to such African foods as bananas, melons, cucumbers, watermelon, okra, tamarinds, palm oil, cola nut beverages, coffee, sugar, millet, sorghum, eggplant, coconut, better strains of rice than those grown in southern Europe, and various fowl and pigs. Black women also enriched their dishes with Indigen foods: chilies, potatoes, pineapples, corn, tomatoes, and others. Living proximate to the Caribbean and along the Atlantic, they used all kinds of fish and shellfish. Such a grocery list begins African Latin cooking, but preparation completes the cuisine. Sensuality became a hallmark as color, shape, texture, and smell enhanced taste to provide some simple but important pleasures. The results are amazing. As demonstrated by jambalaya in Louisiana, meat pies in Jamaica, or coconut pastries in Bahia, proof is in the tasting.[21]

Music is the best-recognized African Latin contribution to the Americas, and the world. Singing while working, black vocalists used their bodies to make music. Voice itself was versatile as chanting, shouts, moans, falsettos, whistling, and other expressions became artistic styles. The hands, feet, thighs, and other body parts provided percussion through clapping, stomping, thumping, and tapping. Black music is born of a collective experience, highly participatory, as evidenced by shouts and responses, overlays of octaves, syncopation, and great complexity with few people. Instruments were improvised from junk or from whatever could be gathered from forest, field, or seashore. With loving care, common trash such as boxes, boards, cans, old washbasins, bones, sticks, shells, and empty oil barrels were worked into maracas, drums, tambourines, bells, castanets, horns, flutes, and various stringed instruments. Ingenious in the face of poverty, blacks seemingly made something from nothing. That something was great music.[22]

As with music, African Latins excelled at dance. More than fun, black dance was initially religious and ceremonial: ancestral spirits infused living bodies, and whirling dancers dramatized natural forces through mimicking the movement of animals, plants, rain, waves, and wind. Dance also told stories of people working, of dreams, of the land before the middle passage, of erotic desires. Originally a predominantly male art form, African dance in the Americas was joined by women and eventually formalized into the samba and rumba. Blacks also moved to their own internal rhythms, in the everyday body language of personal cadence evident in hand gestures and arm movements, in walking, talking, laughing, and even listening.[23]

African Latins also show distinctive spiritualism. Slaves blended African beliefs with Catholic and Protestant faiths. The syncretism of Catholicism was obvious as blacks worshiped particular Catholic saints who curiously resembled African deities. Anglo-Africans or Dutch-Africans in Jamaica, Trinidad, or Suriname organized Protestant congregations where simple hymns became emotional existential statements. Everywhere African Latins developed religious cults. Haitians reincarnated Bantu beliefs as voodoo, and in Cuba Santeria blended popular Catholic superstitions with African magic. The same was true of *espiritú* in Puerto Rico. On the hump of Brazil *condomblé* elevated women to priestesses. African spirituality also infused folk medicine, biblical stories, and Aesop-like fables filled with magical animals, personal morals, reverence for elders, and the mysteries of nature. African Latin belief differed from rationalist European religions by emphasizing emotion, relationships, and experience rather than theology, dogma, and ritual. And while Christianity promised slaves an afterlife, African spirituality was a daily salvation.[24]

To a nonscribal people, verbal communication becomes currency and oral tradition a bank. Since slaves were universally prohibited from writing to convey and reading to remember, their oral legacy became a cultural glue. Building on the African art of expressive storytelling, black women and men employed chanting, singing, poetry, improvisation, cadence, and intonation to enrich an oral legacy. Preserving one's history and identity depended on retelling events, fables, and odes through many generations. Officially denied writing (although some were literate from previous training), slaves learned spoken Portuguese, English, Dutch, French, or Spanish and infused them with Africanisms to create patois and creole, something very different than speech in Lisbon, London, Paris, or Madrid. A twentieth-century catalog of Cuban Spanish lists 1200 commonly used African words and phrases. A similar African influence characterizes Jamaica, Brazil, Haiti, and wherever slaves were forced to use a European idiom. So massive was the blending of European and African language that Jamaicans visiting elsewhere in the Caribbean are called *Inglés,* that is, "the English."[25]

BLACK DEMOGRAPHICS

Black populations today constitute about 6 percent of Latin America and are identifiable mainly in regions that experienced heavy slave imports. Some Caribbean nations—Jamaica, Haiti, and the smaller eastern Antilles—are predominantly black. Other Caribbean countries—the Dominican Republic, Puerto Rico, and Cuba—have fewer blacks and many more mulattoes. The mainland Caribbean nations—Belize, Honduras, Nicaragua, Costa Rica, Panama, Colombia, and Venezuela—have coastal zones of predominantly black or mulatto peoples who differ in culture, religion, and language from typically highland criollo and mestizo majorities. Many of these African Latins descend from ancestors who escaped slavery on Caribbean islands. In the nineteenth and twentieth centuries, English Caribbeans were hired by U.S. companies to build railroads, cultivate bananas, and dig the Panama Canal in Central America. In the Guyanas, blacks usually constitute half the population, the other half being Asians from India or Indonesia. On the hump of northeastern Brazil, African Brazilians concentrate in the port cities of Bahia and Recife, but they have also migrated in more recent times to Rio and São Paulo in the south.

Some places of former slave importation show little present evidence of earlier black densities. Veracruz and Acapulco in Mexico, and Buenos Aires, Argentina, once imported numerous Africans, but the immigrants blended with Indigens, mestizos, and Europeans. And where African Latins existed as servants and artisans—places like highland Mexico and Peru—little remains to affirm a former presence.

Population statistics only suggest the powerful influence of Africa in the Americas. At the milepost year 2000, African Latins will number about 33 million, similar to the African-American community in the United States. But with almost twice the total population, almost 500 million inhabitants, Latin America has half the percentage of blacks as does the United States. Yet such numbers are estimates at best, for clear delineations between "white" and "black" are a fiction. In the United States, as in Latin America, mixing and "passing" have been common.[26]

The ledger book of racial demographics only suggests the powerful and pervasive influence of Africans in the new world. In countries like Cuba and Brazil—where more modern immigration from Europe came in floods—African Latins constitute 10 to 15 percent of the population. Yet the pulse of national rhythm often sways to an African beat. In music, dance, food, even body language, those without black genes became partly Africanized through centuries of association. Who could have guessed that enslaved people would command such legacies?

THE AFRICANNESS OF THE AMERICAS

The impact of Africa on others in the Americas came in many ways. Nannies, wet nurses, and servants shared love as well as culture and sustenance with slaveholders' children—in effect, their future masters. African Latin stories, music, movements, and dispositions subtly entered white consciousness and rippled through society. Black culture also reached whites directly through Latin American institutions. During colonial times *cabildos de nación* (fraternal clubs or ethnic associations) were organized by both free blacks and slaves to serve as social centers and cultural preservation societies. Some *cabildos de nación* operated as banks and loan agencies to buy freedom for slaves. They also transmitted African Latin culture to whites by using Christian holy days, such as the Epiphany (one of the three wise men was black) and Mardi Gras, for festivals where African dance, music, and food were plentiful. Whites joined the fun of carnival and began to dance and sing differently.[27]

Recognition of African Latin culture has grown during the twentieth century. A key factor in strengthening black awareness was reaction to invading U.S. Marines who brought Jim Crow racism, particularly to Cuba, Haiti, and Central America. A decade later, black consciousness invaded the United States when Marcus Garvey left Jamaica to excite racial pride in U.S. cities; today his Rastafarian followers use reggae music and Trenchtown culture, and reach mixed-race audiences throughout the world. On a professional level, whites and blacks have promoted awareness of African Latin culture since the Afro-Brazilian Congress of 1934. At Recife, anthropologists, linguists, historians, folklorists, and others formalized African Latin culture as an academic topic. Since then, scholarly journals, books, popular magazine articles, festivals, films, and recordings have spread recognition of African Latin culture.[28]

Like mestizos, African Latins are a new people in the new world, but they are not totally new. Blacks melded African customs with new world cultures in thousands of ways and in hundreds of places. The result was magic on the loom. Today, many different African Latin legacies exist. And the weaving continues.

THE IMMIGRANT

Representing their nations, presidents of countries also demonstrate ethnic heritage. During recent times Latin American presidents with names like Frondizi, Menem, Stroessner, Goulart, Kubitschek, Grove, Jagan, and Fujimori have represented not only Argentina, Paraguay, Brazil, Chile, Guyana, and Peru but the achievements of immigrants from Italy, Syria, Germany, France, Yugoslavia, Great Britain, India, and Japan. Our list might also include the independence-era hero of Chile, Bernardo O'Higgins, whose ancestry needs no identification.

The most recent additions to Latin America's ethnic tapestry have been arriving in large numbers since the mid-nineteenth century. They came from Europe, east and south Asia, and Arab lands in three migratory waves: first from 1880 to 1914, then following World War I, and again after World War II. These modern arrivals far outnumbered earlier *peninsulares* and equaled slave trade immigration, which they replaced. Argentina received the greatest numbers, with immigration there creating higher rations than in the United States: in 1914 one of three persons was born abroad. The highest ratio for the United States was half that.[29]

Modern immigrants arrived poor and initially seemed to contribute little more than sweat and diversity. But their cultural baggage included beliefs, behaviors, and ambitions that were revealed as children and grandchildren ascended in status and power. Where immigrants were predominantly male, marriages to African Latins and mestizos were common. Growing family wealth also brought criollo suitors. With intermarriage came Catholicism and Latin culture, already familiar to many migrants from southern Europe. When immigrant women arrived, the customs of the old land lasted longer.

PEASANTS AND POSITIVISM

People leave ancestral lands for two reasons: things are bad where they are and better elsewhere. Such "push" and "pull" factors characterized mass European migration in the nineteenth century when growing populations drove the rural poor to seaports leading elsewhere. Meanwhile, in Canada, Latin America, the United States, and Australia, "pull" factors included the promise of farms (or farmwork), industrial and service jobs, and the dream of progress, perhaps even owning land.

Latin American elites initially encouraged white immigrants. By the 1860s, criollos governed almost everywhere, and while some still dreamed of feudal estates with nonwhite workers, most envisioned modern nations of order and progress based on a philosophy called positivism. Positivism included pseudoscientific concepts of race: industrious whites would replace supposedly less efficient darker races. "To govern is to populate," said the criollo president of Argentina Juan Bautista Alberdi in the 1850s. What he meant was that Argentina "must construct our population to fit our system of government; . . . we must increase the Anglo-Saxon population in our land. They are the ones who are identified with the steamship, with commerce, and with liberty." However, few Anglo-Saxons arrived, even after criollos made immigration a mandate in Argentina's constitution of 1853: "The federal government will encourage European immigration."[30]

Criollo ideals became policy across the Americas as African Latins, mestizos, and primarily Indigens were displaced by white Europeans, albeit poor ones. On the prairies of Canada, the plains of the United States, and the pampas of Argentina, poor European peasants colonized Indigen lands. In Buenos Aires the philosopher, educator, and president, positivist Domingo Faustino Sarmiento elaborated criollo ideals in his rambling newspaper essays later assembled as *The Life of Juan Facundo Quiroga: Civilization and Barbarism.* Sarmiento depicted a titanic struggle between wild *castas* and civilized white citizens. Criollo progress included wars to exterminate Indigens, replacing them with European immigrants, as in the United States. Typical for criollos, Europe supplied both philosophical ends and practical means: positivism and peasants.[31]

Positivist ideas were as much a path to European immigration as the gangplanks of ocean freighters. Mexican liberals recruited German, British, and "Yankees" to settle the northern provinces of Texas and California. In Argentina, railroads and steel ships took away meat and wheat and returned with Italian and Spanish peasants. Brazil exported rich coffees and imported poor Portuguese and Italian coffee pickers. Chile shipped nitrates and timber while bringing Italian miners and German lumberjacks. During the decades surrounding 1900 the stream of Europeans arriving in Latin America—particularly in temperate southern climates—became a flood. The arriving peasants dreamed of owning farms. And there existed plenty of land, or at least work on other people's land.

The immigrant numbers were substantial. Between 1850 and World War II (with an interruption during World War I), 11 million Europeans arrived in Latin America. Nine decades of immigration virtually equaled almost 400 years of the Atlantic slave trade. Nearly 3.5 million Europeans went to Argentina, and almost as many moved to southern Brazil. Three out of every twenty migrants sailed for Cuba, and smaller numbers journeyed to Uruguay, Mexico, Costa Rica, and Chile. After World War II, smaller numbers of refugees arrived in almost all Latin American nations.[32]

Table 3-2 lists six European nations that made significant contributions to the region's ethnic tapestry.[33] More than three-quarters of the region's modern immigra-

TABLE 3-2
MAJOR SOURCES OF EUROPEAN MIGRATION, 1850–1940

Nation	Numbers, millions	Percent of total
Italy	4.2	38
Spain	3.0	28
Portugal	1.2	11
Germany	0.3	3
France	0.3	3
Russia	0.3	3

tion came from Italy, Spain, and Portugal. Language and national customs attracted Portuguese peasants to Brazil, but criollo families and arriving farmworkers were separated by the chasms of land ownership, wealth, education, status, and access to political power. Similar gaps characterized immigrants to Spanish America, and here a long-standing pecking order derived from Castile's early domination of other Iberian peoples widened and deepened the breach. Original *peninsulares* usually prided themselves on a Castilian identity—bequeathed to criollo descendants—while most modern arrivals were Basques, Asturians, Catalans, Galicians, and Andalusians. Differences were evident in customs and lifestyles but also in well-defined accents and even separate languages (Basque and Catalan). Criollo slurs against immigrating Iberians labeled them *gallegos:* persons from Galicia in northwestern Spain. But *gallego* also meant "hick."[34]

Italians also came to Latin America in large numbers, and their descendants now concentrate in Argentina, Uruguay, and southern Brazil, with lesser numbers in Chile. Italians constitute the largest percentage of modern European immigrants to Latin America: 38 percent of arrivals between 1850 and World War II. Many of these Italians were blond, blue-eyed, and fair-skinned. They were *northern* Italians from the Po Valley, Trieste, and parts of the former Austro-Hungarian Empire. Nicknamed "swallows," many initially migrated twice yearly between Italy and Argentina, following the sun to summer farmwork. Eventually many nested in the new world as either rural workers or urban proletarians. Some Italian families achieved great success in the new world, arriving as peons and advancing each decade through owning a general store, managing grain or pork distributorships, constructing processing plants for canned lard and milled flour, producing soaps, harvesting lumber, and so on. And Italians entered politics, becoming presidents of southern South American nations.[35]

Non-Latin immigrants arrived from Europe in smaller but significant numbers. Germans migrated to the forested mountains of southern Chile and Argentina, which still retain a distinct Teutonic flavor in architecture, crafts, music, and cuisine. German immigrants also settled in the mountains of Venezuela, Colombia, and Guatemala. One descendant of German immigrants, Alfredo Stroessner, served for three decades as the autocrat of Paraguay. More common professions for Germans included dairy farming, lumbering, managing coffee plantations, and merchandizing European products from film to pharmaceuticals. Welsh and other British islanders settled in mainland colonies opposite the Malvinas (Falkland) Islands, in southern Argentina. Swiss, Welsh, Irish, and French colonists also arrived in Uruguay and southern Brazil. People from Poland, Yugoslavia, Russia, Ukraine, and other eastern European nations settled in Venezuela, Mexico, Cuba, and Brazil.

Since about two-thirds of the arriving European immigrants were males aged eighteen to forty, intermarriage and learning customs from mestizo or African Latin wives were common. In Argentina, seven of ten immigrants were single men aged thirty to forty. In 1914, a census counted three men to every two women in the country. When immigrant women came, the European heritage lasted longer. But immigrant children raised in Latin American barrios with mestizo or mulatto children also helped blend races and cultures.[36]

Immigrant dreams of easy achievement lasted briefly. Newly arrived workers were exploited by criollo landlords accustomed to legacies of cheap labor and personal authority. Despite some immigrant achievements, upward mobility was difficult for the *descamisados,* an Argentine term meaning "shirtless ones" and designating a largely immigrant proletariat. *Descamisados* herded cattle and tended sheep, or planted and harvested wheat on the pampas. In Buenos Aires, *descamisados* were meat packers, stevedores, construction workers and sweatshop operatives.

In his careful case study, *The Prairies and the Pampas: Agrarian Policy in Canada and Argentina, 1880–1930,* Carl E. Solberg tells the tale of contrasting immigrant fortunes. Immigrants to Canada were granted land but also provided loans, schools, access to markets, and more. Life was still difficult, and many faced discrimination, but owning land, forming cooperatives, and developing leadership gave Canadian immigrants a vested interest in politics and progress. In Argentina, immigrants lived on haciendas as tenants. They owned next to nothing, and Argentine society made little investment to empower them. Victims of authoritarianism, they grew frustrated and often fatalistic. Much the same happened elsewhere. From coffee pickers in Brazil to miners in Chile, immigrant laborers faced elitist attitudes about work and workers little changed from the days of encomiendas and plantations.

Ships bringing peasants also brought class consciousness and worker militancy. While criollos read positivist prophets like Comte, Spencer, and Gobineau, their hirelings studied revolutionary pamphlets written by followers of Marx, Bakunin, and Proudhoun. More than happy folk with ethnic customs arrived from Europe. Immigrants were—or soon became—socialists, communists, anarchists, and syndicalists. Instead of viewing a growing landscape of either yeoman farms or pliant peasants, criollos were aghast to watch immigrants form unions, stage strikes, create political parties, and, eventually, win elections. After 1900, workers struck in Chile's northern mines and on the docks of Buenos Aires. Criollo governments suppressed these and other protests, killing thousands of workers during one Chilean strike. In the 1930s and 1940s, Argentine *descamisados* found political allies in Juan Domingo Perón and Eva Duarte de Perón, and for a generation worker wages increased, benefits grew, and living standards improved. After Eva died and Perón was overthrown in the 1950s, criollos found willing allies in the military. Only in the 1990s have the scars of ethnic antagonism begun to mend.

The story of European immigration has been one with many endings—or perhaps more like continuing chapters. Some immigrant families have been so successful as to enter criollo society, using politics, education, and entreprenuerial skills as calling cards. This happened with the Allessandri family in Chile, where the young reformist father charged from northern mining regions to become a populist president following World War I. His son later guarded elite privileges following World War II. Juan Perón himself followed a similar road in Argentina; hailed as a savior by *descamisados* in the 1940s, he returned from exile in the 1970s to oppose change. A quest for propriety occurred in business as well as politics: families once laboring as workers now own construction and industrial conglomerates that resist worker consciousness. Many European immigrants assailed criollo status—not to overthrow privilege but to join it.

Other European immigrant families write different stories, usually with chapters about professional achievement and middle-class status. As doctors, engineers, teachers, and journalists, grandsons and granddaughters continue the immigrant's dream of respectability and material success. Those struggling for working-class consciousness also have middle-class sequels. Some unions have secured contracted wages and hours, pensions, savings plans, unemployment compensation, and other benefits. Where unions and labor parties succeeded—even temporarily—the immigrant goal of security was accomplished.

IMMIGRANTS FROM ASIA

Columbus may not have found east Asia, but Asians have discovered the Americas. Asian migration began in the sixteenth century when the solitary Manila Galleon made its annual trip between Acapulco and the Philippines, linking Spain's Asian colony to empire. Mexicans went to Manila, and one official ship per year returned to the land of the Aztecs loaded with people and products from Asia. Many more illegal ships made the journey, bringing contraband goods as well as Filipino, Japanese, and Chinese crews and slaves. The influence of the Manila trade remains in Mexico, where Asian motifs and artisans created a legacy of design and color.[37]

More modern Asian migrations occurred when U.S. and British companies brought Chinese workers to many new world locations. After the United States excluded Chinese immigration in the 1880s, contracted workers from California—as well as new recruits from China—were taken to Latin America. In Mexico the industrious Chinese formed construction crews in North American–owned mines, on railways, or in oil fields. Staying in Mexico after their contracts expired, the Chinese sought professions in agriculture or commerce. In northern Mexico, Chinese farmers irrigated the desert and made it bloom with cotton, rice, sugar, vegetables, and their famous fruit orchards. In towns and cities, the Chinese became merchants, beginning as traveling vendors and eventually owning general stores, clothing shops, and pharmacies. Using family and friends overseas, local merchants brought products from the United States and Asia. The more prosperous entered banking and real estate, some eventually owned small factories.[38]

Despite economic success, Chinese social life in Mexico was difficult. Males far outnumbered women, but few Chinese men took Mexican wives. Instead, immigrants dreamed of returning wealthy to China or brought "picture brides" from their homeland. Social links with Mexican society were rare, as the Chinese preferred living in isolated agricultural communities or in "Chinatowns." The mix of material gain and social isolation made for explosive politics as during the early twentieth century the Chinese were repeatedly targeted as exploiters. Riots, looting, and killing decimated Chinese communities during the violent and nationalistic Mexican Revolution. Thousands died, and most fled for their lives.

Chinese workers entered Central America with U.S. companies building railroads. They labored on the Panamanian isthmus route in the 1850s and extended rails into the banana lowlands and coffee highlands of Costa Rica, Honduras, and Guatemala. Today, Chinese restaurants throughout Central America testify to early working-class immigration. The Chinese also went to Caribbean islands, with Cuba receiving the largest number: 150,000 between 1849 and 1875. Many Chinese fled from race riots in the western United States and were nicknamed "Californians." In the Caribbean, they not only pushed rail lines through sugar fields but cut cane. But plantation life was dismal, as malaria and yellow fever combined with endless exploitation and sparse opportunity. Social life was minimal, and virtually all immigrants were men. Homesick and melancholic, many committed suicide. But once labor contracts expired, Chinese workers usually drifted to nearby cities, where they married African Latin women or brought wives from China. Today, both Asian-Africans and Chinese Latins are seen on Caribbean islands.[39]

Asians arrived early to Peru. A Lima census in 1613 recorded thirty-eight Chinese or Filipinos, twenty Japanese, and fifty-six persons from the East Indies. As in Mexico, large numbers of Chinese went to Peru with railway companies in the nineteenth century, but the British also contracted workers to dig guano on desert islands. Dusty bird droppings were dug and hauled with pick, shovel, and cart, all in intense heat. Since no one freely chose such work, recruits in China were promised work as household servants and, once unloaded on Peru's Chibcha Islands, held in chains. Breathing and eating surrounded by guano dust led to high mortality, including death from suicide. Those who survived fifteen years of this hell were allowed to migrate to the mainland. Working initially as day laborers, they climbed the economic ladder through effort and enterprise. Today, Chinese descendants are found among professions, in business, and as large-scale farmers in most west coast nations.[40]

Brazil and Peru are the two Latin American nations with sizable Japanese populations. In the nineteenth century, Japanese migrants initially went to Hawaii, California, Canada, and Peru. When racism restricted migration to the United States in 1908, the first trickle of farmers from Iwo Jima and Okinawa arrived in Brazil. By World War II, when Japanese migration ended, about a quarter million countrymen had joined them. Today, well over a million persons of Japanese descent live in Brazil. The early immigrants first picked coffee, but with ceaseless effort they advanced from field hand to tenant, to yeoman farmer, then to employer—usually over two generations. Enterprise was a family affair, since wives and children also migrated to work gardens that were leased or bought near large cities and developed intensively to supply growing urban markets with produce, fruits, eggs, and poultry. Some Japanese truck farms became big businesses. Today, many Japanese Brazilians have moved from family businesses into such professions as medicine, law, and education. Through marriage, blending with other cultures is common, yet devotion to ancestral tradition endures; in this sense, Japanese values reinforce those of Latin America. Cooperation within families is intense, hard work is often communal, and individual profits are pooled.[41]

The other Latin American nation with a notable Japanese population is Peru, which in 1990 elected Alberto Fujimori as the first president of Japanese ancestry in a western hemisphere nation. Japanese immigrants—numbering only 30,000—arrived in Peru between 1926 and 1941, typically worked in agriculture, and saved and invested. Valuing education, many became professionals; Fujimori, for example, earned a doctorate in agronomy from the University of Wisconsin. In presidential politics, he opposed novelist Mario Vargas Llosa, a prominent criollo. In 1995, he was reelected over another criollo icon, former UN Secretary General Javier Pérez de Cuellar.

Asians began arriving in the Caribbean as the slave trade ended in the nineteenth century. Since Caribbean planters still needed workers, labor recruiters in Calcutta became busy supplying more than a half million Indian immigrants to Trinidad, Jamaica, Guyana, and other British colonies between 1838 and 1918. Most were Hindu, but about one-fifth were Muslim. And once their labor contracts expired, many moved to vacant lands and founded communities with names like Chandernagore, Fyzabad, and Madras Settlement. With muscle and persistence, they diked and drained marshes to create farmland. Today, most Indians in the Caribbean are still farmers, small-town artisans, or merchants, but Indians have also become doctors, lawyers, journalists, scholars, and a family of famous authors: the Naipuls from Trinidad. Some have become prominent politicians. In Guyana, ethnicity became the dividing line of politics as presidential candidates Cheddi Jagan and Forbes Burnham personified ideological contrasts. Jagan was Indian and a Marxist; Burnham was African and friendly to British corporations. A generation of intense rivalries often exploded into riots and killing. In contrast, the story of ethnic diversity has been peaceful in nearby Trinidad. There, Indians and Africans achieve harmony, particularly in cuisine and music: disco stars are often accompanied by both sitars and steel drums.[42]

What the British did with Indians, the Dutch did with Indonesians. During the 1930s, Dutch developers resettled many Indonesian families from Java to Suriname, on the South American mainland. Again the demand was for plantation workers. And again those who came brought their heritage. In the process, another Latin American location became the crossroads of culture: this time Dutch, Indonesian, African, and Indigen.[43]

JEWISH IMMIGRANTS

Some small groups play large roles. From the beginning of European contact, Jews helped weave Latin America's ethnic tapestry. In 1492, Spain was a doorway between two worlds, a threshold of time and place. The Moors were conquered after

700 years, the monarchy of Isabel and Fernando imposed conformist Catholicism, and a small speculative expedition crossed the Atlantic. Jews participated in all these events, caught as in a whirlwind. Forced to convert, many Jews left Spain. But others felt complex personal motives—from maintaining homes, to preserving wealth, to feeling national greatness—and converted to Catholicism. These *conversos* were no poor folk, for the Jews of Spain, including conquered Moorish Spain, were a powerful class of doctors, lawyers, scholars, and bankers. Some sought legitimacy through lending resources to Isabel and Fernando. Thus, the financing of Columbus's journey—the equivalent of funding a modern journey to Mars—came from Jews demonstrating a necessary or useful patriotism.[44]

During colonial times Jews remained important to the new world. Despite their conversions—some ardent, many superficial—"New Christians" were considered suspect by jealous Iberian elites. Increasingly, *conversos* were denied sensitive or lucrative opportunities, like living in the Americas. Yet *converso* money continued to open forbidden doors, and new world documents frequently labeled affluent immigrants as "New Christians." But Iberian Jewish families driven to European exile eventually arrived in the Americas. In the mid-1600s, when Holland seized major parts of Brazil for a generation, Dutch Jews with Iberian ancestors sailed from Amsterdam to become Brazilian planters. Synagogues and temple schools were opened in Recife and Bahia. When the Portuguese reconquered the region, the Jews did not stay to test Iberian tolerance a second time. Instead, many sailed with Dutch fleets to the Caribbean, taking sugarcane cuttings, plantation technology, slaves, and capital with them.[45]

Sizable Jewish migration to Latin America did not occur until the early twentieth century. And unlike earlier Jewish immigrants, these people did not come from Iberia or Holland with cash and credit but from the eastern Mediterranean with little more than integrity and ambition. Their destinations were many. Argentina ranks third after modern Israel and the United States as a haven for Jews. Brazil also has a substantial Jewish community, and smaller numbers are found in Venezuela, Mexico, and elsewhere. When Jews escaping Nazi persecution were barred from the United States in the 1930s, many went to "Hotel Kuba," so named for its role as a generational halfway house. Many Jews coming to the United States during the 1950s were children or young adults with Cuban passports and European parents.[46]

Immigrants from the former Ottoman Empire formed the largest Jewish migration. During the early twentieth century, young single men from Romania, Syria, or Lebanon typically visited Argentina or Brazil to establish a business before returning for a bride and moving permanently to Latin America with a family. Although poor, these petty entrepreneurs brought the wealth of literacy and the ability to keep ledgers and compute finances. They began as itinerant peddlers and progressed to owning general stores. Trips to the old world resupplied these merchants with their best-selling items: religious relics from the Holy Land. The more practical also sold everything from hardware and fuel to seeds and advice. Jewish immigrants were also haberdashers, watchmakers, locksmiths, bakers, pharmacists, book dealers, cobblers, and optometrists. Their most important "item" was credit. They financed consumer buying as well as their own purchasing and production. Women and children joined men in crafting and selling, and many family businesses grew into major industries. A deep commitment to learning led later-generation Jews into the professional world as journalists, doctors, lawyers, and engineers. Young Jewish women—accomplished in languages, music, and the arts—initially tutored and later became teachers and school administrators.[47]

But success, together with fascist dictatorships during the cold war era, targeted Jews for anti-Semitism, particularly in Argentina. Prejudice drew upon an Iberian legacy, emulation of Hitler and Mussolini, training in terrorism, and military resentment of civilian critics. Jewish editors, professors, attorneys, and students were frequent targets of anticommunist regimes. They were tortured in chambers adorned with swastikas and desecrations of Judaic symbols. Lesser campaigns accompanied similar repressions in Brazil, Uruguay, and Chile during the 1970s. While those regimes are gone, bitter memories remain.

Never numerous, Jews in Latin America have nonetheless been prominent. They have played key roles in history and have attained significant economic success.

ARAB IMMIGRANTS

Arabic influence in Latin America was planted before the conquistadores left Spain. For 700 years Iberians had absorbed Arabic culture: its language, food, religion, art, architecture, music, literature, and science. During medieval times, Córdoba was one of three great Arabic cities in the Mediterranean world. The Arabic influence reveals itself in Latin American mosaics and patios, vocabulary and cuisine. In modern times, Arabic influence arrived more directly with immigrants from the eastern Mediterranean.

Arabs in Latin America are often misnamed "Turks" since they arrived from the Ottoman Empire, generally from Lebanon and Syria. Some were Muslim, but most were Christians: Greek Orthodox or Maronite rather than Roman Catholic. In their escape from ethnic conflict, their destinations and destinies were often determined by cheap space on transatlantic freighters. Like the Jews, Arabs went to many places. They formed the second-largest foreign community in Buenos Aires by World War I. Today, about half a million descendants of Arab immigrants live in Argentina, and an equal number reside in neighboring Brazil. Mexico and Venezuela also have significant Arab communities. Argentina's president in the 1990s, Carlos Menem, had Arab ancestors, as did the former Colombian president Julio César Turbay.[48]

The Arab experience in Latin America is predominantly urban and either commercial or artisan. Like the Jews, Arabs moved from itinerant selling to owning general and department stores or wholesale distributorships. They also made and sold shoes, clothing, perfumes, toys, and other household items. Many businesses became prosperous industries allowing children and grandchildren to gain university educations and enter professions. And when prosperity arrived, so too did acceptance.

A DYNAMIC TAPESTRY

The ethnic tapestry of Latin America is complex. Mere description is formidable since no other world region shows such mixing of large native populations with so many different immigrants from around the world. But the complexity is more than a roster of Indigens, Iberians, Africans, Asians, and European immigrants. Latin America's ethnicity is also synergistic: blending created new elements. Among these are mestizos and mulattoes, groups created by the historic encounters of conquest and slavery. The arrival of Asians produced another synergism. It appeared early as art following the Manila Galleon and recently as entrepreneurship among Japanese immigrants to Brazil. Synergism also remade definitions of criollo as the energy and effort of poor European immigrants blending with "old whites" softened the boundaries of exclusion.

Perhaps the most potent synergism in the Americas is the least understood: the mixing of Africans and Indigens. Since many more blacks than whites arrived in colonial times, the African-Indigen blending of culture and race was great. Outlawed by colonial white regimes, the mixing was proscribed and little documented—but ubiquitous. It appeared wherever blacks and natives met: among the Mashpee and Naragansett of New England, as Seminoles and "Buffalo Soldiers" in the American south and west, as "black" mestizos in Acapulco and Veracruz, along dense Caribbean coastlines such as the Miskito region of Nicaragua, as *mamelucos* on Brazilian plantations, as gauchos in Argentina, and in new world *quilombos* everywhere. As comprehensive as our account seeks to be, it remains incomplete until the Indigen-African synergism is better studied and better understood.

In Latin America, the mixing of race and cultures has created a multifaceted debate. On the one hand, racism exists. It is evident in everyday discriminations—against Indigens and African Latins—but also in the subtleties of a ladino preference for things European. It shows as the desire of families—black or white—wishing their sons and daughters to marry persons of light complexion so that grandchildren will be whiter. It is subliminally evident in advertising, which portrays role models as affluent, happy, and—often—blond.

Opposing this racism is a historic esteem for dark-skinned peoples, evident in popular culture and the arts. During the colonial era, slave masters often flaunted and adorned their mulatta mistresses. In Mexico, the *puebla china—mestiza castas* such as street vendors—were considered mesmerizing sirens. Flattery surrounds the *cafe con leche* ("coffee with cream") racial blending of black and white in Colombia and Venezuela. A tradition reaching from cabaret singing to modern videos idealizes *morenos* ("colored" gals and guys) for their beauty and vibrancy. Artistic views of Indigen and African Latin culture in the twentieth century have been both powerful and positive, from Mexican murals to Brazilian movies, in songs, novels, dance, and carnival pageantry.

Regardless of current debates, the synergism of race and culture is Latin America's future; indeed, mixing is a world prospect. While pockets of ethnic strife in Bosnia and elsewhere scream from headlines, places like Latin America are quietly pioneering a more likely scenario. Here, ironically, campaigns for tolerating differences are becoming anachronistic as humankind moves toward a condition both ancient and forthcoming: a blending of supposedly distinct genes. Recent scientific evidence points to common ancestors for all humans. Meanwhile, a half millennium of racial mixing in Latin America indicates that Indigens, Europeans, Africans, and Asians will have common children. Esteem for a racially mixed "cosmic race" in

Latin America was first voiced when Mexican essayist José Vasconcelos coined the term in the 1920s. What Vasconcelos meant was the unlimited blending of races to create a totally mixed community: Latin America. He argued that the region's destiny lay not with its divisive past but with its mixed and creative future: the synergism of a growing mestizo/mulatto presence.

Ethnic dynamism abounds in Latin America. But so does diversity. Whites, blacks, Indigens, and others are still evident. Latin America is as much home to a Guatemalan Mayan, an Argentine criollo, or a Haitian black as it is to numerous Mexican mestizos and Brazilian mulattoes. Thus, conflicting characteristics—dynamism and preservation—further compound understanding Latin American ethnicity. The tapestry of peoples evolves while much remains unchanged.

SCENES FROM THE TAPESTRY

In previous times the bare walls of castles were adorned with colorful tapestries. The weavings covered cold and hard stone with human stories: texture created patterns and pictures of people in their daily lives. A much broader tapestry covers the new world with lives more diverse than any castle weaving. This Latin American tapestry is made not of wool and warp but of individuals of many races and cultures, some found only in the new world.

The scenes on the grand tapestry are many, and each is detailed. A black girl in crisp pinafore and shiny shoes walks to school in the Caribbean sun, carrying a book of short stories by Jamaica Kincaid. An elderly Indigen woman in a black derby and colorful clothes sits with other Ecuadoran villagers to separate potatoes from a recent harvest. A young man of Italian ancestry studies law at a university library in Buenos Aires. A mestizo businessman in Mexico City uses the Internet to check closing stock prices in New York. An Amazon hunter stalks a monkey with his blowgun. A criollo woman drives her German car to visit her brother, a priest in nearby Medellín. A barefoot youth in a Haitian village whistles as he sells fresh fish caught by his father. A Central American soldier stands guard beside his military base, watching passing buses filled with ladinos and Indigens. A Costa Rican of Chinese ancestry prepares an air cargo shipment of refrigerated flowers for shipment to London. A baby is born to a Lima house servant who migrated from her Quechua village last year. A Brazilian worker—part Indigen, part African, part European, and thoroughly modern—assembles Volkswagens at a São Paulo factory. These are sample scenes from Latin America's ethnic tapestry. In its complexity, diversity, and dynamism, this tapestry reflects the making of a new world.

SUGGESTED READINGS

Conniff, Michael L., and Thomas J. Davis. *Africans in the Americas: A History of the Black Diaspora.* New York: St. Martin's Press, 1994.

Curtin, Philip D. *The Atlantic Slave Trade: A Census.* Madison: University of Wisconsin Press, 1969.

Klein, Herbert S. *African Slavery in Latin America and the Caribbean.* New York: Oxford University Press, 1986.

Mannix, Daniel P., with Malcolm Cowley. *Black Cargoes: A History of the Atlantic Slave Trade: 1518–1865.* New York: Viking, 1965.

Martínez Montiel, Luz, ed. *Asiatic Migrations in Latin America.* Mexico City: El Colegio de México, 1981.

Mattoso, Katia M. de Queirós. *To Be a Slave in Brazil, 1550–1888,* trans. Arthur Goldhammer. New Brunswick, N.J.: Rutgers University Press, 1986.

Mintz, Sidney W., and Richard Price. *The Birth of African-American Culture.* Boston: Beacon Press, 1992.

Morrissey, Marietta. *Slave Women in the New World: Gender Stratification in the Caribbean.* Lawrence: University Press of Kansas, 1989.

Rawley, James A. *The Transatlantic Slave Trade: A History.* New York: Norton, 1981.

Solberg, Carl E. *The Prairies and the Pampas: Agrarian Policy in Canada and Argentina, 1880–1930.* Stanford, Calif.: Stanford University Press, 1987.

Thompson, Vincent Bakpetu. *The Making of the African Diaspora in the Americas, 1441–1900.* New York: Longman, 1987.

4

THE WORLD OF FAMILY

My world isn't based on right and wrong, mi hijito. *It's based on love and doing whatever a mother needs to get done to survive.*

Doña Margarita, in Victor Villaseñor's *Rain of Gold*[1]

In the North American ethic the center is the individual; in Hispanic morals the true protagonist is the family.

Octavio Paz[2]

No other affiliation in Latin America—not school, church, occupation, politics, or neighborhood—touches daily life so thoroughly as family. Like parents contributing genes, the family bestows individual identity. To be born Indigen, criollo, mestizo, African Latin, or immigrant marks ethnicity. And children who are born privileged, peasants, or professionals inherit their families' relative status. But more than ethnicity and rank, the Latin American family bequeaths fortune and fame, feuds and friendships, the psychologies and philosophies of kin. And Latin American families are more than blood relatives: families include trusted friends and associates. In Latin America, an individual without family is considered an incomplete person.

The Latin American family is difficult to discuss because so many kinds exist. Historic dynamism supplied ethnic models that were reworked through conquest, colonialism, slavery, illegitimacy, immigration, and urbanization. Resulting patterns now face forces such as mass education, migration, television, advertising, and demographic factors resulting from birth control and greater longevity. Thus, ancient legacies and modern changes create many designs for gender roles, parenting, sibling relations, generational esteem, and family networking. And, as elsewhere, generalities about family life confront personal specifics.

Despite modern fluidity, the legacy of kinship is still central to Latin American life. Families provide identity, loyalty, contacts, comfort, welfare, and a goal for those who suffer its loss.

THE IMPORTANCE OF FAMILY NAME

Latin American naming customs are Iberian and, while seemingly complex, are actually logical, simple, and instructive. Both maternal and paternal names are used. For example, if a father's family name is Sánchez and a mother's family name is Gómez, the child's family name (recognizing *both* parents) is Sánchez Gómez. This name is used both legally and commonly. In our example, if a child's given name is María, she would be called María Sánchez Gómez. Note carefully: the first surname (Sánchez) is paternal, the second (Gómez) is maternal. If a Latin American name is to be shortened (as when confronting confused U.S. clerks) the mother's family name is usually dropped. Thus, our María would carry a U.S. driver's license typically saying María Sánchez, not María Gómez.[3]

Latin American naming customs perpetuate family identity. For example, since a female changes neither her being nor her heritage when wed, women typically maintain natal names after marriage. Should María Sánchez Gómez marry José Martínez Chávez, she would legally (and often in everyday use) be known as María Sánchez Gómez de Martínez Chávez. (Latin American women often sign checks this way.) However, a husband does not add his wife's name: our José would *not* be known as José Martínez Chávez de Sánchez Gómez. As elsewhere, women historically gain identity from the men in their lives, not vice versa. And maternal names are dropped after one generation. Thus, the children of María Sánchez Gómez and José Martínez Chávez would carry a relatively simplified surname: Martínez Sánchez. A child, Miguel, would be Miguel Martínez Sánchez. The marriage of our María and José shows not only unity of two individuals but the bonding of families.

Naming also provides clues to ethnic heritage. In Guatemala, a neighborhood child proudly told me she was Yolanda Ixmay González: her father was Mayan and mother mestizo. In Costa Rica, a bank clerk was named Pedro Chang Wilson; upon conversing I learned his father was Chinese, his mother African Caribbean.

A simple logic underlies Latin American naming customs. A woman remains an identifiable member of her parental family after marriage. And children recognize family names from both father and mother. In Latin America, an individual is *family,* and *family* marks the individual.

THE INNER WORLD OF FAMILY

Latin America families and homes are designed for strength and privacy. Throughout Latin America one finds traditional Mediterranean-style homes of adobe, masonry, or poured concrete with barred windows, massive doors, and walled enclosures. Picture windows are rare. The ambience is one of seclusion.

The Latin American home is typically a refuge, a secure inner world for its members. In a society that deeply values personal contact, the family is the most intense center of touching. *Abrazos* (hugs), kisses, playful poking, teasing, running fingers through another's hair, and love pats are common. Family touching is also public: a Latin American teenager may hug and kiss a mother when parting on a street corner. Children and parents, or grandparents, or aunts, uncles, cousins, nephews, and nieces also walk down city streets arm in arm, leaning into each other with jokes, teasing, and comments. Latin American homes indulge the senses: usually with natural beauty through adorning either graceful patios or stark barrio windows with potted plants and singing birds. Whether rich or poor, Latin American homes typically feast the senses—sight, sound, taste, and scent—in an atmosphere adorned with fountains, color, cooking, singing, music, laughter, and storytelling. Such sensual homes encourage self-expression and enjoyment: members share emotions, possessions, burdens, and dreams. Prestige is earned when one's failings and weaknesses—as well as one's challenges and accomplishments—are shared with family members. Confession and forgiveness, as in Catholicism, renew mutual support and common dedication. But such intimacy and trust are guarded within the family.

Latin American families usually confer dual membership: in an immediate conjugal group and in an interactive extended network. Usually husband, wife, and children live together as a unit, but each conjugal unit relates closely to the larger network of an extended family. The extended family includes all blood relatives and many persons recruited through marriage, godparenthood, and friendship. The extended family serves as a huge and connecting canopy protecting and uniting its many conjugal groups.

Warmth and support characterize both conjugal and extended families. Individuals, particularly children, circulate informally among other conjugal families of aunts, uncles, cousins, grandparents, and godparents. Brothers and sisters also treat cousins (and aunts and uncles of near age) as siblings. Older aunts and uncles commonly serve as surrogate parents and share raising one anothers' children. While staying with a Mexican family of four children one summer, I struggled to keep a chart of conjugal and extended family members, including married relatives, godparents, and friends. In a month's time more than fifty names were scribbled on my crib sheet, including addenda on the back. All entered this home as welcomed members. The attitude toward family and friends within a Latin American household is typically *mi casa es su casa*—my home is your home.

The conjugal family remains a unit as long as it includes two or more persons. While both husband and wife live—as elderly as they might be—they almost always maintain their own home. But when grown children leave and one parent dies—usually the more elderly father—this unit is a group no more. Since the grandmother is normally revered, one of her children (usually the eldest daughter) will take *abuelita* (grandma) into her home. The idea of a grandmother living alone or being sent to a retirement apartment is foreign to Latin America, where the old cherish the young and youngsters still generally respect the elderly.

Of course, family stability and security are often ideals. In practice, two major factors weaken both conjugal and extended families: poverty diminishes family resources, while migrations strain family networking. Coping with any combination of meager resources, threatening environments, or physical displacement weakens family traditions. For example, rural families moving to congested cities often leave Grandma with village relatives, since urban apartments are crowded. When they do so, important links between children and the extended family are loosened.

Where it operates well, the Latin American family is an intense and secure inner world. It is a comfortable haven where mutual trust and support abound. The opposite applies to the *outer world,* which is everything beyond the family. The outer world is unknown, potentially hostile, and difficult to master. Family becomes a greater asset as it successfully permeates the outer world.

EXTENDING THE INNER WORLD

The world beyond one's home becomes understandable and manageable only as it becomes familiar, that is, like family. Thus, both individuals and families establish ties between inner and outer worlds, employing many stratagems to link family with village, city, school, market, church, government, army, and employment.[4]

The simplest way to extend inner worlds is merely to place family members in outer-world posts. From the early Columbus and Pizarro clans to modern families, Latin Americans prefer relatives as representatives, officials, foremen, policeman, loan officers, accountants, or corner grocer. This is not to say family is always trusted: Fidel Castro's sister campaigned for Republicans in the United States, and Chamorros in civil war–torn Nicaragua published rival newspapers. Such exceptions are all the more dramatic because they violate the principle of family loyalty.[5]

Another mechanism for linking inner and outer worlds is *compadres* (godparents). Choosing *compadres* is an art. Parents seek prestigious and well-connected persons who are also psychologically strong. The poor and powerless typically solicit the affluent and influential. Middle- and upper-class parents use *compadres* to solidify and extend control. The choice is perfect when the *madrina* (godmother) and *padrino* (godfather) provide financial and material assistance, introductions to other important people, arrangements for schooling, useful advice, encouragement, and love. Formally, *compadres* attend or send gifts to a godchild's family celebrations and grant favors when asked. More intimately, *compadre* and godchild may visit each other's home and truly act as parent and son or daughter. For *compadres,* godchildren enhance their own connections to the outer world and add prestige: families are linked as parents entrust someone else with their most prized possession, their child.

Amigos (friends) are another mechanism for linking inner and outer worlds. During childhood and as young adults, Latin Americans often develop lifelong friendships among a few neighborhood chums or schoolmates. Good amigos or amigas can be closer than siblings—who, as elsewhere, often bicker and compete—and the home of a friend usually becomes a child's second home. Parents of amigos informally coparent each other's child and assist each other as needed.

Marriage also extends the inner world of family. During courtship, relatives pay close attention, for marriages also bind families. If a match is favorable, love is encouraged. If families lack mutual respect, roadblocks multiply. Either way, families typically try to monitor or supervise the couple—strictly in the past, less so today. Since the family will prosper or suffer with each marriage, the family is involved.

All mechanisms for linking inner and outer worlds depend on the key component of children. Children extend family links exponentially: securing more outer-world positions, gathering amigos, acquiring more *compadres,* and cementing more families through marriage. Latin American families have traditionally been large not because the Catholic church forbade birth control but because—in the Latin American context of family—having children is practical.

THE STRUGGLE FOR PRESTIGE

Prestige in Latin America is not measured by how much one makes, although this is changing. Rather, prestige is measured by how one shares success, particularly with family members. Sharing the struggle to achieve prestige enhances one's status even more. *La lucha* (la LOU-cha, from *luchar,* "to struggle") is an Iberian concept of overcoming odds. The word is heard frequently in Latin American speech, and for both individuals and families *luchas* are everywhere. The poor struggle for sustenance and daily gain. And such struggles are typically shared as daughters and sons commonly contribute to a hardworking mother and vice versa.

Professionals *luchan*—usually via the telephone—networking through family connections and resolving business or career issues using a group approach and contacts. Even the rich *luchan.* Those born to privilege gain further prestige through struggling to achieve education, authorship, high political office, contacts, or sometimes social justice. Whether one is poor or privileged, *luchando* (struggling) is common.

A person who neglects relatives is considered *orgulloso* (or-gu-YO-so: egotistic). Prestige can be forfeited if individual ascent does not also involve family. Just as *mi casa es su casa,* so too is success shared. Sharing also applies to effort. A personal *lucha*—to make a living, to be educated, to prosper, to overcome challenges—should involve relatives. *Mi lucha es su lucha* (my struggle is your struggle) signals respect, not shame. Those assisting—*su lucha es mi lucha* (your struggle is mine too)—gain prestige by helping. By either giving or receiving, one feels needed. And being needed by family is deeply important in Latin America.

SEX AND BIRTH

Sex and birth, like families themselves, are human constants. And Latin American characteristics are not unique. But Mediterranean, Indigen, and African legacies—together with particular historic realities— emphasize certain aspects of gender relations and procreation.

Since illegitimacy is common in Latin America, legal families are obviously not the sole domain of sex. However, sex and particularly birth are integral aspects of families. And births create families: often simple ones of mother and child. Ideally, birth in Latin America is viewed as both a spiritual and a natural fulfillment. It is a sacred event, a culmination of God's will or nature's plan, for each birth provides both a new soul for eternity and a reaffirmation of human existence. Pregnancy and birth also represent strong psychological and social bonding: between two lovers, between two parents, between two families. With births, family members celebrate continuance and expansion. Conception, pregnancy, and birth in Latin America are normally esteemed as practical, magical, even mystical.

But sexual attitudes of male dominance and female vulnerability result from historic realities. Conquering men once took what they wanted, particularly Indigen and African Latin women. Today, male wealth and power still often exploit women in poverty. In the past, mestizo meant "nixed" as well as "mixed." Today, many fatherless (and more frequently motherless) children share a similar fate, scavenging rags and cardboard, begging and thieving on urban streets. The birth of a child is not always sacred. Sometimes it is tragic.[6]

Birth control, now commonly available, also affects sexual and family values in Latin America, and Catholic opposition has become less strident and rarely effective. Yet having children is still prestigious. Only "family planning"—the preferred parlance—is gaining favor, particularly among the middle class, poor women, and government planners. Children are desired; only the desired number is smaller.

CHILDHOOD

Childhood typically involves both cherished affection and immense responsibility. Where protected by a strong and stable family, children are not only loved but usually respected. Through children, adults renew the spontaneity and joy of discovery. In the process children are encouraged to inquire and create. Latin American youngsters are usually very social. Moving about frequently, they visit extended family members and amigos. Children also assume family responsibilities. Girls train for motherhood by caring for younger siblings, while boys model manliness by mimicking adult male behavior. Tactile emotional support is common throughout childhood, and children are normally embraced, bounced on knees, playfully teased, and shown much affection by inner-world members. Catholicism imparted an attitude that the young are innocent: uncorrupted until adulthood (or at least puberty). They are considered angelic joys in a devilish world.

Poor rural children are often economic assets, and early in life they assume sometimes immense responsibilities. Young boys on foot or horseback are often seen herding sheep, goats, or cattle down a country road or village street. Little girls often tend either the family cantina or the market stall while mother runs errands or tends younger siblings. The resourcefulness and responsibility of working-class Latin American children is amazing.

Latin America's urban orphans assume an existential *lucha.* Denied childhood, they face adult challenges while still very young. Street orphans typically recreate informal "families," gathering into nuclear groups that network extensively. They locate food and shelter, and devise group strategies to escape vigilante shop owners and paid assassins, mostly off-duty policemen. Denied homes, urban orphans try themselves to replicate family.

THE LEGACIES OF WOMANHOOD

Any discussion of historic models for Latin American women confronts great contradictions. On the one hand, ancient Iberian ideals—still resonant—surround women with protective mechanisms. This was particularly true for white women—*peninsular* or criollo—who secured for their children not only racial and ethnic identity but also property rights. On the other hand, most women—Indigen, mestizo, and African Latin—were often exploited. But these women enjoyed greater personal freedoms.

During a millennium of invasions and conquests, including crusades by Christians and Islamic Moors, Iberian women were tutored in seclusion. Historically, the home of a Spanish, Portuguese, or, later, Latin American woman was a fortress with shuttered windows and balconies, barred doors, and enclosed patio. The Spanish verb for marriage, *casarse,* comes from house (casa) and literally means "to enhouse someone." Seclusion extended to public modesty as clothing took on protective layers of skirts, shawls, mantillas, and capes, sometimes hiding all but the eyes. Iberian women traveled in groups or with chaperons. Such "ladies" also had their mentalities bound, usually by both church fathers and family traditions. The colonial ideal—imposed by males and practiced by females—was that ladies should be chaste, shy, pious, servile, and compliant. An Iberian lady was supposed to spend one-tenth of her waking time in prayer: asking God and the saints to assist family members, particularly her children. Women were also taught to obey men: father, husband, confessor, and king. *Patria potestad* was common. It held a woman subject to her father's authority until either age twenty-five or when she was married, usually following a parentally arranged match. Once "enhoused," Iberian women in the Americas typically endured philandering husbands. According to a popular aphorism, "The loyalty of the wife sanctified the disloyalty of the husband." Female chastity and forbearance were long cherished as ideals. They protected femininity and purity. Such "virtue" also protected white racial purity and dominance.[7]

A contrasting legacy surrounded lower-class women of color, the *castas.* Poverty and political weakness victimized these women, but social mores were less stringent. Whereas white females in Latin America were typically guarded by families, even being killed by irate fathers or husbands if unfaithful, female *castas* (racially mixed people) were punished for resisting sexual advances by domineering men. Forced to submit, their promiscuity came to be assumed; prostitution and keeping of mistresses were common. But women who were either fatherless or lacking husbands operated more independently. They prospered as artisans, merchants, or neighborhood businesswomen, and many managed their own market stalls or entered the service economy as washerwomen, maids, cooks, wet nurses, midwives, fortune-tellers, and curers. In Mexico, *castas* historically formed about one-third of the total workforce, leading lives very different from those of "enhoused" Iberian ladies.[8]

Few Indigen women ever enjoyed any liberties. Tribal traditions and European domination both decided their fates. Among the Aztecs, a woman's destiny was determined by the month of her birth: girls born under particular signs were trained as weavers, potters, and so on, and one month was reserved for prostitutes. The European conquest added further fatalism. Spanish households demanded personal service as well as concubinage. Even when officially outlawed, such customs continued. Indigen women additionally faced the collective burdens of their communities when villages endured *encomiendas* and *repartimientos*. Today, fatalism still attends native girls: village tradition and a mother's trade set parameters. Young Indigen women are typically trained in maternal skills: as weavers, potters, herbalists, and so on. And tribal customs still govern daily lives.[9]

Despite a legacy of exploitation, African Latin women often enjoyed far greater liberties than their Iberian or Indigen counterparts. While slavery suppressed, other factors liberated, albeit within a context of forced labor. Relatively few in numbers, black and especially mulatta women were often indulged by both more numerous black men and white males seeking sexual favors. Freed from restrictions guarding racial purity, they were more open in dress, body language, and speech. Torn from African traditions, black women differed from Indigens raised on ancestral lands with ancient customs. Black women held many leadership roles: as cult matrons, managers of markets, and participants in festivities. At *carnaval,* African Latin women fulfilled fantasy roles as princesses and queens, angels or devils, African goddesses, animals, and natural elements. Periodically, they escaped their destinies. Although legacies differed according to ethnicity and social class, Latin American women did fulfill common roles. Most important was motherhood.

WOMEN-CENTERED HOMES

The greatest irony in Latin America is that men dominate virtually all institutions except the most significant: the home. If anyone doubts the impresario skills of a housewife, let them visit a Latin American household. Whether a wealthy *patrona* managing domestics or a destitute woman making ends meet, the Latin American woman is a marvel at managing resources, schedules, tasks, and often competing egos.

With men frequently busy in outer-world affairs, homes became women-centered. And nurturing remains the norm, as young girls practice with siblings and neighbors to be mothers first, then women or wives. For a girl, her mother is both model and mentor. Young girls practice organizing the home, and not in play. If the family is poor, the young girl becomes a workhorse, sharing tasks of kitchen, garden, shopping, and laundry, and helping run a family business. If the family is wealthy, the girl becomes a *patronita* (little boss), ordering servants about and trying to arrange the home her way. The prestige of a woman begins with family and home. Thus, middle-class and working-class women earn both esteem and money in the outer world. But they, not their men, also assure that household tasks are completed.[10]

While times are changing, a wife's home is still viewed as refuge and her husband as the provider-protector. For centuries it seemed as if women traded childhoods, leaving a father to gain a husband who also expected esteem, support, and obedience. Whether a man succeeds or fails in the outer world, he typically returns home as autocrat, wishing to be served. Rather than rebel, most women comply, having been taught to arrange, to accommodate. In one revealing study, a working-class Mexican woman apologetically explained that men are naturally irresponsible, *"como niños"* (like children), adding that men act foolish because they "can't help the way they are." However, since the home anchors the Latin American universe, it cannot fall into foolish hands. Thus, at home women assume responsibilities: they get things *done,* and done *right.*[11]

Husbands may rule, but women manage the household. Once children arrive, the chores of parenthood fall to women, as few fathers change diapers or push carriages. And while both parents increasingly hold outer-world jobs, the husband usually has only one profession. Working-class women sew clothes or assemble components, and also manage the home. Professional women serve as journalists, lawyers, or teachers, and also manage the home. Upscale women escape household drudgery by managing domestics, the largest and lowest-paid category of female employment in Latin America. But as mothers and daughters, domestics must still manage their own households. Women have historically organized markets, maintained convents, governed estates, and ruled barrios. Except for nuns, they have also managed households.[12]

MARIANISMO

Latin American femininity derives from many sources. Ethnic models include an Indigen *pacha mama* (earth mother) and African *Iemanjá* (water mother). Modern inspirations range from Hollywood sex symbols to women's rights activists. The historical queen mother of all such imagery is the Virgin Mary.

Of all Catholic icons in Latin America, the most pervasive and popular are the many manifestations of the Virgin Mary. She is portrayed as an immensely strong and confident young woman nurturing a totally dependent male child. She is the pietà, grieving for her martyred son's *lucha,* the *mater dolorosa,* suffering life's fates. She is the Virgin of Guadalupe, patron saint of Mexico, mother to mestizos. She is the Virgin of Carmen, blessing soldiers. She is a dozen other incarnations. Remarkable in these images is the absence of husband or father. (One wonders what role model Joseph signals for Latin American males.) Except for a child and adoring cherubs, Mary stands alone.[13]

The very founding of Latin America was a consequence of feminine leadership. In the late 1400s, the unity of Spain, the defeat of the Moors, and the expedition that discovered America were all policies undertaken by Isabel of Castile. But these achievements rested on a more immediate task: establishing her legitimacy. Isabel's strategies were creative. She enlisted burghers to oppose barons, made alliances (including a marriage to Fernando of Aragón), and employed powerful and subtle symbolism to legitimize her sovereignty. The latter included commissioning artists who traveled Spain painting images of the Christian Madonna as flaxen-haired and fair-skinned, like Isabel. Such imagery was already popular in Europe, but Isabel used it to promote her own ideals. Carried to the new world, Mary became the most popular feminine icon of Latin America. Today, more modern "Madonnas"—the MTV persona, rock star clones, pop magazine idols, even television teen sex symbol Xuxa in Brazil—have seized major space among feminine imagery. *Mary* faces many challengers.

Modern life casts women in many roles. Romance now mixes with motherhood in childhood dreams. With puberty a young woman faces the desires and designs of men. And young women have their own strategies. Traditionally, the family united to protect a young woman, often against her will. Virginity today is not the prize it once was: a badge of family honor and certificate of marketability to "good" families. Although a fading tradition, chaperoning was long common due to such practices as *el rapto,* whereby a young suitor desperate in the face of family rejection kidnapped his *novia* (girlfriend). When she was no longer a virgin, the lovers returned for a wedding, grudgingly accepted by her family. Courtship is increasingly a private matter, but modern romance is idealized no less than earlier *marianismo.* However, motherhood reminds women of more traditional values.[14]

In Latin America, giving birth culminates a woman's femininity. Usually marriage leads to a quick pregnancy, which brings esteem to the young woman. Her child is a dedicated and dependent love. In a society that values human contact, pregnancy, birth, and infancy create a bonding like that of Madonna and child. With children a woman has her own family and becomes the center of home life and its impresario. A Latin American household sees men come and go, sometimes for long periods. Without a regular female chieftain—either wife, mother, grandmother, aunt, or elder daughter—the immediate family disintegrates.[15]

As time passes, the mother becomes more respected, even venerated. Flaws are typically forgotten as her qualities—many real, others assumed—grow in memory and magnitude. Her suffering, her sacrifices, and her dedication are raised to supreme levels. As a woman becomes a grandmother and great-grandmother, she begins to enter the realm of legend, more a cherished force than a real person. In Latin America, grandmothers are normally as close to living sainthood as any mortal can be.

LATIN AMERICAN WOMEN: MODERN TIMES

Tradition is tendency, not determinism. Today, new technologies and changing economies confront old traditions. Among the dramatic forces is health technology. Until late in the nineteenth century, family size was limited by infant and childhood mortality. But with early-twentieth-century improvements in public health, childhood deaths declined and family size mushroomed. For most of the twentieth century, Latin

American women were consumed with mothering until late in life. Today, birth control is another health technology impacting women and motherhood. Increasingly, Latin American families have about three children, born while parents are young. Thus, at about age forty most Latin American women face empty nests. And due to greater longevity, women live longer. Hence, mothering only partially defines what it means to be a modern woman.[16]

Another force changing women's status is education. Women today receive both more years and different kinds of education than earlier. During the late twentieth century, higher education for women not only tripled to one-third of all enrollments but professional study moved from almost exclusively teaching and nursing toward training in law, journalism, medicine, engineering, social services, research, business administration, computers, and university teaching. University education for Latin American women now emphasizes empowerment rather than nurturing: imparting autonomy and the ability to compete in a male-dominated outer world.[17]

Employment itself is another force changing women's roles. When men were breadwinners, women were bread makers. Increasingly women of all classes do both. Poor rural women have long been heavily involved in artisanal or agricultural work. They operate cottage industries or labor in the fields with children tagging along. Today, many rural women work in canneries and food processing plants. Some campesinas (women field hands) assume leadership roles in farm cooperatives and labor unions. After agriculture, the second major area of female employment is the service sector. Half the region's total service economy is made up of household domestics, mostly young women migrating to cities. Latin America has the world's highest percentage of household servants. But because domestics receive very low pay, many poor women seek factory employment. In urban and industrial areas, women are often more employable than men. Mothers and elder daughters often hold multiple jobs: as domestic servants, sales clerks, and factory operatives. To contend with low wages and long hours, family females pool paychecks and coordinate work schedules. They still manage the household but also become—as a group—major money earners. The impact on male authority and family priorities is dramatic. A majority of middle-class women now hold outer-world jobs. They also demand greater equity in family gender roles. Growing objections to traditional tasks have led men to assume greater responsibilities for children and household chores. The new demands of middle-class women also lead to higher divorce rates and, more commonly, separation. (Latin America has very low divorce rates by world standards.) However, as women's roles change, so does the traditional family.[18]

Women increasingly impact outer-world affairs. They typically achieve well in both business and politics, areas long dominated by men. Modern success in both corporations and government derives from skills learned in women-centered homes. As managers of enterprises called families, women daily perfect skills of scheduling, personnel management, organization, negotiating, and compromise. Typically patient, permanent, loyal, and stable, women show both long-range vision and attention to immediate details. Such administrative skills lead to success in business careers.

In government, women adapt traditional roles to modern politics. During the mid-twentieth century, Eva Duarte de Perón in Argentina used multiple images—vamp and victim as well as Cinderella and fairy godmother—to gain political power. In death, she became an icon in the image of the Virgin Mary: long-suffering and dedicated to her vicarious children, the working classes of Argentina. In the 1990s, Violeta Barrios de Chamorro was elected president of Nicaragua. She used a modern media blitz and massive support from the George Bush administration—but most of all *marianismo.* Widow of a slain national leader, she constantly posed for pictures beside either his grave site or his bullet-ridden vehicle. Projected as symbolic *mater dolorosa* (sorrowful mother) to a sorrowfully divided nation, Violeta Chamorro was a real mother to a family torn by civil war. As the patient and compassionate grandmother, she defeated the Sandinistas, symbols of heroic machismo. Elsewhere in Latin America—in Brazilian shantytowns, among the mothers of "disappeared" children in Argentina, in church kitchens, in labor unions, and in political parties—women emerge as leaders. In Argentina, Mothers of the Disappeared held weekly vigils seeking information about victims of military repression. Increasingly, women everywhere serve as mayors, congresswomen, and governors. As power brokers, women succeed by transferring to the political arena the many skills of home management: negotiation, compromise, delegation of responsibility, and the seemingly simple ability to get things done.

MACHISMO

The ancient Latin American concept of machismo, or manliness, is at a turning point. For centuries men typically ruled (but did not manage) homes and flaunted double sexual standards by demanding faithfulness from wives while themselves visiting prostitutes, having affairs, or keeping a mistress. And with sometimes great bravado, men made outer-world activities a public arena for personal competition. But modern times demand other roles, or at least old values affirmed differently. Other aspects of multifaceted machismo are now preeminent. One is *personalismo,* the art of personality, and some Latin Americans—men and women alike—dazzle with charm. Another side of machismo is the drive for public acceptance, for esteem. As prestige is defined by new standards—such as higher incomes—men seek esteem in new ways.

A male learns manliness as a child. The first lesson is not fatherhood as much as male authority. The ancient Mediterranean tradition of paterfamilias is that the eldest male is both king and judge. For a young boy, the father commands but also shows how to command. Whenever Papa is away, elder sons practice "manliness" by ordering others about: usually sisters and younger brothers. The goal is to exert power, to persuade others, to be the authority, if not an authoritarian.[19]

If the Virgin Mary provides a role model for girls, another woman becomes a boy's feminine ideal: his mother. From infancy through adulthood, the Latin American male is typically indulged: a Madonna and her *male* child forge a mutual dedication (or at least understanding) early in life. A mother will find many reasons, excuses, rationalizations, and immense reserves of patience in coping with her son's transgressions, which multiply during puberty. Does this form the young man's expectations for a wife? Usually.[20]

Puberty brings a lifelong preoccupation for most Latin American males. When Islam conquered Spain it introduced a dream that still inspires the imagination of Latin American men, young and old. In Muhammad's heaven, willing women serve the warrior's wish. The old Spanish phrase *"El hombre por la lengua y la mujer por las piernas"* (A man for his speech and a woman for her legs) repeats a dying but not dead dream. Through either persuasion and graciousness or intimidation and strength, machos seek to dominate women. Among themselves, machos use sexual "conquests" as currency: like a game of poker, they try to "trump" each other with boasts about how many, how often, and how good.[21]

Machismo is also part of everyday behavior, an attempt to exert authority over other men, as well as women. Machos typically dominate conversations, granting permission for women and "inferiors" to speak, answering when others are addressed, and interrupting at will. Machismo also contributes to violence against women. Wife beating and double legal as well as sexual standards long shielded abusive males from censure and punishment, particularly when lower-class women lacked recourse. Men long claimed a right to kill a wife's lover, even the wife herself. Why did courts and custom vindicate such violence? A macho's prestige was at stake.[22]

THE SEARCH FOR PRESTIGE

For Latin males, manliness extends beyond sexual authority. As a male approaches adulthood, *la lucha,* the struggle for outer-world prestige, looms larger. As the security of childhood ends, it is time—as they say in Chile—"to put the long pants on": to test manliness in public.[23]

The outer world is where men struggle for prestige. Since Roman times, Mediterranean man's quest for status has depended upon competition with other men in the forum, plaza, bureaucracy, arena, street, court, café, bar, barracks, factory, legislature, school, office, corporation, or literary anthology. Wherever men congregate to create civil life, outer worlds are filled with *luchas.* The goal is to be recognized, to achieve authority, to overcome oblivion, to bequeath prestige.[24]

But such struggles are not solitary. Part of success is learning to exercise familial support in outer-world *luchas.* And a family's status and standards help or hinder a young man. A youth may adopt a father's *lucha,* sharing the elder man's legitimacy. Occasionally, rebellious sons reject father or family and adopt their own *lucha.* One such example is Fidel Castro, who rejected the power and prestige of his rich landowning father to achieve his own revolutionary dignity. Either way, family inheritance (wealth but also values and training) imparts certain initial strengths or challenges. Those born to notable families compete in universities, newspaper editorials, or legislatures. Campesinos (peasants) and poor laborers vie in lesser arenas: local neighborhoods, a village square, or a town bar. Family values, attitudes, and skills deeply mark a young man. The self-expression, diplomacy, logic, and dedication learned in childhood affect his *lucha.*

At school, in business, work, or politics, a young man's challenges multiply. For campesinos, the struggle is often for land and to not be cheated. Urban workers *luchan* for decent jobs with dignity as well as better pay. Middle-class men compete for quality educations and career advancement. Even privileged men are expected to *luchar:* to augment family fortunes and fame, to be successful diplomats, to achieve political office, or to pen quality literature.

Money matters in all societies. Equally important in Latin America is how money is used. Sharing one's wealth enhances prestige, whether with family, by endowing prestigious universities, or at the corner bar. Ironically, making money matters less than having and using it. Selfish accumulation often stigmatizes, since wealth is not an end but a means: to gain wisdom, talent, influence, and a good marriage. The goal is not money but using wealth to acquire culture, refinement, authority, or recognition. What matters is not money but the prestige that money buys. However, prestige is also currency—one that secures its source.[25]

For those without inherited privileges the quest for prestige is by *lucha* or luck, and success is minimal for peasants and the urban poor. For many lower-class men status is achieved through begetting children, winning a bet, knowing the boss, having a good *compadre,* learning a skill, or helping their children complete school. Perhaps the dearth of prestige among poor men explains why traditional machismo still thrives: the mixture of booze and frustration often creates bully behavior. Too often, the only authority a poor men exerts is at home or among his amigos while drinking.[26]

For artists and artisans, prestige comes as quality and achievement. Iberian society has traditionally disdained men who labor physically and esteemed those who speak and think. Thus, braceros (from *brazo,* "arm"), campesinos (peasants), and assembly line workers typically lack prestige, but respect is earned by those who craft well or serve graciously. Quality builders, carvers, weavers, groundskeepers, painters, musicians, and architects—anyone who creates beauty—is esteemed. Likewise, able waiters and salesmen—anyone working effectively with the public—can gain esteem. In this way movie stars, toreros, and sports heroes gain esteem and often amazing fame. And high honor goes to those who influence others.

PERSONALISMO

Traditionally, prestige comes to persons who display a complex of values called *personalismo.* One route to personal charisma is *palabra* (expressiveness), and men or women who influence others by speech are respected whether they be priest, politician, professor, or a good salesperson. *Palabra* is also the written word, and authors—particularly well-known novelists and poets—often enter the realm of public worship in Latin America. On an everyday level, *personalismo* is found in *simpaticismo,* which is well renowned as typical Latin American friendliness and charm. A frequent compliment heard in Latin America is that a person (male or female) is *muy simpático* (outgoing and engaging). *Personalismo* often dovetails with *poder* (power). In reality, charm *is* power, a subtle and sweet attraction that uses persuasion to gain allies and advocates.[27]

Personalismo also reveals different kinds of *dignidad* (dignity). Those who not only speak for a cause but overcome obstacles show *dignidad.* The prestige of personal action, of bravery in the face of fire, explains why protest, rebellion, and revolution are important features of not only Latin American politics but self-worth and self-esteem. While some Latin Americans show bravado or courage, the *dignidad* of others derives from a personal elegance: not wealth or apparel but inherent styles of grace and virtue. Caballeros (formerly "horsemen," now "gentlemen") have *dignidad:* graciousness and charm. Men and women who treat customers or clients as one would a respected family member also show *personalismo.* For Latin Americans, *personalismo* is character.

TRADITION AND TRANSITION

Heritage is not deterministic. In Latin America today, social change is rapid. The agents include technologies, new goods and services, mass media, advertising, education, female employment, growing individualism, democratic ideals, increased materialism, mass migrations, and more. Many changes are resisted by traditionalists, yet historic definitions of male and female are being rewritten. As change confronts constancy, the Latin American family is not breaking but bending: adapting new functions to old forms.

Much resistance to change—of the family, of female and males roles—is institutional. Despite undergoing great recent change itself, the Catholic church still projects old roles. Only men are priests, only men hear confession, and only men are bishops who determine policy. While the image of Jesus Christ has been updated to that of reformer or revolutionary, *marianismo* still presents Mary as a prideful or sorrowful mother, not a working or professional woman with family. And militaries resist change. Barracks machismo exhibits a phobia of outer-world women. Officers denounced Eva Perón's ambitions in Argentina, and when Chilean generals seized power in 1973, soldiers walked the streets, scissors in hand, making sure that women wore skirts, not pants: *una mujer por las piernas.* More recent confrontations in Argentina saw officers oppose the Mothers of the Disappeared, whose children were raped and killed by soldiers. While Latin American militarism is in recess, any resurgence will likely be rationalized as "defending the nation" not only from political "subversives" but against "radicals" who challenge old-time family values: that is, traditional male authority.[28]

In Latin America some institutions considered agents of change also perpetuate tradition. Commercial media is one. Carefully scripted television and radio dramas, magazine and newspaper stories, and popular *foto revistas* ("soap opera" picture periodicals) depict traditional plots. Well-worn gender roles show men as authoritarian, irresponsible, and full of bravado, while women are passive, homebound, wistfully romantic or suffering martyrs. For the modern media, the traditional family is a convenient stage.

Even new roles for women reveal subtle adaptations of tradition. As middle-class women balance personal freedom, marriage, family, and careers, many have decided to cut the least rewarding responsibility: their husbands. With financial security from a career and old-fashioned family networking, such women rule as well as manage their homes. The same holds true for increasing numbers of poor women. A mother and her working daughters can make ends meet without men around.[29]

Men are also changing. Historic macho home behavior—*"Aquí, yo mando"* ("Here, I command")—is yielding to democratic decision making and acceptance of household chores. In an amusing scene witnessed on a Costa Rican bus, a baffled young father with what seemed like ten thumbs tried to change his daughter's diaper. His encouraging wife was adamant that he learn this parental responsibility. Occasionally, on city streets and in the park, one sees men pushing baby strollers. As women and families change, so do men.[30]

Migration and urbanization change poor families greatly. Rural poverty drives Latin America's poor to large cities or across Mexico's northern border. Today, sixteenth-century beliefs confront twenty-first-century behavior as rural isolation ends. Men are often absent, gone to work in cities or on distant farms. Often such separations become permanent. And everywhere women are less inclined to keep quiet and endure either physical abuse or endless male carousing.[31]

Upon reflection, tradition and transition occur together. While challenges derive from modern occupations, innovative technologies, educational trends, and awareness of other societies, the impact of change has not destroyed the Latin American family. Divorce and separation are much less frequent than in the United States. Families with both parents are still a common feature of Latin American life. Families are smaller, but children are still cherished, often lavished with even more individual attention. Women work outside the home, but motherhood remains primary. Individuals are more self-reliant, but families still influence the fortunes of personal life.[32]

SUGGESTED READINGS

Beneria, Lourdes, and Martha Roldán. *The Crossroads of Class and Gender.* Chicago: University of Chicago Press, 1987.

Bermúdez Q., Suzy. *Hijas, Esposas y Amantes: Género, Clase, Étnia y Edad en la Historia de América Latina. (Daughters, Wives and Lovers: Gender, Class, Ethnicity and Age in Latin American History).* Bogotá: Universidad de los Andes, 1992.

Bingham, Margorie Wall, and Susan Hill Gross. *Women in Latin America: From Pre-Columbian Times to the 20th Century.* St. Louis Park, Minn.: Glenhurst Publications, 1985.

———. *Women in Latin America: The 20th Century.* St. Louis Park, Minn.: Glenhurst Publications, 1985.

Dealy, Glen Caudill. *The Latin Americans: Spirit and Ethos.* Boulder, Colo.: Westview Press, 1992.

Hahner, June E., ed. *Women in Latin American History: Their Lives and Views.* Los Angeles: UCLA Latin American Center Publications, 1980.

Hellman, Judith Adler. *Mexican Lives.* New York: New Press, 1994.

Jelin, Elizabeth, ed. *Family, Household and Gender Relations in Latin America.* London: Kegan Paul International, 1991.

Lavrín, Asunción, ed. *Latin American Women: Historical Perspectives.* Westport, Conn.: Greenwood Press, 1978.

LeVine, Sarah. *Dolor y Alegría: Women and Social Change in Urban Mexico.* Madison: University of Wisconsin Press, 1993.

Nash, June, and Helen Icken Safa, eds. *Sex and Class in Latin America.* Boston: Bergin and Garvey, 1980.

———. *Women and Change in Latin America.* Boston: Bergin and Garvey, 1986.

Pescatello, Ann, ed. *Female and Male in Latin America.* Pittsburgh: University of Pittsburgh Press, 1973.

5

A HOUSE OF MANY SPIRITS

"In the Kingdom of Heaven there is no grandeur to be won, inasmuch as there is an established hierarchy, the unknown is revealed, existence is infinite, there is no possibility of sacrifice, all is rest and joy. For this reason, bowed down by suffering and duties, beautiful in the midst of his misery, capable of loving in the face of afflictions and trials, man finds his greatness, his fullest measure, only in the Kingdom of this World."

Alejo Carpentier, *The Kingdom of this World*[1]

Perhaps it's a Catholic belief in saints and souls. Maybe it derives from Indigens giving personality to natural forces. It appears both as African Latins invoking ancestors and as Pentecostals welcoming the Holy Spirit. Even language is a factor.[2]

Whatever its origins, animism—the belief that spirits manipulate material things—is prevalent in Latin America. Many believers feel that plants, hills, a river, the wind, birth, death, or daily events are governed by nonmaterial forces. These themes are explored in such mystical novels as Gabriel García Márquez's *One Hundred Years of Solitude* and Isabel Allende's *House of the Spirits.* Readers of Allende's novel assume the "house" in question is the characters' home. Some see Chile, the site of the story, as a metaphorical house. But the real house of spirits is all Latin America.[3]

Latin America is a temple of many spirits. Catholicism has been long identified with the region, yet the religion of Rome was never unitary nor universal. Both coercive and compassionate, Catholicism often mixed with indigenous and African beliefs—in different ways in different places. The Catholic church of compassion remains strong, evident today as the radical theology of liberation: a political movement more active than Marxism. Indigenous spiritualism continues both as a subtle presence permeating Latin American thought and as specific beliefs in rural areas from Mexico to Chile. African Brazilian and African Caribbean spiritualism strengthens daily, among shantytowns in Brazil, Caribbean nations, and immigrants to Florida and New York. Meanwhile, Protestant Evangelicals mount a Latin American reformation, preaching the gospel on street corners, radio and television stations, and doorsteps everywhere. The Latin American house of spirits has acquired many rooms.

Across an indigenous past, during and since the conquest, and in modern times, spiritual belief has been a mighty presence in Latin America. To comprehend the region one must understand the profoundness of mysticism: how it motivates humans and modifies their behavior.

A WORLD OF SPIRITS

According to indigenous cosmology, nature rules humankind and supernatural forces govern nature; and all these—humans, nature, and the mystical—are closely associated. For Indigens, *whos* rather than *whats* usually make things happen, and natural *whos* are spirits. Unlike Christian angels and devils, these native spirits are not all good or all bad but rather—like humans—changeable: competitive, peevish, jealous to the point of causing evil, benevolent, demanding of attention, and responsive to flattery. For humans to succeed—or just endure—the spirits must be understood and mollified, as one would placate a temperamental boss or an irascible neighbor. Spirits determine the winds and rains; earthquakes, tempests, and tremors; good and bad harvests; success or failure in hunting, fishing, or business; an illness or fine health; even birth and death. Other spirits are ancestors: not specific progenitors but the once-living of a clan, village, or tribe who have journeyed to the mystical world and mediate for the living. Perhaps the foremost spirit is *pacha mama,* the Andean term for earth, the mother of all life.[4]

Unlike the transcendent masculine god of Christians, *pacha mama* (or Coatlicue, the demonic and demanding Aztec mother goddess) is immediate and feminine. *Pacha mama* is dirt underfoot, the land of your valley, soil for crops, and death's burial blanket. *Pacha mama* is a woman inseminated when farmers seed or plant, whose fertility yields harvests, a mother who suckles humankind and enfolds her children at life's end. Thus, land—*pacha mama*—is essential to Indigens: farming is sacred. More than growing crops for sustenance or market, planting and harvesting are hallowed rituals, reaffirming human bonds to life's source. Land also links individuals to family and community. Because Indigens establish identity through ancestors, burial sites become shrines. Special holidays ("Day of the Dead," on November 2 in Mexico, or the Monday before Ash Wednesday in the Andes) mark a bittersweet rite, a reunion of living generations and ancestral spirits on hallowed ground—an earth shared by both—as tombs are cleaned and decorated with confetti, streamers, candies, fresh flowers, and candles. In the cemeteries, meals are served, fireworks ignited, and alcohol, coca, or cigarettes left for the spirits. Such rituals bind an individual to cosmic forces of time and place: origin, domain, and destiny. In the central Andes and Mexico the favor of *pacha mama* is ritually requested at these celebrations, as it is on other special occasions when land or animals are bought or sold, and when baptisms, weddings, or holidays are celebrated. In Peru the brief ceremony is called *ch'alla,* and in Mexico it is offering *aguardiente:* alcoholic beverages or coca leaves are shared among those present, then poured, dropped, or spit on the ground as offering, blessing, and bonding. "May *pacha mama* share with mankind as humans share with earth, the mother of all life."[5]

For Indigens, spirits exist everywhere and many—even an angry *pacha mama*—may cause trouble. Some spirits are mere pranksters, like the dwarfish duendes who spill drinks, hide eyeglasses, and misplace tools. Others are satanic, with fangs and flaming breath, incarnated as a bearlike forest creature or a female temptress who changes to a ghoul. Just as spirits threaten evil, so do haunting times and places. Sunset and night require vigilance as the known recedes before the emerging mysteries of forest shadows, dim village paths, or dark household corners. Here harmful spirits may linger, transforming into animals or making neighbors into witches and sorcerers. Cemeteries and sites of previous human tragedy are also *malos puntos* (bad places). The white crosses beside treacherous roadways in Latin America both commemorate loved ones and mark a mystical site. Other *malos puntos* are breaks in the earth's crust where underworld *espíritus* may emerge: a cave, ravine, volcano, anthill, or animal burrow. Children and women are considered especially vulnerable to spiritual malevolence. The "evil eye" *(mal de ojos),* bad night airs, or similar exposures may cause illness, weakness, accident, or misfortune. But such misfortune is not due to spirits who are totally evil in the sense of the Christian Satan or devils. Evil is done not by bad spirits but by spirits in a bad mood.[6]

Because spirits cause trouble, Indigens search for spiritual allies. The most common human mediums with mystical forces are *curanderos* and *curanderas,* male and female native "curers" who employ herbal remedies and mystical rituals to diagnose and treat illness or accident. Other allies include Catholic saints and clerics. Highly dualistic, Indigens do not rely on one philosophy to the exclusion of others: any devotion or priesthood that works is used. Perhaps the greatest spiritual allies of native peoples are "the ancestors." Not necessarily immediate progenitors, ancestors are those humans from earlier times who initially mastered the mysteries of life, created the wisdom of tradition, and still exist just beyond consciousness. Typically ascribed as belonging to one's own village, clan, or tribe, ancestors are reached through dreams or visions and are valued because they understand two realms: the endless travail of human existence and the eternal world of spirits.[7]

After the European conquest, syncretism—the fusion of similar beliefs—occurred when Indigen converts recreated the Virgin Mary as an earth goddess mother. During the 1540s the Virgin of Guadalupe appeared before a peasant boy at a hillside near Mexico City, and Catholics soon built a huge basilica there to honor Mexico's new patron saint. Today the shrine of Guadalupe is the most venerated site in Mexico, and she is seen as the mother and patron saint of a mestizo nation. In Peru, a Catholic missionary during the 1970s recounted his initial bewilderment when native worshipers threw potatoes at a statue of the Virgin Mary that was paraded through village streets during Holy Week. He later learned that local Indigens viewed her as *pacha mama* and annually—as they had since the 1500s—made such offerings of select seed potatoes. Syncretism linked many forms of native animism and Catholic spiritualism. Andean peoples had used the term *huaoqui,* meaning an individual's "personal essence" or "spiritual friend." To Catholics, it was the soul.[8]

Today, Indigens frequently employ the Catholic term *espíritu* for the spiritual essence of a person, animal, plant, or place. But Christian and native understandings of *espíritu* differ. While Catholic doctrine holds that venerated statues and images only *represent* heavenly *espíritus,* Indigens believe spirits actually *abide* in things and places: plants, rivers, and mountains but also statues, images, and shrines. Thus, when a native mother pins a locket of hair from a dead child on a Catholic statue in a village church, she may not be entreating a heavenly deity. She is probably joining two *espíritus:* child and god.[9]

THE SHAMAN OF QAQACHAKA

Case studies do not generalities make. Nor do they illustrate varieties and variations found elsewhere. But case studies reveal concepts through using sometimes complex, dynamic, and personal details. For this reason, we consider the shaman of Qaqachaka, a *curandero* practicing during modern times in an Aymara community of a thousand or so families in the cold highlands of Bolivia. The dramatis personae are Severo Laura (a young government health worker), Inés (his wife), Zacarias Chiri (a shaman or *curandero*), Saxra (an underground spirit who causes sickness), and the ancestors. This story is based on the personal experience of American anthropologist Joseph W. Bastien.[10]

A remote indigenous community, Qaqachaka became home in 1982 to Severo Laura, a government health worker—a scientifically trained mestizo nurse—and his wife, Inés. Severo sought to bring modern medicine (inoculations, prescriptions, and such) to people long familiar with only native herbalists, curative plants and shamans, who "doctored" by mediating with spirits. Of course, Qaqachaka's *curanderos* and clients considered Severo an intruder and modern medicine as a threat, with its mysterious stethoscopes, syringes, and antiseptics.

Severo's chief antagonist was Zacarias Chiri, the head shaman of Qaqachaka. Zacarias achieved his remarkable credentials by surviving tests of fire and water: he was once stricken by lightning, and on another occasion nearly drowned. However, each event bestowed mystical powers. Surviving sickness showed skill at manipulating spiritual possession. Lightning linked him to upper-world sky spirits and imparted an ability to resuscitate the dying. Submersion introduced Zacarias to both lower-world spirits and the river of life. His baptisms of fire and water led to subsequent success as a shaman.

The rivalry between modern and traditional curing became personal when the government health worker's wife enlisted the services of Zacarias. Inés was childless after five pregnancies. The problem was high blood pressure, which caused miscarriages, and the condition persisted despite modern treatment. After much argument, Severo reluctantly agreed to employ the shaman; the fee was one llama, worth about forty dollars.

The curing ritual was lengthy. Zacarias and an assistant joined Severo and Inés at their home, arriving before midnight. The group sat around a simple room with a dirt floor. To begin, coca leaves were exchanged and chewed, alcohol drunk, and *ch'alla* offered to *pacha mama.* Then the shaman spread a ceremonial cloth on the ground and with ritual prayers and movements repeatedly threw down handfuls of coca leaves, each time "reading" their patterns. When he divined Inés's coca leaves, his insights were many: the cause of miscarriage was far greater than some simple failing of Inés. Repeated castings told him that ancestors were present and requesting ritual meals from Inés and Severo, who had neglected to venerate the village's forebears. In retribution the ancestors had claimed Inés's pregnancies. Zacarias instructed Inés to offer special rituals that would dispel past evils and separate any future children from previous misfortunes.

Continuing, Zacarias declared that Severo had a mistress. This provoked heated denials by the husband and accusations by his wife. Soon the shaman deflected blame by announcing that a mysterious enemy had hexed Severo, causing the affair. Various names were offered, and repeated castings finally divined a culprit.

At two in the morning a new phase began. Calling for total silence, Zacarias extinguished the sole candle and began rhythmic blowing on a whistle. In the dark he confronted Saxra: underworld lord of the night, symbol of a jealous and meddling uncle, agent of evil. Speaking into a cardboard box, the shaman projected voices imitating Inés, Saxra, and himself, creating a trialogue of questions, accusations, and countercharges. Eventually Inés joined the conversation as Zacarias alternately spoke for either Saxra or himself (in the role of mediator). When Saxra and Inés argued heatedly, the shaman spoke for himself and shouted, "Saxra, you've hurt Inés and we're going to castigate you," and began slapping the box with a broken rosary, an image of Santiago (Spain's patron saint), castanets, and the local equivalent of a lasso. Zacarias then had Inés—and eventually all present—lean over the box while he ritually pounded their backs and exhorted Saxra to remove his evil. The shaman then fell into a deep and prolonged trance that ended only when he repeated the entire exorcising process with Condor, sky spirit and protector of nests.

After a long session involving Condor, Zacarias concluded the curing ritual. He anointed Inés and the others, announcing that they had been exorcised of evil spells. As communion, everyone was given a hard-boiled egg as the shaman intoned: "These eggs are eaten on behalf of the hills for all the miracles brought forth from earth shrines" and "Eat this for the health of Inés." During following days Severo and Inés offered rituals in their courtyard while Zacarias—representing them—presented sacrifices of chicken, coca leaves, and llama fat at local shrines dedicated to either the Condor or Qaqachaka's ancestors.

Within a year Inés gave birth, and more children followed. Severo eventually reflected on the interplay of ceremony, symbol, catharsis, and health. He viewed the curing ritual as a form of psychological therapy: removing tension, which, in turn, lowered Inés's blood pressure. Severo was more relaxed, too. He and Zacarias began cooperating: the shaman handled health problems having social and psychocultural roots, the nurse treated illnesses with biological origins.

Other case studies of indigenous spiritualism in Latin America are similar, and still others are different. The protagonists, settings, rituals, and spirits vary. In some examples Indigen traditions are less intense, the modern more evident. But as the shaman of Qaqachaka demonstrates, native spiritualism is still integral to daily life 500 years after the European conquest.

THE CHURCH OF COERCION: THE CATHOLIC CROSS AND SWORD

Catholicism seemingly unites a region splintered by endless ethnic, political, and social divisions, yet an apparently universal Catholic heritage presents opposed legacies. The "church of compassion" is idealism, reaching from early Spanish missions to the modern theology of liberation. Opposed is the "church of coercion," Catholic authoritarianism that supported conquistadores and modern dictators. To understand Catholicism in Latin America one must realize its dual legacies.

Catholicism arrived in the Americas as a weapon. The role of enforcer was earlier forged on the anvil of Spain's *reconquista:* the seven-century crusade of Christian against Moor. In 1492, the successful crusade against the Moors turned westward, across the Atlantic. In the Americas, a potent military religious frenzy—a holy war equal to the Crusades—was unleashed on Indigens. Securing souls as well as soil, Catholic orthodoxy became the test of political loyalty. Now, after almost five centuries of virtual domination, the Catholic monopoly is ending—its dwindling control hastened by a shrinking priesthood, ever greater secularization, and challenges by Protestant and African Latin rivals. But the psychological legacy remains. Catholicism once dominated Latin America.

The church of coercion is exemplified by the interchangeable symbols of cross and sword. Following combat, conquistadores celebrated triumph with a Catholic mass. Without a church, the battlefield was used. For want of a crucifix, a large sword would stab a bloody hillside; with point down and horizontal hand guards, the sword resembled the cross of Christ. Both victors and vanquished knelt before the sword-cross emblem of Christian victory and native defeat. Soon European men in sandals sought a spiritual conquest in the boot prints of soldiers. Iberian crucifixes would complete what Iberian sabers had begun. Missionaries visited indigenous communities, catechized, and built churches. Kneeling before a mission altar, Indigens felt the power of defeat and redemption, dominion and salvation: both Christ's crucifixion and their own.

The cross and the sword also personified Spain's patron saint, Santiago. In a distant century, in remote northwestern Iberia, retreating Christians faced advancing Moors and prayed. One starry night an apparition appeared: a monklike rider brandishing a sword charged about. The warrior-monk reappeared during battles, rallying the armies of Christ and slaying Moors with invincible conviction. Soon, ancient bones were unearthed, and popular myth affirmed the ghostly horseman had been St. James, the missionary apostle of the first century who was rumored to have died nearby. Santiago de Compostela (St. James of the Field of Stars) became a shrine, at times the most popular destination of medieval European pilgrims. For centuries the name of Santiago was also part of a battlefield cry in the throats of Spanish soldiers.

Spain's patron saint visited the new world as a spiritual presence from California to Patagonia, his name given to cities from Santiago, Chile, to Matamoros ("Moor Killer"), Mexico. And Santiago still celebrates his victories annually in Guatemala, Peru, and wherever natives use dance and drama taught to their ancestors centuries ago by Catholic priests. Still reenacting the pageantry of Spain's imperial mission, defeated Indigens—resembling vanquished Moors—ritually fall before a dancer who wears the mask of Santiago, the white-faced conquistador. After ritualistically slaying his foes, Spain's patron walks among his prone victims brandishing not a sword but a crucifix. The foremost conquistador in the Americas was neither Pizarro nor Cortés but a spirit: Santiago.[11]

Catholic coercion in Latin America was more than symbols and saints. Religious institutions also dominated. One such institution was an arrangement between church and state known as *el patronato real* (royal patronage). As gratitude for expanding Christendom—and as political repayment for helping "elect" a Spanish pope—the new pontiff rewarded Isabel and Fernando with the privilege of themselves appointing church officials to conquered territories. Thus, clerics promoted to high church office first demonstrated loyalty to Spain. But *patronato real* also enhanced Catholic power: church and state acted together, sometimes as one person. For example, in New Spain a Catholic priest, Pedro de Moya y Contreras, served as archbishop and *inquisitor-geral* (local head of the Inquisition) but also as viceroy (representing the king) and *visitador-geral* (special judicial prosecutor). Earthly and spiritual domination were one. Such complete authority in modern times is achieved only by those rare dictatorships that command belief as well as behavior.

Catholic orthodoxy was also reinforced by the Spanish Inquisition. Reactivated from dormacy by Queen Isabel, the Inquisition was a church agency that used the sacrament of confession as a lethal weapon. Because Indigens were considered neophytes, they escaped its jurisdiction, but the Inquisition persecuted Moors, Jews, *con-*

versos, and Protestants. Suspects were *desaparecidos* ("disappeared"): seized without warning and interrogated with torture. Naming other "suspects" allowed some leniency, but confession brought public condemnations and punishments of imprisonment, confiscations, or death in an auto-da-fé: ritual execution by strangulation or burning. And ideas were suspect. Condemned books, pamphlets, plays, and other writings were also burned in fiery autos-da-fé.

Other institutional coercions were subtle but substantial. The Catholic church received a tithe (or tenth) of all personal income. Ecclesiastics commanded forced labor from Indigens and African Latins who not only built churches, convents, monasteries, and residences but also cultivated church estates. Clerics also monopolized schools, hospitals, and orphanages—indoctrinating people at all levels of society—and held jurisdiction over births, marriages, divorce, and death, which entailed judicial power over inheritance, endowments, and personal property.[12]

With Catholic bishops and Spanish governors explaining and defending each other, religious faith and political loyalty were synonymous. Thus, the independence movement of the 1800s was viewed as both blasphemy and treason: the Catholic church opposed liberty for Spanish America. In Venezuela, liberal Simón Bolívar was denounced as a heretic. In Mexico, revolutionary priests Miguel Hidalgo and José María Morelos were defrocked and released to the state for execution. Catholicism was an instrument of faith but also of authority, power, and legitimacy.

When Spain's colonial empire ended on mainland America, the Catholic church stood alone as society's most powerful institution. *Patronato real* and the Inquisition were gone; otherwise, the church of coercion changed but slightly. Leaders of new nations eventually named Catholicism as their official state religion, allowing Rome continued control of birth, marriage, burial, inheritance, and other civil matters. The church also preserved many *fueros* (privileges), including its own courts and the tithe. Ties of cross and sword were also renewed, more informally and with local dictators rather than Spanish viceroys. In Argentina, for example, General Juan Manuel Rosas granted the church many favors. In return, priests placed his picture beside images of Christ in churches and praised the bloody tyrant in their sermons.

Catholicism also remained dominant in economics and education. Three hundred years of accumulating land grants from Spanish kings and inheriting estates from *peninsular* and criollo benefactors made the church the largest owner of property in Latin America. Following independence, the Catholic church owned almost half the homes of Lima, about two-thirds of those of Mexico City, and fully half the properties of some new nations. The Catholic church was also Latin America's largest banker, sometimes the sole source of credit. It loaned to friends and withheld money from those who questioned its *fueros.* And the church still demanded tithes. The power, wealth, and influence of the church carried into education: its virtual monopoly of schools, hospitals, and orphanages—and hence political indoctrination—lasted long after Latin America gained independence.

Meaningful separation of church and state in Latin America developed around the mid-nineteenth century, when secularizing liberals challenged ecclesiastical influence in secular life. The liberals wanted to sell church lands, create civil instead of ecclesiastical courts, open public schools, and more. Of course, the Catholic hierarchy cried heresy and fought back, and not just with words and edicts. In Mexico the struggle between church and state erupted into a vicious civil war. On one side was Benito Juárez, champion of secular society. On the other was an alliance of clerics, landowners, Hispanophiles, traditionalist peasants, and, eventually, European imperialists. The pulpit became a potent weapon, as priests threatened their rivals with excommunication and damnation while giving God's blessings to Christian crusaders. When Juárez won, the Church arranged with Napoleon III of France to intervene in Mexico. After a century and a half, a Hapsburg monarchy returned to Mexico in the person of Maximilian, who was blessed by Mexico's Catholic church and supported by French soldiers. He, too, was defeated by Juárez. But the intransigent Mexican church of coercion would not die, even though it lost its lands and legal jurisdictions. In Mexico, and in nations spared such bloody church-state conflicts, liberals eventually accommodated their clerical opponents. The cross and sword did not become ardent and open allies. But they did work together. In Mexico, the Machiavellian Porfirio Díaz built his thirty-year reign, in part, upon church support. And the church again controlled schools and conducted its affairs openly.

Arrangements between traditionalist leaders wanting authority and authoritarian prelates protecting tradition became common in twentieth-century Latin America. Conservative bishops, wealthy landowners, and autocratic generals often united to oppose labor organizers, secular educators, social reformers, or peasants seeking land. When reformers pressed for change, resistance became church policy. In Mexico, seventy-year-old wounds of church-state rivalry opened again when revolutionary governments during the 1920s pushed education and land reforms, again seeking to create a modern, secular nation. Lacking large landowners or foreign allies, church fathers armed and propagandized their peasant flock and marched once more to war. Called the Cristeros, Catholic counterrevolutionaries in Mexico, assassinated hundreds of social reformers: teachers, health workers, agrarian reform agents, and soldiers who sought to defend them. A religious fanatic even assassinated Mexico's president-elect, Álvaro Obregón, when he won his second term in 1928. In Nicaragua during the same time, Agusto César Sandino led a peasant revolt against both landlords and U.S. Marines. Here bishops urged Sandino's followers to abandon their "sterile struggle" and return to family values: work, religion, and traditional authority. Sandino was later assassinated by Anastasio Somoza, who became dictator. The archbishop of Managua eventually celebrated the new and bloody regime by personally coronating Somoza's daughter as "queen of the army" during a huge public ceremony: the crown placed on the young woman's head belonged to the nation's patron saint, the Virgin of Candelaria. Such renewed ties between the cross and sword were intensified when the Spanish civil war reverberated throughout the Hispanic world. In Spain, secularizing socialists fought a bloody war with the self-proclaimed military defender of Catholicism, General Francisco Franco. Fearing atheistic communism, Catholic prelates in Latin America cozied up to many fascist tyrants who tortured and killed in the name of religion and tradition. Catholic clerics also prayed for CIA troops in Guatemala and Cuba during the 1950s and 1960s. From 1492 until the mid-twentieth century, Catholicism remained both orthodox and allied to traditional elites—seeking, like them, to perpetuate privileges acquired during the European conquest.[13]

Yet seismic changes were occurring. During the 1960s internal change shook the very foundations of Latin American Catholicism. Today, the lower clergy of the Catholic church—called the Ti Legliz (the Little Church) in Haiti—is a revolutionary force in Latin America: struggling against what it had been for half a millennium, and often struggling against the church of the bishops, still a force for conservatism. The church of coercion—Catholic traditionalism in Latin America—has been dramatically weakened by competition with a new and radical religious movement: Catholic liberation theology. The legacies of militancy, of shared sovereignty, of the Inquisition—of orthodox belief and behavior—have faded dramatically. A past of religious colonialism is ending. The symbols of coercive Catholicism remain in the physical monuments its once-powerful authority erected. In virtually every city and town, village and valley, massive churches still dominate the region's landscape. Although often empty, they form an imposing facade for the Latin American house of spirits. Meanwhile, great changes occur.[14]

CATHOLICISM: THE CHURCH OF COMPASSION

The bravest Latin American voice for justice today is the Catholic church—or at least a sizable portion of the church. Since the 1960s, probably most Catholic priests, nuns, and bishops have spoken for the poor, powerless, and oppressed, replacing secular Marxists as the foremost advocates for social revolution. Preaching an idealistic yet pragmatic "theology of liberation," Christ's gospel was wedded to both Marxism and modern social science, rekindling a humanism as old as the missions. But liberation theology is only the most recent manifestation of Catholicism's other face: the church of compassion.

The voice of Catholic compassion was raised during the first generation of the European conquest. In Hispaniola, the tragic island colonized by Columbus, a Dominican friar named Antonio de Montesinos rose to his pulpit one Sunday in 1511 to address Spanish colonists. His sermon would reverberate—sometimes loudly, other times as a whisper—during five centuries:

> In order to make your sins against the Indians known to you, I have come up on this pulpit. . . . This voice says that you are in mortal sin, that you live and die in it, for the cruelty and tyranny you use in dealing with these innocent people. Tell me, by what right or justice do you keep these people in such a cruel and horrible servitude? On what authority have you waged a detestable war against these people, who dwelt quietly and peacefully on their own land? . . . Are these not men? . . . Have they not rational souls? Are you not bound to love them . . . ?[15]

Antonio de Montesinos was an early member of the church of compassion. Through time, many others would join.

The most important early advocate of Catholic conscience in the Americas was Bartolomé de Las Casas. Las Casas arrived a conquistador, became an *encomendero,* and exploited Indigens. At age forty he renounced exploitation and became a Dominican priest. His major polemic, the *Very Brief Recital of the Destruction of the Indies,* cataloged Iberian abuses against Indigens. He not only wrote but acted. In Spain he argued that the crown should protect native peoples. When colonists evaded the resulting New Laws, Las Casas and his associates began a series of social experiments in Venezuela, Central America, and Mexico: the early Spanish missions were conceived as utopian societies.[16]

The journey of Las Casas—from coercion to compassion—became a familiar route in Latin America. In Mexico after the conquest, young Spanish priests studying Nahuatl (to better preach among former Aztecs) learned more than language from their native teachers. While prelates elsewhere burned indigenous artifacts as satanic, Catholic clerics like Bernardino de Sahagún and Fray Toribio Motolinía created "Indian schools" and themselves began learning: sitting with elders, transcribing their stories, collecting their documents, and compiling multivolume histories of Indigen civilization. Fray Toribio even took a Nahuatl name: he had been de Benavente, he became Motolinía (the poor one). The Catholic scholars faced opposition from their own countrymen: angry colonists wanting workers, church authorities favoring strict indoctrination, and civil officials resenting priests who defended an empire's victims.[17]

During 300 years of colonial history, the Catholic ideals of paternalism and personal compassion occasionally came close to realization in the Spanish reductions (known as missions in the United States). Organized by religious orders such as the Franciscans, Dominicans, Capuchins, and Jesuits, the reductions left a checkered history from California to Argentina: benevolent at some times in some places, corrupt and exploitative elsewhere. The Spanish state favored reductions as a cost-effective way of "civilizing" or "domesticating" natives, making them into docile peasants. Idealistic Catholic clerics saw the reductions as a way of saving souls. More worldly clerics viewed these fiefdoms as private estates. Typically, reductions were well-ordered villages where all members ideally sought salvation: Indigens from colonial avarice and churchmen from worldly vice. Both objectives became dramatic during the late colonial era, when the Jesuit *Guaraní* reductions in Argentina resisted slaving raids by Portuguese *bandeirantes*. After government officials and church prelates ordered the militant Jesuits to abandon their reductions—leaving natives to be enslaved—the priests resisted: they armed their Indigen followers and fought. Here were church—at least the church of compassion—and state fighting one another, the cross and the sword opposed. In pitched battles, the physical might of Spanish and Portuguese soldiers overcame the moral right of Jesuit priests. Shortly later, in 1767, all Jesuits in the Spanish empire were arrested and exiled. Such mass deportations of Jesuits had occurred earlier in Brazil.[18]

Another Catholic struggle for justice occurred during independence. In Mexico, revolt was begun by one priest, Miguel Hidalgo, and continued by another, José María Morelos. Hidalgo was a criollo intellectual and idealist, a Catholic priest who gave moral authority to ideals of political independence and social justice. The mestizo Morelos shared the same goals but was more practical. Facing great odds, both leaders were eventually captured, sentenced by the Inquisition, and "relaxed to the secular arm," that is, executed by the Spanish government.

The choices confronting Latin American priests—now as earlier—create dual Catholicisms: compassion as well as coercion. Until the reforms of Vatican II in the 1960s, clerics rarely began life poor since the impoverished could not acquire the basic education necessary to qualify for priesthood. Thus, most priests came from highly literate, typically elite families. Following seminary studies, a young priest in his first parish assignment still encounters profound realities: he must decide to either accept the many gifts and invitations proffered by leading privileged parishioners or choose to serve the poor, ministering to prostitutes, campesinos, and street orphans. In associating with the rich, he not only identifies with them but inevitably justifies and defends them. To embraces the *lucha* of the poor is to accept a profound challenge: to his own identity as well as to entrenched social forces. The decision between coercion and compassion is as old as the conquest and as recent as now. Las Casas and Sahagún chose. So do priests, monks, and nuns today.[19]

LIBERATION THEOLOGY

The church of compassion is today stronger than ever. Guided by liberation theology, Catholic clerics since the 1960s have encouraged nothing less than social revolution as an answer to Latin American injustices. During this time a renovation of the church has occurred.

Theology of liberation derives from the times. It began with anticolonialism, a movement for self-rule in Asia and Africa. Although few new world places were directly governed by foreigners, Latin Americans lived colonial lives: Europeanized elites—including representatives of the Roman church—dominated a basically nonwhite poor. Clergy from Latin America's upper classes (joined by U.S. and European missionaries) preached a well-worn message of denial, deference, and deferral: seek not material things, obey the church, reward will come in heaven. Historically, Catholicism justified worldly pain—starvation, disease, and oppression—as a moral test, suffering on earth assured salvation in the afterlife. In other lands similar beliefs and behaviors were challenged as Gandhi in India and Martin Luther King in the United States used consciousness and courage to empower the poor. Young Latin American clerics adopted these themes. Nicaraguan poet-monk Ernesto Cardenal wrote: "I used to be concerned that there might be souls in hell. Now I'm concerned with the hell of misery suffered by millions of my brothers and sisters."[20]

Another stimulus to liberation theology was the Cuban Revolution. The early achievements of communist revolutionaries—often the poor themselves—were not just health clinics, literacy campaigns, and new housing but defeating colonialist fatalism. For some Catholics, "Castroism" was a challenge, not a threat. Many young clerics discovered similarities between Marx's *Communist Manifesto* and Christ's Sermon on the Mount. Often personal interest in Marxism derived from epithets by critics designed to discredit liberation theologians. As explained by Father Miguel D'Escoto, a leader of Nicaragua's Sandinista revolution, "At thirteen I was called a communist for the first time. . . . I didn't know what a communist was . . . it seemed to be someone who felt sorry for others when they were suffering." His colleague, Ernesto Cardenal, elaborated, "It was the gospel of Jesus Christ that made a Marxist of me. There's no incompatibility between Christianity and Marxism."[21]

State oppression, the soulless materialism of capitalism, and simple neglect of conscience radicalized a generation of Catholic seminarians practicing compassion among the region's poor. The early theologian of liberation was the Peruvian Gustavo Gutiérrez, who found faith not in sterile seminary libraries studying for theology exams but among the urchins and poor of congested and dirty shantytowns. Other writers explored Christ's revolutionary message in Brazil. There Leonardo Boff and a bishop, Dom Helder Cámara, became increasingly political on behalf of the poor. They opposed Brazil's military government and foreign domination via international capitalism. In Haiti, liberation theology came to be known as Ti Legliz (the diminutive Little Church or Dear Church), a grassroots movement closely associated with Rev. Jean-Bertrand Aristide. Aristide himself transformed from scholar to activist to president by serving as chaplain of an orphanage. Many of his children were victims of political repression that killed their parents. Aristide inspired these children—and a generation of fellow clerics and countrymen—through playing his guitar, singing, and preaching mystical sermons. Eventually, his parish was torched and many followers slaughtered by thugs of Haiti's repressive regime. Undaunted, the "Little Church" movement spread. In 1990, UN-monitored elections for president delivered a massive landslide for Aristide. When he was driven from power in a military coup eighteen months later, over fifty Catholic priests and many others followed him into exile. Through this all, only one of eleven Haitian bishops has consistently supported Ti Legliz. Allied with elites and the military, the church hierarchy became alienated from the vast majority of Haiti's poor who supported Aristide and liberation theology.[22]

More than the sociology of Marx, it was modern social science that created liberation theologians. Professional studies and civic action were both joined to theology as clerics became social workers, psychologists, nurses, dietitians, educators, administrators, and journalists. Study abroad included reading the works of Protestant existentialist theologians and involvement in both the American civil rights movement and César Chávez's California farmworkers' campaigns. As students, many Latin American clerics learned to be active: opening parish literacy centers and medical clinics, organizing campesino associations, publishing neighborhood newsletters, and conducting community discussion groups.

Demographics pushed Catholicism to change. A declining priesthood and growing Latin American populations meant that many poor Catholics rarely saw priests and nuns, or almost never received the sacraments and formal religious instruction. Church attendance was infrequent, often only at Christmas and Easter. During the 1970s, as liberation theologians trained parishioners themselves to conduct local ministries, Chile had a ratio of one priest per 4300 Catholics and Brazil one priest per 8500 believers. Catholicism faced the prospect of becoming folklore rather than an organized church.[23]

Liberation theology also grew from reforms known as Vatican II. During the 1960s, Catholicism renovated itself: vernacular replaced Latin in public, celebrants of the mass turned to face parishioners, folk music supplanted Gregorian chant, local art replaced classical statuary, and the congregation—including women and children—participated in ceremonies and administering sacraments. Equally important were new goals: by publishing *Mater et Magistra* (1961) and *Pacem en Ter-*

ris (1963), Pope John XXIII reoriented Catholicism from abstract traditionalism toward a profound humanism emphasizing social reform.

In Latin America, Vatican II reforms were affirmed and enlarged, particularly at the Medellín Conference of Latin American bishops held in 1968. At Medellín, the church of compassion triumphed over the church of coercion. There Catholic prelates endorsed a revolutionary agenda which held that social systems of great inequity and repression could be even more sinful than evil individuals. In this light, political action—reform or revolution—was legitimized as liberation from sin. Shortly afterward, a meeting of Brazilian bishops—led by the charismatic Dom Helder Cámara—issued a formal letter identifying specific institutions as not only harmful but immoral: they condemned both the nation's repressive military government and exploitation by foreign capitalists.[24]

During the 1970s and 1980s, the conflict between entrenched elites and liberation theologians intensified. Liberationists projected Christ as a revolutionary who overthrew money changers at the temple and redistributed wealth by feeding loaves and fishes to the hungry. When Latin America's powerful did not change, further analogies were drawn: landowners were equated with the Pharisees, and local armies were equated with Roman legionnaires. Repression escalated and, as in the times of the catacombs, Christians became martyrs. One priest—Father Camilo Torres of Colombia, who died in 1966—gained notoriety as an actual guerrilla warrior. He explained himself, saying, "When circumstances impede men from devoting themselves to Christ, the priest's proper duty is to combat these circumstances. . . . the revolutionary struggle is a Christian and priestly struggle." Hundreds more priests and nuns—fighting with ideals and compassion rather than physical weapons—would also die as dictatorships in Guatemala, Haiti, Nicaragua, and elsewhere formed death squads composed of "off-duty" soldiers who murdered followers of liberation theology with impunity. In El Salvador death squads brandished such slogans as "Be a soldier, kill a priest" and assassinated European, Canadian, and U.S. as well as Latin American clerics—nuns as well as monks and priests. When the archbishop of San Salvador, the peaceful Oscar Romero, called for soldiers to obey their consciences rather than their officers, he was assassinated in 1980 by members of a death squad. In Nicaragua, liberationist priests blessed Sandinista guerrillas who opposed death squads and the Somoza dictatorship. When the Sandinistas triumphed, liberationist priests served the revolutionary government as cabinet members, roles reminiscent of the earlier cross and sword but with a modern and *revolutionary* irony.[25]

Essential to liberation theology is a concept that authority emanates not from "church fathers" but from common parishioners: the church as the "people of God." Liberationists practice *basismo,* use of grassroots *comunidades de base* (Christian base communities) for consciousness-raising. These communities reinterpret theology, seeing Mary not as queen of heaven but as a peasant woman, and her child not as a martyr but as a dedicated revolutionary. Moving beyond theology and religious imagery, Christian base communities also discuss modern wealth and poverty, political authority and public submission, lack of government services, and action to achieve change. *Basismo* empowers participants, as by teaching literacy through a "pedagogy of the oppressed" whereby the poor originate their own written vocabularies, write their own stories, and enact dramas: often tales of alcoholism, domestic violence, worker exploitation, and police repression. Pioneered by Brazilian educator Paulo Freire during the 1960s, "pedagogy of the oppressed" was quickly adopted as a central feature of emerging liberation theology. *Basismo* is as much action as awareness. The poor not only conceptualize themselves as victims but develop action plans: creating clinics, building schools, forming cooperatives, organizing petitions, sometimes holding strikes or boycotts. When desperate in the face of governmental repressions, liberationists form guerrilla armies.

Through liberation theology, Catholicism—or at least a major part of it—has emerged from centuries of orthodox lethargy to be militant again: but ardent in support of justice, not conquest, and liberation, not domination. Despite decades of counterpropaganda from both regional elites and Washington policy makers who together decried outside communist infiltration, the most successful inspiration for meaningful change in modern Latin America has been the home-grown gospel of Jesus Christ as revolutionary.[26]

Today, Latin American Catholicism is divided. Opposing the liberationists are more defensive traditionalists, who still see the hierarchy as the bastion of moral authority. The leader of the traditionalists has been John Paul II, who after becoming pope in 1978 both appointed antiliberationist clerics to high office and visited Latin America frequently to support conservatives. One consequence of the counterliberationist movement has been the success of Archbishop Miguel Obando y Bravo. Leader of Catholic traditionalism in Nicaragua, Obando y Bravo used the pulpit to help elect conservative Violeta Chamorro as president in 1991. The pope has also stripped some liberationists of their authority to speak on Catholic doctrine. As in past times, the Catholic church persists with dualism: the church of compassion continues as liberation theology, and the church of coercion as modern orthodoxy.

During the late twentieth century the Latin American house of spirits has witnessed its most thoroughgoing renovation since the European conquest. Theology of liberation is one innovation, Protestant Evangelicalism is another. A third modern surprise is the reemergence of old religious forms, the growing popularity of African Caribbean and African Brazilian cults.

THE BOTANICA

Let's walk through a store. Well, it's more than a store, it's a warehouse of strange artifacts, a museum of odd potions, lotions, and products. The store is located where people of African ancestry share a Latin American identity: Rio de Janeiro, Santiago de Cuba, a sleepy Caribbean town, or busy Miami. The store has different names. In Puerto Rico—and New York City—it's called the botanica.

An initial impression on entering the botanica is immense clutter. In fact, the door opens only partway, with so much piled behind, and narrow walkways make getting around difficult. Everywhere burdened tables verge on collapse, and shelves are stacked as high as the ceiling. Fetishes include African warrior statuettes of ebony, miniature cigar store Indians carved from pine, mythical Asian dragons cut from onyx, plaster of paris Buddhas, and painted plastic mermaids. The smells are many and competing, although some have grown stale with time: sweet herbs and scented waxes, strong incenses and pungent dried seaweed. Despite poor lighting, colors are evident: red peppers, candles of every hue, yellow and blue ribbons, and bins with endless earth tone powders. Barrels and boxes contain shells (from conch and sea urchins to sand dollars and wampum), bark from trees and bushes, berries, dried roots, feathers, horns from bulls and goats, rabbit's feet, plastic beads and buttons. A pole holds garlands of garlic. Elsewhere huge tobacco leaves hang like elephant ears. Corncob dolls with skirts of dried husks stare out from a shelf. Herb racks and broken spice bins contain perhaps hundreds of strange powders, each with a different color, texture, and purpose. Soaps for household cleaning and "psychic purification" line one wall. Faded pamphlets explain herbal cures, and dusty tomes on Hindu mythology are partially hidden by copies of African chants. Catholic holy cards with pictures and prayers of the Virgin Mary and Saint Barbara are stacked next to jars of aphrodisiacs—some for men, others for women. For those with modern lifestyles, instructions on aerosol cans tell how to "spiritually cleanse your home . . . and protect the environment." The botanica is endless accumulation, like being suspended in nonspecific time and place.

We visit the botanica because it represents the pilgrimage of African Latin spirituality, where everything was gathered and kept, accepted and remembered. Like *la botánica,* African Brazilian and African Caribbean belief is eclectic and chaotic. But even confusion shows heritage: for just as slavery ripped lives from ancestral traditions and affronted black pilgrims with endless novelty, this store sells things of Angola and Dahomey, Christian European masters, native American and immigrant Asian neighbors. The botanica is a collection of artifacts from everywhere, but also an erratic time line: the future arrives unexpectedly, life's legacies spill over one another, and the past always reemerges. During the slave trade and slavery, resistance normally meant death: one better accept the new—however confusing—not just because the boss says so but because the new might actually help cope with later surprises. Certainly holy water and holy cards, cigar smoke and corn seeds, chants and mantras proved their worth for Europeans, Indigens, and Indians.

From the botanica, history can be reconstructed. Things African—fetishes, materials for rituals, accounts of myths, images of old world deities—recount origins. A fishing heritage and the watery hell of a "middle passage" reveal themselves in marine life, statues of mermaids and water goddesses, objects of an undersea afterlife. From Europeans come images of powerful saints, biblical stories of enslavement and redemption, notions of witchcraft, and even gypsy tambourines. From Indigens we see tobacco and herbs, corn and *pacha mama.* Although the botanica shows all these things, it is more than a museum. Since blacks were long forbidden their own temples, the closest thing to an African Latin church is this botanica.

But much of African Latin belief is hidden, even at the botanica. Slavery and servitude forced African Latins to obscure beliefs, to mask what and how they felt. Their spirituality existed underground for centuries: in subtle multiple meanings for speech, dance, and song, in meetings held during darkness, in making fetishes as toys, in telling bedtime fables of animals with human attributes, in raising women—less challenging to white male authorities—to the priesthood. Even carnival was more than just fun: under the guise of Shrove Tuesday or saintly festivals, African Brazilian and African Caribbean societies celebrated their own heritage, built floats to unforgotten deities, danced in homage to ancestors, and drummed coded rhythms of African spirits. The desire to thrive imparted lasting dynamics of duality, of erasing precise boundaries, of mixing form and substance, of combining what appears and what is. Through it all, African Latins and their cults became innovative and imaginative.

Black spirituality is multifaceted, profound. Ripped from Africa, slaves lost a connection to their native lands but not to the land itself: gone were the venerated springs, rivers, mountains, trees, and ancestral burial grounds of their homelands. But slaves brought a reverence for the spirituality of local places to the new world. In the Americas, Catholic churches became new shrines for old African gods as the statues of favorite saints were adorned with fetishes. Indigens instructed African immigrants in the animism of nearby hills, trees, rivers, and plants. In more recent times, Asian arrivals gave African Latins ideas of karma, of reincarnation, of yin and yang.

But central to African Latin belief are deities. Hundreds, even thousands, exist, as ancient spirits divide and multiply their personas, combining and reincarnating both with each other and with deities from Europeans, Indigens, and Asians. As an example, slavery introduced the Yoruba divinity Orixá to many African Latins whose ancestors never knew him. In the new world Orixá blended with gods from Angola, the Congo, and elsewhere. Orixá also combined with favorite saints of French Catholics in Haiti to appear as multiple identities in voodoo. He blended with saints preferred by the Portuguese in Brazil to reincarnate with scores of different personalities in *condomblé.* In Cuba and Puerto Rico, Orixá joined with various Spanish Catholic saints in the cults known as Santeria and *espiritu.* Syncretism of African and Catholic spiritualism occurred wherever the two met. Ogum (who protects travelers) united with St. George; Mamae Oxum (the solicitous grandmother) blended with the Virgin of the Immaculate Conception; Nana Buruque (arranger of marriages and finder of lost objects) found a home in the character of St. Anne; the list seems endless. And many African gods and goddesses exist without Catholic masks. Iemanjá is ubiquitous and prolific; she is the water mother with large breasts and extended womb, immersed in sea symbols, often pictured as a mermaid in a castle beneath the sea, or as the deity of a river or lake. However, Iemanjá also appears as the mother of Jesus, and as *pacha mama.* African Caribbean and African Brazilian gods and goddesses are as numerous as the many situations faced by pilgrims from Africa.[27]

Also integral to black belief in the Americas is priesthood. African Latin mediums differ significantly from indigenous *curanderos,* who *exorcise* spirits. African Brazilian and African Caribbean priests and priestesses move spirits the other way: into people. Called a *mae-de-santo* or a *pai-de-santo* in Brazil (literally, a mother-of-a-saint or father-of-a-saint) one's neighbor or fellow worker might develop followers and establish part of a village or a few city blocks as his or her "territory." *Maes-* or *pais-de-santo* succeed because they evoke the spirits—or the spiritual emotions of followers—bringing hosts and visiting spirits together to create *encantados* (enchanted ones) during frenzied rituals of rhythmic music, whirling dances, screaming incantations, and sometimes animal sacrifices. *Maes-* and *pais-de-santo* also pioneer new relationships between old forms and emerging trends. Perhaps the most successful *pai-de-santo* in Brazil was a teenage African Brazilian who in 1908 became an *encantado* of an Indigen deity. His charisma created a cult, *umbanda,* which still attracts new adherents. His followers improvise, combining the past with new circumstances. And political personalities are an ever-popular source of African Latin faith. The *encantados* of one *mae-de-santo* evoke the spirits of Jesus Christ, Iemanjá, Omolú, and John F. Kennedy.[28]

African Latin spirituality is complex and intense, and almost everywhere coexists informally with Catholicism. As an example, one anthropologist recounts the story of the African Brazilian alligator deity, Japetequara. Seeking a human god-child, the spirit Japetequara used a *mae-de-santo* to transform a peasant into his *encantado.* This *encantado* of Japetequara then stood as godfather during a Catholic baptism of a neighborhood child. The *encantado* scowled through the ceremony because the alligator spirit detested being in church. Except for the Catholic priest, everyone present knew of the enchantment and accepted Japetequara, not the peasant neighbor, as the child's godfather. The parents of the child hoped that someday their son could become a *pai-de-santo* for the alligator spirit, with his own territory and following.[29]

The popularity of cults in Brazil and other Latin American nations with large black populations derives from poverty and oppression. Whites with wealth and power have long been comfortable with the singular male authority implicit in European monotheism. But a different sociology for African Latins creates a different spirituality. In Brazil, only 0.5 percent of doctors or lawyers are African Latins, as are only 30 of every 1000 government bureaucrats. But 997 of every 1000 male cargo handlers and 999 of every 1000 women domestics are African Brazilians. Such circumstances affect income, education, status—and spirituality. For example, the poor of Brazil do not *choose* between modern medicine and African Brazilian faith healing: modern medicine is not an option. It is unavailable or unaffordable. But one can visit (or be!) a faith-healing *pai-de-santo.* When one *mae-de-santo* was criticized for practicing spiritual healing, she retorted, "Maybe you don't understand. . . . The poor man, when he is sick, has to grab a hold of anything he can."[30]

Today, the Latin American house of spirits has many rooms with sometimes noisy African Latin believers. Voodoo is still strong in Haiti, serving many purposes. It inspires the beautiful paintings of folk artists and was used by dictator "Papa Doc" Duvalier, himself a voodoo priest, to instill fear. Santeria from Cuba and *espíritu* from Puerto Rico arrived in Florida and New York with immigrants. Sometimes they appear as street games of chance. But American courts and town councils must now deliberate whether ritual executions of chickens, cats, and dogs—traditionally part of these African Caribbean cults—are protected by constitutional guarantees of religious freedom. In Jamaica Rastafarianism is a twentieth-century convergence of English, African, and Caribbean experiences. It is an eclectic blending of the Bible, Anglican Protestantism, Marcus Garvey's 1920s "Back-to-Africa" movement, cult worship of Ethiopia's former emperor (Haile Selassie), use of *ganga* and political themes from the 1960s. It is best known in the United States for its reggae music.

In Brazil, African Latin cults rival Protestant Pentecostals in gaining new adherents. In the countryside two very old cults—*condomblé* and *macumba*—were long suppressed by authorities but are now practiced openly. In Brazil's large cities, the fastest-growing African Brazilian cult is the newest, *umbanda.* All these now attract whites, *mamelucos,* and others as well as African Brazilians. Today African Latin spirituality is more socially accepted, more popular, and more successful than at any other time in the long history of Africans in the new world. Botanicas are a growing business.

EVANGÉLICOS: "THE GOOD NEWS"

In Brazil, the nation with the most Catholics on earth, more people attend a Billy Graham rally than gather to honor the pope. In Argentina, a quarter million persons participated in Graham's 1991 crusade, with the choir alone exceeding the number who first heard him preach in Buenos Aires thirty years earlier. Guatemala counts 400 separate Protestant groups: one-third of the nation is Evangelical, and it is likely to be the first predominantly Protestant country in Spain's former empire. All over Latin America, growing numbers of people are reading Bibles on buses, singing with tambourines on city streets, and knocking on doors with Christ's "good news." Some observers are asking: "Is Latin America turning Protestant?"[31]

The greatest spiritual transformation since the era of the Spanish missions is currently sweeping Latin America. From Mexicali, Mexico, to Bahia, Brazil, to Concepción, Chile, old movie theaters are becoming temples, vacant stores serve as Bible schools, and believers are "born again." *Evangélicos* (Evangelicals) are remodeling the Latin American house of spirits.

Evidence of changed spirituality often shocks observers. Some years ago, my wife and I spent Christmas in Mexico, hoping to observe such traditional seasonal pageantry as *la posada,* the parade of children who accompany a boy and girl dressed as "Mary" and "Joseph" and travel from house to house recreating the search for lodging in Bethlehem. The children encounter numerous rejections but finally enter a home prepared for a fiesta: with decorations, music, and a piñata filled with candies and toys. However, our plan to witness a *posada* met with continual frustration. As we left our hotel lobby, Mexican guests were gathering before a large television, watching a satellite-transmitted Christmas special from Las Vegas complete with Elvis look-alikes and scantily clad showgirl skits of Rudolph the Reindeer and Frosty the Snowman. No one—neither hotel staff nor guests—knew where we could find a Mexican *posada.* As we wandered almost empty streets, the children's parade was nowhere to be found, no one knew anything about it, and commercial refrains from the Las Vegas special kept echoing from open doorways. Finally, another stroller said she had seen people celebrating Christmas just a few blocks away. Following her directions, we approached the address, anticipating mariachi music and children singing. Instead we heard an electric guitar, rhythmic tambourines, an amplified preacher, and shouts of "Thank you, Jesus." It was a storefront church, and *evangélicos* were celebrating. We entered: both the Pentecostal temple and the modern realities of Latin American spirituality.[32]

Protestants have been active in Latin America for at least two centuries, but only in recent decades has conversion been intense. During the nineteenth century, immigration introduced Lutherans to Brazil and Argentina, Mennonites to Paraguay and Mexico. In the twentieth century, missionaries from Europe and the United States gained some converts to Presbyterianism and Methodism. The newest wave of Protestantism is more emotional, more messianic, and more successful. These are fundamentalists—Seventh-Day Adventists, Baptists, Jehovah's Witnesses, Mormons, and many more—holding to a wide range of beliefs. The largest group—and a term that encompasses other ardent Protestants—are Evangelicals: seeking spiritual rebirth, practicing puritan values, preaching the Bible, and relentlessly proselytizing neighbors. In many ways they differ. The Baptists are ardent democrats, adamant about autonomy for local congregations. The Mormons are highly centralized, governed by groups of elders. Seventh-Day Adventists are millennialists, believing Christ will soon return to establish the kingdom of God on Earth. Many *evangélicos* accept a literal interpretation of the Bible and oppose modern secular humanism, yet others pioneer modern technologies and business methods. Meanwhile Pentecostals, infused with the Holy Spirit, speak in tongues, use faith healing, and exorcise devils.[33]

The appeal of *evangélicos* in Latin America is understandable. Converts are mainly poor, lower-class persons—usually mestizos, Indigens, or African Latins—who are lavished with attention by proselytizing recruiters. With a new sense of personal worth, converts abandon fatalism and begin a life of self-reliance and group activism. They testify about past sinful behaviors and accept new responsibilities. In a sense, *evangélicos* become puritans: hardworking, clean-living, and dedicated. The Evangelical message is one of personal rectitude: to save your spiritual life one must discipline the physical life. The changes are empowering. Often for the first time in their lives, these "born-again" Christians feel as if they are agents rather than victims of destiny.[34]

Evangelicalism creates communal as well as personal change. Conversion is reinforced by relentless networking of Christian friends, not unlike an extended family, as the convert interacts with others to achieve common goals: preaching in public, visiting door to door, organizing church schools, or managing soup kitchens. Mutual trust and confidence grow as together individuals achieve tangible results.

Evangélicos employ emotionalism. Stirring hymns, foot-pounding music, charismatic oratory, speaking in tongues, and proselytizing allow self-expression but also deeply shared feelings. Although *evangélico* temples are simple places—often former stores—they come alive with boisterous activity whenever members gather to pray and preach, sing and celebrate.[35]

The Evangelical reworking of values brings many advantages. The quest for self-perfection leads adherents to abstain from alcohol, drugs, crass entertainment, and gambling. While such changes make one morally "clean," they also impart self-esteem and allow once-wasted time, money, and energy to be directed toward personal and community improvement. *Evangélicos* typically repair, clean, and paint their homes, their churches, and their neighborhoods. Among *evangélicos* the cult of machismo usually weakens as men take pride in both physical work and home involvement. Women, too, change. Once secluded, women begin to accept public roles as Christian teachers, preachers, and managers. *Evangélico* families save more and reinvest more. Literacy is a requisite, for one must read the Bible to save one's soul. But reading also helps at work, at school, and in society. Spiritual perfection has social and material benefits.[36]

A key factor in *evangélico* success is leadership. In Catholicism, even liberation theology remains significantly authoritarian: priests may be encouraging and supportive, but as consecrated ministers they hold elevated leadership. Among *evangélicos* leaders are "grassroots": neighbors, coworkers, family, or self. Personal interpretation of the Bible, the absence of highly trained professionals, and a missionary zeal all mean that individuals lead. Thus, common people develop the gift of *la palabra,* speaking on street corners, on radio and television, and on doorsteps. Charismatic *evangélico* leadership rewards people—male and female—who are spontaneous, creative, expressive, and diligent; formal ordination is not necessary.[37]

Catholic realities also encourage *evangélico* conversions. Converts from Catholicism abandon a religion that historically favored the rich and powerful, relegated believers to periodic displays of feudal fealty, and in modern times has been vastly understaffed. Even liberation theology helps *evangélicos:* converts desire personal involvement but without the political repression that marks government actions toward revolutionaries. Often, the more rewarding (and safer) path is that of original Protestant Reformationists centuries ago in Europe: leave Catholicism for a new faith.

EVANGÉLICOS: THE BAD NEWS

The success of modern Latin American Evangelicalism raises disturbing issues. Five hundred years ago spiritual conquest completed Iberian imperialism. Today, a revolution of belief follows U.S. commercial and political dominance. Evangelicalism, the most recent form of colonialism, thrives in Latin America only because U.S. missionaries proselytized relentlessly. And the impact of *evangélico* conversion on Latin American families and communities is also often disruptive, sometimes violently so. The news of *evangélicos* is not always good.

Evangelicalism often appears as imperialism. Of course, domination by conversion—which may be the ultimate form of control—is nothing new in Latin America. Modern conversions began and are sustained by missionaries from the north: Billy Graham's early effort was joined by those of televangelists such as Jim and Tammy Baker, Jimmy Swaggert, Oral Roberts, and many more. Success in Latin America matched or exceeded what these ministries accomplished in the United States. Tens of thousands of North American missionaries recruit daily on Latin American doorsteps. The Mormons alone send 17,000 young men annually to evangelize in the region. Logistic support includes Bibles, billboards, books, pamphlets, radio broadcasts, audiotapes, leasing buses, bringing converts on pilgrimages to New Orleans and Dallas, real estate rentals, and television satellite time. Using American business strategies (which have proved successful in the home marketing of soaps and cosmetics), missionaries employ techniques such as keeping a message simple, recruiting and training local staffs, pyramiding personnel with "down lines," offering bonus incentives, and having converts produce inspirational testimonials.

One North American mission alone operates forty-four Latin American publishing houses (printing religious material in 200 languages from Spanish and Portuguese to Quechua and Quiché Maya), produces 1050 radio programs per week on more than 850 Latin American radio stations, and transmits television programming to 160 television stations. Other Protestant missions are likewise active, flooding Latin America with missionaries and media messages. The "made in America" Evangelical movement is more powerful abroad than at home.[38]

Perhaps the main reason why U.S. Protestant missions have prospered in Latin America (rather than in other world regions) is television. When communication satellites became available in the 1970s, a handful of North American ministries pioneered new applications of this innovative technology. With equatorial orbits straddling Latin America, the region became a target for godly messages: transmitted from North American churches and beamed from the heavens. The sale of used black-and-white television sets in poor neighborhoods completed the electronic link from preachers in Oklahoma and Ohio to Latin American hearts and minds.

Evangelicalism also profits from the popular belief in North American infallibility, an idea common among Latin America's poor and powerless. U.S. domination of Latin American business, military, and politics since World War II has facilitated missionaries from Topeka, Cleveland, New Orleans, and other U.S. cities in spreading a message that America is blessed: in this case with superior spirituality. As with clothing styles or fast foods, Latin Americans are asked to buy another American dream: being "born again." Encouraged to adopt North American ways, some converts just decide to adopt North America: to be born again as immigrants to *el norte*. Los Angeles, Miami, New York, and many other communities have replaced Boston as proverbial Mecca for spiritual perfection, the "City upon a Hill."[39]

Evangelicalism also distorts Latin American families and neighborhoods. Once he or she is born again, an individual can become insufferable around relatives, particularly if family members do not also convert. Domestic feuds develop as the *evangélico* relentlessly pressures loved ones, wearing down their resistance or patience. Communities, too, endure *evangélico* intensities. With truth as a simple message—often literal interpretation of the Bible—confrontations abound. Chiapas, Mexico, is an example. Here native peoples have long blended community, spirituality, and politics. When Evangelicals from Dallas, Texas, began winning Indigen converts, traditional unities were broken. Long before the January 1, 1994, rebellion, a civil dispute ensued as differences over finances and politics became intractable confrontations over ideology and authority. In 1992, *evangélico* converts denounced Indigen and Catholic religions as idolatrous, and refused to pay taxes for local festivals and shrines. Indigenous officials retaliated by expelling *evangélicos* from communal farms. The opposing sides used boycotts, protests, and provocative parades through one another's neighborhoods. When young ministers preached that elder caciques (chiefs, like a justice of the peace) were disciples of the devil, the caciques had the charismatic *evangélico* leaders jailed. The violence escalated as armed *evangélicos* abducted local judges and barricaded streets. Pitched battles with rocks and bottles resulted in deaths and injuries, and intervention by federal authorities achieved only a temporary peace.[40]

Evangélicos are also politically active. In Central America during the 1980s they allied themselves with right-wing regimes. It is no irony that ultraconservative Christians like Pat Robertson and Jerry Falwell influenced policy both in Ronald Reagan's administration and in Central American capitals: they spent money, marshaled legions, and helped advance leaders in both places. In a cynical cycle, U.S. aid and policy supported Latin American dictators, who encouraged *evangélicos,* who followed U.S. televangelists, who campaigned to elect right-wing Republicans, who lobbied for U.S. support of Latin American dictatorships. Oliver North assisted in organizing this system. Elsewhere, *evangélicos* have also achieved political success. In Peru, they worked to elect President Alberto Fujimori, a political outsider who conducted a grassroots effort composed mostly of Christian Fundamentalists well experienced with pushing both doorbells and their message. With Evangelical support, Fujimori defeated Mario Vargas Llosa, scion of Peru's social elite.

Whether Latin America becomes Protestant remains to be seen. And whatever Protestantism it does adopt will surely be as much Latin American as it is Protestant. But clearly the impact of *evangélicos* is profound. The Latin American house of spirits will never be the same.

CHANGE AND PERMANENCE IN THE HOUSE OF SPIRITS

In the long run, the main tendency in Latin America may be secularism, or at least some form of agnosticism: a nonchalance toward spiritual issues. Catholic men, in particular, are notorious for religious laxity: after attaining adulthood they typically attend church only for family marriages and baptisms, sometimes at Easter and Christmas, and eventually their own funerals. And Latin American spiritualism also confronts the pervasive force of simple materialism, a mighty reality throughout the world. The emergence of modern commercialism and middle-class life has fostered secular materialism and a preoccupation with financial security rather than religious salvation.

But even people who avoid church are often unconsciously religious. In Latin America even atheists evoke God. In Spanish, *adiós* (good-bye) derives from *a-Dios* (to God). And among Latin Americans it is common to see *fútbol* (soccer) or baseball players make the sign of the cross. These behaviors may be habit or superstition, but the message is that deeper beliefs exist. Success in sports may depend on forces greater than one's kick or the swing of a bat.

Spirituality—if not religion—remains important because Latin Americans still ponder mysteries. The unanswered questions of life are both immediate and cosmic: why one works hard and has little, why a neighbor dies in a fire, why rains flood part of the village, why we exist on earth, whether we exist afterward. Science and factual cause and effect only partially explain such questions. The chance unknowns of time, place, and process remain mysteries.

The house of spirits will also endure because Latin Americans feel emotionally connected with forces greater than supply and demand, national identity, and television programming. Personal identity reaches beyond the clothes one wears and the place one lives. Acquiring material goods, and living a secure life have not yet dominated the Latin American soul. Peasants and patricians alike ponder how and why the nuances of daily experience accumulate into a lifetime.[41]

Complex spiritual legacies will always influence Latin America. Indigen and African Latin traditions are deep wellsprings from which to draw, even in modern times. Iberian spirituality and that of Notre Dame or Canterbury in the Caribbean are powerful magnets. Pockets of Judaism and Islam are also evident in Latin America. Each tradition is an enduring spiritual legacy. And beliefs such as liberation theology and those of *evangélicos* seem new but incorporate past behavior and belief. For these many reasons, Latin America has been and remains a house of many spirits. Sanctity is still a goal of life.

SUGGESTED READINGS

Bastide, Roger. *The African Religions of Brazil.* Baltimore: Johns Hopkins University Press, 1978.

Brundage, Burr Cartwright. *Two Earths, Two Heavens: An Essay Contrasting the Aztecs and the Incas.* Albuquerque: University of New Mexico Press, 1975.

Cabestrero, Teofilo. *Ministers of God, Ministers of the People.* Maryknoll, N.Y.: Orbis Books, 1982.

Dover, Robert V. H., et al., editors. *Andean Cosmologies through Time: Persistence and Emergence.* Bloomington: University of Indiana Press, 1992.

Hanke, Lewis. *The Spanish Struggle for Justice in the Conquest of America.* Philadelphia: University of Pennsylvania Press, 1949.

Ingham, John M. *Mary, Michael, and Lucifer: Folk Catholicism in Central Mexico.* Austin: University of Texas Press, 1986.

Kita, Bernice. *What a Prize Awaits Us: Letters from Guatemala.* Maryknoll, N.Y.: Orbis Books, 1988.

Lernoux, Penny. *Cry of the People.* New York: Doubleday, 1980.

Levine, Daniel H. *Religion and Political Conflict in Latin America.* Chapel Hill: University of North Carolina Press, 1986.

Martin, David. *Tongues of Fire: The Explosion of Protestantism in Latin America.* Oxford: Basil Blackwell, 1990.

O'Gorman, Frances. *Aluanda: A Look at Afro-Brazilian Cults.* Rio de Janeiro: Livaria Francisco Alves Editora S.A., 1977.

6

ECOLOGY, TECHNOLOGY, AND EMPIRES

Your Highnesses are as much lords of this country as you are of Jérez or Toledo. Your ships can come here as safely as if they still lay at home. They will bring back gold from here. . . .

Gold is most excellent. Gold constitutes treasure, and anyone who has it can do whatever he likes in the world.

Christopher Columbus, from the new world[1]

The world's trade flourishes at the expense of the peoples of America . . . , the riches they draw from the bosom of the fertile earth are not retained.

Petition to the viceroy of Mexico, 1723[2]

In autumn 1993, a young Indigen traveled to the United States from Ecuador's rain forest. His name was Moi, and during a lifetime of about twenty-five years he had seen North American petroleum companies invade his homeland with helicopters, chain saws, bulldozers, drilling rigs, and dynamite. Seeking energy for international markets, the companies demolished rain forests to construct pipelines, roads, electrical transmission towers, storage tanks, and boom towns. Every day they poured tons of toxins into pristine watersheds. They reduced 300-foot stands of ancient trees to piles of smoldering ashes. Native peoples, including Moi's tribe—the Huaorani—suffered. Without ancestral hunting lands, the Huaorani were driven onto neighbors' territories, resulting in conflicts and killings. Denied their natural habitats, Indigens migrated to sleazy oil towns. Here Huaorani men sold souvenirs such as stuffed alligators and captured monkeys. Huaorani women often became prostitutes.[3]

Moi traveled to Washington, D.C., seeking to understand why distant people invaded his homeland and obliterated natural habitats. He wanted to inform others about the destruction. He also sought a meeting with the North American president.

En route, Moi studied everything. He noted technologies and the energy consumed by airliners, taxis, elevators, and streetlights. He pondered what made hotel water hot. Meditating on the interplay of ecology, technology, and faith, Moi reflected: "So many cars. . . . How long have they been here? . . . [What] will you do [when] your world will be pure metal? Did your god do this?"

In Washington, Moi pressed his case. He gifted the representatives of international agencies with woven palm purses made by Huaorani villagers. He met with ecologists and journalists. And he daily visited the White House, whose previous occupant, George Bush, had nominated a Texas oil company executive to be U.S. ambassador in Ecuador. Now a new chief governed, one perhaps sympathetic to Moi, but very busy. Unable to meet Bill Clinton, Moi left him a palm purse and a letter that read in part: "The whole world must come and see how the Huaorani live well. . . . We live with the spirit of the jaguar. We do not want to be civilized by your missionaries or killed by your oil companies. Must the jaguar die so that you can have more contamination and television?"

A JOURNEY OF FIVE CENTURIES

Moi's story transcends time and consciousness as well as distance. The reasons for his journey began five centuries earlier, when evolving international markets and new technologies drove Europeans to exploit resources throughout the Americas. Looking for gold, Columbus dug Haitian mountainsides and devastated native Tainos. Colonial regimes repeated similar scenarios across two continents and three centuries, using Indigen and African labor to produce silver, dyes, sugar, tobacco, diamonds, and more. Nationhood only brought new exploitations: of copper, nitrate, tin, coffee, cocaine, bananas, and many other exportable commodities. Now satellite imagery and computer programs locate resources in South American rain forests. Eastern Ecuador is dug and burned. The Huaoranis are displaced or destroyed.

Imperialism has long been a conquest of consciousness as well as territory. Exploitation created terms that have been employed as weapons. Attacking "wilderness," Europeans also assaulted presumed "wild" people with words such as *pagan, uncivilized, heathen, backward, barbaric, ungodly, wild, savage,* and *primitive.* Such dehumanization supposedly exonerated new masters who seized laborers as well as land. A series of ideologies sought to justify new empires with labels like *civilizing, Christianization, mercantilism, expanding frontiers, free trade, manifest destiny, positivism,* and now *free markets* and *privatization.* Devised in Europe or North America and sent to Latin America along with armies, navies, mining equipment, and drilling rigs, these philosophies colonize consciousness.

Of all the resources extracted from Latin America, labor was the richest. Minerals remain mountains and tropical foodstuffs only seeds or stalks until somebody digs or plants, refines or harvests. From the early days of *encomiendas,* through centuries of plantation slavery, until present-day campesinos pick coffee or strawberries and employees sew clothes or baseballs, working Latin Americans create wealth for others, usually distant others.

THE EMPIRE OF *PACHA MAMA*

Although natural and spiritual, early Indigens were also scientists and engineers. Their planning created a cornucopia of food, built impressive cities, and domesticated natural products. But Indigen technologies also respected earth, the mother of life.

Long dismissed as primitive, Indigen agronomy in fact was sophisticated. It began simply and created a new world rendition of the agricultural transformation. In early times, men normally hunted and women usually gathered. Whoever thought of saving seeds and roots for planting instead of throwing them in the porridge created agriculture. Sedentary communities allowed urbanization, accelerated technical innovation, and provided the leisure necessary for developing culture. As Indigens noticed relationships between celestial movements and seasonal growing, astronomy developed. The Mayans became particular masters of math, making calendars and unifying religion and scientific farming; for example, Mayan art depicts priests in cornfields. However, these spiritual leaders were also technicians. While entreating the gods of nature, they also scientifically manipulated plant genes, soil nutrients, and crop propagation.[4]

A simple but important technology involved seed selection. Indigens reviewed and planted seeds individually (Europeans broadcast grain in handfuls, usually without examination). Although labor-intensive, individual selection reinforced desired plant characteristics. Early geneticists also pollenized plants and propagated stocks through cutting and grafting. The benefits of such technologies were immense. Growing wild, corn produced cobs little larger than human fingernails. Under Indigen guidance it fed empires. Yet Indigens prayed to corn gods: the life force within the plant. Similar science and religiosity characterized genetic control of potatoes, squash, pumpkins, and other foods.

Indigen technologies also managed the soil. Lacking draft animals, Indigens neither plowed the land nor planted in furrows. Instead, selected seeds, roots, and tubers were sown in individual holes made with foot plows, a narrowly pointed shovel with a step for applying human weight. Individual plantings reduced erosion and retained moisture. Natural fertilizers enhanced soil nutrients. These ranged from guano and fish meal to marsh mud and human waste. Soil management enhanced consistency, fertility, and crop production.[5]

Indigen agronomy included companion planting. Best illustrated by the triad of the "three sisters"—corn, beans, and squash—Indigen gardens sought to replicate the biodiversity of nature. Each "sister" supported the others: beans enriched the soil by fixing atmospheric nitrogen, corn shaded tender bean shoots and provided stalks for climbing vines, and spreading squash (or pumpkins) served as mulch, both retaining moisture and suppressing weeds. Such companion planting lessened damage from fungi, viruses, and insects by disbursing potential hosts and introducing other species. With their raised beds and irrigation trenches, Indigen farms resembled manicured gardens rather than broad fields of single crops.

Indigen engineers redesigned the natural conditions of different terrains to maximize potential advantages. In dry, hilly areas, natives built and irrigated terraces. Some are still used in the Andes and the American southwest. Hillside plots retained moisture and retarded erosion while stone retaining walls held daytime heat during cold nights, lessening the effect of frost. Bringing water to plants turned once-rocky hillsides into lush farms.[6]

Indigens also brought plants to water as wetlands horticulture was a stunning achievement. Around Lake Titicaca in the Andes, Indigens constructed productive marshland farms that sustained a long series of evolving civilizations. Engineering riverbanks on the Pacific west coast and in Mayan areas also created rich and well-watered farmland. However, the most famous wetland farms were located in the Valley of Mexico. Known as *chinampas,* some remain as a tourist attraction, the "floating gardens" of Xochimilco. But *chinampas* did not float: garden "rafts" were actually small islands interlaced with canals. Alternate digging and piling turned marshes into a matrix of canals and raised plots, the *chinampas.* Dikes and dams regulated water levels, and periodic applications of canal dredgings rich in humus and minerals renewed fertility. Farming continued throughout the year, with seedlings prepared at one end of the *chinampas* immediately replacing harvests with new plantings. Indigens loaded produce onto rafts or canoes and used the canals to easily transport these heavy loads to lakeshore cities. Other canoes and barges brought human waste from cities to fertilize the *chinampas.* Before the Spaniards arrived, Xochimilco comprised about 23,000 acres, with soil estimated to be five times more productive than later European-style fields. *Chinampas* were among the world's most productive farms.[7]

Agriculture was the basis of Indigen empires. With productive heartlands, Mayan, Aztec, and Incan armies invaded neighboring people and different ecological zones. Indigen elites sought diverse commodities to enliven diets, provide comfort, and beautify cities. In tropical Latin America, moving up or down a steep mountainside replaced crossing distant oceans to obtain exotic products. The ever-systematic Inca moved settlers to high and low, wet and dry ecological zones. Inca colonies on the eastern Andes sent tropical feathers, coca, and corn, while those from dry coastal lowlands along the Pacific produced salt, fish, and guano. From high mountain meadows came woolen textiles and dried alpaca meat. Inca social engineers consulted their own detailed relief maps before sending colonists anywhere, hoping to limit illness from too great a climatic change and contrasting oxygen levels. Size itself necessitated careful planning: if Inca domains were superimposed on the United States, they would trace a wide swath between New York and Los Angeles filled with *tierra templada, tierra fría,* and *tierra caliente.* For Incas, exploiting ecological diversity created wealth, power, and empire.[8]

Productive heartlands and dispersed ecologies were linked by imperial transportation systems. Without sailing ships and with pack animals limited to the Andes, Indigens devised vast transportation and communications networks employing their primary asset: intensive human labor. Indigen farms fed armies but also immense "armies" of runners and porters. These bearers utilized well-engineered roads and trails, including the famous Inca highway network with high suspension bridges and stone warehouses. A notable North American route was the Santa Fe Trail, which carried Indigens, their goods, and ideas between the American southwest and midwest long before a Spanish explorer named Vásquez de Coronado traced it into Kansas or U.S. engineers laid rails along its path. On Indigen trails, runners conveyed messages more than a hundred miles per day. Porters carrying two-thirds their own weight moved products twenty miles per day. So reliable were these simple but effective systems that Europeans used both Indigen roads and native porters for centuries.

Another successful transportation technology developed by Indigens was inland and inshore boating. Like the wheel, sails were an old world discovery, but native American canoes and dugouts—human-powered—turned rivers, lakes, and straits into commercial thoroughfares. The Mississippi may have been used by Olmecs trading between eastern Mexico and Cahokia, near St. Louis. In the Caribbean, Columbus noted huge inter-island dugout *canoas* loaded with commercial products. While his sailing ship tacked endlessly into the wind, Indigens in canoes quickly gained headway using paddles and muscle power. Fishermen in the Andes built boats with marsh reeds. The Aztec capital, Tenochtitlán, used flotillas of canoes and rafts to sustain its imperial consumption. When Europeans arrived, the French—of all Europeans—best appreciated native watercraft: lightweight canoes were the basis of their North American fur empire.

The first new world empires were Indigen. From tropical biospheres to semipolar heights, contrasting ecological zones were tapped for diverse products. Throughout the Americans, mines, quarries, and clay beds supported local cottage industries that produced goods for long-distance commerce. Indigen empires appropriated these many products through tribute as well as trade: Indigen elites realized early that concentrated wealth entailed exploitation. Yet, unlike later empires that took new world wealth to distant continents, Aztec and Inca tribute never left the region: some was even reserved for public relief.[9]

THE EUROPEAN ASSAULT

The impact of European technology on American ecology is hard to overstate. The changes were twofold. First, Europeans extracted a growing list of products for expanding international markets: minerals and timber, plantation crops like sugar, coffee, and cotton, or ranching products such a leather, mutton, and tallow. A second profound ecological change involved replicating European life in the Americas: building cities, introducing animals like sheep and cattle, and monoculture such as raising wheat. Whether extracting wealth or replicating familiar ecologies, Europeans dug, cut, plowed, and pastured new world environments.

The most subtle but significant alteration involved attitude. Indigens viewed the earth as family: partner, mother, or ancestor. Europeans approached the American earth as sexual aggressor. Historian Ana María Bidegain de Urán sees parallels between the invaders' rape of Indigen women and their views of nature: "Europeans represented the New World as a naked woman. . . . The allegory told the Europeans that to dominate Latin America one must sexually seduce it." Reflecting this view, an early European visitor to Brazil typically described the region as a "country that hath yet her maidenhead, never sacked."[10]

The "rape" of America commenced with Columbus, who sought neither a new world nor proof that the earth was round. He wanted nothing novel except a shortcut to the silks, silver, gold, ivory, spices, and other lucrative commodities that had long crossed Asia to enrich Mediterranean ports like Venice and Genoa. Failing in his quest to reach the "Orient," Columbus introduced to the Americas schemes for extracting wealth learned by Europeans in the Black Sea, west Africa, and the Atlantic islands: garner local resources, including land and labor. Since Vikings from Scandinavia had long traded with the Inuit of Canada's Baffin Bay, transatlantic commerce was not new. The newness of Columbus's voyages lay in the use of advanced technologies of ship design, instrumentation, and chart making learned from Africans and Asians, or devised in Europe. Unlike the Vikings, Columbus also linked tropical resources to expanding European markets.

Other than Europeans who fished eastern Canadian waters, Columbus was the first outsider to extract new world wealth systematically to benefit outsiders. The initial exploitation came as subtle commerce: trading glass beads, broken pottery, and small leather strips for golden face ornaments. Columbus also abducted Indigens: servile labor was another commodity sought by Europeans. These simple transfers began an ever larger process. During five subsequent centuries, foreigners used sailing vessels, then steamships, now seagoing containerized transports. The outsiders always extract more wealth than what returns in trade. Of course, the owners of transportation systems decide what goes where to benefit whom.

In 1492, seaborne empires exploiting scattered ecologies were not new, just newly enlarged to include the Americas. Phoenicians and Greeks had cut cedar and cyprus forests to create pastures and fields for growing exportable commodities like wool, wheat, and wine. Romans engineered environments for commercial advantage from Egypt to Spain. Eventually, merchants in the Mediterranean region grew rich turning mythical wealth into real money: showing that sturdy ships and new navigational technologies could transport highly profitable commodities to Europe from the Black Sea and Arab lands. Columbus and his contemporaries merely brought this historic process to the Americas. Soon, tiny European nations like Portugal, Holland, and England would replicate the achievements of the earlier city-states of Athens, Carthage, Venice, and Genoa. Ports would create immense overseas empires.

The immediate objective of European exploitation in the Americas was precious metals and gems. Since gold and silver were the basis of coinage—and then, as now, money bought virtually everything—Europeans lusted for bullion. In the Caribbean, Columbus demanded gold as tribute and hillsides were scoured for mines. Natives were slaughtered when they produced little and few mines were found. However, gold, silver, diamonds, and other precious minerals were located in huge amounts where heaving geologic plates or worn mountains exposed once-buried minerals, primarily along the Pacific Rim and in the ancient shield geologies of Brazil and, eventually, Canada. The history of Europeans in the Americas traces a succession of mining "rushes": from early Mexico and Peru, to the interior of Brazil and Colombia, to California and Nevada, to Alaska and the Yukon. The most valuable lodes were the silver mines of Mexico and Peru.[11]

From colonial silver mines to twentieth-century oil drilling, Latin America's mineral riches were long exploited with few questions asked. Powerful foreigners—always white—told where to dig or drill. Poor Latin Americans—usually dark-skinned—dug, drilled, refined, and shipped. And many intermediaries explained the imperial process, justifying exploitation of both natural environments and nonwhite workers. Nowhere was extraction more evident than in the mother lode of silver known as Potosí and the nearby mercury mines of Huancavelica.

Located in Bolivia (called Upper Peru in colonial times), Potosí produced the greatest yield of high-grade silver ore in human history. Stories of Potosí's discovery include tales of bivouacked Spanish soldiers amazed to witness silver streams issuing from their campfires as rich surface deposits melted beneath their burning embers. If true, the Spaniards were probably led to Potosí encampments by Indigen miners. During subsequent centuries the silver mountain and its surroundings became an anthill of excavations and tailings, dug and refined by Indigens condemned to *repartimiento.* When the mountain was finally emptied, and all nearby forests denuded for fuel and building materials, descendants of *repartimiento* Indigens continued reprocessing the tailings and slag dumps, searching for any wealth that may have been missed the first time.

Spaniards also forced Indigens to mine mercury, a toxin used to refine silver, in the mines at Huancavelica. Mining mercury was debilitating when not deadly. Indigen workers at Huancavelica had a life expectancy of four years, and those who survived carbon monoxide inhalation, pneumonia, and accidents remained invalids due to mercury poisoning. Fear of losing sons to Huancavelica's mines prompted Indigen mothers to break and deform the bones of male infants so that as adults they would be rejected by mine recruiters. And those living downstream from Huancavelica were consistently exposed to mercury toxins.[12]

Together with silver from Mexico, the Potosí mines underwrote almost two centuries of European affluence and power. Peruvian and Mexican silver paid the salaries of imperial bureaucrats and soldiers. Silver coins from America bought slaves from Africa. Spanish American bullion stimulated England's and Holland's commercial expansion; its shining metal adorned Italian altars and became elegant French dinnerware. Smugglers from New England exchanged barrel staves and black slaves for contraband "pieces of eight" in the Caribbean. And some of Potosí's wealth remained in Peru: rewarding colonial elites—bishops as well as bureaucrats—who justified and managed the empire. Today Bolivia's silver mountain is an empty shell, a pit of poverty, and an ecological wreck.[13]

Mining sent Europeans throughout Latin America. Mexican cities—Taxco, Zacatecas, Guanajuato, Pachuca, and others—developed around silver mines. Colombia was a source for gold, rubies, and emeralds. In the eighteenth century *bandeirantes* discovered gold and diamonds in Brazil's interior, a state now known as Minas Gerais (General Mines). In the nineteenth century industrial minerals gained value as Latin American metals helped construct worldwide transportation infrastructures using rails, bridges, and steel ships. Latin American lead, iron, and copper helped build both foreign merchant marines and North Atlantic navies. Shells and explosives from Latin American brass and nitrate killed soldiers around the world during the two world wars. The region's petroleum fueled other nations' industries, automobiles, aircraft, and motorized armaments. Petroleum was also processed into plastic items, from milk jugs and toys to computer hardware and airline interiors. Latin American bauxite became aluminum beer cans, windowsills, and home siding but also air cargo freight systems, military aircraft, and outer-space rockets. Despite these immense innovations, the exploitative themes of Potosí remain. In eastern Ecuador—and elsewhere—entrepreneurs devastate local landscapes to generate wealth elsewhere. New empires profit from old imperial methods.

The European assault on new world environments included cutting trees. Latin American forests supplied fuel and building materials but also dyes and farmland. Cutting, shipping, or burning began early and continues today as rain forests are demolished for lumber and cropland. European conquerors used American trees to achieve both local and international domination. Columbus used them for forts and scaffolds, the latter to hang Indigens. During his two-year conquest of Central America, Cortés cut a huge swath through rain forests, sometimes building a bridge per mile; one of these spans required a thousand trees. In the age of wooden ships, Atlantic maritime powers depended on American trees, since most European forests were depleted. Beginning with Columbus and lasting into the nineteenth century, American forests shrunk as European vessels and fleets grew larger. Of course, ships of new world origin also carried Europeans to Africa and Asia, as well as slaves to the Americas.[14]

Europeans in the new world required trees for many purposes. Building cities and towns required scaffolding and construction beams. Mines consumed lumber as shoring timbers, ladders, sluices, and buildings. Charcoal was the ubiquitous fuel in the era before coal and petroleum: it boiled cane juice into molasses, crystallized sugar, or distilled molasses into rum. After the Caribbean was stripped of trees, distilling often occurred elsewhere, such as New England. Of course, wooden ships and barrels took Caribbean molasses to North American charcoal supplies. And charcoal was the common fuel for Latin American blacksmiths, cooks, and miners until the modern age of gas and electricity. Charcoal is still used by poor Latin Americans who chop and burn forests for a cheap source of fuel.

Latin American hardwoods have been esteemed since the seventeenth century, when they paneled offices in Amsterdam and London. Now rosewood and other Latin American exotics adorn suites and form furniture in Tokyo, Berlin, and Miami.

Meanwhile tropical softwoods today become plywoods and composite boards as rain forests are clear-cut to make flooring underlays and roof sheathing used in urban sprawl around the world. Once, seemingly inexhaustible brazilwood supplied regal red and purple dyes for European clothes. The tree's name designated a coast, a colony, a region, then a nation. Today brazilwood is scarce, but Brazilians still log the rain forest and sell timber abroad.

CHANGES IN THE LAND: PLANTATIONS AND HACIENDAS

Europeans devised two major agricultural institutions, one of which characterized the tropics and the other the regions of *tierra templada.* The first was the plantation, a botanical factory. The second was the hacienda, called the *fazenda* in Brazil and sometimes the *estancia* elsewhere. Haciendas were huge rural estates, often growing crops but devoted to ranching.

The sugar plantation exemplifies the colonial interplay of ecology, technology, labor, and empire. Iberians had earlier adopted sugar production from Arabs, but it was on the Canary and Cape Verde islands where sugar and slavery promoted new forms of corporate capitalism. Demand for sugar and molasses (used for rum) multiplied after 1492, spreading the plantation system to Brazil, Mexico, Cuba, Paraguay, and the Pacific coast. The major planters during the long colonial era were not Spaniards as much as the Portuguese, Dutch, French, and British, who also became the major slave importers. International markets, mill technologies, ship design and size, processing, and packaging all drove expansion—requiring more land, more fuel, more wood, and more slaves. Profitable with sugar, Europeans also used plantations to produce cotton, indigo, tobacco, cacao (used for chocolate), coffee, nutmeg, and coconut. But in the Americas, sugar was the sweetest success.

Plantations were engines of empire, driving Europeans to fight over Caribbean islands and African labor supplies. Plantation profits drove the Puritan Oliver Cromwell to seize Jamaica for England in 1650. French diplomats in the eighteenth century ceded Canada and Louisiana for the return of small but sweet Guadeloupe in the Caribbean. Meanwhile, Europeans scoured the globe to meet the endless need for workers. Portuguese *feitorías* (factories) exploited the west African coast. Brazilian *bandeirantes* raided South America's interior. British bounty hunters kidnapped both Irishmen and New England Indigens for sale to Caribbean sugar estates. England also fought a war to gain the *asiento,* the exclusive right to sell slaves in Spanish colonies. When slave regimes ended, European planters turned to contracted cane cutters from India, China, and Indonesia. Sugar and servitude created world empire.[15]

Long before modern mechanized agriculture, Europeanized farming remade new world landscapes. Huge commercial estates broke the intimate connections between Indigens and *pacha mama:* land became a commodity, another factor in fiscal equations involving masters and slaves, international shippers and buyers, supply and demand. Indigen work had been family-based, shared among clan members who bonded with each other and the land, making work social and spiritual as well as productive. Europeans demonstrated little personal or spiritual bonding with the American land. Often, absentee owners lived in distant cities, even in Europe. Salaried overseers usually rode horseback about estates, commanding slaves or *repartimiento* Indigens. And oxen with plows and harrows became intermediaries between man and land. Rather than numerous Indigens tending small plots with many crops, Europeans favored large fields where few workers grew single crops. Fields of wheat or oats and meadows of hay and alfalfa replaced raised beds growing squash, corn, beans, and other companion plants. But the main European crop was meat.

Europeans depended heavily on animals, and arriving Spanish galleons resembled Noah's ark. As slave hunters depopulated Caribbean islands, aboriginal people were replaced with feral pigs, goats, sheep, and cattle, at a terrific cost to local flora and fauna. As large-scale herders, Iberians were renowned as shepherds and ranchers raising oxen, donkeys, mules, and horses in addition to animals used for meat. These many animals produced leather, wool, lard, tallow, and cheese, and served as beasts of burden. Meat was initially dried or salted, but in the nineteenth century it was shipped to Europe refrigerated, and in the twentieth century it has been frozen or air shipped fresh. In the Americas, Iberians found land and created pastures. Populating landscapes with animals instead of Indigens altered ecologies profoundly.

Replicating Iberian environments, Spaniards typically ordered Indigens to fill canals and drain lakes, creating drier, level land. Valley floors were ideal pastures for larger animals like horses and cattle. Goats and sheep grazed hillsides once terraced and irrigated by Indigens. Both plowing and pasturing replaced luxuriant ground covers with sparse vegetation: often no vegetation during fallow intervals, during dry seasons, and where overgrazed. Of course rain, drought, and wind quickly eroded such land. Within decades once lush hillsides and valleys lost valuable humus and loam. Many dry and rocky Latin American landscapes were made so during an ecological conquest by European animals.

After 1492, Indigens and animals often competed for food. A common complaint throughout the Americas during early colonization was that European farm animals—particularly pigs and cattle—trampled fences and devoured Indigen gardens. In New England, natives killed invading pigs only to themselves be hunted by vengeful colonists. In Latin America roaming animals brought Spanish sovereignty: courts often favored Iberian ranchers over Indigen farmers. As Indigen populations grew leaner, herds of European animals fattened.

Changing demography affected land use. Due to high Indigen death rates and *encomienda* demands, labor-intensive native farming could not be sustained. Meanwhile, European estates increasingly occupied better land in valley floors, forcing Indigens onto more sterile mountainsides. There, even today, Indigens and poor mestizos continue the Latin American legacy of *minifundia* (small-plot farming). On remote mountainsides, poor farmers often grow crops that require less attention and fertility but are more easily transported. Maguey in Mexico becomes pulque, *aguardiente,* tequila, and mescal: all intoxicants. And cocoa in the Andes produces the mild narcotic used to suppress hunger and fatigue. These intoxicants and drugs historically met a heightened demand for escapism among Indigen consumers in fields and mines. Then, as now, they earned much more than selling potatoes, beans, or corn.[16]

If the plantation was the dominant ecological institution in the tropics, the hacienda evolved to meet European needs in temperate zones. From the late 1500s well into the twentieth century, the hacienda was the great and dominating institution of rural Latin America. Like feudal lords, *hacendados* ruled land and local society. So pervasive were haciendas that people traditionally identified themselves not as Mexicans, Peruvians, or other nationals but as residents of their hacienda.

Haciendas differed from plantations in many ways. The main ecological difference was dedication to ranching rather than profitable monoculture like sugar or cotton. Seeking long-term security rather than immediate incomes, haciendas favored traditional and feudal-like relationships of lord and serf became common. Documentary films from the 1940s show Peruvian campesinos genuflecting before the visiting *hacendado* and kissing his hand. Unlike slaves, who were traded on open markets, hacienda workers went with the land. If estates were sold or consolidated through marriage, indebted peons were part of the package.[17]

Haciendas evolved in the colonial era as a response to changing demographics. With a 90 percent decrease in Indigen populations, *hacendados* loaned money to local tribes facing tribute bills. Unable to repay, *hacendados* acquired land—and people—through foreclosure. Caciques (chiefs) interested in personal profit also transferred lands to haciendas. And many Indigens gravitated to haciendas: sharecropping or work as a ranch hand was preferable to paying village tribute.

A host of fiscal mechanisms kept hacienda peons in debt peonage. These included sharecropping, the company store, and payments for religious services. Often, priests *were* landlords as the church inherited vast estates. Priests and *hacendados* also worked together, often as relatives, certainly as members of the dominant class. Loans to peons from the hacienda paid the peasants' church fees: in nineteenth-century Mexico, baptisms cost one peso, marriages fifteen pesos, and burials ten. Monthly hacienda wages of only five pesos prolonged indebtedness. For these reasons, many peons were never officially born, married, or buried.[18]

The Hispanic desire for land was fueled by prestige. As in Spain, those who raised sheep or cattle controlled real estate but also belonged to the governing class. Ranchers formed a powerful guild, the Mesta, and as colonial wealth grew, so did requirements for membership. In 1537, owning 20 large animals (cows, horses, burros, and mules) or 300 small animals (sheep, hogs, and goats) gained one membership in Mexico's Mesta. By 1574, requirements were raised to 1000 large animals or 3000 small ones. Such standards strengthened elitism but further wrecked ecologies through overgrazing.

The trend to latifundia, elitism, and ecological waste continued through the colonial era. In the late eighteenth century, German visitor Alexander von Humboldt observed:

> All the vices of the feudal government have passed from one hemisphere to the other; and in Mexico these abuses have been so much the more dangerous. . . . The property of New Spain, like that of Old Spain, is in great measure in the hands of a few powerful families, who have gradually absorbed the smaller estates.[19]

Haciendas in Latin America expanded after independence. In nineteenth-century Mexico, nationalistic liberal governments seized and sold both church estates and communal Indigen lands, usually to wealthy bidders. In one Mexican state, four concessionaires gained 5.7 million acres; one family's haciendas equaled the size of Connecticut. In Argentina, governments fought Indigens for land. During the 1840s, just 825 estates controlled 33 million acres on the pampas, averaging 40,000 acres per hacienda. Later, one program distributed 5 million acres among 88 *hacendados.*[20]

Industrialism turned ranching from an arcadian pastime into big business. In colonial times, feral cattle were slaughtered for hides and tallow and were shipped from shanties dotting quiet bays from Argentina to California. But as international shoe factories and processing plants multiplied during the nineteenth century, the demand for leather and grease, as well as bone meal, salted beef, mutton, and gelatin, grew enormously. After 1870, refrigerator and even freezer ships delivered increasing tons of fresh and frozen meat to European consumers. Slaughterhouses were built in port cities from southern Brazil through Argentina as barbed wire and railroads spread across the land. As haciendas were linked to international markets, pressures on grassland ecosystems increased.[21]

Haciendas continued as instruments of imperial domination into the twentieth century. When Mexican revolutionaries in the 1920s seized haciendas under the nation's land reform program, they sometimes discovered estate profits being mailed to French and Italian descendants of ancestral *hacendados* who long ago returned to Europe. The only connection between existing owners and Mexico was via occasional correspondence with the hacienda overseer—and periodic checks.[22]

MONOPOLIES

The commodities produced by Latin American mines, plantations, and haciendas fed global imperial monopolies. Since technologies of sea commerce preceded by 300 years any equivalent advances in land transportation, good ships came far earlier than good roads and railroads. The open sea provided a smoother path than rugged and rutted trails through either high mountains or dense tropical forests. For more than three centuries, Latin American colonial enclaves generally were isolated from each other while being bound through seaborne commerce to distant markets and the destinies of foreign planners.

When Spain's empire commenced, Isabel and Fernando pondered how to control its commerce. Genoese advisers at court suggested precedents from prosperous Italian city-states that carefully regulated their own colonies through a *casa de contratación* (house of trade). During the next three centuries, Spain's *casa de contratación* was the singular institution for managing commerce in "the Indies": its new world and Asian colonies. The *casa* regulated every detail of maritime trade: tax schedules, fleet timetables, customs collections, cargo invoices, authorized imports and exports, licensing ships and captains, training pilots, and chartering merchant guilds called *consulados.* The *casa* became a powerful bureaucracy as, for two centuries, major decisions regarding imperial trade were made at its offices in Seville. All Spanish trade with the new world went through this one city until the final decades of colonial rule, when the restrictive monopoly ended.[23]

Castile's attitude of monopoly derived from psychology as much as policy. Never much for seafaring, Castilians conceptualized the world with a terrestrial rather than a maritime mentality. When they did go to sea, they carried a vision of securing dominions, which succeeded well during the reconquest of Iberia. In the Americas, the Spanish Main came to be dotted with colonial forts facing seafaring enemies, just as castles in Spain confronted rival Moors. The armed convoy was another defensive Castilian strategy. Beginning in 1552, the *casa de contratación* ordered that Spain's Atlantic shipping would be done in armed flotillas, as protection against attack but also as a means to regularize and monitor commerce. Armadas sought to halt smugglers as well as pirates and maximize crown revenues. For almost two centuries, sailings from Spain were limited to two fleets per year, one going to Veracruz, Mexico, and another to both Portobello, Panama (for transit to Peru), and Cartagena, Colombia. In the Pacific, the solitary Manila Galleon made an annual round-trip voyage between Acapulco, Mexico, and the distant Philippines. The Atlantic port of Buenos Aires was officially closed to maritime trade until 1778. Legitimate Argentine commerce followed a circuitous route through secured lands: Peru and Panama. Each spring, one armada destined for Spain gathered at Havana, Cuba. (Figure 6-1 depicts colonial Iberian-American trade routes.) While a generally effective defense, the restrictive timetables and limited routes stymied commerce. However, until the mid-eighteenth century, Spanish imperial policy favored monopoly more than growth.[24]

Commercial monopolies were also fostered by feudal-like *consulados,* licensed by the *casa de contratación.* Consulados were guilds of merchants, often members of one or a few families joined by marriage, *compadrazgo,* and regional origin. Each *consulado* monopolized trade in a particular commodity: silver, sugar, textiles, and so on. With representatives acting as lobbyists in major colonial cities and in Spain, *consulados* stubbornly defended lucrative privileges and constantly resisted reforms. Power and profits were preserved through restricted membership, undersupply of captive markets, secrecy of operations, well-placed bribes, and paying dowries to place candidates in the imperial bureaucracy. *Consulados* monopolized the legal commerce of Spain's empire until the monopoly of empire ended.[25]

Imperial monopolies were eventually given a philosophical defense, mercantilism, which held that colonies exist to enrich and empower the mother country. A corollary held that a nation seeking grandeur needed its own maritime commerce, a closed economy with colonies in different biospheres supplying diverse resources to the metropolitan center. Mercantilist thinking also prohibited commerce among colonies, outlawed enterprises competing with home industries, and normally banned trade with rival European nations.[26]

Enriching some, monopolies impoverished the many. In Mexico, New Spain's general standard of living was significantly lower a century following the conquest than it had been when the Aztecs ruled, yet some families were fantastically rich. Eventually, imperial monopolies were wasteful, as two centuries of commercial warfare consumed resources. In a report to the crown, one Mexican viceroy reasoned: "If Your Majesty used but a small portion of those sums [spent on international warfare] in New Spain, the country could become the best in the world and the Crown's revenues would be much increased. For there is no reason why your Majesty should lose what you have already won in order to seek at such expense what you have never had."[27]

FIGURE 6-1

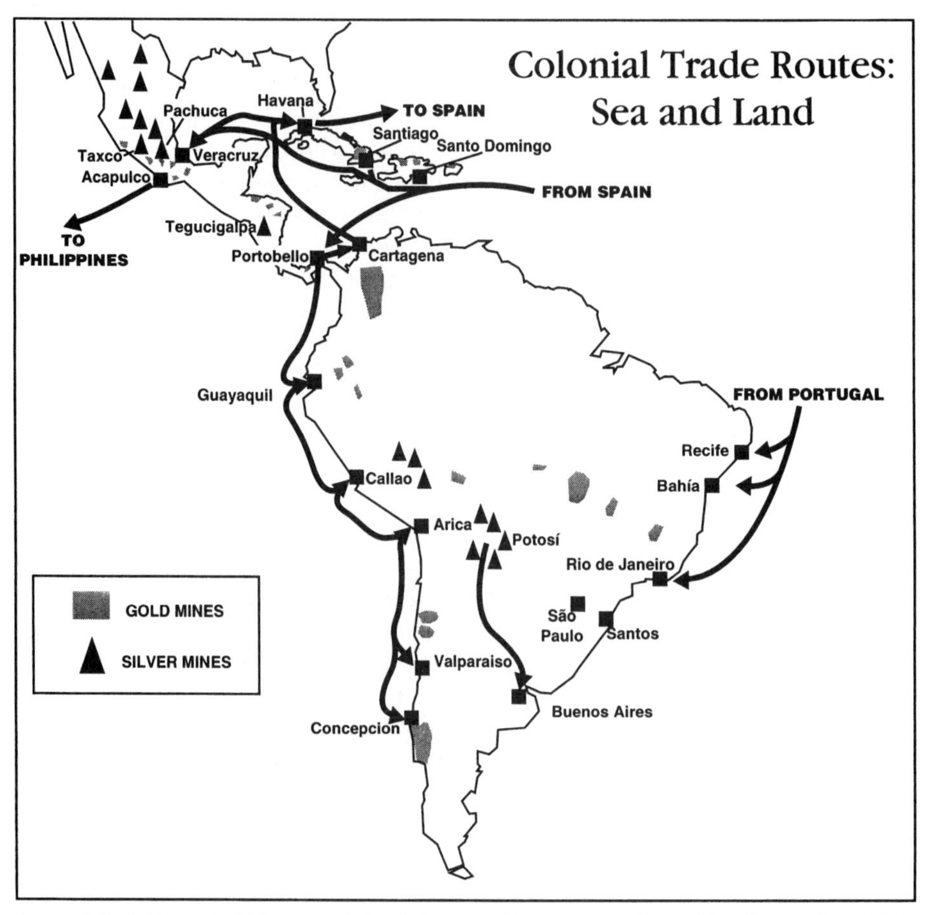

Source: Adapted from David Preston, ed., *Latin American Development: Geographical Perspectives,* Addison Wesley Ltd., 1987. Reprinted by permission of Addison Wesley Longman, Ltd.

European empires were far from uniform. Symbolized by their names, the Portuguese (from *O-porto,* meaning people of "the port") differed greatly from the Castilians (from *castile,* meaning "the people of the castles"). As fishermen and commercial traders, the Portuguese knew that ports were mutual gateways between land and sea. In Romance languages, one word is used for both "port" and "doorway." Keeping commercial doors open through innovation and entrepreneurship led to Portuguese profits and progress.

Because Portuguese commerce with Asia was initially so lucrative, Brazil was not immediately a gem in the imperial crown. During more than a century, the colony was neglected, even partially and temporarily lost to the Dutch and French. Unlike the Castilians who limited colonization to *gente decente* (decent folk) and restricted commerce, the Portuguese encouraged migration to Brazil and eventually sent beggars, thieves, Gypsies, and prostitutes. Brazilian colonists could also normally ship anything, anytime, anywhere. Like coastal towns in the mother country, new world ports such as Recife, Bahía, and Rio were busy doorways between land and sea.[28]

Similar liberalization came to the Spanish colonies after the Bourbons inherited the monarchy in 1701. Eighteenth-century reforms included tax simplification, administrative honesty, improving infrastructures, ending the armadas, opening more ports to trade, allowing commerce with other nations, and involving colonials in self-governance. However, Bourbon reforms faced resistance from entrenched bureaucracies, comfortable *latifundistas,* and privileged *consulados.* Reform's slowness was painfully demonstrated when British forces occupied Cuba during one of many imperial wars. Previously, one merchant ship per month had typically visited sleepy Havana. Under British rule in 1762, more than sixty ships per month from England and New England flooded Cuban markets with ironware, furniture, animals, luxuries, everyday conveniences, and an endless supply of that cheap British staple: African slaves. After Cuba was returned to Spain, the Bourbon reforms accelerated, but the hour was late: independence would make even reformed empires increasingly obsolete.[29]

INFORMAL EMPIRES OF CORRUPTION

Informal economies are a new world reality. Smuggling and bribery long evaded detection and documentation, particularly by officials who shared their illicit gains. Yet corruption has been a major historical force, from smuggled bullion and slaves in the colonial era to twentieth-century rumrunners, cocaine cartels, and money laundering. The personal fortunes of numerous wealthy families today can be traced—to ancestral "pirates" and "freebooters." And new world societies from Canada to Chile have felt corruption's quiet touch as legal monopolies spawned many more that were illicit.

From colonial times until today, evading "the system" has been a system. Dollars became the official currency in North America as New England colonials evaded the British Navigation Acts and exchanged goods with England's rivals to obtain Mexican and Peruvian coins. Illicit British American profits enriched colonial "first families" and, eventually, prestigious universities and philanthropies. French stockings in Peru and German autos in Colombia—centuries apart—somehow made it through customs without detection. Pirates in the Caribbean turned from evading to making the law as they bought land and slaves to become the planter class. In North America, smugglers became patriots during the movement for independence. The slave trade remained a major means of illicit gain, even after its official closing. During the twentieth century, Prohibition in the United States spawned vast networks of rumrunners using Caribbean bases. Other bootleggers later did the same with marijuana and cocaine. The more successful underground entrepreneurs entered politics and banking—earlier as the Mafia in New York and Cuba, subsequently as money-laundering "drug lords" investing in U.S. banks and shopping malls. Without holidays and heroes, contraband and corruption have helped write the history of the hemisphere.[30]

Enforcing official policy has always been difficult. Today, law enforcers use sophisticated equipment, and smugglers still deliver the goods. During earlier centuries, both "mouse" and "cat" shared similar technologies: muskets, mules, and sailing ships. Smugglers even innovated superior technologies: the small, swift sloops created in New England were not designed to catch haddock or herring. However, they easily escaped heavily armed pursuing British, Spanish, or French men-of-war.[31]

Distance, terrain, and human nature have always deterred law enforcers. The Americas form a vast landscape of open seas, rugged mountains, huge deserts, and thick forests where smugglers can easily hide their illegal activities. Bureaucratic procrastination inhibited enforcement as policy waited upon deliberative councils in Europe or the sailing of an annual armada. Unexpected tragedies hampered communication and coordination when appointed officials died or written instructions were lost through shipwreck, earthquake, flood, fire, or enemy attack. Thus, from Argentina to Acadia, Americans usually lived by their wits, developed private ethics, and substituted personal wishes for imperial policies.

Many inhabitants of the Americas belonged to no empire since many stateless societies existed between the frontiers of European colonies. Unaware of imaginary lines on maps, these autonomous peoples were the gauchos, *zambos,* and maroons of Spanish America, the Acadians, Métis, and Cree of Canada, the Seminoles, mountain men, and bayou dwellers of the United States, and buccaneers throughout the Caribbean. The only loyalty of these fiercely independent people was to self-survival. But as go-betweens among empires, they dealt with any Europeans who offered them autonomy, guns, and profitable barter. Any resulting alliance was temporary—and subject to smuggling with anyone else.[32]

Considering American ecologies and technologies, smuggling was facile and frequent. Remote coastlines with rugged terrain allowed goods to be off-loaded from shallow draft ships anchoring in coastal estuaries. From there, shipments disappeared on mules into surrounding hills and forests. Caribbean islands and inlets favored smugglers, as did the many bays of western Mexico and western South America that received illegal shipments from Asia. And small fishing villages from Nova Scotia to Patagonia took in more than the daily catch. No European empire had enough ships or sailors—or honest captains—to patrol its proclaimed dominions.

Eventually, even off-loading in remote bays proved cumbersome. Armed with bribes rather than muskets, smugglers entered major new world ports to conduct their business. Few locals (including law enforcement officers) could refuse a good buy on scarce goods—or becoming a silent partner in lucrative illegal trade. Thus, Spanish Americans traded regularly with New Englanders, Brazilians bargained with rival Dutch and French colonies, and English captains with African slaves and Birmingham steel traded with Latin Americans everywhere. Decrees, rules, forts, fleets, and guards mattered little. Imperial control was illusive. The greatest illusion was official honesty.[33]

So porous was imperial enforcement that illegal practice overwhelmed mercantilist policy everywhere. Nor was trade a textbook pattern of simple bilateral or triangular trade. Instead, Atlantic commerce was complex and changeable, substantial but subtle. Typically, North Americans had cheap provisions, the British had cheap slaves, French colonies sold cheap sugar, and Spanish colonies supplied bullion.

Given the opportunities for mutual enrichment, commerce flowed everywhere, but the Caribbean was its hub. The American historian Philip Curtin explains one of many early scenarios:

> A New England ship might sail to [British] Jamaica with a cargo of barrel staves, horses, and salt fish. These could be sold for bullion, derived in turn from smuggling slaves into Spanish America. . . . In addition, the captain might buy a few slaves for sale on the North American mainland, but his "middle passage" would carry him only to [French] Saint Domingue [Haiti] to complete his cargo with sugar and molasses, bought with bullion. On the way north, he could stop in Chesapeake Bay to sell the slaves, then back to New England where he would sell the molasses to be made into rum for the fur trade. The French sugar could then be relabeled "product of the British West Indies" for sale in Britain, where it and any leftover bullion could pay for British manufactures.

Long before revolutions achieved political independence, contraband freed the colonies. Officially closed to maritime trade until 1778, Buenos Aires existed on smuggling. Its location on the Río de la Plata (Silver River) acknowledged that this port was a shortcut to the fabulous mines of Potosí, Peru. In Spanish Venezuela, commerce in colonial salt was virtually monopolized by smugglers as 125 Dutch ships and 25 British vessels per year loaded at the Punta de Araya salt pans. Merchants smuggled because profits lost through official but infrequent confiscation were less than taxes and markups paid for legally imported goods. Bribed officials were a relatively minor overhead.[34]

Contraband corrupted not only officials but the imperial system. From seamen, stevedores, and customs agents in American ports, to bureaucrats and ministers in Seville, bribes moved goods. Foreign merchants paid illegal "commissions" to use the names, shipping licenses, and seals of Spanish *consulados*. "Placemen" were "insiders" appointed to bureaucratic offices after paying bribes to the crown. "Placed" customs officers, captains, and even viceroys facilitated illegal trade. Evidence of gross corruption comes from officials themselves. The retiring viceroy of New Spain wrote to his successor in 1716: "Justice is sold like goods in a market-place where he who has money in his pocket buys what he wants. In this market-place mystery and secrecy rule. . . . Interested parties are prepared to elude [judgments] or to prevent appeals by the injured. . . . Such justice is like a worm consuming the wealth of the Kingdom."[35] Corrupt viceroys embezzled huge amounts and typically held their posts only long enough to retire in splendor. When caught, officials played the system according to its own informal rules: they "bribed" the crown. In 1715, the duke of Albuquerque paid the court a 700,000-peso "fine" after four years of personal enrichment in the Americas. Albuquerque, New Mexico, is named for this aristocratic embezzler.[36]

Even imperial reforms were quickly corrupted. In 1565, the program of *corregidor de Indios* (*corregidor* means one who "corrects" or punishes) was instituted to eliminate abuses in Spanish-Indigen relations. With low pay, short terms, and no merit, the main attraction of being a *corregidor* was extorting Indigens, colluding with caciques, undervaluing tribute paid in kind, and selling confiscated commodities for personal profit. Like many other colonial officials, *corregidores* usually bought their posts.[37]

An eighteenth-century viceroy pondered the problems of administering a far-flung empire in a letter to the king: "These lands are so far removed from the presence of your royal Majesty, and the remedies for the evils committed are so late in coming, that many bad servants are raised up and we all stretch our consciences, and some never think that your Majesty will remember to punish those who are disserving you here and who so shamelessly go against your service."[38] One doubts that this message came as a surprise to Spain's sovereign.

Corruption still plagues Latin America. Called *la mordida* (the bite) in Mexico, it pays a policeman for "fixing" a traffic violation (real or supposed) or compensates a customs officer for looking the other way. But the noun *mordida* comes from the Spanish verb *morder,* which also means "to gnaw away gradually." During recent decades, Latin American corruption has supported a hemispheric drug trade, illegal toxic dumping, evasion of taxes, and many more abuses. Colonial regimes did not create such modern misfortunes, but corruption during their era became endemic. Endless attempts to reform have failed.

LATER INFORMAL EMPIRES

During the Napoleonic era, England's foreign minister, Viscount Castlereagh, pondered launching an expedition to conquer Latin America. He wanted to expand a commercial empire already rich from centuries of smuggling but wrote that any invasion would encounter "the hopeless task of conquering this extensive country against the temper of its population." He acknowledged that English contraband was a "system of measures, which, on grounds of political morality, ought to be avoided." In the end, Castlereagh decided to expand "the silent and imperceptible operation of our illicit commercial intercourse." Why suffer in blood the right to officially enjoy long-standing illegal profits? During the nineteenth century, Latin America became Britain's informal colony as England monopolized regional commerce, located mines and refineries, built processing plants, constructed railroads and ports, influenced politics, and controlled policies. In 1896 a leading Argentine writer lamented: "English capital has done what English armies could not do. Today our country is tributary to England."[39]

Long before Castlereagh's decision, Great Britain had reduced Iberian empires and Iberia itself to commercial outposts. Ironically, such dependency on England emerged from the very success of Spanish and Portuguese conquests. Incoming wealth and outgoing populations inflated the cost of materials and wages in Spain and Portugal making it cheaper to buy manufactured goods abroad. Needing everything from woolens to weapons, Spanish and Portuguese merchants increasingly purchased these manufactures in lower-priced northern European markets. Eventually, Iberia became a revolving doorway: riches from the Americas entered and exited to buy imported manufactures. Imported manufactured goods from London or Amsterdam landed in Seville or Lisbon for transshipment to the colonies. By 1800, Spain imported 90 percent of what it then shipped to Latin America, from French silks and Italian silverware to British guns and German gunpowder.[40]

The circuitous route of imperial commerce was sometimes bizarre. A customer in Buenos Aires might buy from a local vendor supplied by a merchant in Lima, Peru. The Lima merchant would have purchased goods at a trade fair in Portobello, Panama, when the annual fleet arrived from Spain. The Panama seller probably represented a Spanish *consulado,* which had acquired the goods during the previous year in Holland or England, warehousing them in Seville until the Atlantic flotilla sailed. Such items may have been moved among warehouses, ships, and mules ten times during two years, suffering damage from vermin, seawater, and tortuous transit. While quality deteriorated, handling and commissions multiplied costs. Thus, American consumers increasingly turned to foreign vendors: typically an English or New England captain bringing better products at a fraction of their "official" price. In Buenos Aires, the British traded for Peruvian bullion and products from pampas cattle. As long as Spain's colonies remained politically loyal and paid most imperial bills, American commerce was abandoned to the British.[41]

English mastery of Portugal and Brazil was more direct. Unlike immediately rich Spanish colonies, Brazil struggled economically as over 300 years both commercial and territorial expansion pulsated to rhythmic "booms" and "busts" involving brazilwood, sugar, Indigen slave raiding, gold, diamonds, and rubber. Ties to England strengthened as Portugal sought assistance defending itself from covetous Castile, which temporarily annexed its Iberian neighbor during the seventeenth century. In Brazil, the French and Dutch invaded and occupied territories.

With mutual interests and common foes, Portugal and Britain allied. King Charles of England married Princess Catherine of Portugal in 1661, and in the Treaty of Methuen (1703) Britain promised military assistance to Portugal in exchange for access to Brazil and the African colonies. British merchants subsequently controlled so much Portuguese trade and finance that the Marquês de Pombal, prime minister from 1756 to 1770, struggled to reassert Portugal's autonomy. He thought he had succeeded when gold and diamonds were discovered at Minas Gerais in Brazil. When British imports and interest rates overwhelmed his plans, Pombal fumed, "Since the discovery of the mines, . . . all the gold became the property of other nations. What riches, great God! the possession of which involves the ruin of the state!" Great Britain did save Portugal—or at least its monarch—when Napoleon invaded Iberia in 1808. As French soldiers approached Lisbon, the Portuguese king and court boarded English ships bound for Brazil. However, salvation had its price as the British minister boasted that the alliance was like "Sovereign and Subject," with "Obedience to be paid as the Price of Protection." Again the dubious benefits of empire were paid by American resources: South America received a Portuguese king as Brazilian resources enriched England.[42]

Eventually, the United States replaced Britain as informal imperialist of the Americas. Its domination was accompanied by a quantum leap in technology not unlike that of arriving Europeans in 1500. Around 1898, the North Americans invaded with steam shovels and steamships, railroads, oil rigs, and mineral refineries. Technological dominance was fortified with naval fueling stations, the Panama Canal, radio communication, and eventually air travel. Imperial legions included not only Marines and Navy bluejackets but automobile salesmen, fast-food franchises, resort developers, Hollywood celluloid heroes, and television advertisers.

The new technological empire of the United States resulted from fortuitous circumstance as much as expansionist policies and native genius. In the century following independence, the United States profited from continually close commercial and technical connections with England, the engine of world industrial progress. Skilled professionals and advanced machine design crossed the North Atlantic and spurred North American manufacture of textiles, firearms, steel ships, steam engines, and the machinery to make more machines. Massive British investments in U.S. railroads, mining, and metal production stimulated rapid economic growth. Without close ties to Great Britain, the United States would not have progressed rapidly. Meanwhile, Latin America derived no similar benefits from its former master. Unlike England, nineteenth-century Spain was an industrial backwater. It had little progressive impact on its recent colonies.[43]

ECONOMIES OF EXTRACTION

When Latin Americans figuratively dine on their region's bounty, they find the dinner meager, for huge platters have been removed before the banquet begins. Like Columbus exchanging glass beads for gold pendants, more value leaves than reaches Latin America. Imperial commerce long ago replaced Columbus's simple barter with a labyrinth of sophisticated techniques and procedures: markups, discounts, investment credits, exchange rates, wholesale and retail prices, user fees and licensing arrangements, interest payments, transport costs, commissions, and so on. One major reason why most Latin Americans are poor in a region of great resources is that historic legacies endure: local geologies and ecologies are exploited with ever greater efficiency. And the technologies are owned by others or by local elites: U.S. companies and wealthy Latin Americans.

At the onset of the nineteenth century, independence seemed promising for Latin Americans. In 1800, Mexico was wealthier than the United States. Its northern territories—from California to Colorado and Texas—promised greater wealth. But decades of political squabbling and resulting economic chaos in Mexico contrasted with industrial growth next door, particularly in the northern United States. Seeking even greater markets and resources, the expansionist United States seized half of Mexico in 1848. Thus, during a critical phase of industrial development, Mexico—and all Latin America—languished. And while political conflict and civil war also characterized the United States prior to 1865, its elites were bolstered by growing technological wizardry. By century's end, the United States was poised to exploit Latin America. After invading Cuba, Puerto Rico, and Panama in 1898 and 1903, the United States built a Latin American empire around new infrastructures: coaling stations and a magnificent canal.[44]

A major aspect of industrialism is the application of power to process. Applying energy to manufacturing and transport allowed owners to make and move more. The seeds of industry were initially simple and local. After 1800, waterwheels in the northeast allowed village entrepreneurs to card wool, cut lumber, and grind grain. Soon, larger hydraulics and locked canals allowed more manufactures to be made and moved to distant markets. The search for greater efficiencies eventually inspired engineers to produce the dynamo, a boiler-powered engine of great mechanical force. First fueled by wood, then by coal, and eventually by petroleum, engines went to the work, eliminating the need to site manufacturing near rivers. Engines dug mines, crushed ore, and drilled for oil. They powered factories, produced electricity, and were adapted as locomotives or ship engines. Steam engines and steel rails guided massive loads up hills, across deserts, and through jungles. With steam and steel, merchant marines were no longer restricted to the tensile strength of wood, the physics of mast and sail, or the directions of prevailing winds. Between 1840 and 1860, the world merchant fleet doubled. By 1913, oceangoing commerce was seven times greater than a century earlier. Most of this traffic crisscrossed the Atlantic Ocean, and much of it touched the shores of Latin America.[45]

The impact of engines on Latin America was profound, as an accelerated rate of extraction was joined by a massive search for petroleum, modern technology's fuel of choice. The British drilled Mexico's first producing well in 1901. Within a decade, a sea of oil was found beneath Venezuela's Lake Maracaibo. Eventually Moi's Ecuadoran rain forest would be another exploited Latin American region. Unfortunately, these oil reserves were Latin American only in a geologic sense, as the tools used to explore, drill, transport, and refine are primarily foreign. Even the land became the private property of North American, Dutch, and British corporations known as the "seven sisters": Esso, Mobil, Gulf, Chevron, Texaco, Shell, and British Petroleum. As in the days of Potosí, Latin American geologies enriched foreign elites, this time private technological empires.[46]

Imperial technologies favor elitism. In colonial times, difficult and costly transportation meant that only goods of high value-to-weight ratios, such as silver, gold, diamonds, and dyes, were carried from remote interiors. A mule could move 300 pounds only twelve miles per day. Thus, through the colonial era bulky commodities—such as sugar, salt, brazilwood, and cotton—were produced near the sea. Since high value-to-weight ratios also filled returning ships, imports comprised luxuries for the rich. Thus early transport technology favored elitism both coming and going. Late-nineteenth-century railroads and steamships reversed value-to-weight ratios, as they carried great bulk. But the legacy of elitism remained since only wealthy entrepreneurs could build and operate expensive transportation networks. For a century, most owners of Latin American transportation infrastructures have been foreigners, mainly North Americans.[47]

INFRASTRUCTURES OF EMPIRE

Economists know the expense of building communication and transportation systems. Great sums are required to construct highways, dams, bridges, ports, railroads, pipelines, canals, airports, electrical generating stations, transmission lines, or other infrastructures. Such projects entail time, effort, and money, including surveys, designs, rights-of-way, construction equipment, wages and salaries (including insurance and pensions), structural materials, vast amounts of fuel and energy, and a host of other costs. When built, infrastructures channel people and goods along engineered paths. Today, these patterns of human behavior are cast in concrete and forged in alloys, rather than determined by mule trails and windblown sailing ships. As in the past, modern infrastructures are normally accepted as "what should be" as well as "what is." Innovations—from telegraphs to satellites and narrow-gauge railroads to air freight terminals—are hailed as advancements. However, new technologies usually do old things better rather than differently. The chart of "who produces what," "what goes where," and "who profits most" usually remains the same. "Modern change" is more modern than change.

Railroads demonstrate how infrastructures serve different purposes. In the United States, railroads created dispersed transportation networks connecting hinterlands with ports but also linking Detroit with Denver, Milwaukee with Memphis, Akron with Atlanta, and so on. Trains moved commodities to port but also fostered intensive internal development.

In Latin America, railroads formed other patterns. In Mexico, *American investors* designed railroads to move ore from remote sites to processing plants in the United States. In Argentina, *British investors* laid rails across the pampas like the spokes of a wheel with Buenos Aires at their hub: trains took wheat, beef, and mutton to waiting ships. Movement among interior towns typically necessitated going to the distant port and changing lines before returning to the countryside. The systems of Chile, Peru, Costa Rica, Cuba, and other Latin American nations were similarly designed by foreigners to extract minerals, bananas, coffee, copper, or sugar from inland. Many railroads were of different gauges: with varying widths, equipment from one route could not be used elsewhere. Freight rates also gave exporters discounts while domestic users paid higher fees. Such infrastructures favored production for export.[48]

The construction of Latin American railroads reveals the colonial nature of the region's early industrialism. Peru is a case study. Railroad building in Peru boomed after 1860 as routes followed paths once trod by mules: from mountain mines to coastal ports. Yet almost everything needed for the railroad was imported. Construction equipment arrived from England. Trains, repair shops, and spare parts were made in the United States. Foreign engineers designed and managed the systems. Chinese workers—some veterans from California—hauled rock and laid track. The dynamite was imported, as were the ties and trestle timbers. The main thing Peruvian about Peru's railroads was the location.[49]

Yet railroads profoundly impacted Latin America. São Paulo, Brazil, shows how. Located at the edge of a broad plateau, São Paulo remained a sleepy town until 1868, when it was joined by rail with Santos, a nearby port. That event subsequently changed regional ecologies, the national economy, and Brazilian politics. Immediately, plantations spreading from São Paulo replaced natural habitats with coffee trees planted in parallel rows. Italian and Portuguese immigrants joined poorly paid *mamelucos* (mestizos) who picked and processed the coffee. And booming coffee exports created a wealthy planter class. As rail lines pushed farther inland, the hub-and-spokes pattern of Buenos Aires was replicated. São Paulo expanded and diversified to include not only coffee processing but rail repair shops, textile factories, iron foundries, and service industries. The city's mushrooming population grew to 65,000 inhabitants in 1890, and a half million by 1920. Increased economic power led coffee barons to challenge Brazil's old sugar elites. Having occupied the land, São Paulo's leaders now filled national positions. Railroads helped reach both.[50]

tually surrendered to petty authoritarianism. And domination by the United States was replaced by dependency on the USSR. When the Soviet Union ended—and Russia no longer paid Cuban economic development bills—the centrally managed island economy almost collapsed.

The nonauthoritarian variant of Marxism, *democratic socialism,* also became popular in Latin America. In Guatemala, Chile, Nicaragua, and elsewhere, various governments experimented with mixed economic models derived from successful private-public planning in Europe, particularly Scandinavia. Never allowed to succeed or fail, these nascent social democracies were destroyed by U.S. policy makers. The CIA overthrew governments in Guatemala, Brazil, and the Dominican Republic. It bombed electrical power stations and mined harbors in Nicaragua and paid truckers to snarl traffic in Chile. The United States "made local economies scream," in the torture metaphor of Henry Kissinger. Costa Rican welfarism was about as far "socialist" as the United States allowed any Latin American economy to travel.

In the 1980s, ISI was displaced from center stage by another major theory. Imported from the United States, the "free market" philosophy was an old idea with new aspects: privatization and formation of regional trading blocks. A free market meant that ISI protectionist walls fell and state industries faced international competition. Privatization sold state enterprises to high bidders as governments retreated from nationalistic goals and entrepreneurial roles. Trading blocks ended national autonomy, as economies merged to create large markets. Mexico made the largest leap into free market economics with the North American Free Trade Agreement (NAFTA). But the Summit of the Americas, held in Miami during December 1994, committed all the Latin American nations (except uninvited Cuba) to free market theories. The first flush of free market economics seemed promising: most local economies prospered as they ended ISI policies in the late 1980s and 1990s. But as with ISI, the long-range promise of free market economics also rides on strengthened consumer demand. That requires income redistribution as well as general economic growth. Certainly upper- and middle-class consumers prefer free market strategies: as tariff barriers fall, they buy quality foreign goods more cheaply. And since about 40 percent of Latin Americans are rich or middle-class, this constitutes about 200 million consumers, a large market. But if the poor remain poor, then those who could not buy nationally made televisions under ISI will be unable to buy foreign-made computers under NAFTA.

As the twentieth century ends, Latin American economies are growing again. But the prognosis is complex and questionable. Mexico and Brazil seem poised for expansion but suffer from periodic debt restructuring. The Mexican devaluation crisis of December 1994 was a painful aftershock of the 1980s debt earthquake. Chile and Argentina have experienced growth as export earnings climb and funds from privatization reduce public indebtedness. Sizable private investments that upgrade newly acquired—and capital-starved—public corporations also generate local growth multipliers. But investors invest for returns: what arrives now will later be remitted manyfold as profits.

The philosophy of Latin American policy makers—evident in projects such as

NAFTA and the Summit of the Americas—is that fair trade should replace dependency and aid. And while NAFTA promises progress, its benefits have still not permeated Mexico. Nevertheless, Latin Americans argue that greater market equity represented by expanding trade blocks will eventually improve everyone's lives. The belief is that Mexicans making windshields and tires for U.S. autos will produce incomes sufficient for local workers to buy toasters and VCRs made in Brazil. Employed Brazilians could then purchase Chilean and North American products. Prosperity would circulate through the hemisphere. Someday it may happen.

MICROECONOMIC PRACTICE

María del Rosario Valdez (a pseudonym) once had a formal job. She was employed as an elevator operator in a Mexican bureaucracy. While her salary was low, regular paychecks and fringe benefits provided security. She lived in subsidized housing, took her children to a state workers' hospital for virtually free health care, and saved money shopping in subsidized federal employee grocery stores. But those days are gone. In a national austerity program imposed by foreign creditors, María was fired from her elevator job during the lost decade of the 1980s. Unable to find formal employment anywhere, she joined millions of Mexicans—and Latin Americans—who entered the region's informal economy by creating her own "underground" business. To maximize meager profits, she buys and sells, bargains and barters without obeying laws, obtaining licenses, or paying taxes. Her only policy is experience. Her only theory is intuition.[40]

María del Rosario Valdez sells used clothing to other poor people. Every Thursday evening, she boards a second-class bus in Mexico City and heads to Texas. Riding through the night, she chats with other mothers and fathers who operate similar businesses in Mexico's informal economy: buying and selling cosmetics, toys, electronic gadgets, kitchenware, tools, and so on. At bus stations and major intersections, they watch similar entrepreneurs: people washing windshields, juggling, making tacos, hawking puppets or cassettes, filling cones with homemade ice cream, swallowing swords, selling pastries.

At the border, María moves with clockwork efficiency. She takes a cab across the border to a cavernous warehouse, where she walks among tons of clothes piled onto plywood tables. Many are used and some are overstock, outdated styles usually, that have been collected from all over the United States. For six hours she fills boxes and suitcases with about 500 pounds of carefully selected items, costing about $150. Later, at the border, in the bus station, and at checkpoints leading to Mexico City, she pays perhaps twice that much as bribes to Mexican customs officials. They, too, earn little under the government austerity program and augment their incomes "informally."

When the bus arrives in Mexico City on Saturday morning, María immediately goes to her downtown market stall. Unsold clothing from the previous week is bundled and sold to another woman who hawks ultracheap clothing door-to-door. María's new stock is laid out, and during the remainder of the week she spends long hours displaying goods, negotiating prices, repacking clothes at day's end, and moving to another neighborhood the next morning. Each Thursday evening, she goes to Texas again.

For centuries, Latin Americans have lived with unofficial economies. "Underground" enterprises once involved slaves and bullion, Manila Galleons, and mule trains. Today the informal economy touches everything from used clothes to cocaine, and the lives of most Latin Americans, who invariably buy things from street vendors. The vast majority of the underground entrepreneurs are poor, like María del Rosario Valdez. They are numerous and increasingly are studied. Their major student has been the Peruvian economist Hernando de Soto, who derived theory from practice in his pioneering book *The Other Path, The Informal Revolution.* De Soto estimates that 60 percent of the total work in his native Peru occurs in the informal economy, where people pay bribes rather than official fees or taxes. In Peru and throughout Latin America, peasants and the urban poor occupy vacant lots, and without legal titles, they build homes with whatever they can collect from dumps, building sites, or each other. They earn incomes delivering water or snow cones from foot-pedaled carts. They work as maids or handymen, and typically neither employer nor employee bothers with tax declarations. Although intense and ubiquitous, the informal economy sustains many but enriches few.[41]

In an interesting but tragic turn of fate, drugs have become the major success of Latin America's informal economy. They are the only Latin American commodity sold directly in North America by Latin Americans themselves. As narcotics shippers evade U.S. enforcement agencies, they also avoid the marketing mechanisms of North American middlemen. Unfortunately, like other items in the hemispheric *mercado,* few drug profits actually reach Latin America. Most drug money remains in the United States or in Swiss bank accounts.

Drugs are among Latin America's major exports. Jamaican "gold" and Colombian "red" have long been favored by discriminating consumers of marijuana. Throughout the Caribbean, Central America, and Mexico, struggling peasants often augment meager bean and corn corps with small plots of lucrative marijuana. Common to illicit drugs everywhere, reliable statistics are illusive, particularly for this economic "weed."[42]

The giant among Latin American drug commodities is cocaine. The coca leaf—but not cocaine—has long been part of South American culture. Before Europeans arrived, coca bushes were cultivated in their natural habitat in the Andes, from Bolivia through Colombia, with Peru as the center of world production. Among Andean Indigens, coca leaves have been a traditional barter item, at times even currency. Chewing coca leaves suppressed hunger and fatigue: it sustained native workers in silver mines and plantations. And coca still accompanies local religious rituals: "Mother Coca" was first offered to Indigen spirits, then to Catholic saints.

Cocaine is the most recent global addiction to a Latin American product. Tobacco, rum, chewing gum, sugar, caffeine (as coffee), and even cough syrups (in the nineteenth century) formed earlier dependencies. And while coca is not new, massive use of cocaine has grown since the 1940s, when simple processing was innovated. As coca production expanded, Peruvian Indigens settled isolated eastern Andean regions. With its high value and low bulk, cocaine was a cash crop easily transported to distant markets: first by mules, then by small aircraft. As the market quickly expanded, so did production and processing. Between 1975 and 1990, cocaine cultivation increased 800-fold. During the first half of the 1990s, Peru probably cultivated a half million acres of coca. Peasants earned ten times as much growing coca for export as they did growing corn and potatoes for local markets.[43]

Cocaine has stimulated bittersweet economic growth in the informal economy of the Andes. The constant infusion of outside money generates higher incomes for poor people and stimulates local economic multipliers. Money circulating in local economies creates new towns with continually expanding services ranging from hospitals to brothels, and consumer outlets selling everything from imported pickup trucks to junk food. Shining Path, the Peruvian communist party, arrived to organize agricultural cooperatives, unite peasants, and demand higher payments from cocaine processors. Meanwhile, the region suffers deforestation, erosion, and water pollution resulting from using kerosene, sulfuric acid, and ammonia to process cocaine. Violence and crime are other occupational hazards of an illicit and competitive industry.[44]

As an informal economy, no one accurately knows the statistics surrounding cocaine. Investigations in 1990 concluded that cocaine's annual street value in the United States alone was $100 billion, of which only $10 billion reached Latin America. Nine-tenths of cocaine profits remained in U.S. bank deposits or investment portfolios, typically in Florida, New York, and California. Of the $10 billion remitted yearly to Latin America, Colombia and Peru receive about half. The remainder goes elsewhere, to pay for transportation in Mexico and Panama as well as remote production and processing in Brazil or Paraguay. As with other commodities, sizable markups benefit middlemen the most. Still, Peru's earnings made cocaine the nation's most valued export commodity during the latter decades of the twentieth century. Viewed as jobs, cocaine provides wages for a third of a million Peruvian peasants in a nation facing 50 percent unemployment. Narcotics may constitute two-thirds of Bolivia's foreign exchange and one-third of Peru's.[45]

In Latin America, profits from narcotics far exceed those from bananas, strawberries, or other foreign-controlled commodities. In a tragic irony of free market economics, Latin Americans match local supply to foreign demand. To do so, they use timeworn traditions of hemispheric smuggling with many North American accomplices. Through avoiding formal economics, many Latin Americans have become informally richer.

CONFRONTING LEGACIES

The quest for wealth in Latin America has left many Latin Americans poor. The legacies are many, and include unfair barter, *encomiendas* and slavery, colonial authoritarianism, and extracting minerals, money, labor, and talent. These many tendencies have encouraged elitism for some and alienation for many. Yet changes are occurring.

The major change in the quest for wealth is decreasing U.S. control over Latin America's economy. The greatest point of mutual United States–Latin America involvement occurred during the mid-twentieth century as each region shipped about half its exports to the other. By 1987, only about one-eighth of each region's exports were exchanged. Both Latin America and the United States have found other trading partners: Canada, Europe, and east Asia for the United States; east Asia, each other, and distant developing nations for the countries of Latin America. During the late twentieth century, 90 percent of what Latin Americans manufacture has been sold domestically or to each other. And trade with less developed countries across the Atlantic and Pacific has increased dramatically. Brazil, for example, supplies manufactured products—including automobiles—to Nigeria and the Philippines. Such trading patterns give Latin Americans greater options.[46]

Domination of Latin America by U.S. corporations is also waning. In 1959, a full 70 percent of major firms operating in Latin America had their headquarters in the United States; by 1976 this had declined to 43 percent. Instead, major corporate players are more typically Latin Americans themselves. U.S. investments parallel this change. In 1959, a total of 38 percent of all Latin American investments originated in the United States; by 1980 this had dropped to 12 percent. U.S. corporations clearly have less involvement and less influence. The quest for Latin American wealth has become more diversified.[47]

Another long-range trend (the 1980s were an exception) is that, economically, Latin America is expanding much faster than the United States. From 1960 to 1980, Latin America maintained far greater growth rates than the United States. During the 1990s, Latin America is again surging forward. Such trends make Latin American economies more important in world trade.[48]

Population trends also indicate change. In 1960 Latin America had 207 million inhabitants and was 1.14 times more populous than the United States. By the year 2000, Latin America will be home to about half a billion persons, almost twice the U.S. population. If poor Latin Americans—60 percent of the population—ever experience major wage improvements, population multiplied by purchasing power will create twice as many regional shoppers as in the United States. Larger markets create not only demand but economic dynamism.

Meanwhile, North American society is changing. With more nonwhites, including a mushrooming Latino population, and changing tastes generally, the United States is increasingly becoming a consumer of Latin American culture. The popularity of Caribbean music and Mexican food, better hemispheric media connections, and greater use of Spanish in the United States all indicate new roles for Latin American culture in *el norte*. Miami, San Antonio, and Los Angeles are hemispheric as well as U.S. trendsetters.[49]

Taken together, these many trends indicate changing hemispheric economic relationships. The growing size, complexity, diversity, and dynamism of Latin American societies lessen the success of outside interference. The waning ability of the United States to control hemispheric destiny is reversing—in strange ways—historic roles of dominance and dependence. In the multi-billion-dollar drug trade, the United States is the frustrated supplicant. And Latin American pragmatics rather than North American ideals determine the realities of immigration. Trade itself may soon reverse the historic scales of who gains how much, particularly as new trade agreements mature. While U.S. corporations gain immediate profits, many Latin American supporters of NAFTA and the Summit of the Americas sense a day when access to huge North American markets will create larger profits for Latin American producers. Relationships are changing, and with them characteristics once thought permament.[50]

CHANGING TRADITIONS

Changing trends will not easily alter traditions. Boom and bust cycles will not end with another wave of prosperity commencing in the 1990s. Renewed growth alone will not bring economic justice. Declining North American involvement will not end extraction. The quest for wealth in Latin America will continue. To modify *how* and *for whom* will take conscious and coherent change of both belief and behavior—no easy task, anywhere.

What must change most dramatically for Latin America to become a region of general prosperity is the distribution of regional incomes. The massive skewing of regional wealth toward a small group of the ultrarich not only harms the poor but deters sustainable economic growth. In a brilliant study, the scholar Carl E. Solberg shows the results of contrasting economic and social policy in two similar ecologies—the prairies of Canada and the pampas of Argentina—seeking to discover why two similar situations evolved so differently. Solberg's book *The Prairies and the Pampas* shows that contrasting land tenure systems generated democratic or authoritarian rule, with resulting policies encouraging reinvestment or extraction. Life on the Canadian prairie was not always easy, but there European immigrants progressed significantly with each generation. In contrast, European immigrants arriving to the grasslands of Argentina were neither enfranchised nor empowered to control their destinies: they were denied both land and political voice; they could not influence credit, transportation policy, or marketing. Paralleling Canada and Argentina shows that democracy is more than an ideal. It is also an economic force and an engine of progress.[51]

In Latin America, economic elitism has deterred material progress. The relatively few who are able to invest are often foreigners or local elites employing trickle-down policies in good times or capital flight when economies turn sour. And purchasing power for a relatively small but affluent few does not allow formation of the broad-based demand necessary for diversified domestic production. For overall economic health, Latin American nations should not import luxury automobiles but rather build bicycles, motorbikes, and small pickup trucks. One case study found that if the yearly earnings of Brazil's richest 1 percent had been distributed to its poorest 50 percent in 1980, the incomes of half the nation would have doubled. Such an increase in purchasing power would be a mighty stimulant to local economic activity. The poor must become viable consumers not only for their betterment but for general prosperity.[52]

Another problem with capitalism in Latin America is that many capitalists lack capital. With so much profit trickling up and out, a huge pool of native entrepreneurs lacks funding. The self-employed poor and the lower middle class of Latin America have long cultivated the pragmatic arts of economic survival. María del Rosario Valdez and her millions of cohorts are living examples of ingenious entrepreneurship. Without capital for materials, they build shantytown homes. Without proper tools, seeds, and fertilizers, they farm small plots. With little investment in human capital, they learn to survive. Lacking jobs with regular incomes, they hustle a livelihood: carving, cooking, cleaning, singing, sewing, selling used clothes, and so on. From campesinos to street and market vendors, many of the poor and marginally poor in Latin America are perfect capitalists: hardworking, saving, inventive, resourceful, practical, and street-smart. The only thing these entrepreneurs lack is capital for growth. Whether it be U.S. foreign aid, international financial assistance, or domestic programs by Latin American nations, more loans and funding must reach struggling producers in local markets: for seed, fertilizer, tools, supplies, further training, and other capital needs. Capitalism can be a dynamic force, particularly when practiced by small-scale entrepreneurs.[53]

Motivated as much by cuts in funding as by new philosophies of aid—trying to do more with less—some aid agencies have begun to support projects that stimulate microcapitalism in local communities. The Inter-American Foundation made small low-interest loans to street vendors who then bought pushcarts instead of renting them at costly rates. Repaid loans were recirculated to Catholic church groups, cooperatives of weavers, cottage industries, and even human capital projects such as training citizen advocates. In Peru and Bolivia, micrograssroots aid has assisted neighborhood women in buying garden tools, pots and pans, and refrigerators, and in receiving technical assistance. The resulting communal kitchens provide better nutrition as well as training and leadership.[54]

Large-scale capitalism is also important, but in Latin America it needs a code of ethics. The modern corporation is an undeniable engine of economic progress: coordinating resources, introducing technologies, rationalizing management, and uniting capital, production, and markets. But too often the "bottom line" of immediate profit has been the only visible one for investors in Latin America, whether they be private or corporate. Corporations need to reduce costs, but not at the expense of driving poor Latin Americans to compete for *lo mas barato* wages in already depressed regions. The search for comparative advantage must acknowledge regional standards: minimum wages, environmental codes, tax policies, plant closing procedures, profit sharing, hiring of nationals, and so on. Whether it be the Organization of American States, the Economic Commission for Latin America (an agency of the United Nations), or another group, codes of corporate conduct need to be agreed upon and uniformly enforced. Capitalism with a conscience needs to replace a legacy of greed.

Fairness must also characterize the international *mercado,* where *lo mas barato* prices have long denied Latin Americans sufficient capital to reinvest. As long as producers gain so little from selling so much, scanty revenues will undercut regional development programs. Quite clearly, a larger percentage of profit from sales of bananas, coffee, strawberries, petroleum, and other products should return to Latin America. Either through hemispheric trade associations or intervention by international agencies, fairness and stability need to become features of hemispheric commodity markets.

Immediate progress in changing painful legacies could begin with ending the debt crisis. For Latin Americans, the legacy of foreigners extracting wealth is a quarterly reality, all the more sublime because nothing physically leaves. And interest payments on unending debt—unlike extracting minerals or fuels—never deplete the source. Some resolution of debt has occurred, but purported "cures" are merely lesser stages of illness. The Brady Plan of the United States contains little actual debt reduction. Instead, it consolidates debt, extends payments, and grants certification by the U.S. government that a Latin American nation is again "safe" for foreign investment. Even this minimal approach renews prosperity. Other approaches—particularly debt-equity swapping—are more fair and creative. In a debt-equity swap, a debtor nation, the creditor bank, and a foreign investor work together: the bank discounts debt certificates from a Latin American government and sells them to an investor, who then returns them to the government in exchange for ownership or lease of land, facilities, resources, or other assets in the debtor nation. Through debt-equity swaps, North American environmental groups have purchased and preserved rain forests in Costa Rica, Belize, Ecuador, and Bolivia. European soccer teams have acquired Brazilian players through mutually beneficial debt-equity swaps. Argentina used the approach to privatize its economy and invite free market competition: the state-owned telephone company was sold to a consortium of Bell Atlantic of the United States and Telefónica de España for $214 million in cash and $5 billion in debt reduction. The deal resulted in Argentina paying $50 million less in monthly interest. These and other mechanisms show that mutually beneficial solutions can be found to reducing Latin American debt. Cooperation and creativity can turn depression to development.[55]

To change any of these traditions will require reversing the legacy of regional disunity. While Latin Americans have long shared their music, dance, literature, and art, cooperation for economic and social progress has been rare. Yet common cultural roots and similar problems call for mutual action. The European Community shows that even recent enemies can work together for mutual progress. Surely Latin Americans with much less to divide them can also cooperate to plan and act for a better future.

Latin Americans must also search their own cultural roots and local heritage for future keys to economic success. Too often Latin American economic models have been European or North American, yet small nations like Taiwan, Malaysia, and Singapore have pioneered being successful by doing little things well: through combining modern technologies and native skills. Latin Americans need to discover the special strengths of their own heritage and environment as they develop new and appropriate technologies and arts. This has been done with synthetic fuels made from sugarcane in Brazil, new strains of potatoes developed in Peruvian laboratories, medicines derived from tropical plants in Costa Rica, and modern crafts inspired by old traditions in Mexico. But richer resources for further development exist in the skills of artisans, in respecting nature, in an ancient agricultural heritage, in using local colors, materials, sounds, and foods. Before Europeans ever arrived, Indigens had created great civilizations using the raw materials and native visions of their own worlds. Latin Americans can do it again.

SUGGESTED READINGS

Breslin, Patrick. *Development and Dignity: Grassroots Development and the Inter-American Foundation.* Roslyn, Va.: Inter-American Foundation, 1987.

Canak, William, ed. *Lost Promises: Debt, Austerity, and Development in Latin America.* Boulder, Colo.: Westview Press, 1989.

Cardoso, Eliana, and Ann Helwege. *Latin America's Economy: Diversity, Trends, and Conflicts.* Cambridge, Mass.: MIT Press, 1992.

Chilcote, Ronald H., and Joel C. Edelstein. *Latin America: Capitalist and Socialist Perspectives of Development and Underdevelopment.* Boulder, Colo.: Westview Press, 1986.

De Jesús, Carolina María. *Child of the Dark: The Diary of Carolina María de Jesús,* translated by David St. Clair. New York: Dutton, 1962.

De Soto, Hernando. *The Other Path.* London: IB Tauris, 1989.

Drake, Paul W., ed. *Money Doctors, Foreign Debts, and Economic Reforms in Latin America from the 1890s to the Present.* Wilmington, Del.: Scholarly Resources, 1994.

Hellman, Judith Adler. *Mexican Lives.* New York: New Press, 1994.

Hoberman, Louisa Schell, and Susan Migden Socolow. *Cities and Society in Colonial Latin America.* Albuquerque: University of New Mexico Press, 1986.

Lernoux, Penny. *In Banks We Trust.* Garden City, N.Y.: Anchor Press/Doubleday, 1984.

MacDonald, Scott B. *Mountain High, White Avalanche: Cocaine and Power in the Andean States and Panama.* Published with the Center for Strategic and International Studies. New York: Praeger, 1989.

Madrid, Raul L. *Overexposed: U.S. Banks Confront the Third World Debt Crisis.* Washington, D.C.: Investor Responsibility Research Center, 1990.

Ritter, Archibald R. M., Maxwell A. Cameron, and David H. Pollock. *Latin America to the Year 2000: Reactivating Growth, Improving Equity, Sustaining Democracy.* New York: Praeger, 1992.

Shehan, John. *Patterns of Development in Latin America: Poverty, Repression, and Economic Strategy.* Princeton, N.J.: Princeton University Press, 1987.

Stallings, Barbara, and Robert Kaufman, eds. *Debt and Democracy in Latin America.* Boulder, Colo.: Westview Press, 1989.

8

EL NORTE: THE NEIGHBOR TO THE NORTH

The United States is grand and powerful. Whenever it trembles, a profound shudder runs down the enormous backbone of the Andes.

Nicaraguan poet Rubén Darío[1]

The North American . . . substitutes social truth for the real truth, which is always disagreeable. We get drunk in order to confess; they get drunk in order to forget. . . .

. . . It seems to me that North Americans consider the world to be something that can be perfected, and that we consider it to be something that can be redeemed.

Mexican poet and essayist Octavio Paz[2]

We did not, in fact, come to the United States. . . . The United States came to us.

Mexican-American writer Luis Valdés[3]

Only one hemispheric nation has repeatedly impacted the fate and fortunes of all others during the last century. Following the withdrawal of Spain and Portugal, the most important nation in Latin American affairs has been *el norte,* the neighbor to the north: the United States.

The story of *el norte* is much more than formal diplomacy or military intervention. It also involves psychology, education, media, music, business, language, technology, religion, immigration, and more. Most accounts of the United States and Latin America emphasize the Monroe Doctrine and list the policies of presidents. The Latin American agendas of U.S. administrations have ranged from idealism to power politics and form a chronology of programs, corollaries, doctrines, plans, treaties, agreements, alliances, and so on. Often neglected in standard texts is a general discussion of pervasive attitudes: those of presidents and public alike. These include racism, moralism, self-righteousness, outright hypocrisy, and honest efforts to confront entrenched legacies. Viewing U.S.–Latin American relations from the perspective of U.S. presidents inherently creates a superior-inferior relationship: it resembles explaining the European-Indigen encounter from the perspective of European conquerors.

The story of *el norte* is much more than what U.S. leaders think. The most pervasive theme is ignorance, as many Americans seem blissfully—sometimes stubbornly—unaware of our hemispheric neighbors. More than fact and truth, they are familiar with the superficial and stereotypical. Rather than shibboleths, our story of *el norte* will confront some neglected aspects and episodes. As the twenty-first century dawns, the United States must face new regional realities. Despite a rocky start, the North American Free Trade Agreement (NAFTA) promises equity in cultural as well as commercial relations. Latin America is also a domestic issue. According to current projections, Hispanics will comprise one-quarter of the U.S. population sometime around 2050. Persons of Latin American ancestry will constitute the second-largest group in a nation of minorities: behind whites but more numerous than African-Americans. While looking forward, the United States must also review its past. Our reflections on *el norte* begin with that process. Among other things, we shall assess schoolbooks, television, and Hollywood films. But we begin with U.S. diplomacy and warfare—viewed from a Latin American perspective.

THE OLD CLOTHES OF THE EMPEROR

I once discussed U.S.–Latin American relations with a friend, a Costa Rican diplomat.[4] I asked her which U.S. presidents demonstrated understanding, compassion, or just simple fairness toward Latin America. From the teaching of U.S. History in the United States, one would have presumed that Woodrow Wilson, Franklin Roosevelt, Harry Truman, John F. Kennedy, and Jimmy Carter would make her list. Wilson publicly rejected both the "big stick diplomacy" of Teddy Roosevelt and the "dollar diplomacy" of William Howard Taft; FDR had his "good-neighbor" policy; Truman proudly hung portraits of Latin America's liberators in the oval office and initiated major technical assistance programs; Kennedy began both the Peace Corps and the Alliance for Progress; and Carter learned Spanish, promoted human rights, and with great difficulty concluded the Panama Canal treaties.

My friend answered, calmly but firmly, "None! *No* United States president ever demonstrated consistent respect for Latin America or Latin Americans. United States presidents are all more alike than different." Neither radical nor un-American, my friend left me dumbfounded. I countered with a recitation of supposed American ideals: foreign aid, support for democracy, the Peace Corps, human rights, and so on. She listened politely, then responded: "All these are public relations, meant to influence opinion." Acknowledging that some good—such as the Peace Corps and the Panama Canal treaties—occasionally occurs, she carefully examined the more substantive record, an account that was always ethnocentric and often racist.

Trying one last time, I asked her to identify at least one American chief executive who at least intended to promote fairness and equity. She thought briefly before unloading her greatest surprise, mentioning a U.S. president almost universally refuted by his countrymen: Herbert Hoover, the true author of the good-neighbor policy.

For Latin Americans the official record of U.S. relations is tragic and sad. While U.S. governments since the 1820s have designed Latin American programs with marquee names such as the Monroe Doctrine, the Roosevelt Corollary, the good-neighbor policy, the Alliance for Progress, and the Caribbean Basin Initiative, actual events have been less bright and glamorous. The "good neighbor" (FDR) sent warships to Cuba and lauded murderous dictators. The Alliance for Progress president (JFK) approved CIA saboteurs and assassins in Cuba and bolstered repressive Latin American regimes. The Caribbean Basin Initiative of Ronald Reagan was accompanied by his invading Grenada, creating a civil war in Nicaragua, and spending $4 billion suppressing social change in tiny El Salvador.

That deeds speak louder than words is evident in any chronology of U.S. aggressions. Its highlights can be summarized. In the early decades of the nineteenth century, the United States repeatedly invaded Spanish Florida, seeking to wrest the territory for itself. During the 1830s and 1840s the United States maneuvered to acquire Texas, California, and the northern half of Mexico. Outright invasion in 1848 completed this campaign. During the mid-nineteenth century, filibusters—mercenaries and ragtag militias from the United States—tried to seize Caribbean islands, Central American nations, and parts of Mexico. In 1898, the United States invaded Cuba and Puerto Rico. In 1903, it invaded Colombia to create a nation and a canal, both named Panama. The twentieth century, then, forms a crowded chronology of U.S. invasions, CIA intrigue, sabotage, and both subtle and overt domination. When Nicaragua was not suffering from U.S. invasions, it was usually governed by U.S. puppets. Much the same happened in Haiti, Cuba, the Dominican Republic, and elsewhere in Central America and the Caribbean. Farther south, military assistance and training programs served as the U.S. equivalent of a Trojan horse: infesting local governments with intimidating or dominating officers more loyal to U.S. officials than to their own elected representatives.

Items from this list became a hard personal lesson during a visit to Mexico's Caracole museum, where the nation's long history unwinds in a spiral structure built onto a hillside. My initial viewing was accompanied by a bus load of boisterous North Americans who quickly flooded the hall. They joked and laughed, sang commercial jingles, and combed their hair using showcase reflections. Quickly they zipped through the museum, skipping the written explanations (in English), and even whole displays. Understanding Mexican history was not a priority.

Meanwhile, I repeatedly found myself in the quiet company of a Mexican mother who carefully explained her nation's legacy to a young daughter. Beginning with the Texas rebellion of 1836, the woman's stories increasingly involved U.S.–Mexican relations. She described how President Polk deceptively provoked war in 1848, the siege of Mexico City by U.S. Marines, the proud but tragic suicides of Mexican cadets who refused to surrender after exhausting their ammunition, of General Zachary Taylor's northern invasion, of the Treaty of Guadalupe-Hidalgo, which forced Mexico to surrender half its national domain. The mother talked about how U.S. investors lauded the long dictatorship of Porfirio Díaz, how in 1913 U.S. Ambassador Henry Lane Wilson negotiated a coup that assassinated Mexico's democratically elected president Madero, and how U.S. bluejackets killed hundreds of Mexicans defending Veracruz in 1914. During these patient explanations the daughter kept glancing at me. The mother continued: U.S. oil companies in Mexico organized private armies, U.S. General Pershing invaded in 1916, North American diplomats coerced favorable terms for exploiting Mexican petroleum during negotiations of 1923.

Finally, the little girl tugged on her mother's skirt, pointed toward me, and asked: "Is he from the United States?" Both stared quizzically and I nodded. With an intense scowl and determined voice, the little girl snapped directly at me: "Why did you do this to us?"

Since outright invasion often causes embarrassment—and is difficult to explain—U.S. officials have preferred more subtle domination. And while labels like the Monroe Doctrine, the Roosevelt Corollary, and national security doctrine name the policies of particular eras, the overall relationship between the United States and Latin America—especially in the twentieth century—has been one of subtle control rather than overt conquest.

"PLATTIFICATION"

Despite many direct invasions, U.S. aggression toward Latin America has usually been indirect: sending Marines or airborne divisions makes for embarrassing moments when a nation professes democracy. Hence, another method of colonialism was preferred. Created as an addendum to Cuban "independence" and named after a rather obscure Senate committee chairman, the United States has preferred the Platt amendment.

The Platt amendment's real author was Elihu Root, Theodore Roosevelt's secretary of state. Root created a framework of attitude and policy that would dominate U.S.–Latin American relations for a century. With fellow imperialists of the generation of 1898, he wanted both business opportunities and military bases, mostly in the Caribbean, and did not trust Latin Americans. Since the American Senate (to forestall public fears of annexing Cuba) had declared that the United States would "leave the government and control of the island to its people," Root sought to "obey, but not comply": to control overall policy while *gente decente* (decent people—i.e., elite Latin American friends of U.S. officials) managed daily affairs in Cuba. His tool was the Platt amendment, which was forced into the Cuban constitution: American troops from 1898 disarmed Cuba's patriots but remained until Root's terms were accepted.

The Platt amendment allowed Washington officials to dominate Cuban national life. Its provisions included the following:

1 The United States controls Cuban foreign affairs.

2 The United States supervises Cuban public finances.

3 Cuba permits U.S. intervention to secure a stable government respectful of U.S. interests.

4 Cuba grants to the United States perpetual use of Guantanamo Bay as a military base.[5]

"Plattification," as Mexican editorialists in the 1920s called it, became longstanding U.S. policy not only in Cuba but throughout the region. "Plattification" reduced Latin American nations to "protectorates," a self-serving term implying some vague defensive benefit while actually conferring colonial status. During the twentieth century, the United States "Plattified" much of Latin America.

Plattification came in many forms. The Roosevelt Corollary was one. Enunciated by Theodore Roosevelt in 1903, it was a self-proclaimed right of the United States as a "civilized power" to militarily intervene when "impotent governments" tolerated local "wrongdoing." Critics dubbed it "big stick diplomacy" and "gunboat diplomacy." Another form of Plattification was financial and replaced invading Marines with accountants and loan agents from U.S. banks. Dollar diplomacy is best defined in a promotional speech by its inventor, President Taft's Secretary of State Philander Knox:

> In Central America the [U.S.] administration seeks to substitute dollars for bullets by arranging, through American bankers, loans for the rehabilitation of the finances of Nicaragua and Honduras. The conventions with those countries . . . will take the customs houses out of politics so that every ambitious revolutionist shall not seize them to squander the resources of his country to impose himself as dictator. By this policy we shall help the people of these rich countries to enjoy prosperity instead of almost incessant revolution and devastation. We shall do a noble work.[6]

Of course, dollar diplomacy's "noble work" paid returns to New York bankers and secured the region for U.S. investors, neither of whom were concerned with issues of local justice. And Knox's "ambitious revolutionists" were often local peasants and patriots opposed to U.S.-backed landlords and authoritarians. Debt management was a means of control as old as company stores and sharecropping. Presidents Wilson, Harding, and Coolidge practiced dollar diplomacy in Latin America. And since the 1980s, "debt diplomacy" has similarly controlled Latin American fortunes.

Plattification did entail occasional invasions to achieve "secure" governments. In 1902, Theodore Roosevelt and Elihu Root placed a criollo living in New York into Cuba's new presidency. One would assume that Tomás Estrada Palma, educated in the United States, would respect democracy. He didn't. In 1906, he rigged his reelection and Cubans took to the streets in protest. Under terms of the Platt amendment, the United States sent troops to "secure a stable government respectful of United States interests."

U.S. "Plattification" of Latin America became a tragic joke. As assistant secretary of the Navy in the Wilson administration, a young Franklin Roosevelt boasted of composing Haiti's constitution: occupied by U.S. forces, Haiti had no option but to accept. Woodrow Wilson turned idealism into a personal and imperialist crusade, boasting: "I am going to teach the South American republics to elect good men!" While his ardor was certain, his judgment was questionable. By the 1930s the United States directly supported tyrants in Cuba, the Dominican Republic, and Nicaragua. Franklin Roosevelt noted the decline from ideals to self-interest—and reduced the Platt amendment to a quip—in defending such despots as Batista, Trujillo, or Somoza, saying, "He may be a S.O.B., but he's our S.O.B." Eventually even surrogate dictators became embarrassing. In 1962 John F. Kennedy was mortified by the blatant tyranny of "friendly" dictator Rafael Trujillo in the Dominican Republic and authorized a CIA hit squad, which smuggled weapons hidden in shipments of peanut butter. In the 1980s, Panamanian dictator and onetime paid agent of the United States, Manuel Noriega, similarly lost favor with George Bush, himself a former CIA director. This time it took the Eighty-second Airborne Division rather than pistols and peanut butter to remove him.[7]

Around the mid-twentieth century Plattification took the form of hired mercenaries. Pioneered by both the secretary of state and the director of the CIA (positions filled by the Dulles brothers, John Foster and Allen), this strategy was used in 1954 by Dwight Eisenhower to overthrow the progressive, popular, and democratic government of Guatemala. John Kennedy endorsed a similar CIA army of Cuban exiles, in the unsuccessful 1961 Bay of Pigs invasion. The largest force of Plattifying mercenaries confronted Nicaragua in the 1980s. Composed of Cuban and Argentine soldiers of fortune as well as veteran officers of a previous Nicaraguan dictatorship, the contras (from *contra la revolución,* "against the revolution") were recruited and paid by Ronald Reagan operatives. These mercenaries were no more successful than CIA troops during JFK's Bay of Pigs adventure. Failing to overthrow Nicaragua's Sandinista government, they instead subjected Nicaragua to almost a decade of U.S.-sponsored murder and mayhem.[8]

Plattification also included training Latin American praetorians. Beginning in the late 1940s, foreign aid monies annually supported Latin American officers who grew more loyal to U.S. interests than to the elected officials of their own nations. These commanders were given wish lists of hardware and training, both in their nations and at the U.S. School of the Americas, located first in the Canal Zone then at Fort Benning, Georgia. During the long era of anticommunism—officially known as the national security doctrine—the United States did not so much dictate policy as define issues. North American officials in Latin America oriented attitude rather than ordered actions. One official neatly summarized the process during the 1970s: "They [Latin Americans] didn't see their problems as clearly as we felt we did." Such paternalism was not new. It originated with Elihu Root.[9]

PRIDE AND PREJUDICE

For nearly a century, U.S. actions and attitudes toward Latin America have been defined by the generation of 1898. Two simple ideas permeated the thought of Theodore Roosevelt, Elihu Root, and their peers: the United States is superior; Latin America is inferior. For the United States to act as it did, as often as it did, as long as it did, imperialism had to become a commonplace concept. Domination of hemispheric neighbors was not just proud policy; it was also popular prejudice.

Even before 1898, American leaders promoted self-superiority. Richard Olney, Democratic President Cleveland's secretary of state, mixed jargon, pomposity, and bully pride when he wrote to the British in 1895:

> Today the United States is practically sovereign on the continent, and its fiat is law upon the subjects to which it confines its interposition. Why? It is not because of the pure friendship or good will felt for it. It is not simply by reason of its high character as a civilized state, nor because wisdom and justice and equity are the invariable characteristics of the dealings of the United States. It is because, in addition to all other grounds, its infinite resources combined with its isolated position render it master of the situation and practically invulnerable as against any or all other powers.[10]

Such attitudes formed policy. Increasingly, they also became public opinion.

The greatest spokesman for imperialism was the "Rough Rider" himself, Theodore Roosevelt. His Roosevelt Corollary, enunciated in 1904, organized Olney's ideas, reinterpreted the Monroe Doctrine, became a Moses-like dictum for later presidents, and initiated the U.S. role of hemispheric policeman:

> Chronic wrongdoing, or an impotence which results in a general loosening of the ties of civilized society, may in America, as elsewhere, ultimately require intervention by some civilized nation, and in the Western Hemisphere the adherence of the United States to the Monroe Doctrine may force the United States, however reluctantly, in flagrant cases of such wrongdoing or impotence, to the exercise of an international police power.[11]

The Roosevelt Corollary summarizes both U.S. policy and popular attitudes. It echoed through ninety years of hemispheric history, most recently as Bill Clinton's Haitian intervention of 1994.

However, public policy often exemplifies private prejudice. This was true with Theodore Roosevelt, who while sending troops to Cuba in 1906 privately raved: "Just at the moment I am so angry with that infernal little Cuban republic that I would like to wipe its people off the face of the earth. . . . They should behave themselves." Roosevelt repeatedly scorned and jeered Latin Americans. During negotiations with Colombia he fumed: "Those contemptible little creatures in Bogotá [Colombia's elected leaders] ought to understand how much they are jeopardizing things [i.e., Roosevelt's securing a canal route in Panama]. . . . You could no more make an agreement with the Colombian rulers than you could nail currant jelly to the wall."[12]

Teddy Roosevelt's prejudices echoed in the mouths of American leaders for a century. Woodrow Wilson's Secretary of State William Jennings Bryan used racial slurs to describe Latin Americans. President Wilson himself and Secretary of State John Foster Dulles (1953–1995) viewed Latin Americans with moralistic self-righteousness born of deeply Protestant convictions. Lyndon Johnson and Richard Nixon described Latin Americans with barnyard humor and bathroom profanity. Harking back to my Costa Rican friend, only Herbert Hoover, Harry Truman, Jimmy Carter, and Bill Clinton approached Latin Americans with candor, equity, and respect.[13]

Even Latin Americans who closely identified with U.S. superiority—its generals—were taught the hard lesson of prejudice. For decades, since signing the mutual defense Rio Pact of 1947, Latin American generals were co-opted by membership in a Washington-led anticommunist crusade. But when Argentina and Great Britain fought each other during the Malvinas (Falkland) War of the 1980s, the cant of mutual defense fell prey to both Anglo-American cooperation and personal friendship between Ronald Reagan and British Prime Minister Margaret Thatcher. Rejected by the United States, Argentina's military dictators turned to the Soviet Union for satellite surveillance and logistical support. To Latin Americans in uniform—and not just Argentine generals—the lesson of the Malvinas War was obvious: despite often ardent praise, Reagan and his conservatives had other loyalties.[14]

Arrogant myopia and ignorant assumption have become commonplace U.S. biases. In the United States one still hears boastful clichés about "our backyard," "our interests over there," "our canal" (Panama), or "our sphere of influence." (Latin Americans could rightfully describe Florida, Texas, or California with similar arrogance!) In the midst of momentous debates—as during the Panama Canal treaties and the North American Free Trade Agreement—the prejudices of the generation of 1898 echo repeatedly, as if platitudes and Plattifications were universal truths. Like superficial tourists in a Mexican museum, North Americans viewing history are trained to see flattering images of self.

THE SCHOOL OF IMPERIALISM

U.S. schoolchildren are indoctrinated in imperialism. Using texts of partial fact, partial truth, and partial honesty, educators unwittingly perpetuate the shibboleths of racism, elitism, and cultural superiority. The result is a blinding self-righteousness that elevates or excuses U.S. aggression while depicting "others"—not only Hispanics but Indigens and African-Americans—as inferior or villainous.

Historically—and according to scheduled lessons—examples come early. U.S. military expeditions into Spanish Florida predate even the self-excusing Monroe Doctrine of 1823 (written by John Quincy Adams). Lamentably, Andrew Jackson's assault against Indigens and African-Americans in Spanish Florida during 1818 already followed precedents, and itself became a step toward subsequent U.S. invasions and annexations. The pattern of military violence and diplomatic intransigence was repeated with Mexico in 1848, Cuba and Spain in 1898, Panama in 1903, and many others.

Usually treated lightly, the account of Florida is first told in elementary school texts and is repeated—with greater offense against justice—into the college years. The narration in popular texts usually derives from historians' borrowing each others' accounts. But the original documentation is that of the winners, the presidents, in this case the participants: James Monroe, Andrew Jackson, and John Quincy Adams. Historians have myopically relied primarily on presidential papers to form a narration. Little is heard from other participants. By omission, we assume the legitimacy of a presidential viewpoint.

Reviewing accounts of the 1818 Florida invasion in U.S. history texts provides a lesson in imperialism. Similar investigations could be done of both school curricula and media coverage of Mexico in 1848, Cuba in 1898, Panama in 1903, Mexico in 1914, Nicaragua in the 1920s, Guatemala in 1954, Cuba in 1961, Chile in 1973, and so on. Compared with these many others, the case of Florida is simple. It should also be familiar, since it has been taught repeatedly. But here again are representative excerpts from history textbooks beginning with middle school and carrying through college. We begin with seventh grade:

> In 1818 General Andrew Jackson received orders from President Monroe to invade Florida and stop Seminole (SEM-un-nohl) Indians from raiding American soil. Spain complained about this invasion of its territory. But Secretary of State John Quincy Adams defended the action. Spain, he said, had not maintained law and order in Florida, and he argued that the United States had to do what it did.[15]

Reflect on the subtle messages of this passage before continuing with a U.S. high school text:

> The United States had long wanted all of Florida. Then in 1818, the federal government ordered General Jackson to protect southern and western settlers against Indian attacks from eastern Florida. He was told that he could follow Indian raiding parties back into Spanish Florida. Jackson—who was no Indian lover—responded to this assignment with enthusiasm. Supposedly chasing Indians, he swept across East Florida, capturing the Spanish strongholds of Pensacola and St. Marks on the way. During this campaign he executed two Englishmen who were suspected of supplying arms to the Indians. . . .
>
> The President's Cabinet was divided. Secretary of State John Quincy Adams supported the rash Jackson. But all the other Cabinet members wanted him to be censured and his acts disavowed. Adams and Jackson prevailed, and the President sent Spain an ultimatum: either control the Indians or sell Florida to the United States.
>
> The weak Spanish government, plagued by revolts in its other American colonies, had no way to control the Indians. So rather than have the United States take Florida for nothing, Spain decided to sell the land for what it could get.[16]

Again, analyze the subtle messages before moving to a college diplomacy text, first published in 1940 and the faraway best-seller for many decades:

> Spain had been forced to weaken her grip on East Florida. . . . Amelia Island, an outpost near the Georgia border which had slipped away from Spanish control, became such an intolerable nest of pirates that an expedition authorized by the Washington officials seized the islet in 1817. Far more irritating were the Indians of Florida. Joined by runaway Negroes, white renegades, and others, they periodically sallied across the international line to pillage, burn, and murder. The harboring of such a villainous lot of outcasts under the Spanish flag was a clear violation of the good-neighbor pledge embodied in the Pinckney Treaty of 1795, but Spain was admittedly powerless to control or restrain these cutthroats.[17]

Just for comparison, we turn briefly to the pages of a more recent college diplomatic history text:

> Adams, in 1818, began negotiations to obtain East Florida from Spain. The Spanish Empire was gasping its last breath in most of Latin America, but its minister to Washington, Luís de Onís y González, used every trick he knew to stall the US advance. "I have seen slippery diplomats . . . ," Adams complained, "but Onís is the first man I have ever met with who made it a point of honor to pass for more of a swindler than he was."
>
> In 1817–1818, drama in Florida radically changed the context of the Adams-Onís talks. Monroe had ordered General Andrew Jackson to the Florida border to stop attacks by the Seminole Indians on the advancing white settlements. Jackson, who was seldom moderate when dealing with Indians or the British, decided to attack the problem's root. He marched into East Florida, destroyed Indian villages, captured and promptly hanged two British citizens who he claimed were egging on the tribes against Americans, and took the region for the United States. Monroe and most of his cabinet were horrified. . . . Adams wrote a blistering public paper condemning the two victims and the Seminoles.[18]

Some of these accounts are cautious. Others raise up heroes and cast down villains. All are filled with crucial omissions. The college texts, in particular, are laded with heavily prejudicial vocabulary. All these accounts also echo fantasy themes stretching from Puritans to modern Hollywood: of Rambo-esque (or Miles Standish–esque) moral authority cutting bureaucratic corners to accomplish a supposedly civilizing mission against hostile and corrupt aliens in the wilderness. Unfortunately, each retelling builds upon previous renditions, compounding lessons of supposed good and evil, superiority and inferiority. Inherent lessons include "might makes right" and "authoritative voice": that is, whose rendition gets told. Yet—upon reflection—questions emerge. Are the Spanish and British really such fools or villains? Who is Andrew Jackson really assaulting? Why must he push deep into Florida to reach them? Are genuine settlers on uncontestable American territory really innocent victims of foreign aggressions?

The story of Andrew Jackson in Florida can be told another way. In place of using only select official records and presidential papers, this rendition emerges from oral tradition, local histories, and a comprehensive review of public documents. The painting of a different picture begins with *The Exiles of Florida, or, the Crimes Committed by Our Government against the Maroons, Who Fled from South Carolina and the Other Slave States, Seeking Protection under Spanish Laws,* the full title of a book written not by recent revisionists accused of being "politically correct" but by an Ohio congressman and abolitionist, Joshua Giddings, in 1858. (Maroons, you may recall, were ex-slaves who did not wait for white liberators: they escaped and defended themselves. Harriet Tubman was a Maroon.) From this and other sources comes the following story.[19]

Prior to 1818, U.S. cotton plantations and slavery expanded westward from the eastern seaboard and eastward from Louisiana, acquired by treaty with Napoleon in 1803. Often the occupation of Spanish land—such as pieces of the Gulf coast east of New Orleans in 1810 and 1812—was done by paid hirelings of U.S. officials who crossed the border claiming to be settlers, tore down the Spanish flag, declared their independence, and asked for annexation to the United States. President Madison issued proclamations granting their wishes, but he also falsified documents to avoid illegalities. Meanwhile, Georgia politicians representing slaveholders made treaties, many fraudulent, with Creek Indians. In the Treaty of Galphinton, for example, white commissioners met representatives from only 2 of about 100 native villages but still concluded a document declaring that all Creeks in the designated region would cede land and "restore all the negroes, horses and other property . . . to such a person as the Governor [of Georgia] shall appoint." This and other bogus treaties—one was never committed to paper—split the Creek people. Some Creeks became bounty hunters serving U.S. officials, living in American-style towns, and even owning slaves. Others—the Seminoles—withdrew and resisted. In the Creek language, *seminole* means "runaway."[20]

As early as the 1730s Seminoles and Maroons escaped to the forests and swamps of southern Georgia and Spanish Florida. Sometimes called Black Seminoles because of racial mixing, tens of thousands of independent Indigens and African-Americans created villages and towns. During four generations they farmed, fished, and raised cattle peacefully. But as cotton plantations expanded, pressure mounted for more land, more slaves, and exterminating native/Maroon sanctuaries. White and Creek bounty hunters raided Black Seminole communities. From 1800 on, U.S. forces repeatedly drove into Spanish Florida seeking to smash Black Seminole communities and enslave their inhabitants. Organized by the Spaniards into militias, the Indigens and Africans resisted and usually repulsed the attacks. During the War of 1812, Black Seminoles were armed by British agents, then an ally of Spain. One of these, Alexander Arbuthnot, was executed by Andrew Jackson during the 1818 invasion. Arbuthnot has been described as "a kindly, seventy-year-old British subject whose commercial dealings with the Indians were so scrupulously honest that his profit-minded superiors in England were annoyed with him."[21]

While John Quincy Adams negotiated to obtain Florida, Andrew Jackson invaded with 3000 soldiers. Jackson, it should be noted, was deeply involved in seizing and selling native lands. This particular invasion was more than a border skirmish: Jackson's soldiers drove deep into Spanish territory. The Spanish forts of St. Marks and Pensacola surrendered. But in the battle of Suwannee on April 19, 1818, Black Seminoles inflicted heavy casualties on Jackson's forces and he temporarily pulled back. Practicing "hit-and-run" tactics, local defenders quickly faded into swamps and forests. An angry Jackson retaliated with a search-and-destroy strategy that found mainly women, children, and the elderly. A descendant of the Black Seminoles, an elderly woman in 1972, recounted her family's oral history:

> Jackson get hurt at Swanee [*sic*], man, the ancestors brutalize him there. He run away, and never come back to face Blacks and Seminoles fighting shoulder-to-shoulder—black flesh touching red and brown—that kind of thing does give the white man nightmare and day-fever all at the same time. But after them Black and Seminole fighters punish Jackson good and proper, he turn on the women and children that the Seminoles did leave behind, and any of them that look like they had African blood, he carry off to sell into slavery. Oh, God! That man Jackson was cruel, eh! He makes slaves of them who was free already for two and three generation. He sell the grandchildren of former slaves to the grandchildren of former slave owners![22]

Spain was unable to resist decades of U.S. assaults. Following Napoleon's Iberian conquests, the Spanish government lay in ruins. And its new world colonies were rebelling. Often working without instructions, Spanish Minister Luís de Onís faced an intransigent John Quincy Adams, whose media propaganda defending Jackson and castigating both the Seminoles and the Spanish in Florida not only whipped public opinion into an instrument of diplomacy but fueled enduring prejudices. According to one reliable source, Onís "proved himself a dogged, skillful advocate of a hopeless cause." In 1819, Spain sold Florida to the United States.[23]

This Florida story is important. Coming early, it set precedents for later aggression and bias against Latin American lands and people. The pattern was repeated in Texas and California. Later, citizen militias known as filibusters attempted the same in Central America and the Caribbean. And early attitudes of superiority and inferiority fostered by Adams and Jackson helped shape expansionist policy in 1898. These sentiments still linger.

Imperialism is brash and overt. But defending it, accepting it, or excusing it involves twisting evasions, gross omissions, and subtle turns of logic. The annexation of Spanish Florida by the United States was probably inevitable. Even the way it was annexed may have been inescapable, given the personalities involved. Even so, such histories deserve comprehensive and forthright accounts. As Aesop knew centuries ago, the telling of a tale leads to the moral of the story.[24]

FRONTIERS OF PLACE AND PERCEPTION

A nation's frontier marks where the known ends and the unfamiliar begins; it is a boundary of self and others. In the United States, frontier was associated with wildness. (In reality, Creeks, Iroquois, Pequots, Onondagas, Cherokees, Navajos, and hundreds of native peoples already had towns and trading networks in supposed wilderness.) But for the Americans of manifest destiny, the westward course of empire was an ongoing re-creation of America: its idealized virtues, citizens, communities, and mission.

That frontier ended in 1890 when the U.S. Census Bureau declared the empty areas of America (native Americans did not count) as filled, populated. National leaders lamented the "closing of the frontier" and speculated on how the change would affect American character and fortune. But in the same decade the United States created two new frontiers. One was territorial: a new southerly frontier of colonies in Latin America and the Pacific. The other was image and imagination: mass media brought pictures of self and others to expanding urban audiences.

The war of 1898 took both frontiers abroad. Leaving the American west, the Rough Riders embarked for Cuba. Leonard Wood, who together with Theodore Roosevelt organized the brigade, went from chasing Geronimo in Arizona to fighting Spaniards in Cuba. The "wild west" psychology of supposed conflict between civilized moral authority and hostile alien anarchy followed a new generation of American "frontiersmen" to foreign wildernesses. But unlike the domestic frontier—which removed Indigens and resettled whites—the mission of the foreign frontier sought to replicate American manners among "little brown brothers" inhabiting the wilderness of alien cultures. Disregarding local dignity and thirty years of organizing their own independence, Colonel Leonard Wood wrote of Cubans in 1902: "We are dealing with a race that has been going down for a hundred years and into which we have to infuse new life, new principles and new methods of doing things. This is not the work of a day or of a year, but of a longer period." The new foreign frontier would not replicate American populations. Instead it spread American values, attempting to remake "others" into North American images of themselves.[25]

The new frontier of image and imagination derived from numerous media technologies innovated in quick succession. The rotary press facilitated both sensationalized journalism and moralizing nickel novels. New wire services carried details of distant events, with stories woven of fact and fiction. Wax cylinders and pressed disks brought faraway sounds that were replayed endlessly. Film and illumination created the preeminent image industry, soon known as "Hollywood." Radio, television, and computerized "virtual reality" programs would later add greater voice and vision to the twentieth-century revolution in programmed perception.

The cognitive impact of these innovations—particularly the motion picture, but they all reinforced one another—was nothing less than astounding. For an expanding population of urban Americans, a mediated reality daily displaced natural observation. Soon, even direct observation fell prey to preconceptions formed by previously edited and totally vicarious experience. For tourists, seeing was believing, particularly when viewing alien lands apparently confirmed what they already "learned" from films and television.

THE BLACK LEGEND, GREASERS, AND OTHER VILLAINS

The twentieth-century frontiers of place and perception built upon long-standing attitudes toward Hispanics. Great Britain's rivalry with Spain had created enduring propaganda known as *la leyenda negra* (the black legend). *La leyenda negra* was born in religious rivalries and military confrontations as old as English Protestantism and the Spanish armada. It was nurtured in competition for American colonies as Francis Drake, Henry Morgan, and Walter Raleigh—pirates on the Spanish Main—became knighted heroes in England. Rulers from Henry VIII and Elizabeth I to the Puritan Cromwell and British prime ministers opposed Spain. London publicists poured out outlandish caricatures of Spain and Spaniards, twisting evidence to fit purpose: including works by the Spanish reformer Bartolomé de Las Casas. Unfortunately, propaganda became belief.[26]

La leyenda negra depicts Hispanic civilization as authoritarian, decadent, and corrupt. Critics of Spain point to the conquest of the Americas, bullfights, and the Inquisition as examples of Spanish bigotry, cruelty, and intolerance. Whether in Iberia or the new world, Hispanics were portrayed as slovenly and dirty, morally and materially backward, and more interested in both medieval religiosity and hedonistic ostentation than hard work and progress. When England's thirteen colonies separated from Great Britain, black legend propaganda was adopted by new leaders seeking a new empire, carved from the hide of Spanish dominions. Steeped in bias, leaders from John Quincy Adams to Ross Perot have in their own ways restated the prejudices of *la leyenda negra.*[27]

During the late nineteenth century, *la leyenda negra* propaganda inflamed the

American public. "Yellow" journalists, imperialist politicians, and anti-Catholic Protestants fueled a firestorm of rumor. Fabricated exposés like *Rosamund, or the Narrative of Captivity and Sufferings by an American Female, under the Papish Priests in the Island of Cuba* and cleverly titled tales such as *Convent Life Unveiled* (also set in Cuba) were serialized in the popular press and reinforced by fake testimonials at religious revivals. Lurid tales of travesty beyond the border—complete with stories of nuns as sex slaves, sadistic Spanish officers, and innocent American maidens—satisfied voyeurs, xenophobes, and prudes: no easy task. Bombast characterized politicians, like the Kansas senator who claimed the following: "Spain has been tried and convicted in the forum of history. Her religion has been bigotry, whose sacraments have been solemnized by the faggot and the rack. Her statesmanship has been infamy; her diplomacy, hypocrisy; her wars have been massacres; her supremacy has been a blight and a curse, condemning continents to sterility, and their inhabitants to death."[28]

La leyenda negra endorsed a simplistic countermyth: *la leyenda blanca* (the white legend). *La leyenda blanca* endorsed a crusade: Anglo virtue would avenge Hispanic vice. Set in type as the war of 1898 unfolded were books carrying such titles as *America's War for Humanity,* with chapters such as "America, Cuba's Good Samaritan." For most Americans, the confrontation of 1898 was a "splendid little war": quick, effective, and cheap, but also popular and godly.[29]

With Spain vanquished, *la leyenda negra* came to characterize Latin Americans. The criteria for inferiority were both racial and cultural. During a decade marked by Jim Crow segregation, the massacre of Indigens at Wounded Knee, legalized segregation via *Plessy v. Ferguson,* and hundreds of lynchings annually, the United States invaded Latin America. Regardless of ethnicity, dark-skinned Latin Americans were commonly described with prejudice, as here demonstrated by an American businessman in Mexico: "The habits of carelessness and inexactness are characteristic of the entire race wherever found. . . . The native Latin American is lazy and filthy." The accompanying political cartoons (pp. 202–203) are visual period pieces, reflecting and endorsing racist diplomacy.[30]

Turn-of-the-century prejudice also imprinted Hollywood at birth. Powerful images on the screen created impressions lasting a lifetime, particularly when children encountered similar scoundrels, heroes, and themes in repeated films, nickel novels, radio serials, and comic books. Because Mexico was proximate to Hollywood, Mexican actors were cast as villains. The scripts were updated versions of *la leyenda negra.*

For early Hollywood, Mexicans were "greasers": poor, dirty, heartless, and lawless. The *Mexican* sources of ranch culture—guitars, campfires, roundups, rodeos, and horsemanship—were denied by an industry that favored *la leyenda blanca* cowboys: Tom Mix, Gene Autry, Hopalong Cassidy, Roy Rogers, and so on. In "greaser" films, the magic of illumination projected screen images of virginal white maidens, crisp Anglo heroes, and slovenly Mexican desperados. A short list of period films includes *The Greaser's Gauntlet* (1908), *Tony the Greaser* (1911), *The Greaser's Revenge* (1914), and *The Girl and the Greaser* (1915). Character actors like Thomas Gómez and Julio Sandoval, denied other roles, turned the sombrero and serape into symbols of malice. Mexican women were cast as treacherous seducers. Standard props for greasers—men and women—were knives. Their signature facial feature was a snarl.

Media stereotypes softened during the 1930s and 1940s, as U.S. officials courted Latin American allies. Hollywood accommodated Washington's good-neighbor policy and the desire for hemispheric defense. Negative images such as the greaser did not die, and superior North American roles remained but they were modified. In *The Man from Monterrey* (1933), actor John Wayne rewrote history as he rescued poor Mexican peasants from ruthless "greaser" landlords: the real land sharks following the Mexican-American war had been Anglos. Greasers were also recast as buffoons. The most notable was Leo Carrillo, whose intrinsic humor and acting skill created "Pancho" (patterned on Sancho Panza from *Don Quixote*) of the long-running *Cisco Kid* series. The Cisco Kid himself was a Robin Hood, a celluloid rendition of the real "Zorro" of California history and a prototype for the later Disney television series. Hollywood also created suave Latin roles, usually filled by Anglo or Italian-American actors such as Tyrone Power, Caesar Romero, or Don Ameche. Carmen Miranda became the archetypal Latin American woman: a caricature of biblical Eve outfitted with a fruity headdress. Walt Disney joined the good-neighbor crusade with his *Three Caballeros* (1945), a pioneer film combining acting with animation and showing Donald Duck being guided through Latin America by two cartoon characters: José Carioca, a Brazilian parrot, and Panchito, a Mexican roadrunner. Hollywood history raised Mexicans, in particular, to simplistic heroism. *Viva Villa,* starring Wallace Beery, was a charming but boozy portrayal of the Mexican revolutionary. *Juárez* was more accurate, and Hollywood's best effort at dignifying Latin Americans was *Viva Zapata!* with Marlon Brando and Anthony Quinn. Despite his Irish name, Quinn was a Mexican-American actor in a genuine Latin American role. But Latin Americans neither wrote scripts nor directed films. The exception was *The Pearl,* based on John Steinbeck's novel, made in the late 1940s by RKO and Emilio Fernández.[31]

The emergence of the cold war in the 1960s again saw Hollywood working for Washington. *La leyenda negra* was reworked into a modern mythology of dictators, drugs, and dupes, all requiring North American saviors. From Woody Allen's comedy *Bananas* to Oliver Stone's deadly serious *Salvador,* Latin Americans were portrayed as chaotic and clumsy. Period pieces include *The Magnificent Seven* (based on the Japanese *Seven Samurai*), its parody *Three Amigos,* Rambo-type films, *"Crocodile" Dundee 2, Scarface,* and many others. The new "greasers" were revolutionaries or drug lords. Only Americans (or Australians, another breed of Anglos) could outsmart the villains. A modern list of sincere movies about Latin America is short. It includes *The Emerald Forest, The Mission, Kiss of the Spider Woman,* and the now-classic *El Norte.* Likewise, Hollywood's quality films on U.S. Latinos are few. These include *Stand and Deliver, The Ballad of Gregorio Córtez* (and other films by Edward James Olmos), *La Bamba, The Milagro Beanfield War,* and *Mi Familia.* Very rarely, a Latin American film is allowed distribution in the United States. The most notable success was the Mexican gem *Like Water for Chocolate.* However, none of these matched the box office draw of *la leyendas: negra y blanca.* For Hollywood, the redemptive mission of 1898 continues.

Decades ago television surpassed the Bijou—and its modern successor, Cinema

JOHN BULL: "It's really most extraordinary what training will do. Why, only the other day I thought that man unable to support himself."
Fred Morgan, *Philadelphia Inquirer*, 1898.

UNCLE SAM to PORTO RICO: "And to think that bad boy came near being your brother!"
Chicago Inter Ocean, 1905.

Six—in generating modern media myths. Television's message is not so much *la leyenda negra* as *no hay leyenda:* a Hispanic legacy does not exist. Television is a poor window for seeing the real world. Viewing television, one would conclude that few Latinos live in a United States that exists in a solar orbit far removed from Latin America. On television, Hispanics have gone from initial low visibility to virtual invisibility. In the late 1990s they are reappearing, particularly in sitcoms. One study revealed that between the 1960s and 1990s, while African-American presence on television jumped from 0.5 to 17 percent, the depiction of Hispanics decreased from 3 to 1 percent. Their status also declined from the talented, prosperous, successful and respected Ricky Ricardo character of *I Love Lucy* (the world's most successful television series) to being poor or corrupt, if depicted at all. Even positive roles, such as that of Edward James Olmos on *Miami Vice,* are surrounded by crime and disorder that implicate Latin Americans.

A major problem for nonwhites in television lies with scripts. One study showed that between 1987 and 1991, only 3.9 percent of television shows were written by minorities, and very few of these were Hispanics. With 96.1 percent of all television entertainment programming written by whites, Latin American images begin with North American imaginations. During the 1980s, there were no wealthy or successful roles (other than drug traffickers) for Latin Americans on U.S. television. Latino fame still derives from greaser-type villainy. One major assessment of Hispanics on U.S. television concluded: "Sadly, the highest-profile Latino characters of the most recent television season have been Erik and Lyle Menéndez, whose trial for the confessed slaying of their parents was featured in two made-for-television movies." Television allows Latins only certain roles.[32]

Like entertainment programming, the news of Latin America on television is usually no news. Latin America is typically terra incognita to American television viewers. One study found the three major networks each giving about twenty-five minutes of news coverage *per year* to Mexico, the Latin American nation most important to the United States. Latin America becomes newsworthy only when "scripted" (i.e., stereotyped) events occur—natural or national disasters such as hurricanes and earthquakes, revolts and assassinations, economic collapse and poverty—or when a U.S. president personalizes policy issues: usually with a pet peeve about some "bad guy" in Cuba, Nicaragua, Grenada, or Panama. The most consistent message of television news is that Latin America is chaotic, tyrannical, and desperate while the United States remains a beacon of orderly freedom. Long ago television network news abandoned the logos approach of substantive analysis for ethos stories of good and evil, and the pathos of pity. Visuals and story lines of both Haitian boat people and Cuban rafters in the 1990s exemplify this process. The biblical accounts of a Latin American exodus to an American land of milk and honey were not accompanied by substantive stories analyzing the impact of U.S. economic warfare against both Haiti and Cuba: of how U.S. embargoes and boycotts (in the words of Henry Kissinger regarding Chile in the 1970s) "make the local economy scream." The plot lines of 1990s television news stories bear remarkable similarity to those of 1890s newspapers: the moralistic United States must intervene to save poor Cubans (and Haitians) from *la leyenda negra* tyrants.[33]

Even when television tries to cover an essentially logos issue regarding Latin

America—trade and a treaty—the themes of ethos and pathos emerge. The most memorable television event during the NAFTA debate was not informative analysis about Canada or Mexico, their economies and leaders, but rather Ross Perot and Al Gore arguing about Mexican latrines and political corruption on *Larry King Live.* Unfortunately, such content sells. And such programming often determines not only American awareness but momentous policy. On American television one hears only brief blips about the Colombian doctor who finally cured malaria, the Nobel Peace Prize awarded to Mayan Rigoberta Menchú, or achievement of democracy. The little news received is usually bad news. And since about two-thirds of North Americans gain their *exclusive* knowledge of political information from television, misinformation abounds. Unless viewers own satellite dishes south of Kentucky or subscribe to a Spanish-language network, regular familiarity with Latinos on television is pretty much limited to Juan Valdez, Speedy González, and Geraldo Rivera. Americans using television as their window on the world can more easily identify commercial and cartoon characters than either the president of neighboring Mexico or renowned novelists like Isabel Allende or Gabriel García Márquez. North American fantasies substitute for Latin American realities.[34]

AT HOME IN *EL NORTE*

The United States is becoming a nonwhite nation, with 29 million persons of African heritage (12 percent of its citizenry in 1990), only a few nations have larger black populations. As the twenty-first century begins, Latinos will outnumber African-Americans: then the United States will be the world's third-largest Hispanic nation, ranked below Spain and almost 100 million Mexicans. Somewhere around the year 2050 the United States will be a nation of minorities: whites will constitute less than half of the population, and one of four Americans may be Hispanic. Since white birthrates are low and Latinos have large families, such changes will occur even without immigration.[35]

Already the United States is significantly Hispanic. Visitors to Los Angeles, Miami, New York, or San Antonio see and hear plenty of evidence. Los Angeles is the Hispanic capital of the United States. However, the United States metropolis with the longest blending of Hispanics and Anglos—and a majority of Hispanics—is San Antonio, Texas. In southern Texas, Anglo and Hispanic cultures combine in the music of Tish Hinojosa and Freddy Fender and such dishes as chile con carne and nachos made with cheddar cheese: often processed cheddar cheese. Similar adaptations occur wherever Hispanics cluster (see Table 8-1). While many Latinos are urban, the most thoroughly bicultural *region* in the United States is the Rio Grande Valley of New Mexico and southern Colorado. Here Hispanics—many tracing ancestors to Spain itself—live in villages and towns. In this rural area, immigrating Anglos fill growing cities.[36]

Hispanic populations form major sectors of many states. Listed by percentage of Hispanic population, U.S. states rank as shown in Table 8-2. In New Mexico, four out of ten citizens are Hispanic. Most have a local heritage measured in hundreds of years.[37]

The ancestors of many Latinos never came to the United States. They merely

TABLE 8-1
TEN LARGEST HISPANIC METRO REGIONS IN THE UNITED STATES
Hispanic population in millions, 1990 census

Los Angeles	4.7
New York City	1.9
Miami	1.0
Chicago	0.7
Houston	0.7
Riverside/San Bernardino (Calif.)	0.7
San Antonio	0.6
Anaheim/Santa Anna (Calif.)	0.6
San Diego	0.5
El Paso	0.4

stayed where they were—scattered from Florida to California—as the United States came to them. Long before the English settled Jamestown or Plymouth, Hispanics lived in Saint Augustine, Florida, and Santa Fe, New Mexico. These residents became American citizens with the annexations of 1819 and 1848. In 1898, Puerto Ricans and Cubans became other annexed peoples—officially or informally. Everywhere "annexed" Hispanics viewed arriving "gringos" with apprehension. Fear derived from Anglo racism evident in relations with Indigens and African-Americans. In the southwest, "Mexicans" faced vigilante lynch gangs, all-white male juries, and Anglo sheriffs. There, as well as in Cuba and Puerto Rico, choice lands were occupied by the invaders, often through fraud. Other agents of discrimination were local courts, school committees, bank loan officers, election board officials, and employers. Except for New Mexico, few Hispanics in the continental United States were allowed political rights until modern times.

The annexed Hispanics preserved and adapted in *el norte.* During more than a century, Hispanics have generally kept the language, religion, cuisine, music, and dance of their Spanish, Mexican, Cuban, or Puerto Rican origins even as they learned English, played baseball, served in the military, and acquired a taste for franchise foods. In New Mexico, Hispanics build ranch-style homes using adobe blocks covered with vinyl siding. In California they introduced pizza tacos and taco pizzas. In Texas, Los Lobos play rock music with a *ranchera* beat. The connections with Mexico have been the strongest, due to numbers and proximity. From Brownsville, Texas, to San Diego, California, Mexicans and Mexican-Americans for a century easily transmitted culture both ways across an invisible border. In Cuba, Puerto Rico, Haiti, and the Dominican Republic, Latin Americans began adopting North American manners before migrating north. They learned from United States soldiers, businessmen, bureaucrats, and Protestant missionaries.

The native Hispanic population of the United States has been joined by waves of immigrants from Latin America. In the nineteenth century, workers from Mexico were recruited to build and maintain a rail network covering everything west of Chicago and New Orleans. Mexicans also herded cattle, dug and refined minerals,

TABLE 8-2
STATES: ACCORDING TO PERCENT OF HISPANIC POPULATIONS

State	Percent Hispanic	No. of Hispanics, millions
New Mexico	33.3	0.6
California	25.8	7.7
Texas	25.3	4.3
Arizona	18.9	0.7
Colorado	12.0	0.4
New York	12.3	2.2
Florida	12.4	1.6
New Jersey	9.0	0.7
Illinois	7.9	0.9

constructed cities, and irrigated the desert. While doing so, they taught Anglo-Americans ancient skills derived from Moorish, Hispanic, and indigenous legacies. Mexican vaqueros (buckaroos) also taught Hawaiians how to ride, rope, and play the guitar. Mexicans were mentors for Will Rogers and a generation of Hollywood actors. Mexico's violent revolution drove many professionals north in search of personal security and employment as engineers, journalists, and educators. But in all occupations, Mexicans and Mexican-Americans were always paid less and promoted less frequently than Anglo workers.

During the federally sponsored bracero program of World War II, farmworkers from Mexico replaced dust bowl migrants who moved into either military service or defense-related industries. Using braceros (officially or illegally) to subsidize profitable U.S. agribusiness continued after World War II. With higher personal incomes, few whites sought jobs gathering California produce or picking Pacific northwest fruit. Whole families of migrant workers were reduced to conditions of semislavery chronicled in a 1950s documentary by Edward R. Murrow (rare for television) called "Harvest of Shame." In the 1960s, migrant workers began organizing under the leadership of a modest but charismatic Mexican-American, César Chávez. The strikes, boycotts, and related campaigns of the United Farm Workers' captured the nation's attention and eventually improved working conditions for braceros, but only partly.

Meanwhile, Mexicans in *el norte* also become gardeners, nannies, and domestics. Immigration from Mexico was relatively light when Mexico prospered, as during the 1970s. But when debt-induced depression shrunk Latin American economies in the 1980s, the Mexican-United States border became the earth's busiest crossing. Walking or wading a few dozen yards still represents a dramatic change from poverty to relative prosperity as *la frontera* (the border) attracts Mexicans, Salvadorans, Guatemalans, as well as economic refugees from South America. Work in the United States represents a threefold gain in personal income for campesinos, who typically recross the border many times, earning money in *el norte* and renewing ties to families back home. Remission of *el norte* wages to poor families supplies scarce cash to debt-depressed economies. Ironically, the 1980s demonstrated "Reaganomics":

"supply-side" labor moved to the booming north. Meanwhile, the profits of U.S. agribusiness and industries, and the domestic comfort of affluent Americans, are underwritten by multitudes of laboring Latin Americans.[38]

In the mid-twentieth century, migration between south and north expanded with cheaper air travel. Cultural ties between Miami and Cuba, New York and Puerto Rico developed as the United States occupied Caribbean islands after 1898. In the 1940s and 1950s, Caribbean connections flourished, and eventually non-Hispanic Jamaicans and Haitians also joined the exodus to *el norte.*

Cubans began arriving in the United States in the nineteenth century. Even before the United States invaded their island in 1898, Cuban workers were rolling cigars in Tampa, Florida. When North American culture flooded Cuba during the decades between 1900 and 1960, Cubans flowed into the United States as informal colonials of an unofficial empire. Middle-class immigration was strongest as Cuban families sent aspiring kin to Florida, New York, or California. In the United States, Cubans typically sought education, entered entertainment careers, or promoted family businesses. Comfortable on either side of a movie camera, Desi Arnaz personified upwardly mobile Cubans equally at home on either side of the Straits of Florida. After Fidel Castro assumed control in 1959, Cuban migration became a cold war symbol, an element of U.S. propaganda. Middle-class migration remained strong, as arriving Cuban entrepreneurs and professionals stoked southern Florida's economic and cultural renaissance. Prosperous and powerful Cuban-Americans were also political, supporting the Republican campaigns of Nixon, Reagan, and the Bushes. Eventually, Cuba's poor also joined the exodus. Refugees during the Mariel exodus of 1980 and those using crude rafts in the 1990s resembled economic migrants from Mexico, coming for material gain rather than political freedom. Few professionals rode dangerous rafts. As the flood of poor immigrants crested, so did domestic opposition: from Florida taxpayers and well-heeled Cuban-Americans. In 1994, the Clinton administration reversed a cold war policy granting preferential status to Cuban immigrants. Few in the United States protested. Meanwhile, Cuban-Americans remain the most prosperous, successful, and powerful Hispanic group in the United States.

Puerto Ricans have been in New York since the 1830s. Large numbers began arriving during the 1950s, congregating first in Manhattan above East Ninety-sixth Street, creating Spanish Harlem, and then in the Bronx. After 1980, *nuevo yorqueños*—the children and grandchildren of these early migrants—began moving in larger numbers to New Jersey, Pennsylvania, upstate New York, and New England. Early flights from San Juan also brought seasonal workers to northeastern tobacco farms: many stayed in nearby cities, forming barrios from Boston to Baltimore. Of all Hispanic-Americans, Puerto Ricans have experienced the least success, despite enjoying U.S. citizenship at birth. In northeastern cities, former island peasants typically found low pay, menial work, and welfare. As with all immigrants, success depends on regional prosperity as well as personal ambition. Mexicans and Cubans arrived in "Sunbelt" areas during times of economic expansion. Puerto Ricans landed in "rust belt" areas that were experiencing deindustrialization, with consequent factory and business closings, high unemployment, and collapsing public services. As the twentieth century ends, mainland Puerto Ricans are finally progressing: they attend schools in greater numbers, organize politically, and express themselves more boldly in art, music, literature, and theater. Before his untimely death, the actor Raul Julia demonstrated how Puerto Ricans bridge two cultures: among his many roles, he was El Salvador's Archbishop Romero, the *Man of La Mancha,* and Gómez of *The Addams Family.*[39]

English-speaking black Caribbeans first arrived in the United States as slaves. They farmed Indigen lands for whites. It still happens. On southern corporate farms Jamaicans and Trinidadians harvest rice, sugar, and winter vegetables from former Seminole marshes. In the northeast, commuters living in woodland developments zip past British Caribbean field workers gathering such Indigen crops as squash, tobacco, pumpkins, and potatoes. These laborers are seasonal, living in farm barracks. But many British Caribbeans and their children are U.S. residents or citizens, some prominent professionals like the author Jamaica Kincaid, the poet Derek Walcott, and General Colin Powell. In northeastern cities Jamaicans form the largest British Caribbean communities: more Jamaicans may live in the United States than on their native island.

Other peoples also migrate north. Portuguese-speaking Brazilians and Atlantic islanders work in New England textile shops. Brazilians Carmen Miranda and Sonia Braga became prominent in Hollywood. Haitian refugees used overcrowded boats rather than an underground railway seeking freedom in *le Nord.* Dominican immigrants first cross clandestinely to Puerto Rico, then take planes to New York. Their more athletically talented countrymen enter the United States via baseball dugouts.[40]

Reviewing statistics, we see that about half the Latinos in the United States are Mexican-Americans. Puerto Ricans constitute about one-quarter of those with Latin American ancestry. The relative size of the three major U.S. Hispanic groups is shown in Table 8-3. Cuban-Americans form large communities in Florida and New York. Smaller Latino populations come from the Dominican Republic, Central and South America, and non-Hispanic places like the English Caribbean, Haiti, and Brazil. In 1990, almost one in ten Americans was Hispanic in origin.[41]

The lives of Latinos are as diverse as their ethnicity. They live in quiet New Mexican villages, modern Miami high-rises, crowded Los Angeles barrios, New York brownstones, New England mill towns, on Texas ranches, in Oregon orchards, and alongside midwestern freight yards. In *el norte,* Latin Americans form their own ethnic tapestry.

Latin Americans have contributed much to American success. Helping feed and clothe a nation (at low wages) is no small achievement. And agribusiness profits de-

TABLE 8-3
ETHNICITY OF U.S. HISPANICS

Group	Percent of Latinos	Number, millions
Mexican	52	13.5
Puerto Rican (mainland)	10	2.7
Puerto Rican (in Puerto Rico)	14	3.5
Cuban	4	1.1

pend on cheap bracero labor as produce is shipped not only to Denver or Des Moines but also to Tokyo, Taipei, and, ironically, street vendors in Latin America. U.S. military power owes much to Latin Americans, from Luís Álvarez (a Mexican-American), who coordinated atomic bomb assembly during World War II, to Latinos serving in Korea and Vietnam, to General Colin Powell (a Jamaican-American), who directed Persian Gulf operations. Hispanics also serve as governors, senators, and cabinet officials. Many Hispanics teach: the most famous is the math magician Jaime Escalante (a Bolivian-American), the real hero of the film *Stand and Deliver.* Gloria Estefan (a Cuban-American), Rubén Blades (a Panamanian-American), and Linda Ronstadt (a Mexican-American) are among many Latino singers who combine the old and new, English and Spanish. U.S. media networks such as Telemundo and Univision broadcast throughout Latin America and give U.S. Hispanics a hemispheric voice. Spanish-speaking Americans also sell U.S. cars and computers, cosmetics and clothes to a burgeoning market of almost 500 million Latin Americans.

Yet demographic change and ethnic dynamism inevitably generate resistance. The story of all hyphenated Americans—Irish, Italian, Japanese, African, and even German—testifies to earlier prejudice. Late-twentieth-century history is no different. The "English as an official language" movement is more about conformity than unity. The 1994 passage of California Proposition 187—denying undocumented workers public services—involves immediate taxation but also a historic process of assimilation. Debate surrounding these topics is usually myopic: it typically neglects considering the reasons for hemispheric poverty and wealth, the legacies of prejudice, the ironies of imperialism, and future U.S. leadership.

Meanwhile, Latinos add a Latin American touch to daily life in *el norte.* Following the first Rodney King verdict, Guatemalan vendors sold beautiful flowers on the charred streets of Los Angeles. In New York City, teachers from Peru and Ecuador spend long hours helping young students write English essays on computers. In Miami, Cuban grandmothers volunteer in public schools. And in San Antonio, restaurants serve amazing menus and margaritas.

BETTER NEIGHBORS

The "good neighbor"—the term of Herbert Hoover and a policy of Franklin Roosevelt—implies self-congratulatory moralism. However, without labels many North Americans have become better neighbors: aware and respectful of Latin Americans. As individuals and nongovernmental organizations (NGOs), these better neighbors confront a legacy of damaging policy and prejudice.

Efforts to understand and appreciate Latin America began early. In the 1820s, U.S. Minister to Mexico Joel R. Poinsett began a holiday tradition when he gave friends a plant he found there, afterward called the poinsettia. A decade later, the young American John Lloyd Stephens initiated both regional tourism and Mayan studies when he hired an artist and hacked through Honduran undergrowth to discover ancient Copán. His account became an early best-seller, and ever since millions of Americans have journeyed to Latin American pyramids and temples. Following Stephens, cooperating scholars from the United States and Latin America continued unraveling ancient mysteries: and encouraged growing North American curiosities with *National Geographic*–type articles and published works. Histories of Latin America also met a growing North American demand for romantic drama. William H. Prescott published his massive *Conquest of Mexico* and *Conquest of Peru,* in the 1840s. For over a century, these stories of Aztecs and Incas, Cortés and Pizarro mesmerized generations of North American readers.

As the twentieth century dawned, journalists stirred the North American conscience. Frequently strident and jingoist, "yellow press" publishers like Joseph Pulitzer and William Randolph Hearst championed military intervention in Cuba and Panama. But correspondents with firsthand knowledge and understanding of Latin Americans emerged with John Reed, who traveled on railway boxcars alongside Pancho Villa's troops and filed dispatches later compiled as *Insurgent Mexico.* Seeking adventure and comradeship as much as bylines and commissions, a generation of North American journalists in the 1920s and 1930s began explaining Latin Americans with insight. Carlton Beals, Anita Brenner, Ernest Gruening, Herbert Herring, and others frequently challenged U.S. policy while writing for *The Nation* and *The New Republic.* Decades later, Penny Lernoux, Lee Lockwood, Alan Riding, Alma Guillermoprieto, and many others did similar work, filing dispatches with publications such as *The Progressive, The New Yorker,* the *New York Times,* and still, *The Nation.*

Education has improved North American neighborliness. In colleges and increasingly at all school levels, students more frequently study Latin America. Herbert Eugene Bolton, a California historian of New Spain and the American southwest during the 1930s and 1940s, was a premier early educator who researched and wrote but also traveled on donkeys and descended mine shafts to gain a personal sense of other times and lives. As president of the American Historical Association, he promoted comparative study of Canada and Latin America, and took U.S. historians to their first meeting abroad, in Toronto. Bolton's personal involvement in Latin America was joined by a generation of scholars, including Frank Tannenbaum, Leslie Byrd Simpson, Vera Lee Holmes, Bailey W. Diffie, Lewis Hanke, Harriet de Onís, Charles Wagley, and many, many more. However, during the 1960s and 1970s, cold war policies and perspectives affected U.S. learning differently. The direct, subtle, and often secret funding of academic research by U.S. agencies had an effect. So did grants by private-enterprise foundations, which promoted North American values as norms for Latin American change. Neighborliness was neglected.

Today, Latin America is again becoming a popular school topic. As late as the 1960s, U.S. foreign language instruction emphasized French and Latin; Spanish was reserved for students with less academic promise. That changed as Peace Corps volunteers prepared for service, corporate representatives traveled more extensively, and Latin American authors composed exciting literature. Spanish is now introduced to students in the elementary grades. Meanwhile, elder learners—vacationers and the retired—attended language schools from Cuernavaca, Mexico, to Quito, Ecuador. Field trips and study-abroad programs also take college and high school students particularly to Mexico. As an area of study in U.S. colleges and universities, Latin America is second only to the United States itself.[42]

Despite legitimate criticisms of profiteering and pushiness, international business is the most pervasive, practical, and powerful force for cultural exchange. Commerce is a change agent transmitting ideas, information, and behavior across borders and nationalities. As North American businesses shift from extraction to marketing, new sensitivities develop. Instruction in anthropology and languages as well as marketing helps U.S. companies sell everything from toothpaste to computers. Meanwhile, Latin American trainees in American corporations gain skills ranging from English fluency to personnel management. Teams of mixed nationalities operate franchises, regional offices, and local branches. Hemispheric cooperation yields mutual profits.[43]

Technological innovations also make better neighbors. In 1926, the U.S. Army Air Corps conducted a goodwill flight through Mexico and Central America, seeking "Latin American affection and admiration." Shortly after, Charles A. Lindbergh and the *Spirit of St. Louis* went courting in Mexico. "Lucky Lindy" promoted neighborliness but also dated Anne Morrow, daughter of the U.S. ambassador. Celebrated in Mexico, Lindbergh enjoyed further Latin American hospitality in Central America and the Caribbean. Back in the United States, Lindbergh hosted Mexico's outstanding aviator, Emilio Carranza, who was officially feted after the two pilots flew wing to wing around various Washington monuments. On his return to Mexico, Carranza crashed and died during a mid-western storm. All this was chronicled by newspapers and radio, which enhanced the romance and drama of inter-American friendship. Substance as well as symbol characterized technological bonding as for decades Pan American Airlines served as the preeminent model of exotic travel and U.S. achievement. Today, flights from throughout the United States make Latin America the favorite destination of *el norte* vacationers going abroad. Other linking technologies include satellites, telephones and television, fax, and the Internet. During the twentieth century, these transportation and communication networks have created two-way streets in the hemispheric neighborhood.[44]

Art also links the Americas. Artists, writers, musicians, and singers have crossed boundaries to share sight, sound, and stories. Mutual creativity became intense during the good-neighbor era of the 1930s and 1940s. Mexico's most famous muralist, Diego Rivera, and his artist wife, Frida Kahlo, visited the United States to paint in New York, Detroit, and San Francisco. José Clemente Orozco completed murals in New Hampshire and California. These and many more Latin American painters introduced North American audiences to their region's immense energy and expressiveness. American artists responded in kind. The painter Georgia O'Keefe and photographer Ansel Adams were most prominent. They reveled in the Hispanic ambience of the American southwest, using magazines like *Life* and *Look* to reach mass audiences. In music, composer Aaron Copland wrote *El Salón México* and brought Mexican and Brazilian conductors to New York City. During the 1950s, Leonard Bernstein moved Puerto Ricans from the streets of New York to both the Broadway stage and generations of summer stock productions with *West Side Story.* Through performances and recordings, both Spaniards and Latin Americans continually bring culture to North American listeners. Great interpreters range from Andrés Segovia and Julio Iglesias to Claudio Arrau and Guiomar Novaes.

Literature is the most timeless link between north and south. John Steinbeck pioneered the connection with *Tortilla Flat* and *The Pearl,* stories involving Latinos and a Mexican parable. The Mexicans Octavio Paz and Carlos Fuentes—longtime residents of the United States—reach American readers through editorials and articles on cultural, diplomatic, and economic relations. Fuentes also created a powerful film series, *The Buried Mirror,* which explains Latin America to an American audience. Latino writers like Richard Rodríguez interpret life in *el norte* for their Anglo countrymen. More generally, Latin American authors have profited from a generation of excellent English translators and North American publishers. North American audiences can read Latin American writers in fine translations.

The most insistent effort at hemispheric neighborliness is the work of NGOs. The success of voluntary NGOs in changing not only attitudes but national policy cannot be underestimated. NGOs linking Latin Americans and U.S. citizens have proliferated and become active in recent decades. A partial list includes Oxfam America, the Sanctuary Movement of the 1980s, the American Friends Service Committee, Witness for Peace, the Maryknolls, Habitat for Humanity, Amnesty International, Americas Watch, the North American Congress on Latin America, and Trans-Africa (despite its name, deeply involved in U.S. Haitian policy). Many others exist, some affiliated with churches, many others secular but deeply ethical. NGOs staff schools and operate soup kitchens, monitor human rights abuses, and help build homes. In the process these associations introduce everyday North Americans to residents of remote villages and city barrios throughout Mexico, Central America, and the Caribbean. Picking coffee, building homes, feeding children, and learning local history in Guatemala or Nicaragua is augmented by publishing newsletters or magazines, and showing slides or videos in Minnesota or Ohio. These activities are augmented by writing editorials, hosting Latin Americans, and—if necessary—staging protests to oppose U.S. policies. NGO activity has both limited U.S. aggression in El Salvador and Nicaragua in the 1980s and promoted intervention in Haiti on behalf of democratically elected Jean-Bertrand Aristide in 1994.[45]

North American retirees also pioneer better neighborliness. While young Latin Americans journey to *el norte,* more elderly North Americans go south for retirement. Often labeled "American colonies," places like Cuernavaca and San Miguel de Allende in Mexico, and many communities in the Caribbean and Costa Rica, have been inundated with aging refugees from colder climates. American retirees want sunshine, warmth, and more buying power for monthly pensions. However, many also attend classes in language, art, local ceramics, and cuisine. These migrants are more than metaphoric neighbors.

Altogether, the most significant history of hemispheric relations has little to do with presidents and official policy. Whether it be northward migration of Latin Americans, the inexorable effects of commerce and technology, North Americans reading books and hearing music, or American volunteers helping villagers, daily life creates a more pervasive record than the annals of "official" actions.

ANOTHER BEGINNING

Periodically, the United States tries to recreate official relations with Latin America. These policy shifts carry labels like Monroe Doctrine, Roosevelt Corollary, Alliance for Progress, and Nixon doctrine. Each seems new. But they all share a presidential origin and a basic intent: keeping control.

Meanwhile, substantive changes occur without official labels. The subtle evolution of hemispheric affairs is measured in degrees, appears in seemingly separate actions, encounters sizable resistance, and is neither conscious nor consistent. One significant evolution is a redefined national security emphasizing trade and treaties, not military aid and alliances. Other trends include greater equity among neighbors, enforcement of Latin American democracy, and American adaptation of Latin American culture. Milestones in evolving relations include the Peace Corps, the Panama Canal treaties, interventions favoring self-rule rather than domination, NAFTA, and the Summit of the Americas.

The seeds of new directions were planted even as the United States extended its domain and dominion. Although the Monroe Doctrine of 1823 was unilateral, addressed only Europeans, and set precedents for hemispheric policing, it declared that the Americas shared a common identity and interests. The Pan-American Union of the late nineteenth century built on this belief by advancing hemispheric solidarity and establishing mechanisms for cooperation. Even U.S. imperialism—although violent, arrogant, and tragic—witnessed ironies. One was a professed idealism, which continually guided, excused, or haunted the subsequent actions of North American leaders. Another irony bound the destinies of invader and invaded. Wherever imperialism intruded—Mexico, Cuba, Puerto Rico, or Haiti—colonials invariably returned. One invasion usually leads to another in reverse.

Leadership has infrequently strengthened the evolutionary movement toward equitable relations. Herbert Hoover's goodwill tour of Latin America in 1928—the first ever by a U.S. president or president-elect—was a major precedent. And the subsequent good-neighbor policy, although not perfect, often seemed so when contrasted with previous and subsequent actions. As president, Harry Truman continued good neighborliness, honoring Mexico's war dead of 1848 before a monument in Chapúltepec Park, extending technological aspects of the Marshall Plan to Latin America, and hanging full-sized paintings of Miguel Hidalgo, Simón Bolívar, and José de San Martín in his executive office. The Peace Corps, conceived by Hubert Humphrey and enacted by John Kennedy, continued North American idealism. As important as these often-symbolic actions were, they still carried the "Made in USA" label. Even the human rights campaign of Jimmy Carter in the 1970s appeared as a mea culpa, an apologetic moralism. True neighborliness is based on mutuality.

The United States has increasingly moved toward mutual respect with Latin America. The Panama Canal treaties of 1978, initiated by Panamanian President Omar Torrijos, witnessed the world's superpower negotiating fairly with a former tiny colony. The treaties faced stiff and jingoistic opposition in the U.S. Senate, and, to his credit, Jimmy Carter labored hard persuading fellow citizens that continued U.S. domination was ultimately self-damaging. Mutuality was later strengthened when Mexican President Carlos Salinas de Gortari suggested to President George Bush and Canadian Prime Minister Brian Mulroney that North America become a free trade zone. Bush supported the idea; however, Democrat Bill Clinton—and Vice President Al Gore—inherited efforts to persuade a reluctant citizenry and Congress.

The Panama Canal treaties and NAFTA debates—negotiated with great difficulty, argued intensively, and passed by razor-thin margins—were major steps away from unilateral legacies of diplomatic dominance and military might. Neither treaty was perfect; such ideals do not exist in a world of compromise. But both were important tools for facing others as equals. The 1994 Summit of the Americas in Miami, a largely symbolic meeting attended by the heads of all Latin American governments (except Cuba), promised even greater hemispheric equity in trade and diplomacy. All these developments revised policies that had characterized U.S. relations from the invasions of 1898 through the cold war.[46]

Another trend of new diplomacy begun by President Jimmy Carter was respect for genuine democracy. In 1978, Carter acted quickly and decisively to assure that election results in the Dominican Republic were respected by all parties, particularly a longtime servant of U.S. interests. Facing reelection, Dominican President Joaquín Balaguer and army chums trained by the United States seized the nation's ballots when counting indicated the incumbent's defeat. Such actions historically preceded ballot box stuffing in the region. Defending the emerging results, Carter personally intervened to convince Dominican officials that they should accept the popular will. His action reversed a U.S. policy begun in 1906, when Cuba's Tomás Estrada Palma—a U.S. spokesman—"won" in a rigged election. In 1989, another electoral crisis built on Carter's precedent by using troops to enforce the popular and—in this case U.S.—will. George Bush sent the Eighty-second Airborne Division into Panama to capture General Manual Noriega—self-declared victor of a manipulated election—and administer the presidential oath to the true winner. While the episode resembled a comic but tragic opera—and was filled with irony, if not hypocrisy—it took the Carter initiative a large step beyond mere persuasion. Meanwhile, in El Salvador, Bush enlisted the United Nations to conduct fair elections, which were won by the incumbent party.

The Bush precedents of using both force and the United Nations were subsequently employed by Bill Clinton in Haiti. There, Jean-Bertrand Aristide was fairly and overwhelmingly elected during balloting supervised by the United Nations. But the theology of liberation priest served only eighteen months before being overthrown by Haiti's military. Subsequent UN and U.S. negotiations to secure Aristide's return encountered endless duplicity from island autocrats. Pressured by NGOs, a flood of Haitian boat people, and Haitian military intransigence, Clinton eventually decided to do as Bush had done in Panama: send troops. With the Eighty-second Division en route, the Haitian generals capitulated to a negotiating team headed by former President Jimmy Carter. Soon, island citizens celebrated: the return of a beloved president, the enforcement of democracy, and the arrival of U.S. soldiers. All were novel joys.

The U.S. role of democratic enforcer is problematic. But in Mexico, U.S. expectations—particularly since NAFTA—have mounted subtle but powerful pressures. Whether the presidential election of Carlos Salinas de Gortari in 1988 was stolen remains debatable. But later scrutiny by the United States, the United Nations, the world, and Mexicans themselves made the elections of 1994 the fairest in Mexico's history. Future U.S. policy and pressure in the region will depend on who governs the United States as well as particular Latin American nations. But the actions of Carter, Bush, and Clinton stand as precedents.

As the twentieth century ends, the United States faces a new century with new populations, new habits, and emerging policies. Certainly prejudice and the legacy of imperialism remain; they are dragons not yet slain. But evolution to new values is as evident as food on the table. And sitting to dine, North Americans now eat fajitas, burritos, and tacos. They may soon be drinking Corona, Dos Equis, Peñafiel, and Señorial as often as Bud, Miller, Coke, and Pepsi. North Americans already spend more on salsa than on ketchup. They listen to a different kind of salsa, as well as reggae and *rancheras.* And since Latin America is becoming more important as a market (rather than a supplier), it will inevitably be better understood as North Americans find ways to influence Latin American consumers. Inevitably, what is good for Latin Americans (rising wages and purchasing power) will be good for North Americans (larger and more lucrative export markets).

Inherent in new lifestyles are new attitudes. Someday soon U.S. television will discover growing Hispanic markets in the United States and Latin America. When that happens, this powerful engine of imaging will also reflect emerging realities. Already Latin Americans shop in Miami and San Antonio, visit medical specialists in Boston and New York, and watch hometown heroes play baseball: either in Cleveland, Toronto, and Los Angeles or on their own television sets. MTV, CNN, HBO, and ESPN are already broadcast in Spanish to all Latin America. MCI, Sprint, and AT&T have discovered the growing hemispheric phone market and compete with Latino specialty companies such as La Conexion Familiar to provide multilingual operators, direct dialing, and cheaper rates. It is both symbolic and substantive that better communications follow the cold war's end.[47]

And despite legitimate criticism of the North American Free Trade Agreement, this treaty may someday appear as a diplomatic watershed. For more than any other initiative, it approximates a true partnership. In the words of Enrique Iglesias, president of the Inter-American Development Bank, NAFTA was more than a commercial treaty: it was an *"abrazo* (an embrace), not just a handshake," the most significant American overture toward Latin America during his lifetime—far more important than Franklin Roosevelt's good-neighbor policy or John F. Kennedy's Alliance for Progress. Iglesias reflects the perspective of many Latin Americans, adding, "We now become partners in a joint venture."[48]

In a sense, NAFTA symbolizes the cold war's end. It also marks the return of the United States to forgotten priorities. After Pearl Harbor in 1941, the United States began a series of crusades that turned its attention to Berlin and Tokyo, Seoul and Hanoi. After winning World War II and spending decades trying to "contain" communism, *el norte* is returning to more immediate tasks: being a better neighbor.

SUGGESTED READINGS

Black, George. *The Good Neighbor: How the United States Wrote the History of Central America and the Caribbean.* New York: Pantheon, 1988.

Coatsworth, John H., and Carlos Rico. *Images of Mexico in the United States.* San Diego: Center for United States–Mexican Studies, University of California at San Diego, 1989.

Dorfman, Ariel. *The Empire's Old Clothes: What the Lone Ranger, Babar, and Other Innocent Heroes Do to Our Minds.* New York: Pantheon, 1983.
Gann, L. H., and Peter J. Duignan. *Hispanics in the United States: A History.* Stanford, Calif.: Hoover Institute on War, Revolution and Peace; Boulder, Colo.: Westview Press, 1986.
Gibson, Charles, ed. *The Black Legend: Anti-Spanish Attitudes in the Old World and the New.* New York: Knopf, 1971.
Johnson, John J. *Latin America in Caricature.* Austin: University of Texas Press, 1980.
Karnes, Thomas L., ed. *Readings in the Latin American Policy of the United States.* Tucson: University of Arizona Press, 1972.
Knouse, Stephen B., Paul Rosenfeld, and Amy Culbertson. *Hispanics in the Workplace.* Newbury Park, Calif.: Sage, 1992.
Langley, Lester D. *The Banana Wars: United States Intervention in the Caribbean, 1898–1934.* Lexington: University of Kentucky Press, 1983.
Lowenthal, Abraham F. *Partners in Conflict: The United States and Latin America.* Baltimore: Johns Hopkins University Press, 1987.
Meier, Matt S., and Feliciano Ribera. *Mexican Americans/American Mexicans: From Conquistadors to Chicanos.* New York: Hill and Wang, 1993.
Novas, Himilce. *Everything You Need to Know about Latino History.* New York: Penguin, 1994.
Pike, Frederick B. *The United States and Latin America: Myths and Stereotypes of Civilization and Nature.* Austin: University of Texas Press, 1992.
Powell, Philip Wayne. *Tree of Hate: Propaganda and Prejudices Affecting United States Relations with the Hispanic World.* New York: Basic Books, 1971.
Villaseñor, Victor. *Rain of Gold.* Houston: Arte Publico Press, 1991.
Weyr, Thomas. *Hispanic U.S.A.: Breaking the Melting Pot.* New York: Harper and Row, 1988.

9

AUTHORITARIAN LEGACIES, DEMOCRATIC ACHIEVEMENTS

This country does not obey the law, it obeys authority.

Mexican businessman and politician[1]

Remove justice, and what are kingdoms but bands of criminals. . . .

Bartolomé de Las Casas, quoting St. Augustine's *City of God*[2]

Soldiers, priests, and bureaucrats laid the foundations of modern Latin American politics as they competed for power during the sixteenth century. All were men. And they began two dominating legacies: military rule and oligarchy (government by the few). In the 1980s, generals ruled almost everywhere.

But during the last two centuries, Latin American citizens have challenged militarism and elitism. During the Enlightenment and independence, Latin American rationalists and idealists strove to achieve dreams of republican government. After initial success, they suffered devastating reverses. During the late nineteenth century, growing industrialism laid the socioeconomic foundations for modern democracy: constitutional rule, middle-class values, and working-class participation. In the twentieth century, this broad movement toward democracy fell prey to militarism, elitism, and a U.S. imperialism preoccupied with hemispheric security. But democratic forces emerged once again. In the 1990s, elected civilians ruled almost everywhere.

While the drama of Latin American politics is filled with despots, democrats, and dramatic reverses, underlying forces write many of the actors' scripts. Comprehending either authoritarians or democrats requires being familiar with socioeconomic dynamics as well as individual resolve. But understanding politics abroad—or at home—is always difficult.

Political misunderstandings arise from faulty, incomplete, and stereotypical stories in the news or schools. For example, media accounts of Haitian boat people and Cuban rafters focused on dramatic pathos, giving viewers and readers painful pictures and tragic testimonies. Pointing fingers at supposed tyrants, such media coverage typically neglected complex background discussions of what causes poor people to migrate: issues like market structures, income levels, debt and interest payments, and such U.S. policies as selling arms, training armies, and imposing embargoes. U.S. news coverage of Latin America creates programmed attitudes: Latin American "news" is usually limited to rebellion, dictatorship, corruption, and chaos. Coverage of ongoing "process" is neglected. Lacking information, the North American public gains little understanding of Latin America's citizen interest groups, candidate campaigns, judicial decisions, and daily democracy.

In addition to receiving incomplete and misleading news, many North Americans superficially contrast Latin American and U.S. political cultures. Unconscious balance scales—loaded with personal assumptions—measure us and them, good and evil, order against chaos, better versus worse. And new information about Latin America is typically measured against North American ideals, not realities. A gut-level pride in American politics—despite its many flaws—derives from nationalistic texts, idealistic teachers, nostalgic elders, ethnocentric journalists, principled preachers, hygienic candidates, eulogizing officials, and a citizen's strong personal desire to believe and belong. Suppositions regarding American order, fortune, and righteousness seem all the more justified when one notices little about Latin America except chaos, tyranny, and corruption.[3]

Hopefully, an analysis of Latin American politics will dispel stereotypes. As we proceed, realize that governing is more an account of power and process than ethics: judging leaders as "good" or "bad" may simplify labeling, but it often obscures understanding reality. Realize also that no leader or government is perfect. Politicians must compromise to survive. Institutions are edifices with flaws as well as grandeur. We all live in a world painted gray. Even the "land of the free and the home of the brave" is not a pure fountain of justice, liberty, and democracy from which others must drink. Each society copes with its own conflicting values, opposing policies, and internal dynamics. And struggles to achieve ideals are endless.

POLITICS OVER HALF A MILLENNIUM

During *la conquista,* opportunistic Iberian soldiers gathered around charismatic officers as they defeated Indigens. Factors like European disease, technology, religion, and imperialism made the contest a foregone conclusion. But warfare—among Spaniards more than between natives and invaders—created a macho political legacy filled with personal ambition, group loyalties, shifting alliances, and psychological as well as physical coercion.

Yet the politics of military might was quickly replaced by the authority of absolute right. Soldiers—and all subjects—eventually submitted to king and God, or at least their bureaucratic and clerical representatives. Colonial institutions such as the church, viceroys (vice kings), royal governors, and ruling councils dominated colonial politics for almost three centuries. Royal edict, aristocratic ascription, and Christian orthodoxy restrained ambitious soldiers seeking to escape low-class status via sometimes audacious adventures. Institutions dominated individuals.

Conquest and colony created the legacies of Latin American politics. The first brief period was militaristic and personalistic. The subsequent long era of imperial domination was oligarchic and institutional. Chaos and rapid change were replaced by order and enduring stability. But both legacies were authoritarian: one individualistic, the other institutional.

The nineteenth century replicated this cycle over a shorter time span. In Spanish America, independence brought violent militarism as criollos rebelling against *peninsulares* were joined by slaves and mestizos in a grand tumult. Home rule quickly degenerated into furious arguments over who should rule at home. Armed men—charismatic warlords called caudillos (commanders or military chiefs)—filled the void of imperial authority with personal ambition. Until midcentury, competing caudillos subjected young nations to uprisings, guerrilla warfare, and dictatorships. Meanwhile, in Brazil, independence happened almost peacefully when a prince refused to follow his regal father back to Europe. In 1821, Pedro I remained in South America and became the Brazilian emperor.[4]

Eventually, the industrial transformation brought orderly change to Latin American politics as provincial caudillos fell before national elites armed with the centralizing powers of railroads, telegraphs, barbed wire, and banks. Generally, governments during the late nineteenth century were constitutional and representative. Presidents were regularly elected, legislatures debated, courts deliberated, and both peace and progress were rarely disturbed. However, democracy did not spring full-blown from this order and progress. Instead, oligarchies ruled: power was limited to those who protected their economic and political prerogatives. Pressures did build for greater popular participation: middle-class parties formed, labor unions organized, journalists campaigned, and the disenfranchised used strikes, marches, and elections to advance meaningful democracy. And some oligarchs were themselves intelligent agents of political and social reform.

For Latin Americans, the twentieth century has been a struggle between despotism and democracy. During the early decades, strikes, protests, and organizing by the disenfranchised encountered more repression than reward. And democratic leaders were sometimes co-opted by oligarchies. In Mexico pressures for effective suffrage brought a bloody revolution that began in 1910 and lasted for a generation. Then, during the great depression of the 1930s, all social classes throughout Latin America clamored for dramatic solutions to economic and political collapse. New authoritarians arose, combining personalism and populism with constitutionalism and progress. During a time when both international fascism and communism held appeal, charismatic leaders—many in uniform—fostered both nationalism and socialism to elicit mass support. From the 1930s even into the 1970s, populist movements seeking economic justice and political power gained strength. Many were headed by popular autocratic rulers, like Juan Domingo Perón—aided by his charismatic wife Eva Duarte de Perón—in Argentina. Established elites felt threatened by authoritarian populism. So did U.S. interests. Even before Fidel Castro's revolution in Cuba, Latin American oligarchies and U.S. policy makers began seeing "red" in regional populist movements.

Pushing its national security doctrine, United States cold warriors allied themselves with Latin American authoritarians—both local oligarchies and military officers. Hemispheric defense pacts, U.S. training missions, and politicized foreign aid created a new kind of praetorian. These were not personalistic and nationalistic caudillos so much as nameless bureaucrats implementing institutionalized anticommunism. Military agencies more than charismatic individuals stood guard against change. From the 1960s into the 1980s, military regimes—headed as often by juntas (committees) as by a singular general or colonel—imprisoned labor union leaders, "disappeared" activist citizens, banned opposition parties, and curtailed populist reforms. Voices for political democracy as well as economic justice were stifled in the name of anticommunism. Encouraged by such national security sovereigns as Kennedy, Johnson, Nixon, Kissinger, and Reagan, Latin America increasingly became a U.S. version of Soviet-dominated eastern Europe: local "apparatchiks" (apparatus people) did the ideological bidding of distant masters.

In the midst of repression, grassroots democratic movements emerged. Driven to mere subsistence, the very poor—often with middle-class assistance—organized self-help programs. The need to operate soup kitchens, cooperatives, and literacy sessions taught poor people how to organize and lead. It also taught resourcefulness. Catholic liberationists empowered the poor by fostering *basismo* (base communities). Relatives of repression's victims—the mothers and grandmothers of *desaparecidos* (citizens "disappeared" by military death squads)—held public vigils, courageously and repeatedly facing heavily armed security forces. Coalitions developed among clergy, labor leaders, lawyers, environmentalists, artists, authors, and even businessmen. These civil leaders were angered by the ecological devastation, the public corruption, the political repression, and the increasing ineptitude of military governments. Cries against human rights abuses also arose from international allies: journalists, clerics, humanitarians, and rock singers. Eventually, even the U.S. State Department of Jimmy Carter began to oppose Latin American militarists.

Meanwhile, economics, diplomacy, and, ironically, *war* removed powerful props supporting repressive regimes. During the debt-ridden 1980s, military rulers lost legitimacy as their national economies stagnated. Argentina's military government virtually collapsed in the aftermath of its failed Malvinas (Falkland) War. And with the cold war's end and U.S. congressional budget cutting, Washington's support of anticommunism declined. The world movement toward economic free markets also carried a corollary of encouraging politically free societies. Meanwhile, the United Nations assumed a greater role in promoting both peace and democracy. With all these changes, repressive regimes withered.

As the twentieth century ends, civilians govern virtually everywhere in Latin America. The death squads and secret torture chambers are gone. The military is in its barracks. Elections are honest, open, and hotly contested by multiple parties. Elected officials are scrutinized by increasingly viable opponents, an often-critical media, religious leaders, human rights activists, and neighborhood associations. In Venezuela and Brazil, corrupt presidents and congressmen have been impeached and removed. In Colombia and Mexico, chief executives have been investigated, and their intimate associates and family members indicted and arrested. Corruption exists, but democratic institutions are strengthened each time it is exposed. Emboldened, citizen advocacy groups from Mexico to Chile petition in capital plazas and march on city boulevards. They also lobby and litigate for electoral openness, judicial justice, and a modern legislative agenda that includes the environment, the handicapped, campesino rights, Indigen claims, open dialogue, better representation, and political accountability. As both process and product, democracy is growing stronger in Latin America.

However, ancient legacies endure. The specter of military intervention is never distant. Entrenched political mafias and vested interests resist displacement. And dreams of hierarchical rule still seduce both elected officials and privileged classes. Despite Latin America's democratic achievements, authoritarian legacies linger.

THE LEGACY OF CONQUEST: MILITARY FORCE IN POLITICS

Armed men from Iberia began the modern era of Latin American politics. As during the Christian reconquest of Spain, soldiers created sovereignty: territories seized by armies evolved first into colonies and then nations. Later militarists would argue that since the army "made" the nation, soldiers could intervene in politics to "save" it: brushing aside constitutions as pieces of paper written by lawyers and removing elected officials debunked as demagogues. For military officers, "protecting the nation" has often justified overthrowing constitutional governments.

Conquest wrote the first violent chapters of modern Latin American politics. The conquistadores were intensely competitive men who employed bravado, machismo, Machiavellian maneuvers, supple loyalties, intense rivalries, threats, and violence.

The soldiers and officers of Iberia were not colonists arriving to clear forests, plant crops, or begin businesses. As conquerors they wanted estates, tribute, personal service, and the political power to secure these privileges.

The Spain of 1492 was a warrior society honed on 700 years of armed struggle. The lure of leaders, the loyalty of the led, and the prospects of victory worked like glue as aspiring soldiers followed inspiring officers. Idealism and self-interest became dual sides of the military persona. Both are evident in Spain's national hero, El Cid, who fought for god and country but also for high-paying lords, monarchs, clerics, and even Islamic princes. He won great fame and honor but also much wealth and territory. The schizoid goals of military honor and personal reward are also explored in the great national novel of Spain, *Don Quixote de la Mancha,* which details the idealistic knight Don Quixote but also his hedonistic squire, Sancho Panza. In the long history of Latin America, many Cids, Quixotes, and Panzas have served higher missions—and also themselves.[5]

The means to metamorphose from lowly soldier to godly ruler has been *poder,* a wonderful Spanish word meaning more than its simple English equivalent. As a verb it translates as "to be able to." As a noun *poder* means "power." Thus, *poder* is both means and end. *Poder* achieved by sword, gun, mounted followers, or modern tanks grants authority, the right to command. Military *poder* has long been shrouded in spiritual righteousness. Modern coups are usually accompanied by pious claims: to guard the sacredness of family, to protect western civilization, or to save the nation (from the left, unscrupulous politicians, or chaos—).

The mystical calling of taking up arms to save the state is an ancient device derived from *la reconquista.* As a homegrown holy war, the reconquest brought monks and soldiers together: one prayed for victory while the other fought for salvation. In some early century, the roles were joined in the character of Santiago, Spain's patron saint, both apostle and soldier. But the role of holy warrior was more than a symbol, for clans of soldier-monks evolved. These *hermandades* (from *hermano,* or "brother," hence, a "brotherhood") also joined mentalities: soldier-saints opposed the infidel with might and right. Known in medieval times as the Knights of Santiago, Calatrava, or Alcántara, each *hermandad* developed unique traditions, symbols, rituals, and leadership. Belonging to a religious-military brotherhood was like being a member of a clan or militia: it imparted a sense of place and primary loyalty; it raised the individual to a higher purpose. *Hermandades* also sought rewards for serving church and state. Payback—sometimes outright blackmail—consisted of *fueros:* grants of land and captives, aristocratic titles, exemption from taxes, and trial by peers rather than civilian courts. Formal *hermandades* were not exported to the Americas, but the soldiers of Iberia did bring the psychologies of military brotherhoods. And ever since 1492, little Santiagos—self-proclaimed soldier-saviors appearing as caudillos, liberation armies, "special forces," guerrilla movements, and juntas—have appeared as either individual "free lances" like El Cid or informal *hermandades.*[6]

Military clans infused with both idealism and opportunism were evident early in Latin America's political history. In Hispaniola, followers of Columbus opposed soldiers of the rebel Francisco Roldán and a third group loyal to Francisco Bobadilla, the crown's emissary. Of course, Roldán's men and Bobadilla's troops also opposed each other. Aided by the Catholic church, the crown eventually won, as authority was imposed on all contesting factions. In Mexico, ambitious conquistadores promised rewards to troops and plotted against each other. En route to Tenochtitlán, Hernán Cortés double-crossed the expedition's sponsor, Diego Velásquez, and opposed numerous rivals such as Pánfilo de Nárvaez, sent by Velásquez to capture Cortés. Cortés used lies, bribery, bluster, charm, and force to win allies and defeat opponents. After gaining Mexico, he struggled against a succession of plotters, eventually losing authority to crown officials before returning embittered to Spain. In Panama, Colombia, Paraguay, and elsewhere, Spain's military was political: and politics were militant. In Peru, more Iberian soldiers died fighting each other than defeating Inca armies.[7]

Key elements in these contests were ambition, greed, and jealousy. While not unique to any nation, such vices form an instructive fable told by the Spanish historian Ramón Menéndez Pidal. Menéndez Pidal's account involves three greased poles at a fair, each topped with a prize:

> The first is a French pole, and the competitor who climbs up does so amid the encouraging applause of the audience: the second is an English one, and the public watches the climber in silent rapt attention: the last is Spanish, but here the spectators yell at the man who tries to climb up and one even pulls him by the legs to prevent him from reaching the top.[8]

Like a bad dream, Menéndez Pidal's story haunted Latin America during conquest, independence, and the twentieth century. Most climbers on regional greased poles organized armed followers. The contestants have been leaders like Columbus, Cortés, Simón Bolívar, Pancho Villa, and Fidel Castro. These aspirants appear when institutional authority weakens and personal ambition dons a uniform.

Following Latin America's violent conquest, audacious soldiers were replaced by dour bureaucrats. For almost 300 years, strong institutions stabilized politics. But when royal authority ebbed after 1810, aggressive men again organized informal brotherhoods and took to arms. During the independence movements, many aspirants climbed many greased poles amidst great rancor.

Independence's first leaders were Enlightenment idealists versed in the Rights of Man and republican government. They were quickly joined by machos with more primitive instincts. Those who initially inspired revolt against European empires—Mexico's Miguel Hidalgo and José María Morelos, Haiti's Toussaint-Louverture, South America's Bolívar, José de San Martín, Bernardo O'Higgins, and the public committees of Buenos Aires—were typically Enlightenment thinkers promoting rationality and progress. However, the military struggle against Spain invited ambitious and impatient warriors who held different passions about the "laws of nature" and scorned such concepts as dividing authority or building checks and balances into constitutional government. Caudillos wanted *poder:* their own.[9]

In Mexico, the era of caudillos was a national disaster. Between 1821 and 1854, more than twenty men served as president; most were soldiers. Antonio de Santa Anna—he of Alamo fame—ruled and misruled Mexico four different times. This caudillo's emotional temperament dictated both national policy and political chronology for a generation as his many moods swung between idealism and hedonism, courage and cowardice, boredom and excitement, *luchando* and fatalism. Santa Anna alternately issued imperial decrees from the capital, hid as a recluse on his Veracruz estate, dissipated on booze and gambling, brooded in exile, or commanded the nation's forces on grand expeditions. Two foreign wars cost Santa Anna his leg and Mexico half its national domain. Rule by Santa Anna and other caudillos repeatedly drained the Mexican treasury. What began as a glittering empire in 1821 ended some thirty years later as an impoverished republic.[10]

In Argentina, Juan Manuel de Rosas was more consistent and more thoroughly despotic than Mexico's Antonio de Santa Anna. As dictator of Buenos Aires Province and much of Argentina during the 1830s and 1840s, this caudillo was lauded as "Restorer of the Laws" even though he governed with "total power . . . for as long as you think necessary." Decrying "blasphemers," he supported a Catholic hierarchy that gratefully adorned churches with images of the tyrant and taught a potent catechism condemning the caudillo's real, imagined, and improbable enemies:

From the marvelous future,
    Deliver us, O Lord!
From the Jacobin reform,
    Deliver us, O Lord!
From the suppression of the religious,
    Deliver us, O Lord!
From freedom of conscience,
    Deliver us, O Lord!
From [Bernardino] Rivadavia [a Rosas foe],
    Deliver us, O Lord![11]

(Not to be outdone, another caudillo also courted church favor, adopting a black banner inscribed with "Religion or Death.") When Rosas commanded a gaucho expedition that slaughtered 6000 Indigens and seized southern lands, his wife, Doña Encarnación, remained behind in Buenos Aires, commanding a private army of thugs and spies called the *mazorca,* meaning "ears of corn": that is, "even the corn can hear." This brotherhood dismembered opponents during the night, leaving body parts prominently scattered about neighborhoods as public warnings. Not all caudillos were as tyrannical as Rosas or as fickle as Santa Anna. Some even sought justice and enlightenment. But all were ambitious. And all used military might to enforce personal right.[12]

Halfway through the nineteenth century, caudillismo yielded to less personal and arbitrary rule. Individualistic caudillos were increasingly replaced by an elite class seeking the political stability needed for industrial expansion. From the 1850s well into the twentieth century, the building of railroads and telegraphs, processing plants and modern ports led to increased education, urbanization, and government centralization. Constitutionalism promoted structured politics, if not real democracy. The resulting era of order and progress lasted well into the twentieth century, when a series of crises—the Mexican Revolution, growing U.S. intervention, and the great depression—encouraged a new breed of authoritarian leaders.

The Mexican Revolution, beginning in 1910, repeated the worst features of Latin American militarism. When the long and stable rule of Porfirio Díaz (1870s–1911) collapsed, ambitious men sprung from every side with armed followers. Political identity derived from persons, not policy. *Maderistas* (followers of Francisco Madero) opposed *porfiristas* (those loyal to Porfirio Díaz). *Reyistas* (from Bernardo Reyes) joined forces with *huertistas* (soldiers of Victoriano Huerta) to fight *villistas* (following Pancho Villa), *carranzistas* (adherents of Venustiano Carranza) and *obregonistas* (dedicated to Álvaro Obregón). These latter eventually fell out and opposed each other. Meanwhile, *zapatistas* (peasants loyal to Emiliano Zapata) fought for land in the south. Finally, *delahuertistas* (supporters of Adolfo de la Huerta) unsuccessfully rebelled against *obregonistas,* who triumphed:—at least until their leader was assassinated in 1928. And this is only the short list of leaders seeking to climb the greased pole of Mexican politics during two decades of revolution.

Authoritarians gained power throughout Latin America during the great depression. But these depression-era leaders differed from the caudillos of a century earlier. The new breed were typically populists promising direct action to fix broken national economies and fractured politics. Some were civilians working within existing political structures. Many were soldiers who kept the trappings of constitutional government while exercising *poder* by twisting elections and the arms of both legislators and judges. Riding a wave of international fascism, many leaders of the 1930s fostered cults of personality: generating mass support with nationalistic symbols, staging elections as grand rallies, and threatening opponents with "the will of the people." Seeking to perpetuate the era of order and progress, these strongmen also pushed import substitution industrialization and state development programs: highways and hydroelectric projects, state factories, and mineral exploitation. Many also promoted schools, hospitals, labor unions, and peasant land reform. Some strongmen were charlatans, enriching themselves while impoverishing the people. Many aligned themselves with economic elites. Some were honest reformers. And along the southern flank of North America, depression-era dictators almost always aligned themselves with the economic and security interests of the United States.

NATIONAL SECURITY REGIMES

When one society tries to reform another, the result is usually a hybrid rather than a transplant. This happened with U.S. efforts to "democratize" and "professionalize" Latin America militaries. Early-twentieth-century Caribbean initiatives sought to train politically neutral police forces. However, instead of molding civil servants, Marine instructors fostered modern caudillos and *hermandades:* national police chiefs with praetorian guards who unabashedly ingratiated themselves with gringos through naming boulevards after U.S. presidents, issuing postage stamps commemorating Washington officials, and even printing currency with images of U.S. ambassadors. As in earlier times, distant sovereigns granted *fueros* to local chieftains securing the frontiers of empire. Twentieth-century privileges included tanks and airplanes, training at U.S. military bases, lucrative business connections, and foreign aid. Meanwhile, the Caribbean and Central American despots crushed democratic labor union leaders, student movements, independent newspapers, and progressive professionals. Many Latin Americans seeking democracy in their nations died in torture chambers, were assassinated, or mysteriously disappeared—even from the supposed safety of North American exile. Wincing U.S. officials dismissed oppression by the Somozas in Nicaragua, the Duvaliers in Haiti, Machado and Batista in Cuba, Trujillo in the Dominican Republic, Ubico in Guatemala, and so on.[13]

From the late 1940s into the 1960s, populism and reform gained strength in Latin America. Strikes, boycotts, marches, and support from reformist military officers often drove dictators into exile. When civilian movements failed, reformers sometimes went into the hills, creating informal brotherhoods—guerrilla movements—usually around charismatic individuals. In the 1950s, Fidel Castro began his political career as a lawyer defending the poor and eventually organized an armed insurrection to forcefully change a corrupt and oppressive government. He was following another Latin American legacy: political action by guerrilla movement.

Guerrillas (from *guerra,* meaning "war": hence, a "little war" or civilian revolt) have long infused Latin America's military legacy. Indigen rebellions challenged colonial authority, and popular revolts marked independence. The twentieth century witnessed many guerrilla movements: from Emiliano Zapata leading Mexican campesinos in 1909 to rebellious Mayan peasants in Chiapas calling themselves *zapatistas* in 1994. Among the more persistent twentieth-century guerrilla leaders was Augusto César Sandino of Nicaragua, who during the 1920s and 1930s fought U.S. Marines in an eerie precursor to the Vietnam War. The guerrilla chief withstood all the United States could muster, including counterinsurgency strategies and state-of-the-art military technologies. After the Marines withdrew, Sandino was assassinated during peace negotiations with U.S.-trained Anastasio Somoza, a local police chief. In Nicaragua—and increasingly elsewhere—U.S. policy was achieved not through direct military intervention but by relying on surrogates.

Fear of losing control drove U.S. policy makers ever closer to Latin American elites and armies. The approach became policy following the success of Fidel Castro in 1959. Initially, the United States encouraged "controlled" change, that is, U.S.-controlled change, such as the Alliance for Progress, which was civilian and economic. But soon all change was suspect as U.S. assistance became militarized. Latin American armies were lavished with U.S. funds, equipment, and training. Presidents Kennedy, Johnson, Nixon, and Reagan each promoted different military projects. Monies for alleviating poverty evaporated. J.F.K. liked elite "special forces" counterinsurgency units designed to gather intelligence: they invariably tortured and established state terrorism. L.B.J. and Nixon felt more comfortable with U.S.-trained generals as chief executives. Reagan lavished mercenaries in Central America. Latin American democracy was the region's greatest victim as U.S. presidents elevated national security into doctrine.[14]

During the cold war, U.S. support for Latin American authoritarians generally changed from backing personalistic despots to strengthening institutional repression.

Promoted by both Democratic and Republican administrations, the national security doctrine dominated U.S. Latin American policy from the 1960s through the 1980s. Its tenets were simple: (1) train Latin American armies to defeat guerrilla and popular political movements; (2) encourage military officers to assume civilian tasks such as administering economic development, transportation, and energy; (3) encourage foreign investment in Latin America; and (4) massively fund military assistance that links Latin American armies to North American command networks. U.S. cold warriors wanted professional, service-oriented armies in Latin America. What they got were armed brotherhoods, modern *hermandades.* Brazil and El Salvador show how Iberian legacies adapted Yankee reforms.

The officers who overthrew Brazil's civilian government in 1964 were a brotherhood united by mutual experience and North American tutelage. The generals leading this *golpe de estado* (blow to the state) were veterans of World War II. They had served with the U.S. Army in Italy, becoming lifelong pals with each other and with certain North American officers. During the 1950s and early 1960s—as Brazil's populist governments encouraged greater democracy—the generals grew apprehensive over labor strikes and peasant organizing. The triumvirate of oligarch, officer, and U.S. official saw "red" whenever reform became meaningful. To defend themselves against potential right-wing coups, Brazil's civilian leaders sent conservative generals to "safe" posts: military academies instead of urban barracks. In schools they organized lectures and commanded soldiers holding pens and pencils rather than guns and truncheons. But exile to the classrooms allowed conservative officers to share plans—and also to socialize with old U.S. friends, visiting instructors preaching the national security doctrine. And their pupils eventually advanced in the ranks of Brazil's armed forces. United by philosophy, experience, apprehension, and duty (i.e., saving the nation from a "flawed" constitution and "irresponsible" politicians), the generals acted. The 1964 Brazilian *golpe de estado* was planned in both Brazil and Washington, and was fully supported by the United States. It unabashedly carried the code name "Operation Brother Sam," acknowledging the U.S. role. As tanks and airplanes secured Brazil's major cities, Congress was suspended, the populist president exiled, union leaders arrested, political parties outlawed, judges dismissed, newspapers censored, and democracy destroyed. From 1964 well into the 1980s, the military ruled Brazil through a council of generals that served as the nation's supreme governing power. When Congress, courts, and newspapers reopened, they all endorsed military policies. In Brazil, a professionally trained military imposed institutional repression.[15]

The blending of U.S. assistance and Iberian military legacy in El Salvador is slightly different. Here a brotherhood formed around a graduating class of the military academy known as *la tandona* (the rotation): the class of 1966. The officers of that year achieved identity amid the sudden arrival of U.S. money, instruction, and attention. During the next two decades, more than $5 billion in U.S. military funding flowed through *la tandona* hands: warfare was tragic El Salvador's only growth industry. The aid was more than spiffy uniforms, polished boots, and sophisticated guns, as Salvadoran troops trained at U.S. bases, officers were entertained during lavish Washington ceremonies, and commanders visited Vietnam as VIP guests. *La tandona* specialized in domestic security, counterinsurgency, intelligence, and interrogation. Its area of expertise was state terrorism.[16]

For more than a generation, *la tandona* intimidated the army, presidents, branches of government, and the nation itself. Defended by personal contacts in the United States, members of the brotherhood of 1966 created private units loyal to individual commanders. Many different "death squads" seized, tortured, and executed a growing list of victims, including tens of thousands of journalists, teachers, students, campesinos, politicians, union organizers, nuns, and priests. Some of these victims were visitors from the United States; others were Europeans and Canadians. The most famous death squad victim was Archbishop Oscar Romero, leader of the Catholic church in El Salvador, who challenged *la tandona* authority by asking troops to obey God, not their bloody commanders. Celebrating mass the next morning, Romero was assassinated by an "off-duty" officer loyal to his own god: *la tandona.*[17]

As the twentieth century ends, Latin American militaries have returned to their barracks. We shall soon see how this remarkable change occurred. Yet, like a potent brew, the elixir of military rule remains a powerful tonic. Ancient machismo has been its closest friend as for centuries the supreme test of male courage was combat: a contest between enemies, a dance with death, a challenge against destiny like matadors fighting the bull. Battle was the most intense adventure, the best *lucha.* Inspired by crusading idealism, dreams of enrichment, or simply military orders, soldiers acted. Troops also formed inner worlds of barracks and battle. In a society that reveres and replicates family, military brotherhoods became sources of inner-world esteem, support, and identity. They provided amigos, fatherly authority, and personal connections. *Fueros* for victory came as land, servants, and wealth but most importantly as *poder.*

Military brotherhoods extend beyond formal armies to guerrilla movements, which increasingly include women. In Cuba, El Salvador, Peru, Nicaragua, and Chiapas, revolutionaries with characteristic beards or ski masks employ distinctive clothing, songs, slogans, and behavior. They are brother- and sisterhoods of Fidelistas, Sandinistas, *senderos,* or just compañeros (comrades).

Military rule has also intoxicated civilians: elites defending privilege, but also reformers seeking change. Since constitutions are cumbersome, democracy contentious, and social change threatening, the quest for authority during political crisis or economic collapse is a mystical belief that military strongmen can get things done efficiently and effectively. For these reasons generals in uniform—or guerrillas in fatigues—seem effective. Swords, guns, men on horseback, tanks, armed helicopters, and death squads command obedience. But so do effective political institutions.

THE ELITIST LEGACY: AUTHORITARIAN RULE

Latin America's first politicians were soldiers who debated strategy, formed alliances, and planned policy around conquest campfires. But this brief and intense struggle for *poder* quickly yielded to long-term institutional stability. During 300 years, Iberian monarchs ruled America through bureaucratic structures laced with despotism but also benevolence and, occasionally, enlightenment. And during Iberian colonialism—lasting almost twice as long as British rule in the future United States (1492–1821 versus 1607–1776, or 329 versus 169 years)—Latin America was tutored in oligarchy, rule by a relative few.

Despite modern headlines and sound bites of coups and revolts—or textbook attention to wars and revolution—the political norm in Latin America has been stable institutional rule. The legacy of authoritarian order began with Indigens, whose hierarchical politics reflected the architecture of sacred pyramids. Inca, Aztec, and sedentary societies saw monarchs ruling succeeding layers of noblemen, bureaucrats, priests, commoners, and slaves. Authority was inherited, often through maternal lines, or entrusted to a governing caste that chose political leaders.

After the tumult of conquest, governance returned to bureaucratic norms as the links between distant kings and American subjects followed hierarchical patterns. In Spain, decisions on policy and personnel were made by the king and the Council of the Indies, an appointive body sitting in Seville and charged with administering far-flung colonies. Viceroys (vice kings) were sent to the Americas—Mexico City and Lima were later joined by Bogotá and Buenos Aires as viceroyalties—to govern with the assistance of local councils called *audiencias,* which acted as courts and governed in the absence or death of a viceroy. Smaller provinces such as Guatemala and Chile had appointed governors. Lesser officials (*corregidor,* alcalde, *regidor,* and intendant) occupied the bottom of the political pyramid and managed local tasks such as Indigen affairs, commercial regulations, crime, and taxes. *Cabildos* were city councils, composed mainly of large landowners or prominent townsmen. Almost always, these many officials were *peninsulares.*

Despite stereotypes of despotism and dictatorship, even authoritarian governments are political. The powerful must also wheel and deal, make compromises, and meet certain expectations to keep their legitimacy. The greatest limits to despotism in colonial America were distance and time. Long travel for officials and endless delays for instructions meant centralized authority waned as power extended across the Atlantic and throughout new world landscapes. In the Americas, viceregal sovereignty often seemed more pomp than power as an endless parade of executives typically governed for about four years each, barely time to master the position. As decades passed, each new viceroy faced ever stronger local interests who used inertia, status, and familiarity as political weapons. Arriving in Mexico City or Peru as outsiders, most viceroys were guided by staff secretaries or the local *audiencia.* Except during the early and late decades of empire, viceroys were actually weak figures. Many bought their office and considered tenure a time for payback. Self-enrichment helped the family, friends, and clients of appointed officials, including merchant guilds, which initially paid "dowries" to get their candidate appointed. Knowing the proclivity for corruption, local interests paid bribes to keep their local privileges.[18]

With generally weak or symbolic viceroys, actual authority devolved to the bureaucracy, other institutions, and vested interests: typically landed classes, merchant monopolies, and clerics. All government has an immediate face, and even imperial rule most affected its subjects as petty bureaucrats executing local policies in barrios, towns, or countrysides. Officials such as the *corregidor,* alcalde, *regidor,* and intendant managed local market prices, tax payments, Indigen *repartimientos,* neighborhood land disputes, and so on. Living among those they governed, local bureaucrats were chin deep in politics: open to influence, patronage, and spoils. The old Spanish adage *obedezco pero no cumplo* (I obey but do not comply) acknowledged a compromise between duty and reward: a blend of ideal and actual. Colonial government was despotic but also pragmatic. It balanced many local interests and the goals of distant imperialists.

The Catholic church was another authoritarian institution. Here the realms of man and God were joined as the *patronato real* (royal patronage) permitted the crown to appoint Spanish bishops and grant them civil responsibilities. The Catholic church had long been an adjunct of government: charged with political indoctrination, administering aspects of civil law, advocating for Indigen and slave policy, managing credit as well as schools, orphanages, and hospitals, and acting as both registrar of deeds and divorce court. In this hierarchical institution, authority descended from pope, to bishops, to priests. But for most citizens, the *cura* (parish priest) was the church, the local and approachable authority on morals, doctrine, and also secular sovereignty: sermons extolled the divine right of kings and obedience to crown officials. Priests were also instruments of social class dominance: they were mostly *peninsulares* justifying conquest.

Colonial society itself was an authoritarian institution. *Peninsulares* bossed criollos, and both outranked poor mestizos, Indigens, and African Latins. *Encomenderos,* plantation masters, and later *hacendados* were feudal-like lords ruling their families, workers, and local communities. In commerce, the imperial *casa de contratación* (house of trade) granted monopolies to families and companies. In virtually all aspects, colonial society was elitist. And the greatest privilege was birth. Ascription rather than achievement almost always determined rank for life.[19]

As stable as it was, the colonial era was not monolithic. Dynasties changed, and so did policies. The Hapsburgs ascended the Spanish throne in 1516 and remained until 1701. As noted by one historian, "The Hapsburgs did not, as a rule, take kindly to subordinates of the brilliant or the inventive sort. . . . The official whom they preferred was the hard working, competent, but obedient type, who would faithfully discharge the duties laid upon him and send back for fresh instructions if they had a case of doubt."[20]

The Bourbons, who ruled Spain after 1701, were different. Arriving from France with Enlightenment ideas, the Bourbons introduced progressive reforms. Carlos III (1759–1788) was easily the most pragmatic, energetic, and enlightened of all colonial monarchs. He encouraged education, scientific inquiry, more open commerce, and greater colonial participation in governance and defense. The Bourbons were benevolent and enlightened but still despotic: constitutional monarchy and representative government were still novel concepts back then.[21]

Like Indigen pyramids, colonial Latin American cities reveal past power. Looking about the central plaza of an Iberian-American city, the visitor sees authoritarian legacies cast in stone. The cathedral symbolizes ecclesiastical power, grand and elaborate. Nearby stands a governor's or viceroy's palace, representing imperial rule. Also facing the central square are the *ayuntamiento,* the seat of city government, and usually the *presidio,* the army barracks. Along side streets, never far from *poder,* are the townhouses of colonial landowners and merchants. After independence, the stone temples of colonial sovereignty were occupied by caudillos. No new monuments celebrated these ephemeral sovereigns. Instead, local chieftains appropriated cathedrals, balconies, and parade grounds as backdrops for their own noisy and gaudy investitures.[22]

Eventually, a new institutional authority called for another celebration in stone. In the late nineteenth century, foundations were laid for new structures to house legislatures, judiciaries, post offices, banks, train stations, and schools. The era of order and progress required its own temples of stone and steel—usually ornate renditions of classical senates and courts—honoring a new sovereignty equal to that of colonial imperium. Unfortunately, the monuments to constitutional rule and representative government commemorated things incomplete.[23]

During the nineteenth century, Latin American elites discussed democracy while preserving hierarchy and privilege. Talk of constitutions and republican government increasingly derived not from love of humankind and representative rule but from enthusiasm over the economic success of England and the United States. In Latin America, an emerging class of elites believed that Anglo and Anglo-American models should be emulated because imported political structures would lead to new economic wealth. However, democracy was less esteemed than Anglo ideas about racism, elitism, and industrialism. The philosophy of positivism, similar to England's Manchester liberalism, grew in vogue. Positivism held that progress enriched everyone: many a little, some moderately, and an elite few immensely. U.S. constitutionalism and a British party system seemed preludes to such economic progress.

Around the 1850s, strong elitist governments emerged in Latin America. Political and economic power increasingly became centralized and stabilized as railways, telegraphs, and barbed wire reached across countrysides. Public and semipublic institutions further linked rural people to urban leaders. National armies eliminated provincial caudillos. Arriving European and Asian immigrants without local traditions displaced or mingled with rural peoples. Formal banks began supplanting the informal, authoritarian, and personalist credit systems of bishops and landlords. And regular national elections superseded sporadic *golpes de estado.*[24]

Between 1850 and 1930, constitutional rule and regular elections characterized Latin American politics. But government was still oligarchic: representative in form, not substance. For example, in a Brazilian election held in 1881, only 2 to 4 percent of adult males voted: the national government was chosen by 142,000 persons from a population of 15 million. Everywhere, suffrage was limited by property, gender, education, and other standards. Even more restrictive was the nomination process: those with power chose candidates. Thus, national and provincial governments, legislatures and courts, army and navy commands, all resembled an interlocking corporate directorate. Descendants of colonial criollos still linked families through well-chosen marriages, amigos, and compadres. Constitutions were carefully crafted to look modern while preserving old privileges.[25]

In some places, caudillos and criollo elites cooperated. In Mexico, mestizo general and dictator Porfirio Díaz staffed his regime with *científicos,* a derisive term for "scientists" who engineered society and economics according to positivist tenets. (In the late twentieth century, *técnicos* perform similar functions for those holding "free market" philosophies.) Similar late-nineteenth-century alliances between caudillos and oligarchies dominated Nicaragua, Venezuela, and many Caribbean-area nations. These dictatorships built railroads and refineries but also wrote constitutions and held regular elections, the results of which were previously known to all.

Authoritarian rule in the guise of democracy became a political art in twentieth-century Latin America. The genre was honed to perfection by the ruling party of Mexico, today called the PRI, an acronym for Institutional Revolutionary party, or the Party of Revolutionary Institutions, or maybe Party of the Instituted Revolution. Some critics call it the Conservative party. Begun under another name in the 1920s, the PRI originated as a coalition of revolutionary factions—peasants, workers, the middle class, and the army—which arbitrated often competing goals.

During almost three-quarters of a century, PRI leaders have accomplished much. From the 1920s until the Chiapas revolt of 1994, political violence was rare in a nation repeatedly torn by nineteenth- and early-twentieth-century civil wars, rebellions, and revolutions. The PRI also ended military rule in a country plagued by *cuartelazos* (army coups) and caudillos. Great economic development occurred during much of the PRI's long tenure. And although a political instrument for a one-party state, Mexico's PRI seemed genuinely popular. However, the PRI was no democracy.

The PRI's authoritarian mechanisms were many. From the 1920s until the 1990s, it held a virtual monopoly on national and state politics, allowing no meaningful opposition. It controlled the press and media through intimidation, bribes, and indirect ownership. Its patronage system rivaled that of the Mafia. Its corporate decisions—including who should be the "official" presidential candidate every six years—have been secret. Even as politics became more competitive, the PRI exercised subtle control. In the presidential election of 1994, 43 percent of national television campaign coverage promoted the PRI candidate and only 12 percent and 11 percent centered on two major opponents. Newspapers were equally biased: 20,746 stories in major media markets favored the PRI candidate, and only 8751 and 6279 chronicled the campaigns of rivals. And as competition for internal control of the PRI raged between reformers and traditionalists, violence intensified. During the 1990s, certain PRI factions plotted against and assassinated their rivals, including the PRI candidate. For most of the twentieth century, Mexico's PRI was the most successful political organization of any Latin American nation. It was constitutional, elected, and civilian—but also authoritarian and elitist.[26]

Civilian leaders in other Latin American nations sometimes employ authoritarian and bloody methods. For decades Colombia lived with an arrangement whereby Conservative and Liberal parties traded the nation's presidency. When Colombia's leftist and reformist Patriotic Union mounted a serious third-party challenge, 2341 of its candidates were assassinated over a decade. In Peru, elected president Alberto Fujimori suspended the constitution, congress, and the courts in order to stifle opposition and push his personal agenda; opinion polls showed high approval of his authoritarian methods. Such modern examples—like those of a century earlier—show that constitutions and regular elections do not a democracy make. Yet Latin American democracy at the end of the twentieth century continues to strengthen.[27]

DEMOCRATIC ACHIEVEMENTS: SOCIAL FOUNDATIONS

Historians trace the precedents of Iberian democracy to medieval city-states. Later antecedents include citizen revolts against growing monarchical despotism in the sixteenth century. In Latin America, eighteenth-century Enlightenment ideas and ideals inspired democratic thought among many intellectuals. Despite these many precursors, the sociological foundations of modern Latin American democracy developed with the industrial transformation.

Democracies need supporting systems. Before common citizens can articulate opinions and associate with colleagues, nations need to be significantly literate, peaceful, and diverse. Constitutions, elections, and political parties are only as effective as the articulation and achievement of constituent goals.

Democracy was not an initial objective of late-nineteenth-century political leadership. Instead, it came with the baggage of economic development. As transportation networks extended into the hinterlands to extract wealth, old politics collapsed. From about 1870 until the great depression of the 1930s, Latin Americans moved steadily toward more diverse and complex societies as they became more economically developed. A middle class emerged as engineers, doctors, accountants, teachers, lawyers, nurses, journalists, secretaries, and architects built and operated more technical economic infrastructures. These many professionals also articulated their own values: education, security, health, consumerism, and so on. As economies progressed, skilled tradesmen also multiplied. Mechanics, plumbers, operators, machinists, electricians, and other technicians were trained to run and repair locomotives, trolley cars, telegraphs, refineries, water systems, and processing plants. Advocating their own values, workers formed unions that sought higher wages, job security, pensions, and safety standards. Industrialism also affected elites, who slowly came to realize that diversified investments in mines, shipping, factories, and processing plants also entailed membership in increasingly diversified societies. Rising incomes made for larger national markets: all levels of society desired modern services and more commercial goods. Politics changed, too. Each decade, more Latin Americans sought stronger voices in public decisions affecting their lives.

While many oligarchs resisted democracy, some encouraged it. As the nineteenth century progressed, dynamic criollo reformers pushed education as well as electrification—and also some amazing political changes. Argentina illustrates educational reform. In 1865, Buenos Aries Province (the most progressive in Argentina) educated only one in twenty-five school-age children. (At the time, the U.S. rate was one in three.) But Argentina moved forward when Domingo F. Sarmiento became the nation's "education president" in 1868. He invited U.S. educators to train Argentine teachers, who helped Argentines double the number of schools within six years. Libraries were built, and specialty schools trained students in technical and agricultural skills. The prime beneficiaries of these educational reforms were poor children. Similar changes occurred in Chile, Brazil, and many Latin American nations. Mass literacy as an underpinning of modern Latin American democracy began in the efforts of late-nineteenth-century reformers.[28]

Some imaginative political reforms were also begun by criollo leaders. One great change agent was José Battle y Ordóñez, son of a criollo president and himself twice president of Uruguay (1903–1907, 1911–1915). Educated abroad, Battle y Ordóñez was a lawyer, journalist, diplomat, and politician. In all these professions he championed organized labor and helped achieve a shorter workweek, the right to strike, a social security system (decades before the United States had one), and a national pension plan. Dedicated to women's rights, he instituted a national education system and secular divorce laws that afforded women greater liberties. Battle y Ordóñez also pondered how to eliminate the authoritarian legacy of personalist rule. Visiting Europe after his first presidency, he studied Switzerland's constitution, particularly its collective executive. Later, as Uruguay's president, he helped create a "collegiate" presidency, a nine-member National Council of Administration. While the subsequent political history of Uruguay did not always rise to Battle y Ordóñez's ideals, he at least confronted authoritarian legacies with creative reforms. Like many criollo thinkers across Latin America, he recognized and encouraged the social changes necessary for political democracy.

The near century of stability afforded by order and progress underwrites modern Latin American democracy. Movement away from despotism and instability is measurable and graphic. Through careful collection and display of data, scholars have projected the changing nature of Latin American politics, particularly its rates of violence and despotism versus democracy. Two charts, Levels of Instability and Levels of Authoritarianism, show these data and depict the region's uneven progress (Figure 9-1).[29]

Figure 9-1 plots information by decade, from independence to the 1970s, when the study was undertaken. "Levels of Instability" catalogs three items: coups, basic constitutional revisions, and "change of executive independent of his predecessor." The total of these changes by decade is then averaged for Spanish-American nations. For example, the 1860s depict about eight abrupt political changes per country. By the 1900s such changes per nation averaged about four. Thus, the level of instability in 1900 was half that of 1860.

"Levels of Authoritarianism" shows change more dramatically. The data total three political conditions: military rule, ineffective legislatures, and nonconstitutional government. (The worst-case scenario would be ten years of rule by a military regime that suspended the constitution and allowed only a "rubber-stamp" legislature: a 30 on the numerical scale.) The chart projects averages by decade for all Hispanic nations. Thus, in the 1840s—during the heyday of caudillismo—the typical Latin American nation (at level 13) experienced three kinds of authoritarian rule almost half the time. By the 1920s, with a numerical value of about 5, civilian, constitutional, and representative government was common.

Of course these charts show averages. Great varieties—even extremes—exist by nation. Still, patterns emerge and distinct periods can be identified: the era of caudillos, the epoch of order and progress, the great depression, a period of populism, and an interval of national security regimes. If plotted into the 1990s, the charts would

FIGURE 9-1

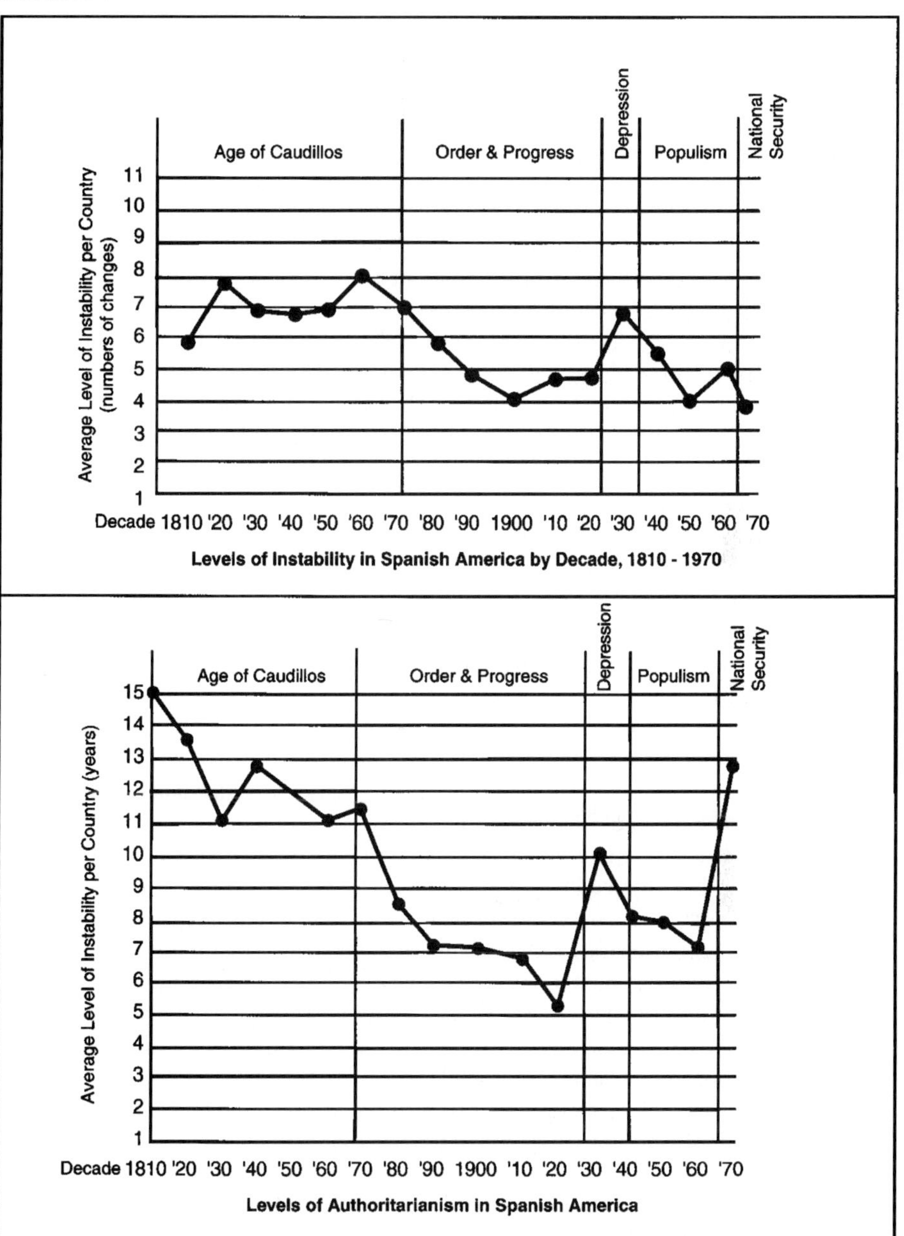

Source: David Scott Palmer, *Peru: The Authoritarian Tradition,* reprinted with permission of Greenwood Publishing Group, Inc., Westport, CT. Copyright © 1980 Praeger, Inc.

depict great stability and very little authoritarian rule. During the twentieth century, Latin America has progressed toward democracy, but as if on a roller coaster.

DEMOCRACY IN THE TWENTIETH CENTURY

During the twentieth century, democratization was shattered twice. The great depression generally ended the long era of order and progress—and civilian rule. Then, after renewal during the 1940s and into the 1960s, democracy experienced a tragic reversal. The cold war—reaching Latin America as the national security policy of the United States—promoted military dictatorships almost everywhere. But as the century ended, so did dictatorship. During the debt crisis of the 1980s, severe economic collapse—as during the depression—again destroyed incumbent governments, this time military regimes.

The achievement of Latin American democracy has not come easily in a land of warriors and oligarchs. Containing militarism was accomplished by Latin Americans themselves. And the United States, despite a civilian legacy and democratic ideology, has often supported militarism and oligarchy in Latin America.

For Mexico, the nineteenth century was mostly a chronicle of *cuartelazos* and caudillos—barrack rebellions and "warlords"—eventually controlled by the thirty-year dictatorship of General Porfirio Díaz. When the octogenarian president left for exile in 1911, he helped trigger the wildest tumult in the nation's history: the Mexican Revolution. For a decade, every political question was argued with a gun, or many guns. Competitive caudillos arose in every region. *Golpe de estado* followed *golpe* as the presidency became a deadly revolving door: for a generation, those who entered were either exiled or assassinated. In 1920, General Álvaro Obregón occupied the presidency—following his own golpe—and eventually faced a *cuartelazo* by half his army. How could such endemic violence be contained? Obregón lamented that generals could solve every national problem except militarism. But generals—and a political party created by generals—would solve even this puzzle.[30]

The overriding achievement of Mexican soldiers in the aftermath of revolution has been terminating militarism. Machiavellian strategies included carefully managed rewards and punishments, what Mexicans call *pan o palo:* bread or the stick. Obregón used bribes—and cynical humor—claiming no general could resist a *cañonazo* (cannon blast) of 50,000 pesos. Money was also spent on the professional training of loyal troops and officers. Meanwhile, proven conspirators faced summary executions and suspect officers were sent on distant missions, such as studying irrigation in Egypt. Eventually, military budgets were slowly reduced. But the keystone of civilian rule in Mexico has been the PRI. Initially, generals had a strong voice in the party, louder than spokespersons for peasants, labor unions, and the middle class. But as militarism waned, so did the political role of soldiers. Since 1946, only civilians have governed Mexico and the army has loyally obeyed elected officials. Given the politicized military and militant politics of Mexico's past, civilian rule has been a major twentieth-century accomplishment.[31]

Armed citizens defeated militarism in Costa Rica, where a ruling party nullified the results of the 1948 election after its candidate lost. When the nation's military supported this travesty, a civilian militia formed, gathered weapons, and triumphed during a brief civil war. The movement's leader, José (Pepe) Figueres, then fulfilled a radical pledge: to abolish the army. He described Costa Rica's military as a waste of money, a threat to lawful government, and about as useful as "a hole in the head." Today, Costa Rica still lacks an army. Its government builds schools and health clinics instead of barracks and arsenals. Costa Rican citizens also enjoy a high quality of life.[32]

In Venezuela, courageous students challenged caudillos and eventually achieved democracy. The nation's young democrats first emerged from classrooms in 1928 to protest Venezuela's military dictatorship. During a generation of relentless opposition, including jail and exile, Rómulo Betancourt and his colleagues struggled to promote Acción Democrática (Democratic Action), both a movement and a political party. Aided by reformist military officers, in 1945 AD overthrew a caudillo, formed a government, and instituted reforms. But granting land to peasants, repossessing foreign-owned oil fields, and restructuring the armed forces created an alliance between landlords, U.S. oil corporations, and generals. Following a military coup in 1948, AD reformers were exiled and imprisoned. For ten more years, Betancourt and his associates opposed dictatorship, this one supported by powerful U.S. officials such as Secretary of State John Foster Dulles and then Vice President Richard Nixon. After Venezuela's military regime was toppled in 1958, Betancourt was elected president. But both his government and his life were continually threatened, and photos reveal his shoulder holster revolver always ready. He faced military revolts, assassins hired by land barons, the opposition of U.S. oil companies, and threats from leftist guerrillas, who thought AD reforms too bourgeois. Tempered by thirty years of struggle, Betancourt and democracy succeeded in Venezuela. Since 1958, Venezuela has witnessed often-raucous politics but neither successful coups nor dictatorships. Meanwhile, a growing democratic legacy has included a chain of fair elections, a multiparty system, a strong legislature, a viable judiciary, free speech, and even impeachment of a corrupt president.

During recent decades, struggles against dictators have included grandmothers, campesinos, and priests as well as journalists, students, and labor leaders. In Argentina the Mothers of the Disappeared led weekly public confrontations against despots after military death squads kidnapped, tortured, and executed tens of thousands of suspected leftists, civilian critics, and even persons of mistaken identity. The *desaparecidos* (disappeared) were mostly young adults: college students, professionals, and workers. Many had families, and numerous imprisoned women who were raped gave birth before dying. Cynically and tragically, children of the disappeared were frequently distributed for adoption by the assassins who had killed their parents. Searching for the remains of executed children and also their kidnapped grandchildren, the mothers of the disappeared—typically working-class women and housewives—uncovered the horrible fates of loved ones. They also defied military authorities by marching weekly in the capital's Plaza de Mayo. For years these simple but dignified and determined mothers and grandmothers in white scarves held placards depicting lost family members and confronted police armed with riot gear, truncheons, and military vehicles. The humble women raised national consciousness by asking simple questions. How did their children die? Who was responsible? Who had their grandchildren?

The answers to these questions have been painful, for the mothers and for Argentina. In the 1980s, the weekly protests, the failed Malvinas War, and economic collapse drove the generals from government. But officers remained political. Whenever subsequent civilian governments brought indicted officers to justice, their "brothers" on active duty staged revolts. Walking a tightrope between personal justice and political survival, President Carlos Menem in 1995 chose to end the dilemma by pardoning soldiers implicated in death squads. Freed from prosecution, some remorseful officers openly confessed to heinous crimes: of drugging victims and throwing them from airplanes over the Atlantic, to torture and mass executions. Much of this testimony was given on national television. Today, the tragic deaths of civilians by military assassins remains largely unredeemed. Yet courageous mothers helped free a nation from military tyranny.[33]

Others have confronted despots. In Chile, Catholic priests and nuns opened the doors of churches and schools for the poor when dictator Augusto Pinochet denied workers the right to assemble and petition. In Brazil, labor unions defied a ban on strikes and bravely picketed. When Brazilian strikers were encircled by heavily armed soldiers and told to disperse, the soldiers, in turn, were engulfed by hundreds of thousands of citizens supporting the workers. In Guatemala, people left offices and shops to march on government buildings in 1993 when the president and his army buddies suspended courts, the congress, and civil rights. Facing a determined nation, the army and authoritarian president withdrew: the chief executive to exile and the military to its barracks. In Mexico City, throngs fill the capital's central plaza pleading for dialogue whenever the government sends soldiers to fight Mayan *zapatistas* in Chiapas. In Haiti, the people defied the colonels and death squads that overthrew elected theology of liberation president, Father Jean-Bertrand Aristide. All across Latin America, civilians have been courageous and determined as they pursue and practice democracy.

A major movement strengthening citizen advocacy in Latin America is the daily practice of "microdemocracy." Since national security regimes spent little on civilians, impoverished citizens organized themselves to provide such basic community services as education, health, and security. In Brazil, small towns and neighborhoods of large cities formed associations called Movimento de Amigos do Bairro (Friends of the Neighborhood Movement), which provide their own day care, schools, clinics, public kitchens, and transit. Middle-class professionals volunteer to teach classes and staff clinics, but the poor themselves—often poor women—develop the managerial skills needed to organize local agencies. With neither political parties nor formal elections, microdemocracy has developed into local self-government.[34]

Growing female activism facilitates Latin American democracy. An obvious but little-noted fact about militarism is that military rulers are invariably males. As long as machos command policy, such issues as child care, birth control, health clinics, and crimes against women get little attention. With more women as lawyers, journalists, engineers, doctors, judges, and politicians, both the personnel and the priorities of government are changing. Poor as well as professional women now occupy government offices, from local mayoralties to federal congresses and presidential cabinets. Women in government typically advance a more democratic agenda than do military governors. They do the same when organized as citizen advocates. One sign of democracy in action was the first international meeting of housewives, held in Buenos Aires during October 1995. Women are moving Latin America into the forefront of modern democratic reforms.[35]

Recent changes in Latin American spirituality—whether theology of liberation, *evangélicos,* or African Latin cults—encourage democracy by giving voice to the poor and adding diversity to a once-authoritarian clerical legacy. In Brazil, the Catholic theology of liberation organized 80,000 Christian-base communities, each practicing microdemocracy. Protestant grassroots churches helped elect Alberto Fujimori as president of Peru. While often arbitrary with opponents and the constitutional process, Fujimori remains popular with a large majority of Peru's poor and won reelection during a fair election in 1995. From Mexico to Chile, new religious groups add fresh and diverse voices to a democratic chorus.

Environmentalists strengthen democracy in Latin America. When the generals ruled Brazil, conquest of the Amazon resembled a military invasion. Roads and airstrips provided logistical support for beachhead clearings in the rain forest, and secured zones had their perimeters enlarged. Critics of this militarized assault against nature included ecologists, Indigen rights advocates, rubber tapper unions, and Catholic activists. Protecting the natural environment necessitated rural people's organizing to protect their lifestyles and their very lives. When these many groups discovered that the military government would not change policy, they politicked to change the government. Similar links between environmentalism and democracy exist in Mexico, Guatemala, and many other nations. In Latin America, the friends of democracy are often Green.[36]

The end of the cold war permits greater democracy. Debate and political competition are no longer reasons for ideological confrontations. During four decades beginning in the 1950s, U.S. and Latin American cold warriors saw "red" whenever Latin American social movements gained strength. The United States meddled endlessly in Latin American politics, reacting with paranoia and myopia but also great determination. In 1954 Secretary of State John Foster Dulles warred on Guatemalan reformers; John F. Kennedy created military brotherhoods to defend the status quo; in 1965 Lyndon Johnson sent Marines to intercept a popular exiled president of the Dominican Republic; in the early 1970s Richard Nixon and Henry Kissinger played endless "dirty tricks" on Chile's democratic president; and Ronald Reagan promoted murderous mercenaries in Nicaragua as if they were Hollywood "Rambos." Many other examples exist as regional reformers were considered suspect for wanting change. Denounced as communists by local militaries and oligarchs, those wanting reforms were either compromised, subverted, or forced to physically fight for change. Among the militant were Castro in Cuba, the Sandinistas in Nicaragua, and El Salvador's guerrillas. But with the collapse of the Soviet Union, the United States is less judgmental. Every political action and actor in Latin America is no longer scrutinized for communist affiliation. Echoes of the cold war still reverberate around Cuba and Castro, but elsewhere reduced paranoia allows a greater range of political voices.

The withdrawal of cold war domination has allowed other international players to assume larger roles in Latin America. Today, nongovernmental organizations (NGOs) such as Amnesty International, Witness for Peace, Habitat for Humanity, Oxfam America, and many more assist Latin Americans who foster peace, civil rights, citizen advocacy, and human dignity. Arriving from Canada and Europe as well as the United States, these goodwill ambassadors are role models of democracy in action. Alongside Latin Americans, these foreigners help create laboratories of democracy as the region's poor develop their own leadership skills.

International diplomacy also underwrites redemocratization in Latin America. While private negotiators like Jimmy Carter have been highlighted in the U.S. press, Latin American leaders have also accomplished much. Former secretary general of the United Nations Javier Pérez de Cuellar (from Peru), Nobel Peace Prize winner Oscar Arias Sánchez of Costa Rica, and Argentine negotiator Dante Caputo have moved armed opponents to negotiations and compromise. Working through the United Nations, the Organization of American States, and in regional conferences, these diplomats have restored democratically elected Jean-Betrand Aristide in Haiti and promoted reconciliation in El Salvador and Guatemala. In Latin America, diplomats have replaced dictators.

Economic changes also underwrite Latin American democracy. Here the debt crisis of the 1980s proved an unlikely asset to civilian governance as falling incomes and rising prices created an unmanageable debacle for military governments. Dictatorships have long been esteemed for their supposed discipline and efficiency: in the popular phrase, "making the trains run on time." But authoritarian economies with few checks and balances are often inefficient and corrupt. They are particularly inept when implementing retraints. According to one study:

> Obviously democracies enjoy strengths that have been denigrated or overlooked, such as legitimacy and popular support; but perhaps more to the point, the rationality, efficiency, unity, expertise, political isolation, and coercive capability of authoritarian governments appear to have been grossly exaggerated.[37]

The failures of military management became evident during the 1980s. In Argentina, the debt crisis coincided with both the failed Malvinas (Falkland) War and vigils by the Mothers of the Disappeared. Generals who claimed expertise in warfare and economics saw their soldiers defeated and productivity crumble. Popular unrest mushroomed. Similar economic malaise occurred wherever authoritarian governments tried to balance budgets using political repression and economic depression. Eventually, officers across Latin America walked away from their fiscal nightmares, leaving the unresolved economic mess to civilians. Even in Chile, the best case for military management, citizens clamored for democracy. When General Pinochet stepped back (not down and out; he still demanded a political role), the economy flourished even more than under military planning.

In the aftermath of military misrule, citizen anticorruption campaigns have furthered democracy. For a while, it seemed that civilian rule in the 1990s was just another turning of the political wheel, that elected officials could squander public trust while enriching themselves. But growing desire for honest and effective government has tightened the political rules. Across Latin America, citizens were not about to jeopardize hard-won democratic rule by allowing civilian charletans to govern in place of incompetent generals. More than in any earlier era, elected officials are accountable—to both public law and their own proclaimed ideals. In 1992, Fernando Collor de Mello resigned the Brazilian presidency after being indicted for embezzlement. In Venezuela, President Carlos Andres Pérez was impeached and convicted on charges of corruption; he was sent to jail in 1993. Emboldened by their accomplishments, citizens advocating clean government formed investigative committees that brought eighteen members of Brazil's congress to trial in January 1994. In Mexico, former president Carlos Salinas de Gortari and associates face indictments and jail terms for implication in political murders during 1994. In Colombia, the treasurer of President Ernesto Samper's election campaign confessed to accepting drug cartel monies. These many revelations of political corruption indict political leaders, but not the region's democratic process. Growing citizen awareness, higher public standards, and strengthening judicial systems bode well for the future of Latin American democracy, despite the failings of individual elected officials. The improvements are evident in Transparency International, a Latin American citizens' action group designed to uncover political abuse. Transparency International creates volunteer teams of anticorruption ombudsmen, reviews political tenure, develops public awareness, aids investigative journalists, and files suits against dishonest officials. Begun in Brazil, Transparency International has branched to Venezuela, Guatemala, Costa Rica, and across the Atlantic, to African nations. In Latin America today, citizens are organizing to promote honest rather than charismatic candidates.[38]

The recent hemispheric emphasis on free trade has also brought freer politics. The ending of state-managed I.S.I. economies encourages the ending of state-mandated politics, such as military regimes in Chile, Argentina, and Brazil, or the PRI's political monopoly in Mexico. Greater competition in politics, like economics, empowers diversity. Labor unions, journalists, business leagues, professional associations, and political parties articulate differing positions. Latin American politics in the 1990s has become a more open marketplace of ideas, issues, and policy debates. Open politics also helps open economies.[39]

Hemispheric commercial treaties—and opposition to them—have also strengthened democracy. Formerly, regional diplomacy was infused with mutual defense issues: soldiers, secrecy, and security dominated the agenda. But the North American Free Trade Agreement—regardless of its economic merits or faults—empowered civilians who as diplomats, economists, lobbyists, businessmen, labor leaders, and consumers entered the political arena. Debates over NAFTA removed military men from arguing their priorities. They had little to say about complex economic issues. The progress and process of NAFTA also moved the United States toward parity rather than dominance of its neighbors. It was originally a Latin American, not a U.S. initiative as the United States and Canada responded to Mexican diplomatic leadership. The future growth of NAFTA to include other Latin American nations will further enhance regional democracy. Generals will be even more removed from central political issues, and the United States will face an ever larger array of voices speaking Spanish and advocating their economic agendas. Growing commercial relations will not bring hemispheric happiness to all, but debating the process should encourage evolution toward pluralism and civilian leadership.

Latin American democracy is far from perfect. But as the twentieth century ends, the future of democracy looks promising. In the stable colonial era, an alliance among bureaucrat, prelate, landowner, and mercantilist dominated public policy issues. But nineteenth-century economic innovations—more than political independence itself—moved Latin Americans toward pluralism, constitutionalism, and democracy. As during the previous century, economic growth still promotes social pluralism and political diversity. Today, public policies are debated by labor unions and peasant leagues, business organizations and consumer groups, environmentalists and professional associations, human rights activists and friends of local neighborhoods. A growing population of lawyers joins the fray using contracts, litigation, and courts as well as lobbying. With many voices advocating many policies, no authoritarian regime can resolve so many conflicting positions. As messy as it sometimes is, democracy is the best instrument for resolving the competitive goals of many different constituents.

With all these factors and forces favoring Latin American democracy, one might assume that constitutional and representative government is assured. Such is not the case. Democracy is a difficult proposition, rarely neat and often contentious. Even a wizard would be challenged to satisfy so many demands in the political marketplace. And democratic politicians are no magicians. In the past, lower-class fatalism made governance among oligarchs relatively easy. Today, with so many demanding so much, the levels of political frustration are always high. In addition, the checks and balances of democracies further inhibit quick and cohesive action. And when democracies stumble, authoritarian rule, including intervention by the military, always looks simple and magically efficient.

But the more profound challenge for Latin American democracy is not efficiency. The real achievement of democracy in Latin America depends on economic as well as political justice. Centuries ago Aristotle noted that patterns of power follow the distribution of property. As long as so few Latin Americans possess so much—and so many own so little—democracy is tentative. To the credit of Latin Americans, they have—for the moment—solved the dilemma of forging democracy in the face of militaristic and authoritarian legacies. But the larger challenge remains. Can economic democracy overcome a legacy of exploitation?[40]

SUGGESTED READINGS

Black, Jan Knippers. *Sentinels of Empire: The United States and Latin American Militarism.* New York: Greenwood Press, 1986.

Bushnell, David, and Neill Macaulay. *The Emergence of Latin America in the Nineteenth Century.* 2d ed. New York: Oxford University Press, 1994.

Guillermoprieto, Alma. *The Heart That Bleeds: Latin America Now.* New York: Knopf, 1994.

Jonas, Suzanne, and Nancy Stein, eds. *Democracy in Latin America: Visions and Realities.* New York: Bergin and Garvey, 1990.

Kryzanek, Michael J. *Leaders, Leadership, and U.S. Policy in Latin America.* Boulder, Colo.: Westview Press, 1992.
Lehmann, David. *Democracy and Development in Latin America.* Philadelphia: Temple University Press, 1990.
López, George A., and Michael Stohl, eds. *Liberalization and Redemocratization in Latin America.* New York: Greenwood Press, 1987.
Lowenthal, Abraham F., ed. *Exporting Democracy: The United States and Latin America.* Baltimore: Johns Hopkins University Press, 1991.
Lowenthal, Abraham F., and J. Samuel Fitch, eds. *Armies and Politics in Latin America.* Rev. ed. New York: Holmes and Meier, 1986.
Munck, Ronaldo. *Latin America: The Transition to Democracy.* London: Zed Books, 1989.
Needler, Martin C. *The Problem of Democracy in Latin America.* Lexington, Mass.: Heath, 1987.
Petras, James, et al. *Latin America: Bankers, Generals, and the Struggle for Social Justice.* Totowa, N.J.: Rowman and Littlefield, 1986.
Wiarda, Howard J., ed. *Politics and Social Change in Latin America: Still a Distinct Tradition?* 3d ed. Boulder, Colo.: Westview Press, 1992.

10

LANDSCAPES BORN OF DREAMS: THE ARTS

We are nothing if not dreamers.

Marcía Watson, Costa Rican journalist and diplomat

The richest resource of Latin Americans is their artistic vision. From formal paintings to native weaving, in architecture, literature, and popular music, the region is filled with wonderful legacies and inspired innovations. Expressive themes emerge from Europeans and Indigens, and from creative adaptations by mestizos, African Latins, and immigrants. Artistic imagination derives from personal visions: passions filled with love, lust, and fear, of respect for nature's beauty and bestiality, the pride and prejudice of families, and struggles for dignity or domination. From these many wellsprings, Latin American artists—professional and folk—have created landscapes born of dreams.

The arts in Latin America originate in its traditions. The Indigen past expresses itself in dramatic weaving, colorful floral arrangements, boldly painted homes, music filled with the sounds of nature, and the storytelling of dance. Colonialism esteemed European models for architecture, murals, sculpture, poetry, theater, and other arts. But European beauty represented its own diverse legacies: from Greeks, Romans, and Arabs, a vast array of folk customs, Christian and Hebraic spiritualism, medieval mysticism, and Renaissance humanism. These entered the artistic landscape of Latin America. Added to Indigen and European visions were arts from Africa and occasionally Asia. African artists in the new world used music and dance, storytelling, carvings, and cuisine. In places such as Bahia, Brazil, and the Caribbean from Cuba to Trinidad, African themes became artistic norms. Asian motifs originated in the Manila Galleon and Pacific smugglers, and in Brazilian trade with the Portuguese East Indies. Asian artisans and artifacts impacted early Latin American styles of architecture, ceramics, and textiles. Later immigrants from China, India, and the eastern Mediterranean brought more personal aesthetics.

Inspiration from many sources entered the mind's eye of Latin American artists, where they mixed with individual visions. The artists were clerical draftsmen, Mozarabic masons, African carpenters and cooks, and Indigen muralists and weavers. For centuries these personal visions interpreted imported European styles:—baroque and classicism, romanticism and realism, impressionism and surrealism. Eventually, North American visions from Edgar Allan Poe and Walt Whitman to Hollywood film and rap music would inspire Latin American artists, although the flow of artistic expression is usually reversed: the pulsating tide of Latin American arts generally flows north. But when imported models of music, painting, architecture, and writing did arrive in Latin America—from anywhere in the world—they were always given a Latin touch, an increasingly strong interpretation using native rhythm, color, shape, and syntax.

Ethnic artistry was sometimes submerged but never drowned during the flood of European dominance. While Indigen cities were leveled or abandoned following the conquest, native song, dance, and decoration were channeled according to European tastes, particularly as Catholic morality plays or decorated churches. African arts flourished as music and movement at carnival, storytelling, or giving shape to everyday objects. Asian styles and tastes appeared in Caribbean cane fields accompanied by sitars from India and woks from China. All these influences—and many others—merged and emerged in a Latin American context.

While artists and artisans adapted many legacies, a truly Latin American aesthetic eventually developed. During the decades surrounding 1900, factors converged to accelerate the formation of a regional identity. The war of 1898 finally ended Iberian imperium in the Americas. The demise of Spain, together with looming U.S. dominance, triggered a search for Latin American consciousness. Mass killing in Europe during World War I diminished esteem for supposed North Atlantic grandeur. Meanwhile, Latin American audiences grew larger and regional artists matured as literacy, wealth, and leisure expanded.

A declaration of aesthetic independence began to form as early as the 1880s. Before this, literature told of encounter and conquest, foreign colonization, and Napoleonic-type struggles for political freedom. Formal painting depicted Christian saints and Europeanized elites. Local architecture copied European buildings. Latin American visions had occasionally parted these dense colonial curtains, but never so strongly, collectively, and creatively as when a generation of young writers pioneered new awareness in the late nineteenth century. Within a generation, Mexico's nationalistic revolution inspired further pride and perception throughout Latin America. Ever since, Latin American artists have proudly used local landscapes to express their profound dreams.

A LANDSCAPE OF LITERATURE

The written word was a European bequest to new world literature. Previously, Indigen expressiveness was pictorial or oral. Forms of writing appeared as colorful figures and symbols adorning the stelae and murals of monuments, or as images in codices. Many of these artistic documents were burned by European clerics as works of the devil. The surviving writings are only now being deciphered by scholars. Yet story*telling* remained prodigious, as human memories supplanted written texts. And with European alphabets and syntax, some Indigens conveyed for posterity the visions of their elders.

While the first modern writings *about* Latin America were penned by European chroniclers, the first literature *by* Latin Americans was Indigen. In the generation following encounter, Catholic clerics helped Aztec, Mayan and Andean authors transcribe poems, songs, and odes into Spanish—or into Nahuatl, Quechua, and other native idioms using a Latin alphabet. The ancients bequeathed many verses, including this haikulike piece:

One by one I bring together
your songs.
I am linking the jades,
with them I make a bracelet
of everlasting gold.

Bedeck yourself with them;
they are your wealth
in the region of flowers
they are your wealth
on the earth.[1]

Perhaps the greatest piece of Indigen literature is the *Popol Vuh,* the expansive Mayan "Genesis" penned by a Quiché nobleman in Central America. It combines science and spiritualism to explain human origins. Other Indigen literature of this early era recounts the ideas and achievements of Inca philosopher-kings, struggles against the Spanish, and the rhythms of daily life.

Indigen sources are a constant wellspring of Latin American arts and letters. Modern authors and painters from Isabel Allende to Frida Kahlo have written and painted in the shadows of ancient Indigen ancestors. The Indigen legacy depicts a world of gods and mystical forces, shamanistic powers and supernatural causation. Native sources are also naturalistic: describing color and shape, of plants and animals, of solar and aquatic forces. Indigen writers bequeathed the burdens of time and place, never forgetting an individual's relationship to either progenitors or the surrounding cosmos. Themes of thirty centuries permeate the Indigen legacy. Consider the relative perspectives of an ancient Indigen myth and a modern poem by Jorge Luis Borges. According to the creation myth of Venezuela's Makiritare, "the [first] woman and the [first] man dreamed that God was dreaming about them." Such imaginative transcendence fills the short stories of Borges, including "The Circular Ruins," but is here succinctly represented in his poem "Chess." After describing a match and its players, he concludes:

God moves the player, he, in turn, the piece.
But what god beyond God begins the round
of dust and time and dream and agonies?[2]

If the Indigen legacy forms one fountain from which modern artists drink, chroniclers from Europe supplied another. European explorers cruising the American coasts and visiting Indigen communities were the first modern writers in the Americas. But even when factual, their accounts read like fantasy as nature and Indigens seemed wondrous to European authors and audiences alike. With great prescience some chroniclers understood the uniqueness of the historic moment: the surprise encounter of unimagined societies. Some writers—such as Columbus—channeled their vision through perspectives born of medieval mysticism, classical mythology, and Christian spiritualism. Others emulated Arabic storytelling as found in Iberian odes. But many European chroniclers pioneered an emerging scientism, where clear description leads to its own conclusions. Still, such accounts are magical. Consider this 1520 journal entry of Antonio de Pigafetta, the Italian chronicler of captain-general Ferdinand Magellan's global voyage. Here he describes an Indigen herdsman in Patagonia:

> One day we suddenly saw a naked man of giant stature on the shore of the port, dancing, singing, and throwing dust on his head. The captain-general sent one of our men to the giant so that he might perform the same actions as a sign of peace. Having done that, the man led the giant to an islet into the presence of the captain-general. . . . [The Indigen] was so tall that we reached only to his waist, and he was well proportioned. His face was large and painted red all over while about his eyes he was painted yellow; and he had two hearts painted on the middle of his cheeks. His scanty hair was painted white. . . . The

captain-general had the giant given something to eat and drink, and among other things the captain-general showed him was a large steel mirror. When he saw his face, he was greatly terrified, and jumped back throwing three or four of our men to the ground.[3]

If it were fiction, Pigafetta's narration would be fantasy. However, it is a careful composition by a person noted for understatement. Similar examples characterize the chronicles of Álvar Núñez Cabeza de Vaca, whose spiritual attributes seemingly raised Indigens from the dead, or Bernal Díaz del Castillo, who described a kingdom that appeared to float on a shimmering lake, or the soldiers of Aguirre in the Amazon, who testified to seeing boats anchored in treetops, or Bernardino de Sahagún or dozens of other Europeans who merely described what they saw: the real, the apparently magical. Centuries later such accounts—together with themes from early Indigen literature—would help create the modern genre called *magical realism.* Writers such as Gabriel García Márquez, Alejo Carpentier, and others created and still employ sometimes bizarre imagery. In doing so, they merely draw on a literary legacy in which the mundane seems magical and the exaggerated is part of daily life.

The meeting of European and Indigen generated more than two perspectives as a complex vision emerged in the dreams of its children, the mestizos. Foremost among the mestizo writers of the colonial era was the Indigen-Iberian known as Inca Garcilaso de la Vega. Garcilaso was born in 1539, following Peru's conquest, of a Spanish captain and an Inca princess. For a lifetime, he served each heritage—and his own alienation. Denied both legitimacy and inheritance by Spanish authorities, he was nonetheless very Catholic, well lettered in Castillian, and accepted by his father's family. From his mother he learned and esteemed an illustrious Quechua ancestry. When twenty-one, he left Lima for Spain to plead before the king—and the court of history.

In Europe, Inca Garcilaso de la Vega's struggles charted his literary life. Although his petitions were dismissed by crown bureaucrats, he was supported by an uncle. He fought as a Spanish officer in the Mediterranean and at age fifty began to translate literature and write narratives that were personal metaphors. His first work was a translation from the Italian, a poetic dialogue composed by an exiled Spanish Jew. This love song gave voice to an outcast like himself. His next work was a revisionist account of conquistador Hernando de Soto's tragic expedition in the American south. *La Florida* reads like a novel. And considering Garcilaso's Spanish audience, the work took a novel approach: native societies were heroic, the Spaniard de Soto was less than noble. Garcilaso's major work sought to balance extremes: Spain's Christianizing mission and the glory of his Inca ancestors. Published as two volumes in 1609 and 1617, *The Royal Commentaries* presented native culture as magnificent, its defeat as tragic. It also praised the culture and Catholicism of Iberia. Written to temper Spanish prejudices, it eventually helped shape Latin American identity. One scholar concludes: "With *The Royal Commentaries* a truly Spanish American literature begins. Garcilaso is its founding father."[4]

Early Latin American literature also had a mother, a poet known as Sor Juana Inés de la Cruz. She lived when solid conventions governed both female and poetic mores. Her courage and creativity confronted both.

In assessing Sor Juana Inés de la Cruz, one must realize that artists reflect their times. As the genre of mundane reports and obtuse sermons, prose was rarely used for literature. By contrast, poetry was painting with words. And colonial audiences preferred epics: poetry of sometimes great length, with rigid structure and florid redundancy. Rather than stylistically free and thematically experimental, seventeenth-century poetry used known models and metaphors derived from medieval odes, classic mythology, and Christian theology. Its authors and audience were a narrow group of *peninsulares* and criollos weaned on European tastes. Poetry was also designed to be social and entertaining more than self-expressive, composed at court and for public contests, read at weddings, funerals, and other ceremonies. With large quantities in high demand, early Latin American poetry was often more artifice than art, and few early poets withstood time's test of changing tastes. Honored by the ages is Sor Juana Inés de la Cruz.

The Mexican Juana de Asbeje was beautiful and brilliant. Born around 1650, she was literate by age three and soon afterward composed witty and intelligent rhyme at the viceroy's court. Adored by many, including scores of love-struck gentlemen, Juana sought the refuge of a convent and took the name "Inez of the Cross." There she practiced many arts: painting, poetry, theater, science, math, music, cuisine, and more. She corresponded with other literati and remained popular at court, although often chided by superiors guarding the "proper" role of women, particularly nuns. Famous in Latin America and Europe, she died in her forties, bequeathing a broad repertoire of morality plays, mildly erotic poems, comedies, essays, drama, and much more. She also left a highly esteemed reputation, addressed in this brief excerpt from "In Acknowledgement of the Praises of European Writers":

Divine Oracles, tell me when,
when, most melodious of Swans,
when did my careless scrawls deserve
to occupy your thoughtful care?

And from what place does so much praise,
so many commendations, come?
Can it be distance that alone
added so much to my portrait?

What stature have you given me?
What great Colossus have you wrought,
entirely ignorant of height,
from this lowly original?

I am not what you think I am;
but over there you've given me
another being in your pens,
and other breath upon your lips,

and, different from what I am,
I walk beneath your pens, and am

not what I truly am, but what
you'd prefer to imagine me.[5]

The audience of Juana Inés de la Cruz spans the ages. Today, her statue adorns parks and boulevards from Barcelona to Buenos Aires. A famous painting of her hangs in thousands of libraries, schools, and theaters throughout the Hispanic world. However, lacking any portrait completed during her lifetime, all these are conjectures based on models, such as a daughter of the artist who, decades after Juana's death, completed the most famous painting. In her own words, she remains "what you'd prefer to imagine me."[6]

The early literary legacy of Latin America owes much to theater. The region produced neither a Shakespeare nor a Molière, and no memorable plays. But in an age when literacy was limited, theater served as mass entertainment. So popular was theater that even great prose like *Don Quixote de la Mancha* employed acting to advance plot. New world theater basked in the illumination of Spain's great playwrights, and the works of Lope de Vega, Calderón de la Barca, and others arrived faster than any royal edict. Most Latin American playwrights feebly mimicked the characters and plots of great Spanish plays, creating local versions of Celestina, Sancho Panza, and the many "Dons": the idealist Quixote, the authoritarian Giovanni, and the rogue Juan. However, even without local genius, the play in colonial Latin America was, indeed, "the thing."

Theater served many masters. It celebrated historic events, reenacted the Christian calendar, satirized foibles, and even—occasionally—criticized local authorities. Titles from the times recapture box office hits: *Lima Founded, The Passion and Triumph of Christ, The Triumphs of Love and Power.* Like period poetry, theatrical dialogue was often metered and rhymed. Then, as now, plays were sometimes polemical. Where officials were despots and playwrights courageous, guerrilla satire and censorship confronted one another. More commonly, patrons hired playwrights as they did politicians, to serve the status quo. Theater was also an instrument of conquest and indoctrination. *Autos sacramentales* composed by friars were sacred plays about Jesus, biblical characters, and the lives of saints. Clerics and Indigens became actors, and spectators participated when casting required a chorus or crowd. *Autos sacramentales* blended play and polemics: belief was literary and literal.[7]

The importance of early theater extends far beyond an often pedantic and polemical output. The significance of plays is deeply psychological. No other genre so thoroughly replaces reality with illusion. In donning costumes, makeup, and following scripts, actors induce transcendence. For a brief moment the imaginary takes precedence as "play" achieves ideals—or the forbidden. Sometimes, then as now, life mimicked art. Colonial actors in real life often displayed mythical stage life: engaging in affairs, scandals, duels, and other high drama. Subverting time and space as well as mores, actors transposed American audiences to European capitals and the Holy Land, as well as heaven and hell. And at a time when women were denied political roles, they often starred in colonial theater. The fantasy of colonial plays fed dreams. Latin America's theatrical legacy is another inspiration for its modern arts.

Early theater was particularly important for Indigens, who long relished the power of masked identity and role reversal. In ancient times soldiers wore the costumes and headdresses of warrior clans, to assume the courage or cunning of the jaguar, eagle, or condor. High priests dressed in the robes of gods. Aztec officials sometimes donned the flailed skins of victims to mimic and mock the dead and death itself. After the Spanish conquest, actors from among the defeated were occasionally allowed victory and virtue in *autos sacramentales.* An Indigen donning the white mask and flaxen wig of Santiago would vanquish Moors and devils. A native actress would portray the Virgin Mary. Following such theater, the honored actors were themselves esteemed. And *autos sacramentales* sometimes became tragically real. Indigen cults reenacted the passion and martyrdom of Christ, even into modern times. Known as *penitentes,* Indigen/mestizo brotherhoods restaged Holy Week, sacrificing a young man in the role of Christ. In the hills of northern New Mexico, such ritual executions were documented as late as the 1940s. Theater has long been a serious Latin American legacy, even deadly so.[8]

NINETEENTH-CENTURY DISCOVERIES

For Latin America, the nineteenth century was a time of rediscovery. It produced regional themes and new means of expression. The early engine of exploration was European romanticism, as artists in the age of growing industry nostalgically reminisced about nature, local habitants, ancient civilizations, and the "natural man." Mimicking European styles, Latin American artists were initially inspired by imported topics and tastes, such as those of ancient Greece and Rome or Napoleonic-type struggles. When they began exploring local color and heritage, they created a Latin American regional identity. Experimentation also led to new means of expression.

In the nineteenth century, Latin American prose literature was experimental since drama and especially poetry predominated. Following independence, nationalistic poets and playwrights won as much fame as the patriots and battles they praised. In Mexico, the play *Guatimoc* (1827), by José Fernández Madrid, typified many works of the era. It staged an Aztec view of the Spanish conquest. While not aesthetically outstanding, such works were important for breaking with a Eurocentric perspective.

Media as well as message evolved as prose writing expanded beyond the pens of bureaucrats and priests. In the hands of independence writers, manifestos and declarations (typically read aloud) gave drama to prose compositions. Some nationalists were intelligent as well as impassioned. Simón Bolívar expressed himself with clarity, conviction, and grace; his "Letter from Jamaica" is a major piece of Latin American writing, important for its literary form as well as its philosophical substance. The independence era also witnessed the first Latin American novel: José Joaquín Fernández de Lizardi's *El Periquillo Sarniento* (The Itching Parrot; 1816), a satire of Mexican middle-class life. Like politics, nineteenth-century prose was active and evolving.

By the mid-nineteenth century, prominent figures were turning from didactic factual writing to occasional fiction. In Chile, the famous educator and editor Andrés Bello experimented with *La Oración por Todos,* a Latin American *Les Misérables.*

Argentine presidents Bartolomé Mitre and Domingo Faustino Sarmiento both published novels. Rather than great literature, these were pioneer pieces, but they were widely read because educational reforms were expanding literacy. With growing audiences and more experienced writers, popular literature was becoming a greater social force.[9]

New themes emerged with new forms of expression. These, too, were initially romantic imports from Europe. Reflecting the popularity of Victor Hugo and Charles Dickens, local writers began to depict the everyday lives of Latin American workers, prostitutes, and beggars. However, such pieces were revolutionary as they moved the interests of an educated literati across class lines. Instead of relating court life or the antics of aristocrats, writers described the poor and local customs. This new regional romanticism eventually had a name: *costumbrismo. Costumbrismo* has been defined as "sketches of manners and customs which portrayed various aspects of contemporary life, amusing or picturesque, usually of provincial regions." From early and brief colorful descriptions of local folk—more like guidebook entries or anthropological notes—writers developed longer stories with plots and characters. *Costumbrismo* quickly evolved into short stories and novels. Woven through these were prominent literary themes such as *indigenismo* and *gauchismo:* the plight of native Americans and the adventures of free-roaming horsemen.[10]

Indigens were ideal subjects for romantic *costumbristas.* They were provincial, colorful, natural, and living examples of ancient civilizations. Like landscape painters going to nearby meadows, *costumbristas* used local Indigens and mestizos as subjects. Initially, writings were nostalgic. *La Virgen del Sol* (The Virgin of the Sun; 1861), a narrative poem by the Ecuadoran Juan León Mera, told of tragic love during the Spanish conquest. Ten years later, León Mera published another romanticized *indigenista* story, *Cumandá,* but as a novel. The transition from poetry to prose was matched by a movement from nostalgic sentimentalism to contemporary criticism. The evolution was clearly evident in the *indigenista* novel *Aves sin Nido* (Birds without a Nest; 1889), by the Peruvian Clorinda Matto de Turner, which explored how Andean Indigens were exploited by large landowners and the Catholic clergy. We shall soon see that *indigenista* themes—propelled by the nationalistic Mexican Revolution—kept publishers busy in the early twentieth century.

The second major *costumbrista* topic was the gaucho, the rough horseman of Argentina, Uruguay, and southern Brazil. To define the gaucho as a Latin American cowboy reverses priorities: the American "buckaroo" (from *Vaquero,* Spanish for cattle hand) was both ephemeral—post-Civil War and passé by World War I—and derived from a long-standing Mexican legacy. Also, the U.S. cowboy was typically a corporate hireling. In contrast, the Hispanic horseman—whether Mexican vaquero, Venezuelan *llanero,* or Argentine gaucho—derived from ancient traditions. And the gaucho was truly independent, even outcast: of mixed Indigen, African, and European background, a tamer of men as well as horses, roaming the fertile pampas, foraging for existence. If found at sea, gauchos might be labeled pirates. As is, they were bootleggers, dealers in hides and tallow, smugglers to passing ships, roughnecks who formed autonomous armies, and loyal to no law except a local caudillo's *personalismo.* Such tough and illiterate men were also poets: not with pen and paper but within an oral tradition. Among gaucho minstrels, rhyming and recitation were highly esteemed.

Gauchos became *costumbrista* subjects as nineteenth-century industrialism invaded the pampas with railroads, barbed wire, plows, and wheat combines. As gauchos became hired hands on fenced ranches, nostalgia for lost freedom on open grasslands fed authors and audiences alike. Among the early romantic pieces was *Santos Vega, el Payador,* parts of which appeared in 1851. The hero's name translates literally as "Sacred Plain"; a *payador* is a troubadour. The unrivaled giant of gaucho writers was José Hernández, who published *Martín Fierro* in 1872 and *The Return of Martín Fierro* shortly later. These long lyric poems were composed in the epic style of gaucho troubadours. They told of macho heroics, a theme as old as Spain's El Cid and as modern Hollywood's latest film. But the success of Hernández—much imitated well into the twentieth century—lay with his use of an oral tradition to overcome illiteracy. *Martin Fierro* sold everywhere, mainly as cheap editions in humble neighborhood grocery stores. Along with flour and salt, this lyric epic was another staple of life. And many avid but stumbling readers became literate pouring over couplets of this macho epic.[11]

The nineteenth century was a period of groping for self-discovery and self-expression. From early patriotic verse, to the experience of writing novels, to the *costumbrista* discovery of local and common heroes, Latin American authors were exploring nearby environments with new tools. Eventually their searchings discovered—or created—a Latin American identity. Regional self-awareness would have profound consequences.

PROPHETS OF CONSCIOUSNESS

It is fully appropriate that the major authors of the late nineteenth century were poets. Practicing a long-established genre, poets enjoyed a legitimacy that nascent novelists lacked. Then, as now, quality poets attained heroic stature. The more renowned still rival visiting dignitaries or soccer stars, and easily fill sports arenas with eager listeners. Such respect is traditional, but it attained mythical proportions when a group of late-nineteenth-century poets helped create Latin American consciousness. Political independence for much of the region had existed for a half century, but local writers still emulated European classicism or romanticism. In rejecting Spain, decades of authors instead esteemed things English, French, or German. With the generation of the 1880s, European ideas were not so much rejected as used to create a consciousness of Latin America. Imported from Europe, the style known as modernism was used by local poets to discover the profound meaning of local landscapes.

In the words of Cuban poet José Martí, modernists focused on *nuestra América,* our America. New identity derived from attention to local environments, popular cultures, Latin American values, and regional personalities. Things of distant origin were not excluded from this new loyalty, particularly when they appeared as daily aspects of local life. Thus, the Spanish language, popular Catholicism, African imagery, and other imported *and adapted* customs were esteemed. But the colonialist legacies of superiors and inferiors, elites and masses, and deference to things foreign were opposed with the zeal of parochial prophets. The modernists instead extolled the colors and shapes of their native lands, the common people, their region's ancient traditions, including its Indigen and African consciousness. They esteemed local landscapes, the blue sky, nearby coastlines, American mountains and valleys, village markets. Modernists gave voice to everyday existence. Inherent in their descriptions was a new identity, a new loyalty. And some would die for the *patria* of poetic visions.

Like a youthful rebellion, the modernist revolt was generational and eclectic. The past was rejected, but not all things old. Foreign sources were suspect, but not all foreigners. The emphasis was on new vision: the war cry of one Peruvian modernist was "old-timers to the tomb; youth to writing." Modernism was a break: from European colonialism, from emerging U.S. dominance, from local hierarchies, from any authoritarianism. But modernists did welcome friends with fresh vision. From the United States, Walt Whitman was esteemed as a North American shaman. Respect for American iconoclasts also included Edgar Allan Poe. The modernists considered France's champion of the poor, Victor Hugo, as a Moses. All these foreign visionaries helped modernists see their own region more intently. And like a child who has learned to walk, the young Latin American poets commenced running.[12]

The two giants of Latin American modernism were José Martí and Rubén Darío. Others, such as the Uruguayan essayist Enrique Rodó, were significant, equally immense in their times, but with hindsight, Martí and Darío loom larger. And while modernism was later challenged by other styles, its impact lingers.

José Martí (1853–1895) was a revolutionary. Had he spent less energy driving Spain from Cuba, he may have written more poems. As is, he was a literary as well as a political prophet. At age seventeen, the young nationalist was imprisoned for his writings. Later, in Spain, he became a lawyer: litigating and lobbying unsuccessfully for Cuban independence. Although travel as a journalist made him worldly, the cosmopolitan man yearned for his parochial Cuba. Once home, revolutionary activities caused authorities to exile him again, this time to New York City. His passion remained *Cuba libre:* and the vision of an intellectually and politically free Latin America. In 1895 he died for his beliefs, fighting Spanish forces in Cuba.

In opposing Spain, Martí emphasized new loyalties. He put his faith in the heritage of common Cubans, the Cuban land itself, and, by extension, the Latin American region. Opposing Spanish political authority also entailed rejecting the subtle props of imperium: hierarchies of race, class, religion, and culture. In their place, Martí promoted a mystical connection to the land, to those who till it, and to their African and Indigen legacies. Becoming a master of the master's tongue, Martí gave literary voice to the dominated: landscapes as well as laborers. And like exploited ecologies and peasants, Martí's poems speak with quiet inference, with subtle rebellion. His descriptions hold double meanings: realities become symbolic and the symbolic becomes real.

Martí's poetry is best expressed not as dry verse on pages but as song. And many of his verses quickly returned to those who inspired him: peasants working and singing in the fields. "Guantanamera" is a song of the Cuban countryside. Many of its verses derive from the poem *Simple Lyrics,* produced in 1891. In it Martí wrote:

I am an honest man from where the palms grow;
Before I die I want my soul to shed its poetry.

I come from everywhere, to everywhere I'm bound:
An art among the arts, a mountain among the mountains.

. . . .

Well do I know that when the livid world yields to repose,
The gentle brook will ripple on in deepest silence.

. . . .

My manly heart conceals the pain it suffers; sons of
A land enslaved live for it silently, and die.

. . . .

I know that fools are buried splendidly, with floods of tears,
And that no fruit on earth is like the graveyard's.[13]

José Martí knew Rubén Darío (1867–1916) mostly through his poetry. And while Martí was an active revolutionary, Darío is remembered as the revolutionary voice of *nuestra América,* the "new America" discovered through modernism. Of African, Indigen, and Spanish background, the young Nicaraguan joined the local literati by age eleven and published when thirteen. Like many aspiring students of his time, Darío was classically trained in Latin and Hispanic tradition, and his particular excellence won a scholarship to Santiago, Chile, then the "Athens" of Latin America. On this trip to the farthest corner of America, the twenty-one-year-old discovered French impressionism and began to paint with words: infusing literary imagery with light. In Darío's poetry, subjects draw life from their very environment. His major literary piece, composed where sky meets sea on the Chilean shore, was *Azul* ("Blue"), published in 1888. *Azul,* and many other writings of this prodigious poet, influenced a hemisphere of readers and generations of writers who, like him, were excited to be living, spontaneous, creative, and Latin American.

Darío's energy is evident in a poem composed when another young adventurer, Theodore Roosevelt, invaded Latin America for the second time. In 1903, the "Rough Rider"—now as president—seized Panama and Rubén Darío composed "To Roosevelt," which is excerpted here:

The voice that would reach you, Hunter, must speak
in Biblical tones, or in the poetry of Walt Whitman.
You are primitive and modern, simple and complex. . . .

. . . .

You are the United States,
future invader of our naive America
with its Indian blood, an America
that still prays to Christ and speaks Spanish.

. . . .

You think that life is a fire,
that progress is an irruption,

that the future is wherever
your bullet strikes.
No.

The United States is grand and powerful.

. . . .

. . . joining the cult of Mammon to the cult of Hercules;
while Liberty, lighting the path
to easy conquest, raises her torch in New York.

. . . .

Roosevelt, you must become, by God's own will,
the deadly Rifleman and the dreadful Hunter
before you can clutch us in your iron claws.[14]

Modernism eventually yielded to other styles. Among later prominent poets is the Argentine Jorge Luis Borges, writing from the perspective of blindness, talking of infinite time and space, probing the vicissitudes of fate. He dissects existential themes with the precision of a surgeon, using words like scalpels. Octavio Paz took poetry in another direction. He explored the vast labyrinth of legacies enfolding life on Mexico's high plateau: geologically elevated, like an offering of humans to the heavenly gods. Paz praises the amalgam of Mediterranean and American peoples as a civilization equal to that of India and China. But Paz was a master essayist as well as poet and Borges was best known for his short stories. They and many other fine poets never achieved the full status of "poet laureate," speaking—like Darío—for a generation of Latin Americans. Such esteem has been achieved at least twice in the twentieth century, and both poets have been Chilean.

Following the death of Darío in 1916, Gabriela Mistral emerged as the quiet and compassionate voice of her generation and was the first Latin American to win the Nobel Prize in literature. Since she did so in 1945, many have joined her. One key to Mistral's success is her identity as a mother and grandmother, despite her being unmarried and childless. Yet, her poetry often reflects a maternal lament, parental passion, and sympathetic guidance. Leaving no singular outstanding piece, Mistral wrote prodigiously, producing love poems, pieces to be sung as lullabies, and works recited as school lessons. Returning to traditional Hispanicism, her topics were popular Catholicism, biblical stories, nature, and timeless morals. Many poems by Gabriela Mistral serve as secular prayers, solitary invocations.

Darío's greatest follower—although he never knew it—was a Chilean who began writing in the 1920s. The poems of Pablo Neruda (1904–1973) praised the grand adventure of life and living, despite its rough edges. Like Darío, Neruda achieved poetic excellence in a hospitable pocket of earth isolated by Andean heights, Pacific expanses, Atacama sands, and polar snows. These boundaries and a canopy of sky formed an amphitheater for Neruda's human drama. In the poetry of Neruda, the natural world bequeaths simple blessings to humankind: from sunlight, stars, and stones to tomatoes, seaweed, and solitude. And the human touch anoints all objects, whether the majestic ruins of Machu Picchu, jetsam collected on a beach, onions in a market, oily machines in a factory, or the seats of an empty railway car. Critics have called the poet a cross between St. Francis and Karl Marx: someone who talked to birds as well as historic muses. To Pablo Neruda, the meaning of life is life itself: whether making love or slopping soup from a spoon. He was profoundly common—and uncommonly profound—whether as a Communist senator, a Chilean ambassador, Nobel laureate, or just someone buying rusty scissors from a junk vendor.[15]

Like Martí, the deeply human and humane Neruda died a martyr. During the fascist Chilean coup of 1973, the poet's home at Isla Negra was invaded and ransacked by soldiers. Forced to lie for hours on the floor while his beloved collectibles were searched and smashed, he suffered a stroke. Like his friend and president, Salvador Allende, Neruda died a victim of the authoritarian intolerance he had long opposed. No single poem can capture the magnitude of Pablo Neruda. He wrote of everything from ancient Andeans to his latest prescription. Our introduction is his adios, "I Will Come Back":

Some time, man or woman, traveller,
afterwards, when I am not alive,
look here, look for me here
between the stones and the ocean,
in the light storming
in the foam.
Look here, look for me here,
for here is where I shall come, saying nothing,
no voice, no mouth, pure,
here I shall be again the movement
of the water, of
its wild heart,
here I shall be both lost and found—
here I shall be perhaps both stone and silence.[16]

Late-twentieth-century poets are still active, but not so renowned as Martí or Neruda. The region's modern literary giants are prose writers: novelists and authors of short stories. But in the land of poets, artists of syntax and symbolism continue creating art and awareness with words. Derek Walcott in the colorful Caribbean uses English to express African Latin imagery. Ernesto Cardinal in Nicaragua employs the theology of liberation to express self and community. There and throughout Latin America, poets are still prophets of consciousness.

LITERATURE FOR A LITERATE CENTURY

In Latin America, Africa, and southeast Asia, modern novelists are writing major works. Salman Rushdie of India, V. S. Naipul of Trinidad, the Nigerian Chinua Achebe, and the Colombian Gabriel García Márquez represent many world authors, a global pattern of thinkers. Their commonality is dual citizenship. Each belongs to the modern world of individualism, civil rights, and materialism. Each also lives among ancient customs: deep religious values, family loyalties, and local authority. The characters in their novels reflect the struggles of traditional societies assaulted by Western values. The promise and perversion of both worlds clash endlessly. Family identities confront entrenched hierarchies. Democracy is compromised by racism. Commercialism undercuts local village markets. Technology empowers multinational corporations, which corrupt local politics. Human dignity struggles to survive both old castes and new classes. Modern learning impugns fables told by elders. Altogether, the complexities of dual citizenship rend the hearts and challenge the minds of fictional characters. Art mirrors society.

The novel is not the singular genre for discussing such tough topics. Poetry and theater are still important, as are short stories and essays. But as mass literacy developed alongside industrialism in the nineteenth and twentieth centuries, the more oral forms of poetry and theater yielded major space to prose. Early in the twentieth century, essays, short stories, and particularly the novel gained popularity among larger audiences with more private time.

In Latin America, the expository essay became a genre with the power to shape perspective. As analysts and soothsayers, Latin American essayists have constructed works that dissect their time and place. The century opened with the most defining of regional essays: José Enrique Rodó's *Ariel.* This 1900 book of essays by Rodó, a contemporary of Rubén Darío, serves as a modernist manifesto. Reacting to the war of 1898, Rodó reaffirmed Latin American cultural as well as political independence from Spain. But he also sounded alarms over a new domination—again both cultural and political—emanating from a predatory United States. Using Shakespearean characters as metaphors, Rodó cast Anglo America as Caliban: an uncivilized military and industrial behemoth, massive and materialist, but blind and selfish. He depicted Latin America as Ariel: a young bird leaving its nest with new wings, aspiring to flight, ready to discover a world of art and beauty. *Ariel* had a tremendous and lasting impact, particularly with Latin American nationalists reacting to U.S. invasions of Panama, the Caribbean, and Central America. With subsequent conflicts—such as the Cuban Revolution in the 1950s and Chilean socialism in the 1970s—Rodó's ideas echoed in later generations.

Another essayist was less idealistic, more self-critical, and employed analytic tools provided by psychology, sociology, and psychiatry. In *The Labyrinth of Solitude: Life and Thought in Mexico* (first Spanish edition, 1950), Octavio Paz explored Mexican and Latin American identity. Educated in both Mexico and the United States, familiar with India and Japan as well as Europe, Paz saw Latin America as the intellectual and cultural equal of any other region. He lamented the fact that prolonged colonialism—first Iberia's, then that of the United States—kept others from appreciating what his region had accomplished: amazing blendings of European and indigenous cultures. Like Rodó, Paz analyzed U.S. influence but without simplistic and dramatic metaphors. With an appreciative but critical eye equal to that of Alexis de Tocqueville—the great nineteenth-century French observer of American democracy—Paz intelligently and honestly dissected both Anglo-American and Hispanic American identities. Written with the syntax of a poet and great knowledge of history, *The Labyrinth of Solitude* typically reads like this:

> Man is alone everywhere. But the solitude of the Mexican, under the great stone night of the high plateau that is still inhabited by insatiable gods, is very different from that of the

> North American, who wanders in an abstract world of machines, fellow citizens and moral precepts. In the Valley of Mexico man feels himself suspended between heaven and earth, and he oscillates between contrary powers and forces. . . . [Here,] reality—that is the world that surrounds us— . . . was not invented by man as it was in the United States. The Mexican feels himself to have been torn from the womb of this [natural] reality, which is both creative and destructive, both Mother and Tomb.[17]

After a half century, *The Labyrinth of Solitude* remains a valuable analysis of subliminal dreams. In its poetic prose, it shows the analytic essay as art.

Latin American novelists produce great short stories, but one author has achieved epic status without a major novel. For most of the twentieth century, the Argentine Jorge Luis Borges crafted poems, essays, and short stories. His fiction resembles that of Poe and Kafka, but it is steeped in ancient Mediterranean and Asian fables and the symbolism of Indigen America. Borges's writings are deeply spiritual but not religious. Liberated by progressive blindness from the hubbub of sight, his mind's eye finds ironic truths in shadows and illusions. Writing with almost Aesopian brevity, his stories are short, his syntax and vocabulary precise. From his personal vistas have come "The Circular Ruins" and "The Babylon Lottery." But like the days of his long life, his stories are many.

In Latin America, as elsewhere, the modern novel succeeds because it is big enough to ruminate on tough topics over many pages. Plays and films would need weeks of performance to match a modern novel's discursive thoroughness. Given modern lifestyles of segmented leisure, the novel is an ideal means for exploring epic issues with patience and reflection.

The modern Latin American novel is a recent invention. Until a widely literate audience emerged in the late nineteenth century, most published prose appeared as legal tomes, theological tracts and such. And "news"—during centuries when newspapers were unknown—used a performing rather than a prose medium. *Corridos* (the Mexican term) were rhymed accounts of events sung by roaming troubadours even into the twentieth century. Earlier, as now, news was entertainment. In Latin America prose literature languished, despite the splendid example and great success of Miguel Cervantes's *Don Quixote,* the world's great early novel. For 200 years, only a handful of prototype novels appeared in Latin America. More popular were picaresque travelogues: rambling accounts of rogues on the run.[18]

During the twentieth century prose writing proliferated. At midcentury the number and quality of Latin American novelists burst forth in a phenomenon termed *la boom.* The reasons for *la boom* derive from both immediate events and rich legacies. Twentieth-century events generated reflective fiction. The Mexican Revolution, particularly its creative period after 1920, inspired Latin American authors who described struggles between authoritarian elites and growing popular consciousness. Meanwhile, the depression-era dictatorships of the 1930s drew Latin American writers to fathom despotism, some from the painful safety of exile. From 1936 to 1939, the Spanish civil war invaded Latin American consciousness: many writers went to the mother country and faced international fascism with guns and grenades. By the 1950s and 1960s, a critical mass of interrelated issues and insight sparked *la boom.* The subjects of the many novels published after midcentury include the Cuban Revolution, women's liberation, national security regimes, liberation theology, the Chilean coup of 1973, modern technologies from auto and air travel to birth control and mass media, and latent Latin American legacies.[19]

While exploring modern topics, regional writers fathomed Latin American traditions. Relevant historic themes include *indigenismo,* elitism, exploitation, spirituality, servitude, Catholicism, ethnicity, and the very magic and mystery of the land. Literary heritage was another important legacy. The naturalism of natives, the fantastic realism of early chroniclers, the realistic fantasy of *autos sacramentales* and other early genres resurfaced in modern novels. Latin American authors also drew upon the rich legacy of Spanish literature as Don Quixotes, Sancho Panzas, Don Juans, and Celestinas were reborn as modern characters. Regional writers also adopted European trends, from Freudian and Jungian psychologies to the artistic visions of Velásquez, Goya, Dalí, and Picasso. And North American media imagery—from Coca Cola and Superman to gangsters and Rita Hayworth—entered the dreams and nightmares of regional writers. By the mid-twentieth century, Latin American writing became a chain-reactive explosion. So many fine writers produced so much that one becomes dizzy trying to contemplate the breadth of subjects and styles. And *la boom* is far from spent.

The writing of Latin American novels progressed with the century itself. *Indigenismo* was its first major subject. In 1904, the Bolivian Alcides Arguedas composed his first nativist novel. It was rewritten and published as *Race of Bronze* fifteen years later, when the Mexican Revolution gave new urgency to Indigen issues: Emiliano Zapata and talk of land reform stimulated hemispheric consciousness and responses. During the 1930s, *indigenismo* emerged everywhere. Jorge Icaza of Ecuador told the desperate story of mountain villagers in *Huasipungo* (1934). Peruvian Ciro Alegría wrote of modern jungles and marginalized natives in *Hungry Dogs* (1939) and *Broad and Alien Is the World* (1941). The Mexican Gregorio López y Fuentes wrote his haunting 1935 novel, *El Indio,* without proper names. Each character fills a ghostly role—*hacendado,* teacher, politician, bride—as fate weaves cycles. Perhaps the most complex *indigenista* novels were those of Nobel laureate Miguel Angel Asturias of Guatemala. His *Men of Maize* (1948) explores ancient Mayan imperium lingering in the cornfields of modern peasants.[20]

Nineteenth-century *costumbrista* topics eventually evolved into a profoundly basic theme: *la tierra* (the land). *La tierra* is more than scenery and stage. It is the story's subtle protagonist, *pacha mama* as primordial force, as a goddess both satanic and saintly. As a theme, the land has had a long existence. In his sixteenth-century Chilean epic, *Araucana,* the Iberian officer Alonso de Ercilla gave literary life to *la tierra:* Spanish soldiers are defeated as much by the power of nature as by native forces. In her late-twentieth-century novel *House of the Spirits,* Isabel Allende again personified a vengeful *pacha mama* as an earthquake smashes the arrogant *hacendado* who seeks to dominate the land. The greatest personification of *la tierra* comes in the writing of Mexican surreal existentialist Juan Rulfo. In Rulfo's short stories and brief novel, *Pedro Páramo* (1955), humans are shadows; the real protagonists are rocks, the arid earth, searing sunlight, heat and dust. Action seems incidental to what remains unchanged: *la tierra.*

In a region where ancient legacies infuse modern realities, Latin American writers easily transcend the limits of chronological existence. But their time warps are not the stuff of North American science fiction, which typically uses technology to go forward. Instead, transcending time in Latin American novels is spiritual and reaches back. It operates within a context of Indigen ancestors, the undead of African Latin heritage, and a Mediterranean fascination with cyclical lives. In modern Latin American novels, time is also personal and arbitrary. This is best displayed in *Hopscotch* by the Argentine Julio Cortázar, who allows readers to choose their own sequence of chapters: each pattern creates different routes leading to the same end. Time itself is a protagonist for Alejo Carpentier, who like all Cubans holds diverse origins. His immigrant Russian mother and French father raised their child in a Caribbean African culture. Training as an architect and musicologist imparted an appreciation of structure and multiple overlays. In his novels characters move about in space and time, sometimes circling upon earlier—or later—manifestations of self. His brilliant short stories include "The High Road of Santiago" and "Journey Back to the Source"; among his many novels are *Kingdom of This Earth* (1949) and *The Lost Steps* (1953). In all these, individuals are baroque facades, a composite of their own legacies and locale.

Writers of *la boom* typically measure time by memory, which is neither linear nor progressive. What a person remembers—and *how* he or she remembers—is more primary for Latin American authors than any clock or calendar. The best example of this is *The Death of Artemio Cruz,* a novel of the Mexican Revolution by Carlos Fuentes. In this story, the elderly protagonist lies dying in a modern hospital. Fading from consciousness, he retrieves personal memories—some romanticized, some supposed, and some painfully insightful—in a nonsequential pattern. Like pieces of a puzzle, episodes from a disorderly lifetime are laid before the reader. The story evolves from initial confusion into a complex amalgam of fact and fiction: national history and world events are permeated with personal ambitions and family betrayals. Politics and sociology mix with popular culture. Gender roles are juxtaposed. Eventually, death and birth are united in one last and long-denied memory of origins. *The Death of Artemio Cruz* is an amazing novel, at once insightful and disturbing.

In modern Latin American writing, personal truth matters more than impersonal fact. How things are perceived and felt is primary. Thus, the nostalgia of a grandmother, the apprehensions of a child, the exaggerations of a macho, and the visions of a shaman may be more honest than what purports to be news, history, or science.[21]

The major themes of modern Latin American literature merge in the omnibus novel by Gabriel García Márquez, *One Hundred Years of Solitude* (1967). Here events are not dates but mist-filled memories. The tierra is magical Macondo, which is as much heat, humidity, mold, and must as a stage for patriarchs, matriarchs, and successive generations of rogues and revolutionaries, virgins and villains: sometimes both in one persona. In Macondo, earlier generations decline into lengthening shadows, which metamorphose into ghostly ancestors. *One Hundred Years* represents a Latin American community and Latin America itself. Here the mundane is exaggerated, exaggeration becomes magical, and magic is mystified. The novel reveals the shallowness of the grand and the grandeur of the common: high ideals degrade into vanity, while a piece of ice enraptures popular imaginations. At numerous times, the reader is shocked to see progress reappear with another round of consequences. Attempts to escape fate design ever more intricate mazes for those seeking glory, wealth, power, and love. In writing this massive novel, García Márquez himself had many progenitors: the chronicles of Pigafetta, stories told in childhood, the history of Latin America, Cervantes's *Don Quixote,* biblical metaphors, Shakespearean tempests, Arabic legends, African superstitions, and Indigen symbolism. If any piece of literature best represents the grandeur of *la boom, One Hundred Years of Solitude* is it.

The wealth of Latin American literature is massive. The cumulative layering of poetry, novels, short stories, theater, and themes has created a resource far richer than mines of silver or pools of petroleum. And late-twentieth-century writing is a mother lode that our survey has identified but barely explored. A more comprehensive assessment would follow many veins: Brazil (with authors like Jorge Amado and Clarice Lispector, and its own Iberian legacy); Cuba (including exiles such as Guillermo Cabrera Infante and Reinaldo Arenas); Peru (where César Vallejo and Mario Vargas Llosa represent the far ends of a vast social spectrum); Mexico (holding generations of writers from Mariano Azuela of the century's opening to Laura Esquival at its end); Argentina (with its own tradition highlighted by novelists such as Ernesto Sábato and Manuel Puig); and many more places with many more writers. The landscape of Latin American literature is vast.

NATIVE BEAUTY

Art seeks to capture human ideals. Whether architecture or painting, dance or music, formal or popular, art reveals personal and collective dreams. It elevates individuals and groups to a higher plane of existence, it surrounds life with a more perfect environment of color, texture, sound, and movement. It also forms consciousness. By understanding art, we better comprehend the aspirations and achievements of those who made it.

Indigen visual arts were highly developed by 1500. Native Americans excelled at using materials, form, composition, and color to express concepts of beauty. Whether textiles or pottery, sculpted metal or choreographed movement, art was an everyday thing. The Indigens' grandest achievements were great and elaborately adorned stone cities. Relics of past dreams remain in the giant Olmec heads of Mexico, the huge but intricate figures at San Agustín in Colombia, and towering granite guardsmen at Tula, Mexico. From Tiahuanaco (Bolivia) to Teotihuacán (Mexico), edifices were carved, cast, and laid up with figures, motifs, and bold colors: in effect, clothing buildings in mammoth renditions of the often dazzling dress still worn by Indigens. Unfortunately, tourists visiting these sites today typically see stones weathered by age and elements. Only in protected nooks and crannies can bits and pieces of original bold coloration be found. Meanwhile, excavations at Teotihuacán and Bonampak have discovered long-hidden rooms with walls covered by rainbow pigmentation. Similar bold colors and murals once embellished exteriors, which were often inlaid with gems and precious metals. Reflecting the sun and replicating nature's palette, the buildings honored the sources that inspired them.

While once-colorful sites are located almost everywhere in the Americas, the most subtly beautiful and practical Indigen masonry is located in the earthquake-prone Andes. In a region where continental plates collide, Indigen craftsmen shaped great boulders often weighing sixty tons and constructed the walls of Inca cities. The genius of such masonry is in carefully fitting stones that lack strictly horizontal and vertical lines. With no mortar, the stones can slide and shift, adjusting to the sometimes shaking earth. They still stand today, while many colonial and modern buildings have fallen to ruins. The beauty of Inca masonry, observed in Cuzco or Machu Picchu, is its austere simplicity. The stone walls replicate the magnitude and majesty, the earth tone colors and deviating lines, the serenity and seeming eternity of surrounding mountains.[22]

From southern Mexico to Paraguay, Indigens still clothe themselves with intricate designs and bold colors. The dyes used by Andean and Meso-American peoples to achieve such beauty are similar to those used centuries ago. The evidence lies in 2000-year-old ponchos found on mummies, including those from the Paracas culture of coastal Peru. These ancient textiles reveal cloth woven from cotton and various wools: llama, alpaca, and vicuña. One mantle contains 190 gradations of color, 22 totally different hues. Such complexity displays amazing technical knowledge of fibers, dyes, looms, and the process of making quality cloth. Weaving also reveals lineage and place. For centuries, particular villages and families have repeated certain colors and designs to mark time and community. Through the patterns of a blouse or shirt, a serape or sombrero, Indigens show ancestry as well as art, their generation as well as village. These ancient stories are told in the colorful dress of modern Indigens, who still weave memories into the fabrics of common life.[23]

Personal decoration complements clothing. When Europeans arrived, they found Indigen elites adorned with massive headdresses and capes of feathers and furs. Subsequent excavations—even today—uncovered death masks of gold and silver imbedded with gems. Such elaborate artifacts have found their way to museums, but daily life remains decorated with less elaborate ornaments: earrings, bracelets, and other jewelry made of copper and silver, stones, shells, and colored threads. These personal objects of art represent more than status, wealth, or just something pretty. They are often symbols of spiritualism. Since ancient times, the attraction of precious metals and gems has been their brilliance: sunshine was considered an Indigen source of life, and objects reflecting light replicated the energy of the gods. Thus, artisans who created jewelry of gold, silver, and copper, imbedded with turquoise, jade, and emeralds, worked in a spiritual medium; they were revered interpreters of mystic forces.

Indigen consciousness came alive in glittering renditions of frogs, fish, birds and snakes, the sun and moon, stylized designs of lightning and rain, and the images of gods. Made into earrings, nose plugs, rings, bracelets, and necklaces, these objects once adorned the statues of gods or—as funerary masks—mummies. And now, as for centuries, Indigen jewelry decorates the living.

Indigen jewelers also worked in larger media. They were the craftsmen who once embellished the shrines and palaces of imperial cities. In Cuzco, the Temple of the Sun was named Coricancha ("fence of gold") for the treasures it held. The volume of golden artifacts accumulated through centuries staggers the imagination. When the conquistador Pizarro captured Atahualpa, the Inca prince was commanded to fill a room as high as the hand could reach with gold objects. When the deed was done—and a golden legacy gathered—Pizarro had the objects melted into ingots. A similar fate for native artistry in gold and silver—usually denounced as idolatry and esteemed as bullion—met Indigen collections from Mexico to Chile. Still, many objects escaped the crucibles of conquest. Today, public museums and private collections—particularly in Lima, Peru—hold some of the world's finest gold and silver artistry.[24]

Ceramics and wood carvings were other Indigen achievements. And here imaginations were grand. Inspired by the natural and mystical, the humorous, erotic, and tragic, Indigens used animals, anthropomorphic images, and intense realism. From New Mexico to Patagonia, natives created a legacy of visual beauty. The artifacts were large and small, with textures approximating human skin, leafy jungles, or animal fur. Coloration ranged from earth tones to the bold. The variety of pottery from the Americas is immense, reflecting many peoples and many millennia.[25]

In the early twentieth century the new science of anthropology discovered the obvious: Indigen performing arts. This realization eventually reached audiences around the world, who discovered native American song and movement through *indigenismo* of the 1920s, the folk movement of the 1960s, or the resurgence of Indigen identity in the late twentieth century. The most commercially successful dance company employing native American music and dance has been the Ballet Folklórico de México, which has repeatedly toured the world. Onstage, Mexican musicians and dancers using replicas of ancient pipes and drums again interpret stories of creation and courtship, hunting and harvesting, human sacrifice and encounters with the gods. In recent years, Indigen performers themselves have brought artistry to public rallies and public squares, from Lima, to Quito, to Mexico City. At the *zócalo* in Mexico's capital, native singing and dancing evoke ancient memories before archaeological digs: excavations of temples that once honored Aztec gods. But the most haunting performances of Indigen sound and movement are in villages. The description of the English author D. H. Lawrence, after he attended a performance at Taos, New Mexico, in the 1920s, captures the subtle power of ancient songs and dance:

> Never shall I forget the utter absorption of the dance, so quiet, so steadily, timelessly rhythmic, and silent, with the ceaseless down-tread, always to the earth's center, the very reverse of the upflow of Dionysiac or Christian ecstasy. Never shall I forget the deep singing of the men at the drum, . . . the wonderful deep sound of men calling to the unspeakable depths.[26]

While some native arts perished following the European encounter, many remained as aspects of daily life. Modern archaeology, anthropology, and Indigen activism have brought native arts to world audiences. But Europeans arriving after 1500 sought to dominate official new world aesthetics. Indigens and enslaved Africans were instructed to create European visions of beauty. Their resulting art was a compromise.

COLONIZED VISIONS

Once Europeans arrived, "official" art in the Americas turned from indigenous dreams to replicating old world visions of architecture, paintings, sculpture, and design. The goal was to construct cathedrals and courtyards resembling those of Moorish Spain, to paint formal portraits in a Flemish or Italian style, and to generally achieve European ideals of beauty. But European standards were neither static nor strict as styles evolved from gothic, to baroque, through (eventually) nineteenth-century neoclassicism. And since the colonial artisans instructed to craft these European visions were often Indigen, African, or descended from Moors or Asians, the result was eclectic: a mix of European principle and diverse practice. Thus, colonial art in the Americas superficially appears European. Upon examination, however, one sees lines bending to African curvature or colors shading to Indigen tones. Once judged inferior for these very reasons, colonial art is instead its own creative genre.

Official aesthetics were propagandistic as well as artistic. Massive public buildings in romance or baroque styles remained colonials of the European imperium. Ornate and cavernous cathedrals anchored European Christianity at the center of colonial life. Opposed to idolatry, Iberian Catholic art also defended against emerging European heresy and profanity: Protestantism and growing secularism. At the Council of Trent, church fathers in 1541 decreed that art should propagate faith: images of beauty should be channeled into Christian symbolism. This broad dictum served as official doctrine in colonized Latin America for 200 years, until Bourbon reforms during the Enlightenment encouraged secular artistic expression.

Until the eighteenth century, colonial art reinforced racial, spiritual, and class dominion. Paintings and carvings depicted the saints, Jesus, and Mary not only as Catholic icons but as white and usually aristocratic rulers. Images of Christ—even the ubiquitous bloodied and tortured symbol of the crucified martyr—displayed a man with distinctly European features. Depictions of the Virgin Mary frequently portrayed a European monarch attended by cherubic retainers and an imperial regalia of crowns, scepters, sumptuous gowns, and sounding coronets. Christian saints from Peter and Paul to Barbara and Anne often resembled European royalty. From building massive cathedrals to assembling humble home shrines, colonial ideals of beauty propagandized imperial power: top-down dreams of grandeur.

But in the Americas, colonial art was filled with popular substance as neophyte Christian artisans carved wood and stone, painted murals, and laid tiles according to ethnic legacies. Plans in the minds of arriving priests or aristocrats could only be envisioned according to the local artisan's own dreams and experience. When instructed to depict a European image, Indigen or African artists and artisans formed local materials and colors into shapes familiar to them. Thus, the baroque art of Mexico is not that of Madrid. The architecture of colonial Brazil is a cousin rather than a clone of buildings found in Lisbon. In one example, Indigen muralists in Cuernavaca, Mexico, were instructed to paint cathedral walls with the story of St. Francis Javier arriving in Japan. What they depicted were Spanish missionaries arriving in Mexico: it was their consciousness. All across the Americas, indigenous dreams remade foreign visions.

Within this adaptive ambience, great artists and artisans emerged. Aleijandinho was one. Aleijandinho was the African Brazilian known as the "Little Cripple," an affectionate nickname for Antônio Francisco Lisboa, born in 1738 of a Portuguese architect father and an enslaved African Latin mother. Aleijandinho was amazing for many reasons. Even as a child, he was renowned as an architect and sculptor. Aleijandinho's most notable aspect became his handicap: at age thirty-nine, disease permanently crippled his hands. Undeterred, he was driven by passion to somehow carve the best works of his career. His most beautiful creations adorn the churches of Ouro Prêto, Brazil. Here stone becomes larger-than-life depictions of human emotion: saints and sinners from Christian mythology meditate and anguish, reflect and repent. Many among Aleijandinho's hundreds of statues look classically Greek and Roman, others have African characteristics. A few, including Jesus, occasionally display an east Asian aspect. But what really distinguishes these biblical characters is their choreography: a great number are frozen in an African Brazilian dance, swaying to an imagined samba in the mind of their creator. Across Brazil and throughout the Caribbean, other artisans shaped and painted adaptations of their African Latin dreams.[27]

Many colonial artisans remain collectively anonymous. As Indigen craftsmen built thousands of beautiful Catholic churches over a span of 300 years and across the Americas, they listened attentively to the plans of priestly architects. However, when finished, these basically European-style churches glittered with colors and decorations as brilliant as those of earlier Aztec or Andean temples. Upon examination, onlookers realize that European architects and Indigen artisans adopted each other's aesthetics. Dozens, even hundreds, of examples abound. Our case study is the Church of San Francisco de Acatepec, near Puebla, Mexico. This small church seems large due to its massive detail and decoration. Its facade is a riot of glazed and unglazed ceramic tiles, which extends the classic baroque repetition of shapes into novel replications of bold colors. As visitors enter the courtyard and approach the portal, they are engulfed by an explosion of reds, blues, whites, and yellows. Baroque curves, Moorish geometry, Mediterranean tiles, and Indigen colors merge into myriad details; the details form a wondrous whole. Observers ponder how human minds could conceive—then construct—such complexity. Inside, indigenous workers carved angels that look like flowers and wove intricate baroque designs that depict the interconnectedness of all living things. Gold leafing above the altar reflects sunlight in an otherwise dim interior, as if heaven illuminates the priest and crucifix. The Indigen artisans who constructed colonial Acatepec descended from craftsmen who once built sacrificial temples to the sun. Under Christian tutelage, they adapted their trades with great skill and irony.

Eventually, after 300 years, colonialism formally ended. Most Latin American nations became independent in the 1820s. However, achieving aesthetic autonomy was a gradual process, beginning long before and culminating almost a century after 1820. The movement away from colonized visions began quietly as Enlightenment ideas infiltrated Latin America in the 1700s. The first manifestation was a transition from religious to secular art. The agents for change—reflecting a paradox of European imperialism—were innovative rulers in Iberia, especially the Marquês de Pombal in Portugal and Bourbon monarchs in Spain. Both new leaderships promoted scientific and secular inquiry in place of religious dicta. Part of enlightened observation was accurately cataloging new world empires.[28]

A revolution in perspective developed as art joined nascent science to clearly depict American habitats. European botanical and naturalist expeditions, complete with highly trained illustrators, scoured the new world. As they pioneered a realistic rendition of new world environments, these illustrators also made America itself the subject of art. The process may have begun when Captain James Cook of England visited western American coastlines from 1768 to 1776, bringing with him artists who carefully painted flora, fauna, and geography. Curious about his own American realms, Carlos III of Spain decided to catalog the plants of his colonies and created the Botanical Commission of New Granada in 1784. For a third of a century, Spanish artists and illustrators drew and painted new world flora and fauna. While the resulting art was not published until the twentieth century, the project fostered broad curiosity. The most famous of the curious was the German scientist and explorer Alexander von Humboldt, who hired a French botanist and artist, Aimé Bonpland. Authorized by the Bourbons to catalog the natural life of their American colonies, the two naturalists traversed Spanish realms from Mexico to Chile between 1799 and 1804, making field sketches, gathering specimens, and filling notebooks. Back in Europe, von Humbolt spent much of his remaining life publishing his findings: thirty volumes over thirty years. The periodic release of quality art on Latin America stimulated continued European curiosity during the nineteenth century.

The late Enlightenment and early romantic passion for knowledge of the Americas formed the final phase of a centuries-long European encounter. Europeans were still looking for an earthly paradise, but instead of Columbus's Cathay and Eden or the explorer's El Dorado, they now searched for the world's last pristine habitat. Some, such as Charles Darwin aboard the *HMS Beagle,* collected specimens to substantiate his theory on the origins of life. More came as artists pursuing the exotic, looking for anything not yet "spoiled." Initially, they drew and painted more or less realistic images of remote mountains, waterfalls, forests, flowers, and strange animals. But romantic interpretation rather than realistic depiction crept into European perspectives. Within decades, paintings evolved from stylized poses of birds and careful catalogs of plants to dreamy portraits of rustic villages and picturesque natives: a Shangri-la of mystical natural wonders and timeless local folk. A few examples of such panoramic bliss are Daniel Thomas Egerton's *View of the Valley of Mexico* (1837), Johann Moritz Rugendas's *View in the Environs of Lima* (1843), and Ferdinand Bellerman's *View of La Guaria* (1842–1846). In Brazil, the French romantic artist Jean-Baptiste Debret portrayed dense jungles and primitive natives. On acres of painted canvas, gentlemen and ladies dressed in top hats and bonnets typically view vast landscapes from some handy lookout, with walking cane or parasol in hand.[29]

The old world interest in natural America held ironic consequences for evolving

European art. One important instance occurred when a visiting artist returned to Europe with more than colored canvas. While traveling in the Caribbean, the Danish painter Fritz Georg Melbye found a local lad, Camille Pissarro, sketching scenes in his native St. Thomas. Eventually, both returned to Europe. In France, the self-taught Pissarro contined painting the way he had in the American tropics: using pastels and broken lines to infuse compositions with bright sunshine. By doing so, Camille Pissarro revolutionized European perspective and launched the French impressionist movement.[30]

Meanwhile, Latin America was experiencing sometimes contradictory transformations. Enlightenment innovations promoted autonomous American visions, as when Bourbon reformers opened art schools that challenged long-standing clerical domination of the arts. The Royal Academy of San Carlos, at Mexico City, opened in 1785. From its inception, this art college taught brushwork and composition but also social consciousness and national identity. As described by one observer: "Here all classes, colours and races were mingled together; the Indian beside the white boy, and the son of the poorest mechanic beside that of the richest lord."[31] San Carlos encouraged artists to envision a more equitable and self-reliant society. But political independence made art serve other masters. In Rio de Janeiro, Brazil, the Academis Imperial de Belas Artes was founded in 1826. Similar art schools opened somewhat later in Spanish American capitals. These institutes were clearly nationalistic. But increasingly that nationalism was also elitist and propagandistic as it celebrated order and progress: and a criollo vision of America.

Patronized by criollo elites, nineteenth-century art schools returned to a colonized perspective, but with a local and modern twist. Gone was the glorification of Catholic spiritualism and Iberian aristocrats. Instead, nineteenth-century "official" art depicted progress by *American* representatives of European civilization. Criollo sponsors hired European instructors and commissioned local painters and architects to replicate slightly Americanized renditions of European art as a way of legitimizing their own rule. Subjects as well as styles extolled the making of criollo America: destiny was displayed in the ideas and actions of white men. Artistic imagery cemented criollo bonds to old world allegories. Nineteenth-century Latin American painting, architecture, and statues generally depicted European content with a thin American veneer. A statue entitled *America* (1830) is merely a stylized Greek goddess with a stereotypical Indigen headdress. One is hard-pressed to find anything Latin American (except the title) in *The Huntress of the Andes* (1891): it portrays a giant white nude sprawled over a lilliputian landscape. More than exploring local identities, most late-nineteenth-century Latin American artists esteemed European images.[32]

Meanwhile, Europeans themselves were looking to Latin America for something more exotic than a Greek goddess in American feathers. Many visiting European artists depicted realistic or romanticized images of natural life. But, as in literature, the taste in European visual arts also ran toward *costumbrismo:* colorful depictions of "rustic" Latin Americans. Most popular were nostalgic images of Mexican Indigens, Afro-Brazilians, and Argentine gauchos. *Costumbrista* subjects were set against panoramic landscapes or were shown using colorful folkloric pottery or weavings. Many were depicted in traditional rites. From these odd dichotomies—Latin American artists looking to Europe and European artists looking to Latin America—some magic occurred. Local artists began to share the European search for a Latin American soul. The quest was initially romantic. It quickly became revolutionary.

LATIN AMERICANS DISCOVER THEMSELVES

As Latin American artists employed European visions to depict nearby landscapes, they discovered a land of subtle force and infinite beauty. Experimenting with form as well as substance, professional artists also advanced truly Latin American expression. From painting murals on public buildings to drawing folk cartoons, to playing music on ancient instruments, Latin American artists fathomed their own legacies. As regional art and artists proliferated, twentieth-century aesthetics became a landscape filled with many dreams.

The transformation from colonized to Latin American visions came in many ways. A late-nineteenth-century painter, the Mexican José María Velasco, was one pioneer. Trained in European techniques, Velasco painted what initially appears to be massive romantic landscapes of central Mexico. But close study shows the grand and obvious to be filled with detail and subtlety as the simple becomes ever more complex—like Latin America itself. In Velasco's paintings, European ladies and gentlemen are replaced by local folk, usually peasants. And rather than standing *costumbrista* fashion to display their dress and artifacts, they are active, chasing dogs, kissing babies, or even riding on railway freight cars. But the major protagonist in Velasco's paintings is the land itself. And one sees both realism and romanticism. Tensions are evident: between humans and nature, between progress and the ancient earth. Latin American themes—such as the interplay of ecology and technology—are revealed in works such as *Bridge at Metlac* (1881). In *El Citlaltépetl* (1879), the snowcapped volcano becomes a mystical backdrop for a locomotive blowing steam and smoke into nearby flora. Between the foreground train and the distant mountain, one views land scarred from earlier human activity. But José María Velasco's paintings are not indictments. Nature and humans, spiritual and material, the old and new: all have their roles, all are one drama.[33]

Another Mexican stylist worked in the realm of popular arts. José Guadalupe Posada was a lithographer, a wood- and tile-cutting artisan producing illustrations similar to London's *Punch* or the cartoons of Thomas Nast in the United States. But Posada put his illustrations on anything and everything, including broadsides, greeting cards, and even cigar wrappers. Much of his art appeared in fifty different Mexico City newspapers and journals between 1888 and 1913. More important than a prolific output was his trademark caricature: the *calavera* (skeleton), representing the duality of lurking death and ghostly afterlife. The *calavera* once preoccupied the dreams of an Aztec priesthood, which decorated temples with human skulls. *Calaveras* subsequently became icons of popular religious art as Mexicans celebrate *el día de los muertos* (the Day of the Dead), which remains an annual festival. Posada satirically used skeletons dressed in cassocks, uniforms, skirts, and sombreros to depict priests and presidents, prostitutes and peasants, generals and even horses, children, and household pets. In these cartoons, Posada's irony was comic and tragic, bitter and compassionate. Although he died in 1913, he elevated both lithography and *calaveras* into popular twentieth-century arts. From Mexico to Chile, during the Spanish civil war of the 1930s, the national security repressions of the 1960s and 1970s, and even today, the art of Posada lingered: like his ghostly *calaveras.*

Velasco and Posada are two examples of the early transition from colonized to Latin American visions. The culminating declaration of artistic freedom came with the Mexican Revolution of 1910–1920, a full century following the region's political independence. In its creative force, the Mexican Revolution impacted all Latin American arts and artists. The full flourish of nationalism and the frontal attack on elitism that characterized the Mexican rebellion inspired creativity as far away as Buenos Aires. While the Mexican peasant general Emiliano Zapata practiced the art of revolution, young admirers developed revolutionary art.

A brief survey such as this can neither chronicle nor catalog the entire twentieth-century chain-reactive explosion of Latin American arts. Decade by decade, across the hemisphere, creativity built upon itself. The endless artistry of Latin Americans has spilled beyond the region, into the streets of Los Angeles, recording studios in Miami, galleries of New York City, and boulevards of Paris. Twentieth-century artistic expression began with frescoes and murals, lithographs and watercolors. It continued with movies and recorded songs: from films starring the Mexican actors Delores del Río and Cantinflas to such great singers and musicians as the Argentine Carlos Gardel and Cuban Célia Cruz. Streams of creativity created new channels. Kinetic art decorated architecture with shadows on raised relief textures. In the hands of avant-garde Latin American artists, wind makes music, moving water induces objects to dance, and potatoes generate electricity. The art of industry includes neon sculptures and murals made from junked cars. Modern adaptations of folk art range from peasant women making papier-mâché dolls of Elvis Presley and Pope John Paul III to African Latin fetishes depicting John F. Kennedy and space astronauts. Whether as old styles or new forms, whether in Haitian villages or the metropolis of São Paulo, the arts in twentieth-century Latin America have boomed beyond the ability of any author to describe in less than a multivolume set: not including supplements.

Mexico leads the twentieth-century revolution in Spanish American arts. And the giant of modern Mexican art—creatively, prodigiously, and physically—has been Diego Rivera. As Latin America's premier muralist, this mestizo employed the ancient Indigen medium of painting public buildings. Mexican colleagues in this craft include José Clemente Orozco, David Alfaro Siqueiros, and Juan O'Gorman. But more than these talented contemporaries, Diego Rivera was a model for devoted artists throughout Latin America. For decades, he inspired an army of artisans who launched frontal attacks on the legacies of colonial domination and local privilege. Here were artists as rebels, using art to inspire action through raising consciousness and encouraging legions of workers and peasants to cast off the chains of tradition. Rivera also inspired New Deal painters in the United States, who painted courthouse lobbies and library hallways across the nation. Of all twentieth-century new world painters, Diego Rivera stands tallest as artist and inspiration.

Rivera's most intimate associate was Frieda Kahlo, his on-again, off-again wife.

Unlike the boldly public murals of Rivera, Kahlo's canvases were boldly private, showing her utmost psychological and physical pain. Few artists in human history have used self-portraits so powerfully and so often to reveal a landscape of emotions. Her pictures draw upon Mexican mythology, colonial religious art, visits to the United States, her own decorated home, but mostly her self. Her greatest resource is her tortured and scarred body. Suffering a near-fatal streetcar wreck as a teenager, Kahlo subsequently painted shattered spines and bleeding veins, alter egos and frustrated femininity. Her art is generally surrealistic but also highly skilled and powerfully beautiful. It projects Mexican identity and the martyrdom of a modern woman.

The old and the new of twentieth-century Mexican artistry culminated in what might be called the traditional modern art of Rufino Tamayo. Tamayo was born a Zapotec in Oaxaca and never forgot his Indigen sense of color and composition. But he lived his adult life in Paris, New York, and Mexico City, amid the urbanity of contemporaries like Pablo Picasso and Marc Chagall. As an artist he drew upon both ancient legacies and a modern ambience. His colors on canvas are the premier signature of his art: they appear as the peeling patina of a sunny Mexican home and the bold mixing of avant-garde pigmentation. His shadowy shapes resemble the ancient distorted morphologies found at Mitla or Monte Albán, yet they could be a takeoff on modern cubism. More than any contemporary, Rufino Tamayo worked in the medium of ancient destinies. His art places one hand firmly on remembered legacies, while the other carefully molds the future.

Beyond Mexico, twentieth-century artists and performers have been equally imaginative and inspired but less concentrated. The Caribbean and Brazil witness endless manifestations of African traditions in modern form. Voodoo folk artists have infused natural objects with African spirituality to form simple street murals and dreamy village sculptures. The Cuban Wifredo Lam did the same with forest greens and African masks for his easel art. Meanwhile, Brazilians dance sambas in the street, and professional companies from Havana and Colombia combine European ballet with African Caribbean rhythms. Urbanization inspires artists from Caracas, Rio de Janeiro, and other regional metropolises who form plated metals, pipes, wires, and cut pieces of rubber and plastic into futuristic shapes with titles like *Five Large Rods, Rubber Grub,* and *Machine Animal.* Celluloid and video have become the chosen media of Latin American photographers and filmmakers from Santiago, Chile, to Santiago, Cuba. Architects use sun and shadow on cylinders and spheres to create mobile effects on buildings. Colored neon tubing has become an artistic palette. Politics promotes new arts. Revolutionary movements in Cuba, Chile, and Nicaragua have each been engines of artistic imagination. And in villages and towns across a hemisphere, folk artists and artisans continue the ancient crafts of embroidery, weaving, carving, and ceramics.

The richest resource of Latin America is its artistic vision. Whether professional or popular, as poetry, stories, paintings, weaving, architecture, music, or dance, all arts in the region derive from eclectic legacies and creative innovations. For many millennia, Indigen visions of beauty created colorful landscapes. After the European encounter, Latin American artists and artisans tutored themselves in the skills of creative adaptation—and sometimes their visions were dominated. But 400 years of colonized art produced a hemispheric museum of art and artifacts. Truly Latin American visions did not emerge until the decades surrounding 1900. During the twentieth century vast artistic landscapes were created from the ancient visions of Indigen and European, African Latin and immigrant. The impulse for creativity became ardently revolutionary, proudly mestizo, and often clearly materialistic. From these many wellsprings—ancient and modern—Latin American artists have crafted landscapes born of dreams.

SUGGESTED READINGS

Ades, Dawn. *Art in Latin America: The Modern Era, 1820–1980.* New Haven, Conn.: Yale University Press, 1989.

Castedo, Leopoldo. *A History of Latin American Art and Architecture, from Pre-Columbian Times to the Present.* New York: Praeger, 1969.

Castro-Klaren, Sara, Sylvia Molloy, and Béatriz Sarlo. *Women's Writing in Latin America: An Anthology.* Boulder, Colo.: Westview Press, 1991.

Englekirk, John E., ed. *An Outline History of Spanish American Literature.* New York: Irvington Publishers, 1980.

King, John. *Magical Reels: A History of Cinema in Latin America.* London: Verso and the Latin American Bureau, 1990.

Manguel, Alberto, ed. *Other Fires: Short Fiction by Latin American Women.* New York: Clarkson Potter, 1986.

Paz, Octavio. *The Labyrinth of Solitude: Life and Thought in Mexico,* trans. Lysander Kemp. New York: Grove Press, 1961.

Rodríguez Monegal, Emir. *The Borzoi Anthology of Latin American Literature.* Vols. 1 and 2. New York: Knopf, 1984.

Townsend, Richard F., ed. *The Ancient Americas: Art from Sacred Landscapes.* Munich: Prestel Verlag and the Art Institute of Chicago, 1992.

Traba, Marta. *Art of Latin America: 1900–1980.* Baltimore: Johns Hopkins University Press and the Inter-American Development Bank, 1994.

CONCLUSION: LEGACIES OF AN ANCIENT FUTURE

Knowledge of the past helps explain the present. And while history is no crystal ball revealing destiny, the future should surprise no one who understands past human behavior.

Like Machiavelli in *The Prince* showing how historical knowledge encourages practicality, comprehending the past should make observers realistic. Before broken machinery can be fixed, its design and functioning must be understood. Likewise, before social, political, or economic problems can be solved, their roots and ramifications must be known. Superficial understanding creates superficial solutions. However, awareness of context—time, place, and culture—does not easily or axiomatically solve long-entrenched problems. Still, awareness of legacies—like knowledge of mechanics—should better identify how a problem originated. And knowledge of beginnings should suggest solutions: or at least a more realistic assessment of how intractable problems are.

This theoretical discussion of legacies can be applied to particular topics. Illegal migration to the United States is one of many issues that can be better understood by reviewing Latin American legacies. Other problems include drugs, debt, worker exploitation, ecological ruin, maldistribution of incomes, and so on. But we shall use immigration as one example revealing how knowledge of legacies illumines modern situations.

During the last decades of the twentieth century, Latin Americans have crossed into the United States in huge numbers. While many immigrants arrive from Caribbean and Central American nations, most are Mexicans, and in modern times the Mexican-U.S. border has been the busiest crossing on earth. Although a fair number of newcomers are professionals, most migrants are poor laborers who usually recross repeatedly as they accumulate higher wages in the north and stretch buying power by either sending money to families in the south or returning home to spend their hard earned dollars. Many poor illegals arrive from depressed economies, and while some seek personal security, quality education, and social services, the primary desire is better wages.

Critics of this migration—politicians, journalists, veterans, and others—have mounted growing protests. They decry an "invasion" that supposedly takes jobs from Americans and burdens public budgets with additional costs for welfare, law enforcement, hospitalization, education, and so on. Protesting higher taxes, critics also claim that illegal immigrants challenge "American identity." They further point to higher crime rates, drugs, and violence. Often immigrant issues assume polarizations of right versus wrong, good versus evil, or just simple authority: "I'm the boss here." Proposed solutions include passing laws denying illegal immigrants access to basic health and human services (including education), increasing security at the border, and rescinding the North American Free Trade Agreement. Police brutality has been another long-standing weapon used against migrants, and in April 1996, a news team in Riverside, California, videotaped U.S. officers mercilessly beating defenseless migrants, including a woman. Despite repeated efforts, stratagems, and frustrations, migration from Mexico and Latin America continues. Knowledge of legacies shows why.

The list of factors drawing particularly Mexicans to the American southwest began 150 years ago when two national destinies collided. In the early nineteenth century, newly independent Mexico was beginning to formulate public policy for its northern territories when invited settlers from the United States declared Texas independent. In a process reminiscent of the Florida annexation—and also filled with legal, political, and military shenanigans—the United States in 1848 waged war with Mexico and seized half its national domain. This act denied Mexico a potentially glorious future, one built on access to California gold, Texas oil, Colorado silver, Arizona copper, Nevada uranium, and other valuable minerals. The modern bounty would have included rich ranches and farmland, hydroelectric power, forests, and a great climate. All these many resources instead enriched arriving Yankees. Had this territory remained Mexican, it would have filled with an expanding Mexican population seeking better lives. To a large extent, it did anyway.

The annexation of northern Mexico in 1848 has been glibly explained and simplistically excused. Some have held that the land was virtually vacant, that Mexico exercised no dominion over this vast territory. But such place-names as Albuquerque, San Francisco, Los Angeles, Nevada, Colorado, and many more argue otherwise. So do the Hispanic populations of 1848 that lived throughout the region. So do subsequent court records revealing land disputes between arriving Yankees and established Hispanic owners. Some say that Mexicans lacked the technology to exploit the land, that possession should accrue to those who make things increase and multiply. However, an honest perspective leads us to ask: Where did invading Yankees learn how to irrigate the desert and mine mountains? From whom did they adopt knowledge of rodeos, lassos *(lazos),* and even guitars? These are Hispanic skills and arts learned from Mexican hosts. Some contend that 1848 was long ago, too distant for modern memories. But many Latino families easily trace their ancestry to the early nineteenth century: old-timers today were raised by their elders, children of the nineteenth century living in a broadly Hispanic landscape without distinct boundaries.

Historical acts are not terminal but seminal. The war of 1848 did not end one destiny and begin another. Instead, the annexation of 1848 joined legacies. Like the U.S. invasion of Cuba and Puerto Rico in 1898, or Nicaragua repeatedly, and many others, streams of history once joined cannot easily or arbitrarily be separated or arrested. One hundred years after mounting the crusade of 1898, North Americans are still passionate about liberating Cubans from supposed tyranny. Actions set precedents and stimulate both unforeseen and long-range repercussions. Encounters begin relationships that build and blend. Instead of an emergent American destiny negating a Mexican one in 1848, two futures combined. And the mingling continues. The "American" southwest displays a distinctly Mexican heritage. It will also bear a markedly Mexican future.

Modern migration from Mexico to the United States was encouraged after 1848 by the legacy of recruiting Mexican workers. Mexican campesinos were hired to build and maintain the Southern Pacific and Santa Fe railroads, to dig mines for the Guggenheim and Kennecott mineral interests, to construct highways and bridges, homes, factories, and offices in growing cities and suburbs, and to work for agribusinesses from Olympia, Washington, to Homestead, Florida. During and following World War II, the U.S. government officially recruited Mexican laborers to work on U.S. farms through the federal bracero program. In the 1960s and 1970s, agri-industries in the west hired Mexican strikebreakers to undercut the unionizing efforts of César Chavez and his United Farm Workers. A century of enticement is not easily reversed as migrations mimic the laws of physics: once a mass moves, it acquires momentum. Humans are creatures of habit.

The lure of the United States also derives from a legacy of exploitation that creates an artificial and porous line between "haves" and "have-nots." In many ways, the U.S. border resembles a leaky dike separating flood and drought: on one side is great wealth, on the other lies significant poverty. One side has many desperate workers, the other many menial jobs. Hemispheric fiscal and commercial policies created both realities, north and south. Inevitably labor will obey economic rather than political laws: supply will match demand when both are high. In an example of "Reaganomic" "supply-side" economics, poor Mexican workers cross the international boundary for better American wages despite political posturing, restrictive legislation, and enhanced surveillance. As long as strawberry pickers in the Bajío region of Mexico are paid three dollars per day (when work is available), many will leave for *el norte* and similar jobs paying ten times more. As long as the Mexican economy—including revenues for schools, roads, and hospitals—is starved by earning *los mas barato* commodity prices and bled white by interest payments to North American banks, petty entrepreneurs like María del Rosario Vásquez will not accrue sufficient capital to prosper without smuggling goods purchased in the United States. Until Latin American economies prosper, the region's poor will seek better incomes by selling drugs in *el norte.*

The motivation to go north also derives from image as well as income. Twentieth-century technologies such as radio, television, and satellites have joined promotional content such as news, entertainment, and advertising to propagandize North American visions and values. Indeed, the medium is the message as Latin Americans are fed a mental diet of everything from jeans and junk food to anticommunism and Evangelical salvation. One time while waiting at a neighborhood bus stop in Mexico City, I was among a group being entertained by three beaming television sets in a nearby department store window. Each broadcast a program from a different Mexican network. All offered images of the United States while promoting American images of Mexico. One station advertised Mexican cuisine sold at a U.S. fast-food franchise, another showed a Speedy González cartoon, the third ran an old documentary dubbed into Spanish: an account of U.S. General John J. Pershing chasing Pancho Villa in 1916. We were all entranced.

The influence of the United States is far greater than its military, commerce, finances, and diplomacy. A legacy of imperialism in the Caribbean and Central America as well as Mexico casts victor and victim into images of power and impotency. North American roles for colonized peoples range from "greasers" and Juan Valdez to boat people and Latino entertainers. Likewise, Latin Americans are fascinated not only with North America but with very different perceived roles within the North American dominion. Whether watching television, praying with Evangelicals, or learning English from tourists, Latin Americans practice joining the "American" cosmos. By crossing the Rio Grande, some take the final step in crossing mental as well as physical borders of consciousness. They decide to join the self-anointed winners in the struggle to control a hemisphere.

The example of immigration shows how past actions illuminate modern problems. Much more could be said. And other case studies would illustrate similar links between past and present. Today, Moi and the Huaorani in Ecuador live in the long shadows of Europeans who clear-cut brazilwood in colonial times. Today, drug runners ship cocaine from Colombia to the United States. Earlier, New England slavers smuggled captured Africans into the Colombian ports of Barranquilla and Cartagena. Both experiences frame the enduring legacy of hemispheric contraband. Today, interest payments from indebted Latin American governments help finance malls and condos in Miami and Las Vegas. Colonial profits from Potosí and Taxco once built palaces in Rome and Madrid. Again, many other examples show links between past and present. Patterns endure.

But legacies are not destinies. Perhaps they are if they are not understood, acknowledged, and countered. But when legacies are evident, cause and consequence may be addressed and altered. Knowledge of the past should help free us from its dictates.

And not all legacies are negative. Certain Latin American legacies are wondrous. Indigen civilizations once delivered broad well-being coupled with significant ecological balance. The Indigen cornucopia of foods, medicines, and products gifted the world. Indigens remain in Latin America, and so do their legacies. The concepts of *pacha mama,* respect for kin and tradition, and establishing harmonies could be lessons for all.

The legacy of Latin American spiritualism includes many aspects. Spanish friars introduced compassion and humanism as well as the conquering religion of Santiago. From Antonio de Montesinos and Bartolomé de Las Casas to modern liberationists, the quest for justice has been a recurring Latin American theme. Early clerical scholarship was also a perecursor to modern anthropology and helped preserve both Indigens and knowledge of their ancient cultures.

The legacy of intellectual excellence emerged early in Latin America and is a cardinal feature of modern life. The genius of both Son Juana de la Cruz and the Inca Garcilaso de la Vega gave voice to early women and mestizo writers. In the nineteenth century, poets like José Martí and Rubén Darío electrified audiences. A strong literary heritage has emerged in the twentieth century as Latin American writers still think profoundly and creatively. Carlos Fuentes, Octavio Paz, Isabel Allende, Jorge Louis Borges, Pablo Neruda, and their many peers reflect a legacy of literary greatness. They also set amazing precedents for future expression.

The legacies of Latin American art are also strong and valuable. The Indigen sense of color, texture, and imagery is mystical. Christian artisans once melded contrasting aesthetics into new architectural styles; African Latins sculpted statues that danced. Latin American arts are still a regional forte. Mexico alone is a trove of twentieth-century talents: Diego Rivera, Frida Kahlo, and Rufino Tamayo are joined by many others. The vast legacy of artistic expression includes folk arts. Latin Americans of all classes have long enjoyed the sensuality of music, dance, and cuisine. Every indication suggests that the legacy of flavors and rhythms will further enliven life.

The Latin American legacy of racial blending has at times been painful. But the modern results—the evolution of a "cosmic race" comprising European, African, Indigen, and even Asian—indicate both an ancient legacy and future destiny: all humans really constitute one race. The evolution of a mulatto and mestizo race and culture lessens tensions based on genetic distinctions as it also encourages cultural creativity. The emerging "cosmic race" in Latin America indicates that the "other" is actually another rendition of the self. The ultimate result of the encounter of 1492 is a blending.

The legacy of Latin America includes domination but also liberation. The heritage of rebellion and revolution is infused with an existential quest for identity, voice, and personal victory. This *lucha* is as much personal as political. The quest for freedom was initially displayed as Indigen uprisings. Maroon communities were another expression. The quest for autonomy infused populations at the margins of empires: the Seminoles, gauchos, Apaches, Araucanians, and others. Today it is evident among courageous grandmothers, students, mothers, and labor leaders who confront either colonels or corrupt civilians. Some of those *luchando* seek the dignity of fair employment and honest representation. Others seek an accounting of *desaparecidos* ("disappeared") family members—and justice for those who executed the innocent. Because the Latin American legacies of authoritarian rule and political corruption are so haunting, the counterlegacy of evolving democracy is all the more inspiring.

The legacies of Latin America are many. But all things must end, including our lengthy reflections. Just as Latin Americans will evolve through struggle and progress, you as a learner will encounter and advance through subsequent understanding. Our sometimes long narration has been a glance backward. But life moves forward. One hopes that this understanding of the past will help us all comprehend our collective future.

CHAPTER NOTES

CHAPTER 1

1 Vespucci, 45.
2 Winn, 215.
3 Societies of small area and/or population have not been included in the text; all but two are Caribbean islands. Information for the textual and following tables derives from Paul Goodwin, Jr., *Global Studies: Latin America,* 6th ed.; *Background Notes.* U.S. Department of State, Bureau of Public Affairs, Washington, D.C.: U.S. Government Printing Office, 1995–96; Barbara A. Tenenbaum, *Encyclopedia of Latin American History and Cultures;* Harold Blakemore, Simon Collier, and Thomas Skidmore, *The Cambridge Encyclopedia of Latin America and the Caribbean 1994 Information Please Almanac.*

Former British possessions with combined populations exceeding 2 million persons and granted independence in the late twentieth century include the following:

SMALL ENGLISH-SPEAKING NATIONS

Nation	Area, sq mi	Population (000)	Literacy	Average income
Antigua	442	64	89%	$6,500
Bahamas	13,934	256	90%	$9,900
Barbados	431	255	99%	$6,500
Dominica	752	87	94%	$2,000
Grenada	344	84	85%	$2,800
St. Kitts	261	40	90%	$3,650
St. Lucia	619	152	78%	$1,930
St. Vincent	340	115	85%	$1,300
Trinidad	5,128	1,300	95%	$3,600

Three Latin American societies comprising almost 1 million persons are part of France, sending representatives to the National Assembly in Paris and subject to French law and governance. These are French Guiana on mainland South America and the Caribbean islands of Guadeloupe and Martinique. Statistics for French America are as follows:

LATIN AMERICAN DEPARTMENTS OF FRANCE

Department	Area, sq mi	Population	Literacy	Average income
French Guiana	35,000	128,000	73%	$2,240
Guadeloupe	687	400,000	70%	$3,300
Martinique	431	400,000	70%	$6,000

A number of Dutch islands in the Caribbean are administered as autonomous provinces of Holland. The largest are Aruba and Curaçao. Altogether they include almost 400 square miles with a population somewhat larger than a quarter million persons. Literacy rates exceed 95 percent and per capita incomes range from $7600 to almost $14,000. Although not independent, Puerto Rico is occasionally included in textual tables because of its relative size, population, and historic importance. Finally, for comparison, Canada's area is one-fourth of the western hemisphere.

4 Niagara is dwarfed in volume by falls on the Paraná River between Brazil and Paraguay. The Niagara River dumps 212,000 cubic feet of water per second over its edge; the figure for the Paraná at Sete Quedas is more than double: 470,000.

5 On June 21, Montreal at 47° north latitude is at the same angle to the sun that Havana and Rio are as the sun crosses the equator.

6 Of course, on December 21, the reverse of a northern "tropics" is created. The "temporary tropics" straddled by the tropic of Capricorn extends from the equator to Patagonia. In January, Buenos Aires has weather similar to that of Norfolk, Virginia, in July.

7 Contrasts are extreme within nations: northern Chile is very hot and completely arid, while the southern region receives snowfall totals as great as anywhere on earth. See: *Worldmark Encyclopedia of the Nations: The Americas,* 77, 215, 282.

8 Conniff and Davis, 19.

9 A more detailed chronology of native events includes the following:

5000–1500 b.c.e.	Settlements in communities, early farming, greater skills, and social organization
1500–200 B.C.E.	Use of advanced materials: metals, ceramics, textiles; intense agriculture in Middle America and Andes
800 B.C.E.	Rise of Chavín civilization in Andes
700 B.C.E.	Rise of Olmec civilization in Mexico
100 B.C.E.	Rise of Nazca and Moche cultures on the coast and the Waru in highland Peru
100–1000	"Classic era" in Middle America: rise and fall of Mayan, Teotihuacán, Monte Albán, others; highly developed agriculture, architecture, religion, mathematics, arts
600–1200	Tiahuanaco theocratic city-state in Andes
1200s–1500s	Aymara warrior kingdoms in Andes
early 1300s–1521	Reign of the Aztec empire, central Mexico
late 1400s–1533	Reign of the Inca empire, central Andes
1492	Columbus encounters Caribbean Arawaks, Caribs
1493–1510s	Spain dominates Caribbean; native extinctions
1519	Cortés invades Mexico, dominates Aztecs
1531	Pizarro invades Peru, dominates Incas
1500s	Portuguese occupy coastal Brazil
1550–present	Repeated revolts of native peoples

1811	Natives join independence movements
1910–1919	Revolt of Emiliano Zapata in Mexico, joined by native peoples
1920s–1930s	*"Indianismo"*: cultural renaissance; communal land grants to natives in Mexico
1960s–1980s	Wide-scale repression of native peoples
1980s–1990s	Sendero Luminoso movement in Peru (native peoples join communist guerrilla warfare)
1992	Rigoberta Menchú, Guatemalan native activist, awarded Nobel Peace prize
1994	*Zapatista* native revolt in Chiapas, Mexico

10 A more detailed chronology of the European component of Latin American history contains the following:

718–1492	*La reconquista:* Christians reconquer Iberia
1385–1433	Creation of Portugal
1415–1500	Portugal colonizes in the Atlantic and Africa
1450–1500	Europeans fish Grand Bank of Canada
1469–1479	Isabel and Fernando unify Christian Spain
1492	Moors defeated in Spain; forced conversion or exile of Spanish Jews; Columbus's expedition
1493–1510s	Spain brings plantation economy to Caribbean
1519–1550	Spain conquers mainland native empires
1500	Cabral in Brazil; exploiting resources begins
1503	Amerigo Vespucci publishes *Mundus Novus:* concept of new world spreads in Europe
1516–1701	Hapsburg dynasty governs Spain
1519–1522	Magellan and Elcano circle world for Spain
1520s–1860s	Europeans ship African slaves to Americas
1600s	Northern Europeans seize Caribbean islands and begin their own plantation empires
1640–1889	Braganza dynasty governs Portugal and Brazil
1701–1807+	Bourbon dynasty governs Spain
1808	Portuguese monarchy moves to Brazil
1810–1821	Independence for Spain's mainland colonies
1822	Emperor declares Brazil independent
1898	End of Spanish empire in the Americas
1960s	Independence, commonwealth, or provincial status granted to remaining Caribbean colonies

11 A more complete modern chronology includes the following:

1791–1804	War for Haitian independence from France
1810–1824	Wars for independence of mainland Spanish colonies
1822	Brazil becomes independent
1820s–1840s	Era of *caudillos:* chaotic period of warlords
1836	Texas gains independence from Mexico
1846–1848	U.S. invades and annexes half of Mexico
1850s–1930s	Order and progress: stabilization and industrialism
1889	Brazil becomes a republic; emperor abdicates
1898	U.S. invades Cuba; later many Latin American nations

1910–1920	Mexican Revolution
1930s	Depression: ascendance of populism
1930s–1990s	Highly nationalized economies
1940–1945	World War II: progress and prosperity
1945–1965	Populism: political and economic progress
1959	Cuban Revolution
1960s–1980s	National Security Doctrine: military regimes
1970s	Economic boom
1980s	"Lost Decade": high debt and economic depression
1985–1994	Movement toward democracy almost everywhere
1990s	Privatization; return of economic growth

12 Because the term "revolution" has been used to the point of confusion, the term "transformation" is being applied to designate those great human changes in agriculture, commerce, and industry. "Revolution" connotes a rather rapid change and is too often confused with political rebellion or national revolutions such as those in China, Russia, Cuba, and so on. "Transformation" better labels the broad and enduring systemic changes in human technologies and social structures.
13 *World Almanac,* 1995, 840; *1994 Information Please Almanac.*
14 *1991 International Data Base,* Bureau of the Census.
15 Statistics on infant mortality and longevity are 1992 figures found in *The World Bank Atlas, 1995.* Diet information is from both Kurian, *Encyclopedia of the Third World,* and Goodwin, *Global Studies: Latin America,* 6th ed. The human development index comes from the U.N. Development Program, *Human Development Report, 1990.*
16 Statistics for gross national product per person are for 1993. Energy use per person is for 1992. Both are from *The World Bank Atlas, 1995.* Data on televisions and radios are from the *Worldmark Encyclopedia of the Nations,* 18th ed., 1995, 340–341.
17 Literacy statistics are from *The World Bank Atlas, 1995.* Data on newspaper circulation come from the *Worldmark Encyclopedia of the Nations: United Nations, 1995,* 340–341.
18 Hauchler and Kennedy, 57.

CHAPTER 2

1 Guy D. García, "Burning with Passion," *Time,* July 11, 1988, 56.
2 Acknowledging he was somewhere other than the "Orient" would jeopardize Columbus's claims to tribute and titles. To verify his mistaken beliefs, Columbus kidnapped Tainos and returned to Spain stating: "I bring with me Indians as evidence." See Jane, 1:16.
3 Vespucci's insightful letter, *Mundus Novus* ("New World"), was eagerly circulated in Europe during 1503, preceding the publication of Columbus's journals and, for a time, making Amerigo more famous than Christopher. Amerigo was Latinized and feminized (like Europa, Africa, etc.) to become "America." Nevertheless, Spanish officials still called the Caribbean the "Indies" and Europeans eventually referred to them as the "West Indies." See Lunenfeld, 118.
4 Another name for native Americans is the Spanish *indio,* an often pejorative and racist term implying "bumpkin" or "stupid."
5 North and South America held between 14 and 100 million Indigens, depending on who is counting and how. Burkholder and Johnson discuss the numbers of native societies. For a discussion of initial populating of the Americas, see the early chapters of Jennings.
6 Jennings; Burkholder and Johnson.

7 Table 2-1 derives from Melissa Meyer and Russell Thornton, "Indians and the Numbers Game" in Colin Calloway, ed., *New Directions in American Indian History;* also Henry Dobyns, *Their Number Became Thinner;* and Francis Jennings, *Invasion of America.*
8 Jane, 4.
9 Jennings, 48–66.
10 Díaz del Castillo, 190–191, 216–218.
11 Klein, *Bolivia,* 20–21, 31–32; Stern, 13.
12 See Padden for further information.
13 Brundage, 96–98.
14 Stern, 39–46.
15 Ibid., 6–8; Stein and Stein, 5.
16 Thornton, 42; Sánchez-Albornoz quoting Cook and Borah, 41.
17 This summary of the conquest from a native perspective derives from León-Portilla.
18 Kicza, xv–xvi.
19 This survey of disease is from Crosby.
20 The 95 percent mortality rate is from CELAM, 32.
21 Quoted in L. Randall, *A Comparative Economic History of Latin America, Peru,* 21. Reprinted by permission of Columbia University Institute of Latin American Studies.
22 Two prominent scholars writing about the *encomienda* are Lesley Byrd Simpson, *The Encomienda in New Spain,* and Lewis Hanke, *The Spanish Struggle for Justice.*
23 Quoted in L. Randall, *A Comparative Economic History of Latin America, Peru,* 23–24. Reprinted by permission of Columbia University Institute of Latin American Studies.
24 Simpson, *The Encomienda in New Spain,* 52–53.
25 Kicza, xix.
26 Curtin, *Plantation Complex,* 103; L. Randall, *A Comparative Economic History of Latin America, Brazil,* 51. For a more extensive discussion of *bandeirantes,* see Willems, 14–17.
27 Velásquez, 560.
28 Brading, 102.
29 Kicza, xviii.
30 Monica Barnes, "Catechisms and *Confessionarios:* Distorting Mirrors of Andean Societies," in Dover et al., 69.
31 Quoted in Sánchez-Albornoz, 56.
32 León-Portilla, 149. From *The Broken Spears* by Miguel León-Portilla. Copyright © 1962, 1990 by Beacon Press. Reprinted by permission of Beacon Press, Boston.
33 Thornton, 13.
34 Using sex and gifting to establish relations between Indigens and Europeans is discussed by Amerigo Vespucci: "It is the exception when they deny you anything; on the other hand, [they are free] in begging. . . . But the greatest token of friendship which they show you is that they give you their wives and daughters; and when a father or a mother brings you the daughter, although she be a virgin, and you sleep with her, they esteem themselves highly honored; and in this way they practice the full extreme of hospitality." See Lunenfeld, 282.

Sometimes ritual gifting was funny. When Nuñoz Cabeza de Vaca wandered among communities in the American southwest, he was accompanied by hordes of Indigens from previous villages. They had been "cleaned out" by other arriving "guests" and now wanted a turn at recouping their losses.

35 This discussion is summarized from Hobhouse, and Crosby. In addition to foods, Indigen cuisine is growing in popularity. Native American dishes include coconut pastries, tropical fruit salads, tapioca pudding, and such Mexican fare as tacos, tostadas, enchiladas, fajitas, and guacamole. In the United States, salsa (an Indigen concoction) now outsells ketchup.

36 For an extensive discussion of Indigen pharmaceuticals, see Plotkin. Other Indigen "gifts" include tobacco products, chewing gum, and coca, used for cocaine.

37 One pound of cochineal dye requires the crushed and dried bodies of 70,000 female insects that live on a type of Mexican cactus and are harvested with tweezers. During the colonial era cochineal was the second most valuable export of New Spain, after silver. Indigo is rendered by another intensive process of leaching color from a tropical plant. Harvesting brazilwood initiated destruction of tropical American rain forests soon after 1500. See Weatherford, 44–48.

38 Ibid., 12–14. Other American native contributions include warfare strategies, musical instruments, methods of farming, and much more.

39 Goodwin, *Global Studies: Latin America,* 3d ed.; Tenenbaum.

40 Strong, 48; Stern, 51–56, 184. Sendero Luminoso opposes rural Indigen leaders and traditions, and proclaims such non-native philosophies as those of Chinese Chairman Mao. However, in practice many Shining Path methods resemble traditional village customs.

41 Menchú, 204. Extensive discussions with Mayan-Cakchiquel women weavers reveal that making native crafts seldom yields much profit for producers. A reasonable income and job security result when Indigens both form cooperatives and win contracts with large-volume vendors: foreign or domestic crafts shops. Competition from rival cooperatives often undercuts profitability, while rivalry among local street vendors often reduces profits to almost nothing. See Bronstein, 225, 240.

42 I earned about $800 a week in 1993, the year of my trip. Statistics reveal that an average Guatemalan Indigen *family* made about the same amount in *two years.* In 1988, the official minimum wage for a campesino was $1.57 per day. Few employers paid that much, as a survey showed that in 1989 most peasants earned about $1.00 per day for field work. In 1989, Indigen family (not individual) income was about $1.50 per day. See Wearne, 12.

43 The discussion of contemporary Indigens derives from personal travels in Mexico and from Oxford Analytica, 32–36.

44 Since Spain had been racially mixed during 700 years of occupation by African Moors, genetic purity was hard to prove. But long-standing religious convictions were easy to document (with Christian birth and marriage records, etc.). *Limpieza de sangre* in the sixteenth century was more a religious than a racial concept.

45 Mörner, *Race Mixture,* 55. Magnus Mörner estimates that 250,000 persons emigrated from Spain to the Americas between 1506 and 1600, and another 200,000 from 1600 to 1650. He laments the lack of evidence for 1650 to 1810. Mörner states that estimating Portuguese emigration is even more difficult. See Mörner, *Adventurers and Proletarians,* 8–10.

46 Further information on *fueros* can be found in Burkholder and Johnson, 185–232. Additional insights derive from various sections of Rivera.

47 Quoted in Stein and Stein, 56–57.

48 The present discussion relies heavily on Suzy Bermúdez's wonderful study *Hijas, Esposas y Amantes: Género, Clase, Etnia y Edad en la Historia de América Latina* (Daughters, Wives and Lovers: Gender, Class, Ethnicity and Age in Latin American History). Other important sources are June Hahner, ed., *Women in Latin American History: Their Lives and Views*; Asunción Lavrín, ed., *Latin American Women: Historical Perspectives*; and Julia Tuñón Pablos, *Mujeres en México: Una historia olvidada* (Women in Mexico: A Forgotten History).

49 *Peninsular* and criollo women in arranged marriages were not just pliant and loyal wives. Many took lovers, frequently their confessors. White women on plantations occasionally had affairs with black or mulatto household servants.

50 Statistics on conquistadores are from Pérez de Barradas, 69. The statistics on percentages of Spanish female immigration are from Sánchez-Albornoz, 66. Tuñón Pablos, 38, estimates the percentage of Spanish women arriving in New Spain (the colony receiving the heaviest early numbers) at a mere 10 percent.

51 This account of colonial life for criollas derives from Tuñón Pablos, 57–65, who also describes the initial attempts by the Spanish to make native princesses into Spanish nobility. They were sent to special schools to learn both the Catholic faith and Spanish customs. During the first generation after the conquest women (probably nuns) were sent from Spain as special teachers. Initially, a fair number of indigenous princesses were educated.

52 Tuñón Pablos, 57–65.

53 The official description of criollos comes from the Council of Indies and is found in Mörner, *Race Mixture,* 28. Hints of inferiority, as in this official definition of criollo, caused constant apprehension: "those who derive from the first *conquistadors* or families that are noble, legitimate, white and free from any ugly stain." Ibid.

54 L. Randall, *A Comparative Economic History of Latin America, Peru,* 58.

55 Comments on the supposed sickliness of *peninsulares* are found in R. Levine, 63. Emilio Willems, in *Latin American Culture,* says that "throughout three centuries of colonial rule there were at least 76 rebellions and uprisings: 15 were revolts of Negro slaves, 31 were major Indian uprisings, and 30 were insurgencies of Creoles *(criollos)* and *mestizoes* against Spanish and Portuguese authorities" (23).

56 Quoted in Tuñón Pablos, 93.

57 Goodwin, *Global Studies: Latin America,* 3d ed.; Tenenbaum; Blakemore.

58 R. Levine, 49.

59 Inca Garcilaso de la Vega, the great Peruvian mestizo chronicler writing of his Indigen mother's family, said, "As soon as the Indians saw that a woman had been begotten by a Spaniard, all the kinfolk rallied to pay homage to the Spaniard as their idol and to serve him because they were now related to him." See Mörner, *Race Mixture,* 24.

Occasionally, sexual relations during the conquest did change the status of Indigens. The clearest example is Malinche—known as Doña Marina—the Indigen slave who became the mistress of Hernán Cortés and the reigning "queen" of Mexico's conquest.

Church fathers were little bothered by constant Spanish or Portuguese sexual relations with Indigen women. The priests were more concerned that Christians not cohabit with pagans: that Indigen partners be baptized prior to coitus, which was often done quickly and as a cursory prelude to intercourse (usually language barriers impeded communication, and sign language was used). See Mörner, *Race Mixture,* 25.

60 Ibid., 26–28.

61 The census of early Santo Domingo is found in ibid., 26. Calculations on criollo and mestizo birth rates are based on my conservative assumptions that a woman would give birth once every three years and that each Iberian man had at least half a dozen Indigen women as sexual partners.

Not all sexually active European men in Latin America were Spaniards or Portuguese. The Hapsburg rulers of Spain allowed Germans to settle Venezuela, while many Italian seamen such as Columbus and Vespucci were probably no less sexually active than their Spanish shipmates.

The growth of the mestizo caste in the Americas parallels the history of sexual activities elsewhere. The Dutch and English in South Africa, the Portuguese in Angola, Mozambique, Goa (India), and Macao (China), and the French in Canada and Vietnam were no less celibate, with dramatic demographic consequences for all locations.

Upon reaching adulthood, mestizos typically intermarried or mated with each other, so the collective rate of mestizo growth may have actually increased with time.

62 Quoted in Sánchez-Albornoz, 66.

63 Arawaks in the Caribbean were sedentary, numerous, and virtually obliterated by Spanish colonists. Those who remained blended with imported slaves to form African-Caribbean culture. The more warlike Caribs resisted the Spanish and today remain in small numbers in isolated areas of the Caribbean. See Curtin, 69. Statistics regarding Mexico are found in Mörner, *Race Mixture,* 31.

64 Sánchez-Albornoz, 132–134.

65 The colonial descriptions of mestizos are found in Mörner, *Race Mixture,* 42, 48, and L. Randall, *A Comparative Economic History of Latin America, Argentina,* 20. More information for this paragraph comes from Sánchez-Albornoz, 129.

66 Stern, 158–167.

CHAPTER 3

1 Wagley, 1.

2 "African Latin" is used to describe the new black culture of Latin Americans, related to but distinct from African. Afro-Cuban, African Brazilian, even Negro criollo have been used to describe new world blacks. See CELAM, 64.

3 Curtin, *Plantation Complex,* 41; Mattoso, 15. An extensive and fascinating account of Atlantic slave trade origins and development is found in Klein, *African Slavery,* chs. 1, 2.

4 A treaty between Spain and Portugal signed in 1479 set the precedent for the *asiento,* the contract allowing others to import slaves into Spanish territories. By this treaty, Portugal monopolized the early importation of African slaves into Spain. Seville became a major European center for the African slave trade with Europe. See Conniff and Davis, 33, 41.

5 Curtin, *Rise and Fall of the Plantation Complex,* provides an excellent discussion of the Atlantic slave trade. See also Rawley, 22.

6 Curtin, *The Atlantic Slave Trade: A Census;* Rawley, 428; CELAM.

7 Sánchez-Albornoz, 138–139. Curtin, *Plantation Complex,* 100–102. During the early national era in the United States, African-Americans constituted about one-third of the population, 90 percent in some southern regions.

8 Thompson, 34–39.

9 Mattoso, 98–105; Klein, *African Slavery,* 160.

10 Quoted in Morrissey, 114.

11 The impact of the slave trade on west Africa is related by Mattoso, 7–33.

12 Rawley, 25, lists these as Portuguese rather than Brazilian imports, but after the early decades virtually all Portuguese imports were for Brazil rather than Portugal.

13 European slavery in west Africa extended from the Senegal River in the North through Angola in the south: a distance greater than the eastern U.S. coast from Canada to Mexico. When the British tried to end the slave trade in the 1830s, slavers moved to east Africa. Whites created client chiefdoms of African middlemen, and used tobacco and rum extensively to extend their dependencies. With European guns and munitions, African chieftains fomented warfare to gather prisoners. See Thompson, 62–98; Mattoso, 7–32.

Information on importing versus breeding is found in CELAM, 152. Trade in children was lucrative and tragic. Children were less rebellious than adults, more cost-effective due to size, but less resistant to disease and more subject to starvation. To escape British west

African patrols, fast clipper ships—many from New England—continued the deadly trade of shipping children well into the 1850s. See CELAM, 52, and UNESCO's *Introducción a la Cultura Africana en América Latina,* 94.

The movement of particular African groups to the new world is presented in the study by CELAM, 44, 63. The British—and their Yankee progeny—used the *asiento* to open doors of commerce everywhere in the Americas.

14 Mattoso, 94.

15 Discussion of work performed by African Latins derives from UNESCO, 41, and CELAM, 34–35. Spaniards rarely used Africans in mines since they were expensive investments for so deadly an occupation. Instead, mostly Indigens mined in Peru and Mexico. They were considered more expendable and suffered mortality rates far greater than the middle passage of the Atlantic slave trade. See R. Levine, 87.

Slave artisans were often rented, and not a few bought their freedom from earnings at extra jobs.

See also L. Randall, *Argentina,* 11, and *Brazil,* 5; Bermúdez, 19.

16 Bermúdez, 74; Klein, *African Slavery,* 197–205.

17 Klein, *African Slavery;* L. Randall, *Brazil,* 41; Curtin, *Plantation Complex,* 100–109.

18 But even after slavery ended in the nineteenth century, Africans were recruited as contracted labor. See R. Levine, 73.

19 Bermúdez, 76; CELAM, 52; Morrissey, 146–147.

20 Manuel Moreno Fraginals has edited *Africa en América Latina,* which thoroughly demonstrates that black culture in the new world was not something preserved from Africa but a new synthesis drawn from many sources. Much of this discussion derives from Moreno Fraginals.

21 Moreno Fraginals, 325; R. Levine, 45; UNESCO, 61. Women enjoyed high status in African Latin societies since imported males outnumbered arriving females two to one. The scarcity of women put a premium on their social roles. Also, African Latin societies are significantly matrilocal, that is, centered on maternal blood lines and mother-centered homes. Due to the central role of women in procreation, guarding culture, and transmitting identity, black females were esteemed.

22 Moreno Fraginals, 217.

23 Ibid., 217, 325.

24 UNESCO, CELAM.

25 Moreno Fraginals, 129, 216; UNESCO, 58.

26 Statistics on black populations are from UNESCO, 51, and Curtin, who estimates the total Africanized population of the United States—not just those officially designated "black"—at over 30 percent. This compares to about 37 percent in Brazil. Increasingly, the United States is becoming not just a nation of many races but also a mixed-race nation. See Curtin, *Atlantic Slave Trade,* 88–92.

27 *Cabildos de nación* are discussed in Moreno Fraginals, 216, and UNESCO, 65. The long history of slavery saw many different cults, often initially secret societies among slaves. *Santería, condomblé,* voodoo, and others had such origins. See CELAM, 63.

Occasionally, Maroons were enticed by white authorities to command expeditions against other renegade slaves and were rewarded with royal grants of freedom, land, and their own slaves. The same incentives lured some black pirates away from piracy. Thus, some African Latins became members of the planter aristocracy. See CELAM, 53.

Rather than reconstituting African societies in the wilderness, Maroon communities often mimicked white plantation society by copying the manners and titles of European elites.

28 The Afro-Brazilian Congress of 1934 is discussed in Mörner, *Race and Class,* 146. African Latins reacted strongly to North American racism arriving during the Spanish-Cuban-American War of 1898. Criticism of U.S. imperialism was raised by blacks who feared segregationist policies. See R. Levine, 58.

White racism was most virulent in the early twentieth century. During previous decades most whites were taught pseudoscientific concepts of evolution which placed Caucasians at the furthest point of evolution. Hitler's racist ideas derived largely from the Englishman Houston Chamberlain and the Frenchman J. Arthur de Gobineau; Gobineau was especially popular among Latin American criollo elites. See R. Levine, 58.

29 Sánchez-Albornoz, 164.

30 Quotations regarding Argentine immigration are found in L. Randall, *Argentina,* 65–66. See also Sánchez-Albornoz, 152.

31 Criollos in Argentina favored European migration after winning political independence. A Buenos Aires proclamation in 1812 stated: "Population is the basis of industry and the corner stone of the happiness of States" and called for colonists from northern Europe. See Sánchez-Albornoz, 147–149.

32 Statistics are from Mörner, *Adventurers and Proletarians,* 39–40, and Sánchez-Albornoz, 154–155.

33 Mörner, *Adventurers and Proletarians,* 36.

34 R. Levine, 55.

35 John Dickinson, "Early Industrial Patterns," in Preston, 84.

36 Sánchez-Albornoz, 163. Statistics on the sex ratio for European immigrants are for Argentina between 1857 and 1926, but the pattern seems typical. See Mörner, *Race Mixture,* 134–135.

37 Much of this discussion about Asians derives from Martínez Montiel.

38 The story of the Chinese derives largely from my personal research in Mexican archives while I was working on a dissertation; and from Martínez Montiel.

39 Martínez Montiel, 23, 53.

40 L. Randall, *Peru,* 88–92. The same British interests forcing China to import opium also recruited and sold indentured workers from Canton to the Chibcha Islands of Peru. British ships were described as "floating hells." Mortality rates were sometimes one-third, and on at least three occasions desperate Chinese immigrants mutinied and murdered the ship's captain. The Chinese were also used on cotton and sugar plantations. Those condemned to the guano beds each day hauled 100 wheelbarrel loads to a cliff and dumped them into a chute loading a ship below. Since water was brought from the mainland, illness from bad water and poor diets was common. Suicide was also a frequent cause of death. And workers were usually defrauded pay after years of servitude, mostly via worthless script. The nitrate and guano industry was lucrative for mining and shipping interests, as demand for fertilizer grew in Europe. Martínez Montiel, 40–41, tells the story.

41 Martínez Montiel, 62. Emigration from Japan accompanied great domestic social and political changes following the Meiji restoration.

42 Ibid., 61–63; R. Levine, 48, 69–70.

43 R. Levine, 72.

44 The main source for information on Jews is Judith Laikin Elkin, *Jews of the Latin American Republics.* She discusses *conversos* on page 9.

45 Curtin, *Plantation Complex,* 82; Elkin, 17; R. Levine, 71; L. Randall, *Brazil,* 12. Jews in Holland financed many Dutch expeditions to Brazil and the Caribbean, seeking to wrest territory from the Spanish and Portuguese. Iberian anxieties and Jewish ambitions were mutually reinforcing.

46 Elkin, 18–20; R. Levine, 71.
47 Elkin, 100–102.
48 Information on Arab immigration is from Martínez Montiel, 131–138.

CHAPTER 4

1 Villaseñor, 379.
2 Quoted in Richard Lacayo, "A Surging New Spirit," *Time,* July 11, 1988, 49.
3 Persons without families, particularly street children, are often runaways who lived at home long enough to remember a family name. They may use it—or the name of a friend, or anyone—as a surname. Some are known only by first names or nicknames.
4 Inner and outer worlds derive from the ancient Greek concepts of *polis* (public life) and *oikos* (home life) as separate domains. The terms characterize most Mediterranean cultures.
5 Such internal family rivalries as the Chamorros illustrate another common characteristic of Latin American life: outer-world rivalries usually end at the family door. Although the children of Violeta Chamorro oppose each other in public, they celebrate family events together.
6 For further reading see Bingham and Gross, *Women in Latin America* (vol. 1), particularly "Women as Conquered People" (33–45), and various essays in Pescatello.
7 Until recently, marriage was primarily an instrument for bettering the financial or social status of families. Often, dowries were more significant than the bride herself. Dowries for the rich preserved ownership of vast estates. Dowries for the middle class allowed upward mobility, such as aspiring merchant families linking with old elite plantation families. For the poor, a modest dowry often secured a marriage and thereby saved a woman from a life of prostitution. See A. J. R. Russell-Wood, "Female and Family in the Economy and Society of Colonial Brazil," in Lavrin, 60–100.

Widowhood provided women great freedom. And despite the legal requirement that wives needed a husband's approval, many were active: freeing slaves, borrowing money, buying and selling property, endowing charities, and controlling their own often sizable dowries. See Lavrin, 25–41.

8 At times colonial Brazil experienced zero demographic increase of white populations. Portuguese officials forbade white women from returning to Lisbon and restricted girls from entering convents. The Portuguese government also tried, unsuccessfully, to recruit poor female emigrants known as "orphans of the king." See Russell-Wood, "Female and Family," 62–63.

White men had illicit relations with but rarely married *castas.* But it was taboo for white women to have illicit relations. Therefore, many just went ahead and married their *casta* lovers. Overall, official marriage between whites and *castas* was rare. More common was the mixture of Indigens with African Latins. See Russell-Wood, "Female and Family," 68; Lavrin, 32–33. Information on Mexico is from Arrom, 198–205.

9 Girls born to prostitutes repeat the pattern of adopting a maternal profession: they have little recourse. The information concerning Aztec fatalism is from Tuñón Pablos, 29.
10 Rivera, 48–51.
11 Evelyn Stevens, "Marianismo," in Pescatello's *Female and Male in Latin America,* discusses the expectations of married women; the quote describing men as *niños* in found in Stevens, 95.
12 See Deere and León for discussions of rural women. See also Pescatello, 106. Change for poor women is often traumatic. Migrating from a countryside of nature, village, and closed

family to bustling cities of asphalt and commerce, these women exchange a life of open air, gardens, and animals for jobs as live-in domestic servants who occupy small rooms of basements or rooftop shacks. The domestic servant's boss is no longer a father (like her, a campesino) but often another woman—the *Señora* of the house—who demonstrates unfamiliar middle- or upper-class values. Whether employed as a domestic, store clerk, or in an office or factory, the migrant rural woman is removed from her family. In cities such women learn a new consciousness as well as new values. The changes in their lives are immediate and substantial, from lipstick and perfume to television and birth control clinics. For a general discussion of women see Bingham and Gross, *Women in Latin America.*

Strict and traditional gender roles govern domestic workers. Women work inside the house doing laundry, fixing meals, and tending children. Men work as gardeners, repairmen, and chauffeurs.

13 Stevens, "Marianismo," 91–95.

14 M. Randall, *Women in Cuba,* 52, explains *el rapto.*

15 Rivera, 54–56; Stevens, "Marianismo."

16 Upper- and middle-class women beyond childbearing age tend to occupy themselves with activities of leisure or prestige. Lower-class women typically work, if they have not been working already. See United Nations, *Five Studies on the Situation of Women in Latin America,* 44.

In 1970, the average number of children per Mexican mother was 6.7 (8 in the countryside). By 1989, the birthrate had dropped to 3.4 children per Mexican mother. Similar changes have occurred elsewhere in Latin America. See LeVine, *Dolor y Alegría,* 6, 11, 197.

17 Summarized from the Economic Commission for Latin America (United Nations, *Five Studies on the Situation of Women in Latin America*).

18 Bronstein, 25. Divorce for women has long been difficult. Until recently, a woman had to prove unconsummated marriage, incompatibility of religion, that a partner had been a hidden Jew or Protestant, or "flagrant" adultery. Divorce was not common but estrangement was: the married partners just went their own ways. Desertion—by men rather than women—was also common. Whatever the process, many "officially" married women were, effectively, heads of their own households. See Russell-Wood, "Female and family," 83–84; also Lavrin, 35.

19 Dealy, 62–65, discusses the importance of male authority. Male esteem in the society is chiefly a matter of successfully commanding others to get things done.

20 Rivera, 54–57.

21 The Spanish proverb is found in Rivera, note on page 2. Dealy's book *The Latin Americans: Spirit and Ethos,* is filled with intelligent insights and pithy examples. He discusses "manliness" on pages 133–147.

22 Machismo also permeates the anthology by Pescatello, *Female and Male in Latin America.* See also Bronstein, 28.

23 Almost all personal struggles are met by first enlisting amigos, who ally for mutual interest and collective power. The task of a young man is to use speech and persuasion to gain leadership, first among friends and family, then in the outer world.

24 The discussion of Roman and Mediterranean backgrounds and reflections on public roles for males and females derives from visits to ancient Ampurias and museums in Barcelona and Madrid. Dealy also discusses classicism, Catholicism, and the Renaissance. He clearly expresses the relationship of prestige and power in Latin American values: "Prestige is to power as credit is to wealth," see notes on page 68. See also Nash and Safa, *Sex and Class in Latin America,* 33.

The urban connotation of civilization is evident in language. When a man is isolated in the *campo* (countryside), he is a campesino or "peasant" lacking civilization. Other derogatory terms for country folk who live in close association with nature are barbarian, heathen, pagan, and "hillbilly."

25 Rivera, 71–75.

26 Nash and Safa, *Sex and Class in Latin America,* 26. In her collection of case studies known as *Dolor y Alegría,* Sarah LeVine tells of repeated wife beatings, 34–35, and elsewhere.

27 Rivera; Dealy.

28 Bermudez, 133–135. Radical reform of women's status emerged during the Mexican Revolution of the early twentieth century when state governments such as those of Tabasco and Yucatán legalized divorce, birth control, and "free love," promoted education for women, and ran women candidates for public office. Women organized political and social organizations that addressed the problems of drugs, alcohol, and prostitution. They participated in national and intentional conferences. Other revolutions and reform movements as in Cuba, Chile, and Argentina also witnessed great change in the status of women.

29 In the *maquiladora* factories lining the Mexican side of the U.S. border, 70 to 85 percent of the employees are women eighteen to twenty-five years old. Paid little, most are unmarried daughters who have become breadwinners for their families. The men of these families have less steady work and are often unemployed. See Thorup's essay in Pescatello, *Female and Male in Latin America,* for quote on irresponsible men and discussion of *maquiladora* factory women.

30 Educational and career information is from the Economic Commission for Latin America (United Nations, *Five Studies,* 87–88).

31 LeVine, 196.

32 LeVine comments on the two-parent family and women spending more personal time with fewer children in the conclusion of *Dolor y Alegría.*

CHAPTER 5

1 Carpentier, 247.

2 Animism infuses the Spanish language. Consider the following. Hearing a crash in the kitchen, an English-speaking parent discovers a child standing before a broken jar and exclaims: "You dropped the jam!" Personal responsibility—if not guilt—is inherent, as children learning English are assumed to control the material world, albeit sometimes clumsily. In the same situation a Hispanic parent uses a reflexive verb, saying: *"Se te cayó la mermelada!"* (The jam fell from you!). The Spanish-speaking child learns that personal will must contend with other forces: either tricky jam jars or fate.

3 My introduction to Latin American animism came one summer while I was living with a Mexican family. The members of the home claimed the stove cooked unevenly "because it likes some foods better than others," a stereo played poorly "because it did not like what a teenager did to it," and a pretty little girl dressed in ribbons and bows was marched around a storm-flattened garden, challenging jealous plants to rise again in splendor. The neighbors shared such attitudes, using animism to explain strange night sounds, closed market stalls, unfortunate accidents, and various illnesses.

4 Brundage, 87, 94–95; John H. McDowell, "Exemplary Ancestors and Pernicious Spirits: Sibundoy Concepts of Cultural Evolution," in Dover, Seibald, and McDowell, 97–98.

5 In both Aztec and Inca society mother earth appeared in different forms and not always kindly. Earth mother was "always recognizable as the giver and destroyer of life and as the supreme oracle. [In Mexico] she was conceived of as a thing of horror and was both eternal and demonic. . . . The Mexica saw her as a demonic colossus gaping and clashing her skeletal jaws. It was a difference not in any essential quality but in the degree of hostility which she showed toward men who lived in her bosom." From Brundage, 91.

Susan Rosales Nelson, "Bolivia: Continuity and Conflict in Religious Discourse," discusses the ceremony of *ch'alla* and the cemetery rituals in D. Levine, 223–224.

In Bolivia, Aymara miners perceive the inside of the earth as a womb and underground streams as veins. See Joseph W. Bastien, "Shaman versus Nurse in an Aymara Village: Traditional and Modern Medicine in Conflict," in Dover, Seibald, and McDowell, 143.

6 Duendes are discussed by Rivera, 156. Extensive discussion of devils occurs throughout Ingham; see particularly 106–120 and 162–164; McDowell, "Exemplary Ancestors," 97–98.

7 McDowell, "Exemplary Ancestors," 108–109.

8 Discussion of the Virgin of Guadalupe is found in Brundage, 94–95. Among the Inca, *huaoquis* were necessary to achieve fullness of humanity. Since commoners were not thought to possess *huaoquis,* they were denied a spiritual existence. See Brundage, 98–99.

9 "Andean peoples tend to perceive or structure their personal and cultural relationships in dualistic terms. How they do this varies according to circumstances." Dover, Seibald, and McDowell, introduction, 8.

10 Bastien, "Shaman versus Nurse," 138–156.

11 Carlos Fuentes, 63. In a further irony of conquest symbolism, the macho Santiago is the patron saint of victorious Spain while the feminine Virgin of Guadalupe is the patron saint of conquered Mexico.

12 Bastide, 43, explains that slaves were presented as gifts by Franciscan monks. One convent in Bahia, Brazil, kept 400 slaves to care for 74 nuns.

13 The account of Sandino and Somoza is found in Philip Berrymen, "El Salvador: From Evangelization to Insurrection," in D. Levine, 59.

14 Kita, xxi.

15 Quoted in Hanke, 17.

16 Always under attack, and trying to balance the ideals of protecting Indigens with the demands of colonists for workers, Las Casas endorsed the African slave trade as a compromise solution. He quickly regretted the suggestion. See Herring, 171–173.

17 Ricard, 39–45; Brading, 104.

18 The first generations of the Spanish missions were marked by idealism, Evangelical zeal, and great dedication. But later Catholic clerics were often agents of repression, younger sons of elites destined by family tradition to serve the church, or even "placemen" who bought their offices and now wanted its rewards. Few were celibate, many kept concubines or mistresses, and most demanded gifts of food and clothing, personal religious fees, and household service. See Stein and Stein, 78.

19 Rivera, 104–108.

20 Cardenal is quoted in Cabestrero, 50.

21 D'Escoto and Cardenal are quoted in ibid., 31, 99.

22 Rother, 3.

23 The statistic for Chile is for 1975. See Thomas C. Bruneau, "Brazil: The Catholic Church and Basic Christian Communities," 108, and Brian H. Smith, "Chile: Deepening the Allegiance of Working-Class Sectors to the Church in the 1970's," in D. Levine, 186.

24 D. Levine, 10–11.

25 Quoted in ibid., 22, n. 5.

26 Lehmann, xi, 96–104.

27 Extensive discussions of African Brazilian deities are from O'Gorman and Bastide. Bastide provides a chart of African Latin deities, 364–369.

28 Bastide, 64–65; O'Gorman, 18. Becoming an *encantado* is not a mark of salvation or holiness; it merely allows the ancestor or the spirit to use the person as a medium. The possessed becomes a *cavalo,* a "horse" which the spirit "rides" during its earthly presence. The possessed is typically selfless, while an *encantado,* behaving and speaking as the spirit, not the host. Riding their *encantados,* spirits sometimes seek human pleasures not allowed them in the other world. And hosts act in uncharacteristic ways: usually shy women strut about smoking cigars drinking vast amounts of alcohol, or shouting obscenities, while otherwise serious men may break furniture in a frenzy, uttering loud vulgarities.

29 O'Gorman, 26.

30 Bastide, 420, provides statistics on occupation and race. The quote from the *mae-de-santo* is found in O'Gorman, 22.

31 Tapia, 28–29.

32 *Posadas* still exist, but their popularity diminishes as North American icons like Santa Claus and Christmas trees make commercial headway. Today they are typically organized by parish churchwomen, many seemingly more enthusiastic about the traditional pagent than its young participants.

33 Goodman and Ryan, 44; Santagada et al., 84.

34 Santagada et al., 21–29.

35 Ibid., 21–24.

36 Coleman, 59–62.

37 Martin and Lees, 30–35.

38 Santagada et al., 35, 41, 93, 102; Goodman, 43.

39 Martin and Lee, 30–35.

40 Althaus, 1992.

41 Santagada et al., 258.

CHAPTER 6

1 Cohen, 299–300.

2 Quoted in Stein and Stein, 86.

3 The account of Moi derives from Kane, 74–81.

4 Richard Smith, "Indigenous Agriculture in the Americas: Origins, Techniques and Contemporary Relevance," in Preston, 39–40.

5 Weatherford, 82–85.

6 Smith, "Indigenous Agriculture," 37–38.

7 Ibid., 46, 56–58.

8 L. Randall, *Peru,* 13.

9 Unlike Aztecs and Mayans, Andeans practiced more extensive animal husbandry, using llamas and alpacas as beasts of burden, for wool, and for meat. Guinea pigs were a common food. See Stein and Stein, 4; Klein, *Bolivia,* 1–12.

10 Ana María Bidegain de Urán is quoted in Bermúdez, 61. The quote on Brazil is by a visiting Englishman and is found in L. Randall, *Brazil,* 15.

11 Bolivia may be the world's most extensive trove of minerals: gold, tungsten, silver, tin, lead, zinc, antimony, bismuth, copper, nitrates, iron ore, natural gas, and petroleum are all abundant. Yet Bolivia is among Latin America's poorest nations.

12 L. Randall, *Peru,* 38.

13 The story of Potosí is recounted in the first chapter of Weatherford, *Indian Givers.*

14 The account of Cortés as Paul Bunyan is noted in Meyer and Sherman, 137.
15 Mannix, 33.
16 L. Randall, *Mexico,* 80–81.
17 Stein and Stein, 31.
18 L. Randall, *vol. 1: Mexico,* 144.
19 Ibid., 92.
20 Stein and Stein, 142–146.
21 Dickinson, "Early Industrial Patterns," 78.
22 L. Randall, *Mexico,* 94.
23 L. Randall, *Mexico,* 29–30. For information on the *casa de contratación,* see Gibson, *Spain in America,* 100–101.
24 Newson, "The Latin American Colonial Experience," 25.
25 Stein and Stein, 49–50.
26 Mercantilism is discussed by Parry, 293–294.
27 Quoted in L. Randall, *Mexico,* 99, 113.
28 L. Randall, *Brazil,* 11. Had Portugal been an island, like Great Britain, separated from its enemies by a channel, its ships could have aided in its defense, as with the English and the Spanish armada, Napoleon's army, and Hitler in World War II. Connected by land to the rest of Europe—and with a small population and army—the Portuguese endured a different fate at the hands of invading Spanish and French armies. One cannot escape geography.
29 L. Randall, *Mexico,* 104–107; Stein and Stein, 96–97.
30 One personal experience with contraband and corruption includes sitting on the wharf of little Tamiahua on the Gulf Coast of Mexico, wondering why Mexican shrimp boats returned empty after a day at sea and yet the crew was loaded with money. Eventually, I was told that American shrimpers from Galveston or New Orleans often had good and quick catches on days when the Mexicans—officially—did not.
31 European diplomats acknowledged the open competition for world empire while maintaining peace at home. Treaties were not enforceable "beyond the line," that is, more than a day's sail from European ports.
32 Curtin calls these persons "transfrontiersmen" and discusses them in *The Rise and Fall of the Plantation Complex,* 92–95.
33 Smuggling and graft were common tools of the Atlantic slave trade, especially after its official prohibition by treaty in the early nineteenth century. Even as abolition gained strength and the Civil War loomed, New England shippers forged papers providing "laundered" investments, insurance, and ships. Few heirs of prominent New England merchants known for smuggling and running slaves have opened family records to public scrutiny. See Rawley, 349–353.
34 L. Randall, *Argentina,* 12; Curtin, *Plantation Complex,* 41, 141–142.
35 Stein and Stein, 50–51; quote on page 68.
36 Ibid., 79.
37 L. Randall, *Peru,* 29, 32; *Mexico,* 68, 112.
38 Quoted in L. Randall, *Mexico,* 59.
39 Castlereagh is quoted in L. Randall, *Argentina,* 31. The Argentine critic of England is Juan B. Justo and is quoted in Stein and Stein, 151.
40 L. Randall, *Mexico,* 5, 9; Newson, "Latin American Colonial Experience," 25.
41 Ibid.
42 The quote from Pombal is found in L. Randall, *Brazil,* 62; see also 84; and Stein and Stein, 23.

43 Stein and Stein, 127, discusses the contrast in English and Spanish colonialism. After 1650, English colonists arrived from a modernizing nation experiencing the throes of change: from religious warfare, to political struggles, to early industrialization, England was a cauldron of social and economic ferment. Out of this emerged certain values: respect for literacy, religious toleration, individual rights, economic liberty, saving and investment. All contributed to growth, which acknowledged change. Meanwhile as an established empire, conservative Spain was elitist and orthodox (except when enlightened despots like Charles III goaded citizens to modernize). In North America, Europeans replicated patterns from their homeland: the French followed rivers, the English clustered on coasts, the *Castilians* went inland. Only after independence did U.S. developmental policies change. The move inland was accompanied by "internal improvements": creation of infrastructures such as canals, turnpikes, and eventually railroads.

44 Although relatively wealthy, Mexico inherited a great disequilibrium between the highly polarized rich and a vast poor majority. See L. Randall, *Mexico,* 57.

45 Dickinson, "Early Industrial Patterns," 73.

46 Nitrates, used in fertilizers and explosives, built the Nobel brothers' industrial empire. Nobel prizes were endowed with gains from the chemical wizardry of European scientists but also from exploiting Chilean minerals. The peak of Chilean nitrate mining was—understandably—during World War I, when munitions were in high demand. But relatively few Chileans profited from this, ironical, "boom." By 1900, the British, German, and Spanish owned 80 percent of Chilean nitrate production; Chileans held only 15 percent of this natural resource. See Dickinson, "Early Industrial Patterns," 81.

47 Newson, "The Latin American Colonial Experience," 22–25.

48 L. Randall, *Mexico,* 162–163; *Argentina,* 80.

49 L. Randall, *Peru,* 107.

50 Dickinson, "Early Industrial Patterns," 80.

51 In shantytowns of large cities and in small villages, merely a used or cheap black-and-white television with an antenna reaching above a poor home is a symbol of achievement. Television viewing is frequently communal, with the apparatus often facing outward from a window for maximum sharing. By 1986, Brazil had 15 public and 1776 commercial television stations. Mexico had no public stations and 840 commercial stations. Satellite dishes are an increasingly common feature of rural Latin America. The world of global television, and its commercial values, reaches throughout the region, bringing its controlled entertainment, news, and commercial values particularly to the lower classes. See Wilkie, Ochoa, and Lorey, 96–97.

52 An extensive discussion of early urban life in Latin America is found in Hoberman and Socolow.

53 Kane, 81.

CHAPTER 7

1 William M. Dyal, "A Government Foundation with a Non-Government Approach," in Eells, 126.

2 Mexico produces about a billion barrels of petroleum per year, Venezuela about 900 million. Other significant producers of petroleum in Latin America, ranked in order, are Brazil, Argentina, Colombia, Ecuador, Trinidad, and Peru. See *The 1994 Information Please Almanac,* 464. See also Hauchler and Kennedy, 316.

3 "A Chasm of Misery," 64.

4 Hauchler and Kennedy, 58, using World Bank statistics for 1993.

5 "Chasm of Misery" states that "the richest 20% of [Latin American] families enjoy a more extravagant life style than that of the upper class in the United States and Japan" (64).

The United States is no longer a model of equality. Since World War II it has grown less egalitarian while western European and east Asian countries with more equitable income distributions have shown more rapid rates of economic growth.

6 Based on figures from the *World Bank Atlas, 1995.*

7 Birdsall and Lowenthal, 6–7.

8 Statistics are from "Chasm of Misery," 65.

9 U.S. governmental assistance to Latin America was greatest during the 1960s with the Alliance for Progress. See Webber, "Announced US, Assistance to Latin America, 1946–88: Who Gets It? How Much? And When?" in Wilkie, Ochoa, and Lorey, 1081–1084. Webber begins his essay unequivocally: "US authorizations for assistance to Latin America are used for purposes of political propaganda in the recipient countries." He also states that "the United States government does not publish data on disbursements. . . . Budgetary 'savings' eliminated the positions of US budget officers whose job it was to know how their respective agencies disburse funds" (1083).

The Agency for International Development, the primary vehicle for U.S. assistance to Latin America, was created by John F. Kennedy in 1961. According to Maizels and Nissanke, 886–887, the original goals of assistance programs were to "promote self sustaining growth, escape the low level poverty trap . . . generate capital, [and achieve] trickle down results." Such idealism was brief, as economic aid became military aid. By the 1970s U.S. assistance did not target the poor. Recognizing this, the U.S. Congress, in its Assistance Act of 1973, reemphasized lost idealism. Maizels and Nissanke summarize its language: "the highest priority" would be to "directly improve the lives of the poorest" people of recipient nations and to improve their "capacity to participate in the development of their countries." The authors add, "This did not occur and, indeed, the aid allocation became even more closely associated with US foreign policy and security interests."

According to Gang and Lehman, 723–732, international lending agencies such as the World Bank and others "adopt policies representing donor nation desires in rough proportions to donor nation contributions." Since the United States has been the major contributor, these agencies reinforce U.S. policies.

10 Levison and de Onís, *The Alliance That Lost Its Way: A Critical View of the Alliance for Progress,* shows that clashing political objectives among American policy makers and between the United States and Latin America interests doomed the greatest effort of the United States to assist Latin America. The quote is from Drake, xix.

11 Girvan and Marcelle, 91–107, discuss the "technological dependency syndrome," including foreign corporations using "restrictive clauses aimed at preserving the supplier's technological monopoly" (91).

12 Information on how Daniel Flood used U.S. foreign aid to build support among his own constituents can be found in the *New York Times:* "Rep. Flood Had Secret Ties to Haiti While Pushing US Aid to Duvalier," 1, 19; and "US to Seek Release of Businessman in Haiti to Hear His Testimony about Rep. Flood," 27.

An ongoing account of the Somozas permeates Lernoux's *Cry of the People.* A detailed case study of congressional lobbying for foreign aid on behalf of a Latin American dictator is found in the discussion of Nicaragua, 103–107. The statement attributed to Franklin Delano Roosevelt calling Somoza "our S.O.B." is found in G. Black, 71. Quotes by aid recipients are from Breslin, 4–5.

13 Breslin, 5.

14 Table 7-1 is adapted from Bailey and Sood, 60. The prices are for 1981. During eight years (1973–1981) the percentage of the retail price paid to actual producers ranged from 16.6 percent (1981) to 11.5 percent, about a one-third decrease of income.

During the 1980s, total income from Latin American commodity sales had fallen to about two-thirds the 1970 level. See "Sharp Fluctuations in Commodity Prices Cause Major External Shocks in Latin American Countries," in Inter-American Development Bank, 6.

15 Robert N. Gwynne, "Modern Manufacturing Growth in Latin America," in Preston, 108. Vehicle production for 1993 shows the following: Argentina 342,350, Mexico 1,080,144, Brazil 1,390,261. See *The World Almanac,* 1995, 208.

16 Correa, 1588–1598.

As with bananas, the advantages in marketing computer software lie with large companies established elsewhere. This applies when Latin Americans are buying as well as selling. In Latin America software products are predominantly of U.S. origin.

17 The "Adjustment of the Banana"—the evasion of paying taxes on exported bananas—is illustrated in Lindqvist, 81–87. He also discusses tax evasion by coffee marketing companies.

The most flagrant examples of foreign companies exploiting Latin America are not corporations with public ownership but private investors, since public corporations are subject to scrutiny. Private investors, sometimes dealing in billions of dollars, are often reclusive.

The case of American Daniel K. Ludwig chronicles the actions and impact of one "lone wolf" investor in Latin America. An American billionaire, one of the world's richest men, and a major supporter of Ronald Reagan, Daniel K. Ludwig built a global financial empire beginning with shipping after World War II and eventually reaching remote Jari, a quiet tributary of the Amazon River. Following a U.S.-sponsored coup in 1964 ("Operation Brother Sam"), Ludwig befriended generals and technocrats in Brazil and used these contacts to secure both hundred-thousand-acre plots of rain forest and Brazilian loans and grants. During the next two decades, with anonymity and autonomy, Ludwig created company towns in the Amazon: hiring workers cheaply, providing no social services, clear-cutting native species for lumber, planting quick-growing trees for paper pulp, and towing from Japan a newsprint mill built on barges. With no oversight other than his own hirelings, Ludwig caused topsoil erosion and river pollution. He also built shantytowns witnessing high rates of prostitution, crime, and other vices. Eventually workers became restive under the authoritarian dictates of Ludwig. When his trees and rice paddies did not produce as planned, he abandoned the project, towed his paper mill away, and left a scarred ecology, people in poverty, and the Brazilian government holding unpaid loans. For a full account of Jari, see Shields, *The Invisible Billionaire: Daniel Ludwig.*

An account of fruit company machinations with Latin American officials in Central America is found in the subchapter "The 'Octopus' " in Lernoux's *Cry of the People,* 115–119. See also Schlesinger and Kinzer, *Bitter Fruit: The Untold Story of the American Coup in Guatemala.*

18 The influence of oil company officials on cabinet members of Warren G. Harding's presidency is part of the "Teapot Dome" scandal of the 1920s. See Hicks, 155; and Brenner, plate 124, 71, and 83.

A full account of the Guatemalan coup is found in Schlesinger and Kinzer, *Bitter Fruit.* The relationship of the CIA and ITT regarding Chile is found in *Covert Action in Chile, 1963–1973,* Staff Report of the Select Committee to Study Governmental Operations with

Respect to Intelligence Activities, U.S. Senate (Washington, D.C., December 18, 1975), 11–13.

19 The term *técnicos* is discussed in Time-Life's *México,* 147–148. A partial list of recent Latin American leaders who were former students in the United States includes Carlos Salinas de Gortari (president of México: Harvard); Alfredo Christiani (president of El Salvador: Georgetown); Violetta Chomorro (president of Nicaragua: Blackstone College); Anastasio Somoza Debayle (dictator of Nicaragua: West Point); Vinicio Cerezo (president of Guatemala: Loyola University, New Orleans); Virgilio Barco Vargas (president of Colombia: Massachusetts Institute of Technology); and José Napoleon Duarte (president of El Salvador: Notre Dame). This brief list could be enlarged a thousandfold by listing aides, advisers, cabinet members, and business leaders. It could also be expanded to include perhaps tens of thousands of Latin American military officers who have trained at U.S. war colleges and institutes.

20 Binswanger, 828; Thiesenhusen and Melmed-Sanjak, 393–415; the documentary film *Controlling Interest* by Adelman and Schmiechen (California Newsreel, 1978); and Schlesinger and Kinzer, 40–41.

21 Rolf Wesche and Michael Small, "Brazilian Amazonia: From Destruction to Sustainable Development?" in Ritter, Cameron, and Pollock, 84–85.

22 The Guatemalan law expropriated only *uncultivated* lands of fruit companies and large estates. During eighteen months, over 100,000 poor families received farms and previous owners were compensated with government bonds. See Schlesinger and Kinzer, 54–56.

23 This case study of Mexican strawberries comes from Ernest Feder, *El imperialismo fresa* (Strawberry Imperialism).

24 Determining ownership is confused by *prestanombres*—Mexicans with either dual U.S. citizenship or on a company payroll who *prestar* (lend) their *nombres* (names) to an otherwise North American enterprise.

25 In California, identical work earned seventeen dollars at the time of this study.

26 Feder.

27 *Annuario Estadístico de los Estados Unidos Mexicanos,* 101.

28 Mexico and Brazil are the most indebted nations. But tiny Costa Rica has the largest per capita debt in the region. See Birdsall and Lowenthal, 6.

29 Three decades of Latin American growth (1950–1980) witnessed a doubling of per person GDP (gross domestic product: the total of goods and services produced in a nation). See Rosenthal, 64. Information on growth of the Latin American economy is from Lowenthal, *Partners in Conflict,* 10.

30 Summarized from Gwynne, *Selling Money: A Young Banker's Account of the Great International Lending Boom—and Bust.* A more specific account of the financial entrapment of Latin America is found in Lernoux, *In Banks We Trust.*

31 Lernoux, *In Banks We Trust,* has an expanded discussion of the late-twentieth-century fiscal history of Latin America. Growth rates are quoted from Enrique V. Iglesias, "The Economic Outlook for Latin America in the 1990s," in Ritter, Cameron, and Pollock, 4.

32 "Money Coming In" is the "net capital inflow" of loans, investments, and transfers *to* Latin America. "Money Going Out" is the "net payment of interests and profits" *from* Latin America to foreign banks and corporations. Wilkie, Ochoa, and Lorey, chart 12.

By the 1990s, investments and loans to Latin America caused a net inflow of moneys: $65 billion in 1993. By 1993, the region experienced a 3.3 percent annual growth rate. See Birdsall and Lowenthal, 6–7.

33 Myron J. Frenkman, "Global Income Redistribution: An Alternate Perspective on the Latin American Debt Crisis," in Ritter, 41. Rolf Wesche and Michael Small, "Brazilian Amazonia: From Destruction to Sustainable Development?" in Ritter, Cameron, and Pollock, 81.

34 "Chasm of Misery," 65; Pastor, 1–18; and Kryzanek, 154. Pastor reports that "much of the capital that exited did so with government approval or acquiescence" (1).

The Wall Street Journal ("Some Latin American Nations' Actions Add to Risk of Holding Cash Accounts," A9c,) reported the following: that Mexican elites sent more than $100 billion out of Mexico during its debt crisis, much of it to U.S. banks and into Texas real estate; the figure for Brazil in 1990 was $40 billion; estimates sometimes differ because of complex currency exchanges, accounting, and secret numbered accounts in Switzerland, the Bahamas, and elsewhere.

Rowan also estimates the capital flight from Latin American elites at somewhere between $300 and $400 billion and explains that as interest rates decline in rich industrial nations during the early 1990s this money is returning to Latin America as investments fostering growth.

The Mexican scholar Jorge G. Castañeda states that "the richest ten percent of Mexicans, those who earned 32.8 percent of national income in 1984, saw their share jump to 37.9 percent by 1989. Conversely, the share of the poorest 40 percent shrank from 14.3 percent to 12.9 percent. The 1990 census, moreover, revealed that 63.2 percent of the nation's inhabitants made no more than twice the minimum wage—$200 per month—while price levels approached those in the United States." See Castañeda, 71.

35 In 1989 the U.S. government promoted the Brady Plan, named after Secretary of the Treasury Nicolas F. Brady. It slightly reduced Mexico's debt, extended repayment periods, and lowered short-run interest payments. For these, Mexico provided incentives for U.S. investors and the United States guaranteed Mexican bonds. See Pauly, 32; Krugman, 141–153. The Brady Plan has been copied by Latin American nations seeking debt refinancing and lower interest payments.

Sherman and Bailey, 3. Sherman and Baily also relate that Latin American governments did not borrow heavily from U.S. banks until the Alliance for Progress brought private bankers and Latin American officials together in the 1960s (3). The authors also show that by 1985, over 5 percent of Latin America's gross domestic product was used just to pay interest on foreign debts: more than Germany paid in reparations following World War I (4).

Rowan explains that while acceptance of the Brady Plan does little to actually reduce debt, it does "restore investor confidence" (5).

36 Lustig, 1327, 1337. Rosenthal, 65, documents a decline in social service budgets of 20 percent during the "lost decade" of the 1980s. She also provides statistics for the following table:

LATIN AMERICA: CHANGES IN GROSS NATIONAL PRODUCT PER CAPITA

1978–1981	+6%
1982	–3%
1983	–6.5%
1984	+1.1%
1985	–0.1%

Explanations of how the rich in Latin America avoid paying taxes is found in "Chasm of Misery," 66. Lowenthal, 1–2.

37 Vessuri, 1544, relates that 250,000 students were enrolled in higher education during 1950 and 5.4 million students in 1980, an increase of twenty-one times. Engineering students concentrated on mineral resources, oil technology, agriculture, nuclear energy (Argentina), and computers (Brazil).

The education of Latin American professionals actually encourages flight by emphasizing the values and standards of more affluent societies. Texts, equipment, and supplies purchased abroad or from foreign companies often rely on examples and methods more appropriate for Boston than Belém. This is true for medicine, energy technology, industrial planning, computer science, communications, and many other technical fields. Thus, Latin American students look abroad not only for answers but for issues. Working on satellite communications for Bell Laboratories is more prestigious than designing electrical supply systems for shantytowns in Brazil. Study abroad also reinforces alienation from Latin American societies. Important subjects at Cal Tech or MIT may not matter much to campesinos in Colombia. And since Latin American societies have few funds to invest in basic scientific inquiry, the region has only 2.5 percent of the world's scientists and conducts only 1.8 percent of global research and development (statistics are from Vessuri). All these factors contribute to professional exodus.

38 "World's Pay Scale," H-3. The contrasts in salaries are most extreme for technical professions but are still significant for low-skilled persons. A sewing machine operative averages $147 per month in El Salvador or $1062 in the United States. Information on emigration is from Mörner, *Adventurers and Proletarians,* 107. The statistic on 17 percent of foreign-born professionals originating from Latin America is from Dillin, 3. Dillin notes that among native-born professionals, Hispanics constitute only 3 percent when their percentage of the total population is about 10 percent. One-third of foreign-born professionals in the United States are from Asia.

39 MacPhee and Hassan, 1112. In 1972 a total of 46 percent of the physicians practicing in the United States were immigrants, from all regions of the globe. Historically, entrance to medical schools in the United States has been both highly competitive and limited. The resulting short supply of doctors contributed to both their long hours and high salaries. A consequence has been immigration of doctors, who are reacting to low supply and high demand in the United States. Thus, limiting enrollments in U.S. medical schools has contributed to decreasing health standards in less developed countries.

40 This account of María del Rosario Valdez is summarized from the wonderful book by Judith Adler Hellman, *Mexican Lives,* 152–159.

41 Hernando de Soto and el Instituto Libertad y Democracia. *El Otro Sendero, la Revolución Informal.*

42 See MacDonald, *Mountain High, White Avalanche: Cocaine and Power in the Andean States and Panama*; Smith, *Drug Policy in the Americas*; and Morales, *Drugs in Latin America.*

43 Strong, 96–103.

44 Ibid.

45 The statistics are from Lima's *El Diario* and are found in Strong, 105; Kryzanek, 153–154.

46 Robert N. Gwynne, "Modern Manufacturing Growth in Latin America," in Preston, 108; Bitar, 5; and "The Other Crumbling Empire," 26.

"The Other Crumbling Empire" cites the Rio Treaty of 1947 as the high-water mark of U.S. hegemony in Latin America: economically, politically, and militarily. It also lists trade relationships between the two for 1987: 12.4 percent of U.S. trade went to Latin America, while 10.9 percent of Latin American trade went north. The United States was still the largest trading partner of both Brazil and Mexico. Bitar, 6, explains that Latin American trade to Europe has also declined since World War II. Trade with other developing regions continues to grow, and regional trade within Latin America is about 22 percent of total exports. Trade with east Asia increased almost tenfold from 1.2 to 10.2 percent of total imports during the 1970s alone.

47 Bitar, 6–10, says that U.S. ownership of 159 major firms in Latin America declined between 1959 and 1976 from 111 to 68. He also says that the decline in investments have paralleled a loss of corporate influence: "Governments have gained power relative to large firms. The ability of any one corporation to impose its interests and to interfere politically has been diminished." He concludes that corporate influence on U.S. policy in Latin America is also less.

48 Ibid.; "The Other Crumbling Empire," 26.

49 Bitar, 5, and Rowan give statistics on population trends.

50 U.S. policy is increasingly superfluous in affecting trends in Latin America. The contra war in Nicaragua disrupted that society but failed in its military objectives. The incursion in Panama captured Manuel Noriega but has not lessened the effects of drug trafficking. In El Salvador and elsewhere, the massive power of the United States has increasingly failed in its objectives. Power brokering in the region is being assumed by such Latin American leaders as Violetta Chamorro, Oscar Arias, and Javier Pérez de Cuellar, or by international agencies like the United Nations and the Organization of American States.

Bitar, 18, discusses many factors that illustrate the decline of U.S. policy making in Latin America. The United States has no coherent program for the region such as the earlier Alliance for Progress; recent efforts have been piecemeal and halfhearted. He mentions the growing role of Spain in both bringing an Iberian consciousness back to Latin America and linking the region with the powerful European Community. Latin America is developing political and economic relations with other world regions: Brazil with Africa and western Latin American nations with Pacific Rim partners. Bitar also mentions that Latin American nations received a strong message when U.S. policy favored Great Britain in the Malvinas (Falklands) War in the early 1980s. Argentina lost, but so did U.S. credibility in the region.

"The Other Crumbling Empire" discusses the drug trade and suggests it may indicate future trends in economic relations between the United States and Latin America.

51 Solberg, *The Prairies and the Pampas: Agrarian Policy in Canada and Argentina, 1880–1930.*

52 Redistribution of wealth would entail new and effective tax structures including not only income taxes but levies on real estate, inheritance, luxury items, and so on. Provisions must also be made to limit capital flight. The eventual result would redistribute property and ownership as well as incomes. For these reasons, such policies have been doggedly resisted by elites.

53 The Brazilian study of income redistribution is from Cardoso and Helwege, 240–124.

54 Breslin, 40, 80; Cardoso and Helwege, 237.

55 See Duggan, 39; "Step up the Pace of Latin Debt Write-offs," 164; and Cardoso and Helwege, 129.

CHAPTER 8

1 Quoted in Rodríguez Monegal, 357.

2 Paz, 23–24.

3 Quoted in Rubén G. Rumbaut, "The Americans: Latin American and Caribbean Peoples in the United States," in Stepan, *Americas,* 279.

4 The title of this section is borrowed from Ariel Dorfman's book *The Empire's Old Clothes: What The Lone Ranger, Babar, and Other Innocent Heroes do to our minds.* Dorfman argues that modern pop culture for young persons teaches imperialistic values.
5 Information about the Teller and Platt amendments is from Karnes, 154.
6 Quoted in Langley, 66.
7 The quote by Woodrow Wilson is found in the essay by Paul W. Drake, "From Good Men to Good Neighbors," in Lowenthal, *Exporting Democracy,* 13. The quote by FDR is found in Patterson, Clifford, and Hagan, 355.
8 The CIA invasions of both Guatemala and Cuba were organized and supplied from bases in Somoza's Nicaragua. Some of Somoza's personnel would be used by Reagan during the contra war.
9 The quote, from a U.S. Agency for International Development official in Brazil, is found in J. K. Black, 216.
10 U.S. State Dept., *Foreign Relations of the US, 1895,* pt. 1, 545–562; quoted in Karnes, 141.
11 Quoted in Karnes, 190.
12 Quoted in Patterson, Clifford, and Hagan, 221, 228. Incidentally, the Rough Riders actually ran up San Juan Hill since the horses—because of poor logistics—were left in Tampa. Also, many of the Rough Riders were African Americans, former "Buffalo Soldiers," many most likely descended from Black Seminoles.
13 Lyndon Johnson is reported to have said that Latin Americans could not pour piss from a boot if the instructions were written on the heel. In the oval office, Nixon commonly used profanity to characterize both his supposed friends and enemies in Latin America. As of 1996, the verdict on Bill Clinton's approach to Latin America is inconclusive. A case for fairness could be made for George Bush in his dealings with Mexico, but in Panama and through debt negotiations, he resembled a Roman emperor dominating the provinces.
14 The Rio Treaty provided for hemispheric signatories to join in solidarity against invasion by outsiders. It was created in the aftermath of Nazi and Japanese aggression but with an eye on the Soviet Union. In 1982 the United States claimed the Malvinas were not part of the western hemisphere and hence not covered by the treaty. The Argentines argued otherwise.
15 Bartlett, Keller, and Carey, 191.
16 Boorstin and Kelley, 172. From *A History of the United States* by Daniel J. Boorstin et al., © 1981, Random House, Inc.
17 Bailey, *Diplomatic History,* 168–174.
18 Lefeber, *The American Age,* 78–79. A more balanced college diplomatic text is that of Patterson, Clifford, and Hagan, *American Foreign Policy: A History.*
19 This story of Jackson in Florida derives from Giddings, *The Exiles of Florida*; Robert V. Remini, *The Legacy of Andrew Jackson*; Anthony F. C. Wallace, *The Long, Bitter Trail: Andrew Jackson and the Indians*; Michael Paul Rogin, *Fathers and Children: Andrew Jackson and the Subjugation of the American Indian*; James W. Covington, *The Seminoles of Florida*; and Jan Crew, "United We Stand! Joint Struggles of Native Americans and African Americans in the Columbian Era," 103–127.
20 Crew, 103–127. Madison's duplicity is from Bailey, 165.
21 Patterson, Clifford, and Hagan, 91–92.
22 Crew, 111–112. Copyright © 1992 by Monthly Review, Inc. Reprinted by permission of Monthly Review Foundation.
23 The quote on Onís is found in Patterson, Clifford, and Hagan, 91. After Florida became a U.S. territory, Black Seminole resistance prompted the costliest Native American war in U.S. history.

24 The final U.S. war against the Seminoles, accompanying their expulsion to the "Indian Territory" (Oklahoma), occurred in the 1830s. President Andrew Jackson referred to hostilities as "this savage [Indigen] and Negro War." One U.S. general in 1836 said: "This . . . is a negro, not an Indian War; and if it be not speedily put down, the South will feel the effects of it on their slave population." See Thompson, 285–286.

25 The quote from Leonard Wood is found in Langley, 16.

26 For a much more extensive discussion of *la leyenda negra,* see Powell, *Tree of Hate,* and Maltby, *The Black Legend in England.*

27 Gibson, *The Black Legend,* introduction, 3–27.

28 The Kansas senator is John J. Ingalls. His speech is found in Gibson, *The Black Legend,* 173–178. Information on the anti-Catholic aspects of *la leyenda negra* come from Tyler, *Freedom's Ferment,* 365–375.

29 *America's War for Humanity* is discussed in Gibson, *The Black Legend.* The chapter title is from Tupper, *Columbia's War for Cuba.*

30 The statement is by George Washington Crichfield, found in Gibson, 179–189.

31 Discussion of Mexico and Hollywood derives from Carlos Cortés's excellent essay found in Coatsworth and Rico.

32 Statistics regarding Hispanics and television are from Michele A. Heller, "Off the Air: Why Aren't Hispanics on the Networks," 34; and "Tuned Out: TV Portrayals of Ethnic Groups," 10. The quote regarding the Menéndez brothers is from S. Robert Lichter and Daniel R. Amundson, "From Ricky Ricardo to . . . the Menendezes?" (excerpts from the authors' *Distorted Reality: Hispanic Characters in TV Entertainment* [Washington, D.C.: Center for Media and Public Affairs, 1994]), quoted in the *Boston Globe,* September 11, 1994, 72.

33 The United States helped create the Haitian dictatorship that drove exiles to the United States.

34 Information on network news coverage derives from Coatsworth and Rico, 65.

35 "Latinos on the Rise," 49. In the 1990 census: almost one in three Hispanics is below age fifteen, compared with about one in five non-Hispanics. And almost twice as many non-Hispanics are age fifty-five or more. Within a few decades, large numbers of young Hispanics will replace large numbers of elderly whites. See Pérez and Martínez, 23.

Immigration to the United States in fiscal year 1993, the most recent year for which statistics are available, lists 904,292 known arrivals. Five of the top ten sources were Latin American nations. Mexico, with 126,561, and the Dominican Republic, with 45,420 immigrants, led all other nations. In descending order, the other top ten nations included India, El Salvador, the United Kingdom, Korea, Jamaica, Canada, Cuba, and Ireland. See *The World Almanac, 1995,* 386.

36 *1990 Census, Social and Economic Characteristics, Metropolitan Areas,* Table 3, 533–540.

37 Ibid.

38 A readable and comprehensive historical survey is L. H. Gann and Peter J. Duignan, *Hispanics in the United States: A History.*

The case study cited found that undocumented braceros from one Mexican village picked fruit in Oregon for six times more than they earned for similar work in Mexico. Net earnings—after deducting for transportation and other travel expenses—were three times greater. Of 379 households in Guadalupe, Mexico, three-quarters regularly sent family members to work in the United States in 1978. During that year 919 people from Guadalupe spent at least part of the year in the United States; all eventually returned. In some families, 79 percent of income is from work in the United States. See Mörner, *Adventurers and Proletarians,* 102–103.

39 The rates of poverty by Hispanic subgroups are Puerto Rican 40 percent, Mexican 28 percent, Central/South American 25 percent, and Cuban 17 percent. See Pérez and Martínez, 17.
40 See Knouse, *Hispanics in the Workplace,* for a comprehensive perspective.
41 Excluding Puerto Rico, Mexican-Americans are 60 percent, Puerto Rican mainlanders 12 percent, and Cuban-Americans 5 percent of the Hispanic U.S. population. See *1990 Census: Race and Hispanic Origin.*
42 Sable, *Latin American Studies Directory;* and Center for International Education, report, March 1993.
43 Wilford H. Lane, "United States Conquest of the Mexican Market as Seen by British Officials, 1895–1905," in Huck and Moseley, 83. Michael Meyer, "Roots and Realities of Mexican Attitudes toward the United States: A Background Paper," in Erb and Ross, 34–35.
44 Wesley Phillips Newton, "The Role of Aviation in Mexican–United States Relations, 1912–1929," in Huck and Moseley, 120.
45 Breslin, 32.
46 Octavio Paz said that NAFTA "is a chance for us to be modern. Our conscious model of modernity has tended to be the United States. This is the first time in the histories of our two nations that we are going to be in some ways partners with each other." See "The World after NAFTA," 57.
47 R. Erlich, "Phone Companies Fight for Burgeoning Latino Market," *Christian Science Monitor,* March 30, 1994, 8.
48 Larry Rother, "NAFTA and the Hemisphere: Latin America Finds Harmony in Convergence," *New York Times,* Sunday, November 21, 1993, E-5.

CHAPTER 9

1 Quoted by Alma Guillermoprieto, 56. The spokesman remains anonymous.
2 Found in Brading, 99.
3 In the United States, religious parables often substitute for political realities. For example, popular stories of Puritans and Pilgrims resemble biblical tales of Moses and chosen people escaping captivity for a holy land. Such stories seek to legitimize American political origins. But the actions of early Englishmen were corporate, undertaken by business enterprises like the Virginia and Massachusetts Bay companies. Colonizing British America was accomplished by businessmen, lawyers, and preachers: sometimes all three in one person, as with the Puritan "Moses," John Winthrop. More than God's will or manifest destiny, fate was a function of efficient English militias that killed defenseless natives at Mystic, Connecticut, or Turners Falls, Massachusetts. Instead of religious freedom (i.e., toleration of plurality), most colonists sought religious *autonomy* (i.e., exclusivity). And colonists wanted "plantations": estates producing marketable commodities through exploiting nature and natives (or slaves). Political rights were conferred by church membership and property ownership: one had to "conform" and be "vested" before being allowed to vote. And *election* was originally defined as salvation through righteous behavior, which qualified one for leadership. Making money helped. Such political realism is neglected in popular political culture.
4 Brazil was spared from excessive caudillismo because the monarchy was not replaced until 1889. The Portuguese court had moved from Lisbon to Brazil during the Napoleonic Wars. In 1822, when the Braganza prince (living in Brazil) was ordered back to Portugal, he merely replied, "I stay." In effect, this was the declaration of Brazilian independence, and

young Dom Pedro—pretender to the Portuguese throne—became the first emperor of Brazil.

5 Curtin, *Plantation Complex,* 60–61.

6 Fuentes, 60–61.

7 Kandell, 95–124.

8 See Menéndez Pidal, 51–52.

9 Comparisons of independence movements in the United States and Latin America shows the critical element of historical timing. U.S. independence and constitutionalism occurred during the 1770s and 1780s when Enlightenment ideas of rationality and natural law were intense. Latin American independence occurred almost half a century later, when romantic notions of dashing heroism ran strong. In between, the fervor of the French Revolution and the imperial rule of Napoleon Bonaparte changed the norms of political leadership. Whereas George Washington and delegates at Philadelphia deliberated in tempered tones in 1787, Latin American charismatic military leaders fought with private and passionate loyalties. Latin America did have many Enlightenment rationalists, but they were overwhelmed by daring men on horseback, little Napoleons mesmerized by personal grandeur. In the United States, Benedict Arnold played a similar role, but he was—in a sense—a man before his time. And one can only speculate on how history would differ had the United States achieved independence when Latin America did in the 1820s. Instead of George Washington, meditate on Andrew Jackson being the "father" of the United States.

10 L. Randall, *Mexico,* 132.

11 Quoted in L. Randall, *Argentina,* 38. Reprinted by permission of Columbia University Institute of Latin American Studies.

12 Ibid., 48; Herring, 701–708.

13 G. Black, 71.

14 Ever the shrewd actor, Castro initially neutralized U.S. opposition by projecting himself in the American media as a modern Robin Hood. Of course, the American media were gullible: *Life* magazine and the Sunday night prime-time *Ed Sullivan Show* showed heroic scenes of Castro's struggle. Thus, U.S. officials backed off the anti-Castro campaign until they could push other messages through U.S. media channels.

15 The story of the Brazilian coup is told in Moreira Alves, *A Grain of Mustard Seed.*

16 A detailed and documented account of U.S. complicity in creating and sustaining the Salvadoran death squads is told in the extensive report by Allan Nairn, "Behind the Death Squads," 21–29.

17 Pamela Constable, "At War's End in El Salvador," 106–11, discusses the *tandona.* See also Nairn, 21–29.

18 Stein and Stein, 72–73.

19 Stern says, "In a society where access to influence constituted the lifeline of wealth and enterprise, high lords and petty tyrants alike spun complicated webs of kinships and placement which enhanced their political reach and stature." Examples are *compadres,* marriage, patronage, placing sons in the priesthood, and dowries. See Stern, 103.

20 Merriman, 3:649.

21 The progressive and democratic Bourbon Juan Carlos is king of Spain today.

22 During the chaotic era of caudillos, the hacienda often became the operative unit of government. As national government descended into anarchy, haciendas armed themselves and politics became a constant game of local diplomacy, not unlike the feudal era, when local fealties and alliances constituted government.

23 In at least one case, an incomplete democracy was represented by an incomplete building. In Mexico Porfirio Díaz's girders for a new congressional palace stood as a rusty skeleton during the revolution. The building was finally completed, but not as a legislature. It was modified to become a monument to fallen revolutionary heroes.

24 Mexico had its first national bank in 1864. L. Randall, *Mexico,* 170.

25 Stein and Stein, 171–173.

26 David Scott Clark, "Mexican Elections Sullied by Claims of Media Bias," *Christian Science Monitor,* June 1, 1994, 4.

27 In Colombia, military officers were hit men for the two major parties. Tried in military courts, they were acquitted. See Ken Dermota, "The Death of a Colombian Party," *Christian Science Monitor,* May 26, 1994, 6.

Before growing smug about U.S. democracy, North Americans should remember a few critical items. As president, Lyndon Johnson regularly blackmailed legislators after having them investigated by the FBI. Richard Nixon short-circuited democracy to win reelection during the Watergate scandal. When American leaders do not respect democracy abroad, they often violate it at home.

28 L. Randall, *Argentina,* 87; Stein and Stein, 172.

29 The source for the figure, here labeled by era, is Palmer, *Peru: The Authoritarian Tradition,* 21, 22. The charts are based on a study by Arthur S. Banks and supplemented with further research by Palmer and others.

30 Randall Hansis, "The Politics of Consolidation: Alvaro Obregón and the Mexican Revolution," (Ph.D., diss. University of New Mexico, 1971).

31 Ibid.

32 Nelson, 43–52.

33 Luis Reneger, "Public Trust and the Consolidation of Latin American Democracies," in Ritter, Cameron, and Pollock, 152.

34 For a case study of Movimento de Amigos do Bairro (in Brazil) see Scott Mainwaring, "Grassroots Popular Movements and the Struggle for Democracy: Nova Iguaçu," in Stepan, *Democratizing Brazil,* 168–204.

35 Sonia E. Alvarez, "Politicizing Gender and Engendering Democracy," in Stepan, *Democratizing Brazil,* 205–251.

36 Rolf Wesche and Michael Small, "Brazilian Amazonia: From Destruction to Sustainable Development?" in Ritter, Cameron, and Pollock, 84–89.

37 Karen L. Remmer, "The Politics of Economic Stabilization: IMF Standby Programs in Latin America, 1954–1984," in Drake, 196.

38 David Clark Scott. "Venezuela's Ex-President Awaits Trial in Prison," *Christian Science Monitor,* May 24, 1994, 7; Scott, "Organization Aims to Shed Light on Shady Deals Worldwide," *Christian Science Monitor,* March 23, 1994, 6.

39 Revolutionary regimes are often as authoritarian and ineffective as conservative military dictatorships. For example, Fidel Castro is intelligent and shrewd but often views problems from an ideological viewpoint. His pet projects in agronomy and industry often fail because they lack sufficient input from different voices that might correct the blindness of stubborn vision.

40 Needler, 15, discusses Aristotle's quote on power and inequity in the Latin American context.

CHAPTER 10

1 León-Portilla, 283. From *Fifteen Poets of the Aztec World,* translated and edited by Miguel León-Portilla. University of Oklahoma Press, 1992. Reprinted by permission of University of Oklahoma Press.

2 The Makiritare legend is found in Galeano, *Memory of Fire,* vol. 1: 3. "Chess" was translated by Alastair Reid, from Borges, 76. Copyright © 1967 by Grove Press, Inc. Used by permission.
3 Pigafetta, 9–10.
4 Rodríguez Monegal, 1:67. Cervantes's *Don Quixote* was also published in two volumes during this same period, 1605 and 1615.
5 Quoted from Rodríguez Monegal, 1:97; "Juana de Asbeje" in *Anthology of Mexican Poetry,* edited by Octavio Paz, translated by Samuel Beckett. Indiana University Press, 1958. Reprinted by permission of Indiana University Press.
6 Englekirk, 27.
7 See ibid., discussion of theater; Galeano, vol. 1: 183.
8 Tate, *The Penitentes of the Sangre de Cristos.*
9 Englekirk, 48.
10 Ibid., 57.
11 Ibid., 74–77. While Hernández defends the gaucho as natural man facing the corrupt injustices of modern life, his countryman Domingo Faustino Sarmiento earlier depicted the gaucho as barbarian in *Facundo* (1845). The most important gaucho novel (rather than epic poem) was *Don Segundo Sombra* (1926) by Ricardo Güiraldes. In Venezuela, novels of the *llanos*—that nation's broad interior plains—would develop themes similar to those of the gaucho on the pampas. *Doña Barbara* (1929), by Rómulo Gallegos, is the most famous.
12 Manuel González-Parada, Peru, essayist and poet, quoted in Englekirk, 105.
13 Foner, 59–63. From *José Martí: Major Poems,* edited and with an introduction by Philip S. Foner. New York: Holmes & Meier, 1982. Copyright © 1982 by Holmes & Meier Publishers, Inc. Reproduced by the permission of the publisher.
14 Darío, 68–69. From *Selected Poems of Rubén Darío,* translated by Lysander Kemp. University of Texas Press, 1965. Reprinted by permission of University of Texas Press.
15 Hamilton Depassier, 76.
16 Neruda, 417. From *Selected Poems, A Bilingual Edition,* translated and edited by Nathanial Tarn. Copyright © 1972. Jonathan Cape, publisher.
17 Paz, 19–20.
18 An early typical picaresque novel is *Infortunios de Alonso Ramírez,* a first-person narrative of a rogue's journey around the world by Carlos de Sigüenza y Góngara (1645–1700), chaplain and close friend of Sor Juana Inés de la Cruz.
19 In Latin America, political novels are as much social and psychological as they are political. Among the notable are *El Señor Presidente* (1947), the exploration of a "banana republic" by Miguel Angel Asturias; *Death of Artemio Cruz* (1962), an epic of the Mexican Revolution by Carlos Fuentes; and *Autumn of the Patriarch* (1975), the stream-of-consciousness story of an aged tyrant who refuses to die, by Gabriel García Márquez.
20 *Indigenismo* was an early theme of Latin American literature. Alonso de Ercilla (1533–1594), a Spanish officer on the Chilean frontier, wrote an epic poem, *La Araucana,* which like Inca Garcilaso de la Vega's *Royal Commentaries* reflects a native view.
21 Gabriel García Márquez (both a novelist and a journalist) is reported to have said that journalists use facts to promote lies while novelists create stories to establish the truth.
22 Castedo, 92–93.
23 Ibid., 71–72.
24 Ibid., 88–94.
25 Ibid., early chapters.
26 Quoted in Richard F. Townsend, "Landscape and Symbol," 36.

27 Castedo, 194–199.
28 Stanton L. Catlin, "Traveller-Reporter Artists and the Empirical Tradition in Post-Independence Latin American Art," in Ades, 42–43.
29 Ibid., 45–55.
30 Ibid., 55–56.
31 Fanny Calderón de la Barca in the 1830s recounting earlier descriptions of Alexander von Humboldt. Found in Ades, 27.
32 Ades, 30–35.
33 Ibid., 101–109.

BIBLIOGRAPHY

SOURCES USED: BOOKS

Abreu, Antonio, S.T. *Dependencia y Brechas entre Ricos y Pobres.* Bogotá: Consejo Episcopal Latinoamericano (CELAM), 1987.

Adams, Walter, ed. *The Brain Drain.* New York: Macmillan, 1968.

Ades, Dawn, *Art in Latin America: The Modern Era, 1820–1980.* New Haven, Conn.: Yale University Press, 1989.

Annuario Estadístico de los Estados Unidos Mexicanos. Aquascalientes, Mexico: Instituto Nacional de Estadísticas, Geográfica e Informática, 1994.

Anzaldúa, Gloria. *Borderlands/La Frontera: The new Mestiza.* San Francisco: Aunt Lute Books, 1987.

Arrom, Silvia Marina. *The Women of Mexico City, 1790–1857.* Stanford, Calif.: Stanford University Press, 1985.

Associaçao Ecuménica de Teologos do Terciero Mundo. Identidade Negra e Religiäo. Rio de Janeiro: Ediçoes Liberdade, 1986.

Avila, Abel. *Alienación, Atraso y Dependencia.* Barranquilla: Editores Grafitalia, 1982.

Background Notes. U.S. Department of State, Bureau of Public Affairs. Washington, D.C.: U.S. Government Printing Office, 1995–1996.

Baddeley, Oriana, and Valerie Fraser. *Drawing the Line: Art and Cultural Identity in Contemporary Latin America.* London: Verso and the Latin American Bureau, 1989.

Bailey, Thomas A. *A Diplomatic History of the American People.* 7th ed. New York: Appleton-Century-Crofts, 1964.

Bakewell, Peter J., John J. Johnson, and Meredith D. Dodge. *Readings in Latin American History,* 2 vols. Durham, N.C.: Duke University Press, 1985.

Balmori, Diana, Stuart F. Voss, and Miles Wortman. *Notable Family Networks in Latin America.* Chicago: University of Chicago Press, 1984.

Bartlett, Richard A., Clair W. Keller, and Helen H. Carey. *Freedom's Trail.* Boston: Houghton Mifflin, 1979.

Bastide, Roger. *The African Religions of Brazil.* Baltimore: Johns Hopkins University Press, 1978.

Bean, Frank D., and Marta Tienda. *The Hispanic Population of the United States.* New York: Russell Sage Foundation, 1987.

Beller, Jacob. *Jews in Latin America.* New York: Jonathan David Publishers, 1969.

Beneria, Lourdes, and Martha Roldán. *The Crossroads of Class and Gender.* Chicago: University of Chicago Press, 1987.

Bermúdez Q., Suzy. *Hijas, Esposas y Amantes: Género, Clase, Etnia y Edad en la Historia de América Latina.* Bogotá: Universidad de los Andes, 1992.

Bingham, Margorie Wall, and Susan Hill Gross. *Women in Latin America: From Pre-Columbian Times to the 20th Century.* St. Louis Park, Minn.: Glenhurst Publications, 1985.

———. *Women in Latin America: The 20th Century.* St. Louis Park, Minn.: Glenhurst Publications, 1985.

Black, George. *The Good Neighbor: How the United States Wrote the History of Central America and the Caribbean.* New York: Pantheon, 1988.

Black, Jan Knippers. *Sentinels of Empire: The United States and Latin American Militarism.* New York: Greenwood Press, 1986.

Blakemore, Harold, and Clifford T. Smith. *Latin America: Geographical Perspectives.* London: Methuen, 1971.

Blakemore, Harold, Simon Collier, and Thomas Skidmore, eds. *The Cambridge Encyclopedia of Latin America and the Caribbean.* Cambridge: Cambridge University Press, 1992.

Blakewell, Peter J., John J. Johnson, and Meredith D. Dodge. *Readings in Latin American History.* 2 vols. Durham, N.C.: Duke University Press, 1985.

Boorstin, Daniel J., and Brooks Kelley with Ruth Boorstin. *A History of the United States.* Lexington, Mass.: Ginn and Company, 1981.

Borges, Jorge Luis. *A Personal Anthology,* ed. Anthony Kerrigan. New York: Grove Press, 1967.

Brading, D. A. *The First America: The Spanish Monarchy, Creole Patriots, and the Liberal State 1492–1867.* Cambridge: Cambridge University Press, 1991.

Brenner, Anita. *The Wind That Swept Mexico: The History of the Mexican Revolution, 1910–1942.* Austin: University of Texas Press, 1943.

Breslin, Patrick. *Development and Dignity: Grassroots Development and the Inter-American Foundation.* Rosslyn, Va.: Inter-American Foundation, 1987.

Britton, John A., ed. *Molding the Hearts and Minds: Education, Communications, and Social Change in Latin America.* Wilmington, Del.: Scholarly Resources, 1994.

Bronstein, Audrey. *The Triple Struggle: Latin American Peasant Women.* Boston: South End Press, 1983.

Brundage, Burr Cartwright. *Two Earths, Two Heavens: An Essay Contrasting the Aztecs and the Incas.* Albuquerque: University of New Mexico Press, 1975.

Burkholder, Mark A., and Lyman L. Johnson. *Colonial Latin America.* New York: Oxford University Press, 1990.

Burns, E. Bradford, ed. *Latin America: Conflict and Creation, A Historical Reader.* Englewood Cliffs, N.J.: Prentice Hall, 1993.

Bushnell, David, and Neill Macaulay. *The Emergence of Latin America in the Nineteenth Century.* 2nd ed. New York: Oxford University Press, 1994.

Cabestrero, Teofilo. *Ministers of God, Ministers of the People.* Maryknoll, N.Y.: Orbis Books, 1982.

Calloway, Colin, ed. *New Directions in American Indian History.* Norman: University of Oklahoma Press, 1988.

Canak, William, ed. *Lost Promises: Debt, Austerity, and Development in Latin America.* Boulder, Colo.: Westview Press, 1989.

Cardoso, Eliana, and Ann Helwege. *Latin America's Economy: Diversity, Trends, and Conflicts.* Cambridge, Mass.: MIT Press, 1992.

Castedo, Leopoldo. *A History of Latin American Art and Architecture, from Pre-Columbian Times to the Present.* New York: Praeger, 1969.

Castro-Klaren, Sara, Sylvia Molloy, and Béatriz Sarlo. *Women's Writing in Latin America: An Anthology.* Boulder, Colo.: Westview Press, 1991.

Cavarozzi, Marcelo, and Manuel Antonio Garreton, eds. *Muerte Y Resurreción: Los Partidos Politicos en el Autoritarismo y las Transiciones en el Cono Sur.* Santiago, Chile: Flacso (Facultad Latinoamericana de Ciencias Sociales), 1989.

CELAM (Consejo Episcopal Latinoamericano). *Los Grupos Afroamericanos: Aproximaciones y Pastoral.* Cartagena: CELAM 1980.

Chiaramonte, José Carlos. *Formas de Sociedad y Economia en Hispanoamerica.* Mexico City: Editorial Grijalbo, 1984.

Chilcote, Ronald H., and Joel C. Edelstein. *Latin America: Capitalist and Socialist Perspectives of Development and Underdevelopment.* Boulder, Colo.: Westview Press, 1986.

Coatsworth, John H., and Carlos Rico. *Images of Mexico in the United States.* San Diego: Center for United States–Mexican Studies, University of California at San Diego, 1989.

Cockcroft, James D., André Gunder Frank, and Dale L. Johnson. *Dependence and Underdevelopment: Latin America's Political Economy.* Garden City, N.Y.: Doubleday, 1972.

Cohen, J. M., ed. and trans. *The Four Voyages of Christopher Columbus.* Baltimore: Penguin, 1969.

Cole, J. P. *Latin America: An Economic and Social Geography.* London: Butterworth's, 1975.

Conniff, Michael L., and Thomas J. Davis. *Africans in the Americas: A History of the Black Diaspora.* New York: St. Martin's Press, 1994.

Considine, John J., ed. *The Church in the New Latin America.* Notre Dame, Inc.: Fides Publishers, 1964.

Coote, Belinda. *The Hunger Crop: Poverty and the Sugar Industry.* Oxford: Oxfam, 1987.

Cortés Conde, Roberto. *The First Stages of Modernization in Spanish America.* New York: Harper and Row, 1974.

Covington, James W. *The Seminoles of Florida.* Gainesville: University Press of Florida, 1993.

Crosby, Alfred W., Jr. *The Columbian Exchange: Biological and Cultural Consequences of 1492.* Westport, Conn.: Greenwood Press, 1972.

Curtin, Philip D. *The Atlantic Slave Trade: A Census.* Madison: University of Wisconsin Press, 1969.

———. *The Rise and Fall of the Plantation Complex: Essays in Atlantic History.* Cambridge: Cambridge University Press, 1990.

Darío, Rubén. *Soledad: Poems of Rubén Darío,* trans. Lysander Kemp. Austin: University of Texas Press, 1965.

Dealy, Glen Caudill. *The Latin Americans: Sprit and Ethos.* Boulder, Colo.: Westview Press, 1992.

Deere, Carmen Diana, and Magdalena León, eds. *Rural Women and State Policy: Feminist Perspectives on Latin American Agricultural Development.* Boulder, Colo.: Westview Press, 1987.

De la Pedraja, René. *The Rise and Decline of U.S. Merchant Shipping in the Twentieth Century.* New York: Twayne Publishers, 1992.

Del Río, Angel. *The Clash and Attraction of Two Cultures: The Hispanic and Anglo-Saxon Worlds in the Americas,* ed. and trans. James F. Shearer. Baton Rouge: Louisiana State University Press, 1965.

Denevan, William M., ed. *The Native Population of the Americas in 1492.* Madison: University of Wisconsin Press, 1976.

De Soto, Hernando. *The Other Path.* London: IB Tauris, 1989.
Díaz del Castillo, Bernal. *The Discovery and Conquest of Mexico, 1517–1521,* trans. A. P. Maudslay. New York: Grove Press, 1956.
Dobyns, Henry. *Their Number Became Thinned: Native American Population Dynamics in Eastern North America.* Knoxville, Tenn.: University of Tennessee Press, 1983.
Dorfman, Ariel. *The Empire's Old Clothes: What the Lone Ranger, Babar, and Other Innocent Heroes Do to Our Minds.* New York: Pantheon, 1983.
Dover, Robert V. H, et al., editors. *Andean Cosmologies through Time: Persistence and Emergence.* Bloomington: University of Indiana Press, 1992.
Drake, Paul W., ed. *Money Doctors, Foreign Debts, and Economic Reforms in Latin America from the 1890s to the Present.* Wilmington, Del.: Scholarly Resources, 1994.
Elkin, Judith Laikin. *Jews of the Latin American Republics.* Chapel Hill: University of North Carolina Press, 1980.
Englekirk, John E., ed. *An Outline History of Spanish American Literature.* New York: Irvington Publishers, 1980.
Erb, Richard D., and Stanley R. Ross. *United States Relations with Mexico: Context and Content.* Washington, D.C.: American Enterprise Institute, 1981.
Escamilla, Manuel Luis. *Cultura del Mestizaje.* San Salvador: Ministerio de Cultura y Comunicaciones, 1985.
Famighetti, Robert, ed. *World Almanac and Book of Facts, 1995.* New York: Press Publishing Co., 1995.
Feder, Ernest. *El Imperialismo Fresa: Una Investigación sobre los Mecanismos de Dependencia de la Agricultura Mexicana.* Mexico City: Editorial Campesina, 1977.
Foner, Philip, ed. *José Martí: Major Poems, A Bilingual Edition,* trans. Elinor Randall. New York: Holmes and Meier Publishers, Inc., 1982.
Friborg, Goran, ed. *Brain Drain Statistics: Empirical Evidence and Guidelines.* Stockholm: Committee on Research Economics, 1975.
Fuentes, Carlos. *The Buried Mirror: Reflections on Spain and the New World.* Boston: Houghton Mifflin, 1992.
Furtado, Celso. *Economic Development of Latin America: Historical Background and Contemporary Problems.* London: Cambridge University Press, 1970.
———. *Economic Growth of Brazil.* Berkeley and Los Angeles: University of California Press, 1963.
Galeano, Eduardo. *Memory of Fire.* 3 vols., trans. by Cedric Belfrage. New York: Pantheon Books, 1985–1988.
———. *Open Veins of Latin America: Five Centuries of the Pillage of a Continent.* New York: Monthly Review Press, 1973.
Gann, L. H., and Peter J. Duignan. *Hispanics in the United States: A History.* Stanford, Calif.: Hoover Institute on War, Revolution and Peace; Boulder, Colo.: Westview Press, 1986.
Gibson, Charles. *The Aztecs under Spanish Rule: A History of the Indians of the Valley of Mexico, 1519–1810.* Stanford, Calif.: Stanford University Press, 1964.
———, ed. *The Black Legend: Anti-Spanish Attitudes in the Old World and the New.* New York: Knopf, 1971.
Giddings, Joshua R. *The Exiles of Florida.* Columbus, Ohio: Follett, Foster and Company, 1858.
González Casanova, Pablo, ed. *Latin America Today.* Tokyo–New York–Paris: United Nations University Press, 1993.
González de la Rocha, Mercedes. *Los Recursos de la Probreza: Familias de Bajos Ingresos de Guadalajara.* Guadalajara: Secretar ia de Programacion y Presupuesto, 1986.

Goodpasture, H. McKennie, ed. *Cross and Sword: An Eyewitness History of Christianity in Latin America.* Maryknoll, N.Y: Orbis Books, 1989.

Goodwin, Paul B. *Global Studies: Latin America.* 3d, 5th, and 6th eds. Guilford, Conn.: Dushkin Publishing Group, 1988, 1992, 1994.

Graham, Richard, ed. *The Idea of Race in Latin America, 1870–1940.* Austin: University of Texas Press, 1990.

———. *Independence in Latin America: A Comparative Approach.* 2d ed. New York: McGraw-Hill, 1994.

Guillermoprieto, Alma. *The Heart That Bleeds: Latin America Now.* New York: Knopf, 1994.

Gwynne, S. C. *Selling Money: A Young Banker's Account of the Great International Lending Boom—and Bust.* New York: Penguin, 1987.

Hahner, June E., ed. *Women in Latin American History: Their Lives and Views.* Los Angeles: UCLA Latin American Center Publications, 1980.

Hamilton Depassier, Carlos. *Historia de la Literatura Hispanoamericana, Segunda Parte Siglo XX.* New York: Las Americas Publishing Company, 1961.

Hanke, Lewis. *The Spanish Struggle for Justice in the Conquest of America.* Philadelphia: University of Pennsylvania Press, 1949.

Hanke, Lewis, and Jane M. Rausch, eds. *People and Issues in Latin American History.* New York: Marcus Weiner Publishing, 1990.

Hauchler, Ingomar, and Paul M. Kennedy, eds. *Global Trends: The World Almanac of Development and Peace.* New York: Continuum, 1994.

Hellman, Judith Adler. *Mexican Lives.* New York: New Press, 1994.

Herring, Hubert. *A History of Latin America from the Beginnings to the Present.* 3d ed. New York: Knopf, 1968.

Hicks, John D. *Republican Ascendency, 1921–1933.* New York: Harper and Row, 1960.

Hoberman, Louisa Schell, and Susan Migden Socolow. *Cities and Society in Colonial Latin America.* Albuquerque: University of New Mexico Press, 1986.

Hobhouse, Henry. *Seeds of Change: Five Plants That Transformed Mankind.* New York: Harper and Row, 1985.

Huck, Eugene R., and Edward H. Moseley, eds. *Militarists, Merchants and Missionaries: United States Expansion in Middle America.* Tuscaloosa: University of Alabama Press, 1970.

Ingham, John M. *Mary, Michael, and Lucifer: Folk Catholicism in Central Mexico.* Austin: University of Texas Press, 1986.

Instituto de Investigaciones Económicas. *Imperialismo y Crisis en América Latina.* Mexico City: Universidad Nacional Autónoma de México, 1985.

Jane, Cecil, ed. *The Four Voyages of Columbus.* New York: Dover, 1988.

Jelin, Elizabeth, ed. *Family, Household and Gender Relations in Latin America.* London: Kegan Paul International, 1991.

Jennings, Francis. *The Founders of America: How Indians Discovered the Land, Pioneered It, and Created Great Classical Civilizations; How They Were Plunged into a Dark Age by Invasion and Conquest; and How They are Reviving.* New York: Norton, 1993.

———. *The Invasion of America: Indiana, Colonialism and the Cant of Conquest.* Chapel Hill, N.C.: University of North Carolina Press, 1975.

Johnson, John J. *Latin America in Caricature.* Austin: University of Texas Press, 1980.

———. *The Military and Society in Latin America.* Stanford: Stanford University Press, 1964.

Jonas, Suzanne, and Nancy Stein, eds. *Democracy in Latin America: Visions and Realities.* New York: Bergin and Garvey, 1990.

Kandell, Jonathan. *La Capital: The Biography of Mexico City.* New York: Random House, 1988.

Karnes, Thomas L., ed. *Readings in the Latin American Policy of the United States.* Tucson: University of Arizona Press, 1972.

Keen, Benjamin. *A History of Latin America.* 2 vols. Boston: Houghton Mifflin, 1992.

Kicza, John E., ed. *The Indian in Latin American History: Resistance, Resilience, and Acculturation.* Wilmington, Del.: Scholarly Resources, 1993.

Kim, Kwan M., and David F. Ruccio. *Debt and Development in Latin America.* Notre Dame, Ind.: University of Notre Dame Press, 1985.

King, John. *Magical Reels: A History of Cinema in Latin America.* London: Verso and the Latin American Bureau, 1990.

Kita, Bernice. *What a Prize Awaits Us: Letters from Guatemala.* Maryknoll, N.Y.: Orbis Books, 1988.

Klein, Herbert S. *African Slavery in Latin America and the Caribbean.* New York: Oxford University Press, 1986.

———. *Bolivia: The Evolution of a Multi-Ethnic Society.* New York: Oxford University Press, 1982.

———. *Haciendas and Ayllus: Rural Society in the Bolivian Andes in the Eighteenth and Nineteenth Centuries.* Stanford, Calif.: Stanford University Press, 1993.

Knouse, Stephen B., Paul Rosenfeld, and Amy L. Culbertson. *Hispanics in the Workplace.* Newbury Park, Calif.: Sage, 1992.

Kryzanek, Michael J. *Leaders, Leadership, and U.S. Policy in Latin America.* Boulder, Colo.: Westview Press, 1992.

Kurian, George Thomas. *Encyclopedia of the First World.* 4th ed. New York: Facts on File, 1990.

———. *Encyclopedia of the Third World.* 4th ed. New York: Facts on File, 1990.

Lang, James. *Conquest and Commerce: Spain and England in the Americas.* New York: Academic Press, 1975.

Langley, Lester D. *The Banana Wars: United States Intervention in the Caribbean, 1898–1934.* Lexington: University of Kentucky Press, 1983.

Lavrín, Asunción, ed. *Latin American Women: Historical Perspectives.* Westport, Conn.: Greenwood Press, 1978.

Lefeber, Walter. *The American Age: United States Foreign Policy at Home and Abroad.* 2d ed. New York: Norton, 1994.

Lehmann, David. *Democracy and Development in Latin America.* Philadelphia: Temple University Press, 1990.

León-Portilla, Miguel. *Fifteen Poets of the Aztec World.* Norman: University of Oklahoma Press, 1992.

———. *The Broken Spears: An Aztec Account of the Conquest of Mexico.* Boston: Beacon Press, 1962.

Lernoux, Penny. *Cry of the People: United States Involvement in the Rise of Fascism, Torture, and Murder and the Persecution of the Catholic Church in Latin America.* New York: Doubleday, 1980.

———. *In Banks We Trust.* Garden City, N.Y.: Anchor Press/Doubleday, 1984.

Levine, Daniel H. *Religion and Political Conflict in Latin America.* Chapel Hill: University of North Carolina Press, 1986.

Levine, Robert M. *Race and Ethnic Relations in Latin America and the Caribbean: A Historical Dictionary and Bibliography.* Metuchen, N.J.: Scarecrow Press, 1980.

LeVine, Sarah. *Dolor y Alegría: Women and Social Change in Urban Mexico.* Madison: University of Wisconsin Press, 1993.

Levison, James, and Juan de Onís. *The Alliance That Lost Its Way: A Critical View of the Alliance for Progress.* Chicago: Quadrangle Books, 1970.

Lewis, Oscar. *The Children of Sánchez.* New York: Vintage, 1961.

Lindqvist, Sven. *The Shadow: Latin America Faces the Seventies.* New York: Penguin, 1972.

Liss, Peggy K. *Atlantic Empires: The Network of Trade and Revolution, 1713–1826.* Baltimore: Johns Hopkins University Press, 1983.

López, George A., and Michael Stohl, eds. *Liberalization and Redemocratization in Latin America.* New York: Greenwood Press, 1987.

Lowenthal, Abraham F. *Partners in Conflict: The United States and Latin America.* Baltimore: Johns Hopkins University Press, 1987.

———, ed. *Exporting Democracy: The United States and Latin America.* Baltimore: Johns Hopkins University Press, 1991.

Lowenthal, Abraham F., and J. Samuel Fitch, eds. *Armies and Politics in Latin America.* Rev. ed. New York: Holmes and Meier, 1986.

Lunenfeld, Marvin, ed. *1492—Discovery, Invasion, Encounter: Sources and Interpretations.* Lexington, Mass.: D.C. Heath, 1991.

MacDonald, Scott B. *Mountain High, White Avalanche: Cocaine and Power in the Andean States and Panama.* Published with the Center for Strategic and International Studies. New York: Praeger, 1989.

Madrid, Raul L. *Overexposed: U.S. Banks Confront the Third World Debt Crisis.* Washington, D.C.: Investor Responsibility Research Center, 1990.

Maltby, William S. *The Black Legend in England: The Development of Anti-Spanish Sentiment, 1558–1660.* Durham, N.C.: Duke University Press, 1971.

Manguel, Alberto, ed. *Other Fires: Short Fiction by Latin American Women.* New York: Clarkson Potter, 1986.

Mannix, Daniel P., with Malcolm Cowley. *Black Cargoes: A History of the Atlantic Slave Trade, 1518–1865.* New York: Viking, 1965.

Martin, David. *Tongues of Fire: The Explosion of Protestantism in Latin America.* Oxford: Basil Blackwell, 1990.

Martínez Montiel, Luz, ed. *Asiatic Migrations in Latin America.* Mexico City: El Colegio de México, 1981.

Mattoso, Katia M. de Queirós, trans. Arthur Goldhammer. *To Be a Slave in Brazil, 1550–1888.* New Brunswick, N.J.: Rutgers University Press, 1986.

McKinney, Joseph A., and M. Rebecca Sharpless, eds. *Implications of a North American Free Trade Region: Multidisciplinary Perspectives.* Waco, Tex.: Baylor University Program for Regional Studies, 1992.

Meier, Matt S., and Feliciano Ribera. *Mexican Americans/American Mexicans: From Conquistadors to Chicanos.* New York: Hill and Wang, 1993.

Menchú, Rigoberta. *I, Rigoberta Menchú: An Indian Woman in Guatemala,* ed. Elisabeth Burgos-Debray, trans. Ann Wright. London: Verso, 1984.

Menéndez Pidal, Ramón. *The Spaniards in Their History,* trans. Walter Starkie. New York: Norton, 1950.

Merriman, Roger B. *The Rise of the Spanish Empire in the Old World and in the New.* 4 vols. New York: Macmillan, 1918–1934.

Meyer, Michael C., and William L. Sherman. *The Course of Mexican History.* 4th ed. New York: Oxford University Press, 1991.

Mintz, Sidney W. *Caribbean Transformations.* New York: Columbia University Press, 1989.
———. *Sweetness and Power: The Place of Sugar in Modern History.* New York: Viking, 1985.
Mintz, Sidney W., and Richard Price. *The Birth of African-American Culture.* Boston: Beacon, 1992.
Mexico. Alexandria, Va.: Time-Life Books, 1986.
Morales, Edmundo, ed. *Drugs in Latin America.* Williamsburg: College of William and Mary, Department of Anthropology Studies in Third World Societies, 1986.
Moreira Alves, Marcio. *A Grain of Mustard Seed: The Awakening of the Brazilian Revolution.* Garden City, N.Y.: Doubleday/Anchor Press, 1973.
Moreno Fraginals, Manuel, ed. *Africa en América Latina.* Mexico City: UNESCO, 1977.
Mörner, Magnus, with the collaboration of Harold Sims. *Adventurers and Proletarians: The Story of Migrants in Latin America.* Pittsburgh: University of Pittsburgh Press, 1985.
———. *Race Mixture in the History of Latin America.* Boston: Little, Brown, 1967.
———, ed. *Race and Class in Latin America.* New York and London: Columbia University Press, 1970.
Morrissey, Marietta. *Slave Women in the New World: Gender Stratification in the Caribbean.* Lawrence: University Press of Kansas, 1989.
Munck, Ronaldo. *Latin America: The Transition to Democracy.* London: Zed Books, 1989.
Múñoz, Heraldo, ed. *Crisis y Desarrollo Alternativo en Latinoamérica.* Santiago, Chile: Editorial Aconcagua, 1985.
Nash, June, and Helen Icken Safa, eds. *Sex and Class in Latin America.* Boston: Bergin and Garvey, 1980.
———. *Women and Change in Latin America.* Boston: Bergin and Garvey, 1986.
Needler, Martin C. *The Problem of Democracy in Latin America.* Lexington, Mass.: Heath, 1987.
Nelson, Harold D., ed. *Costa Rica: A Country Study.* Washington, D.C.: American University Foreign Area Studies, 1983.
Neruda, Pablo. *Selected Poems, A Bilingual Edition,* ed. Nathanial Tarn. New York: Dell, 1972.
1994 Information Please Almanac. New York: McGraw-Hill, 1994.
Novak, Michael, and Michael P. Jackson, eds. *Latin America: Dependency or Interdependence?* Washington, D.C.: American Enterprise Institute, 1985.
Novas, Himilce. *Everything You Need to Know about Latino History.* New York: Penguin, 1994.
Odell, Peter R., and David A. Preston. *Economies and Societies in Latin America: A Geographical Interpretation.* London: Wiley, 1973.
O'Gorman, Frances. *Aluanda: A Look at Afro-Brazilian Cults.* Rio de Janiero: Livaria Francisco Alves Editora, 1977.
Oxford Analytica. *Latin America in Perspective.* Boston: Houghton Mifflin, 1991.
Oxford Atlas of the World. 2d ed. London: Oxford University Press, 1993.
Padden, R. C. *The Hummingbird and the Hawk: Conquest and Sovereignty in the Valley of Mexico, 1503–1541.* New York: Harper Colophon, 1970.
Palmer, David Scott. *Peru: The Authoritarian Tradition.* New York: Praeger Publishers, 1980.
———, ed. *The Shining Path of Peru.* New York: St. Martin's, 1992.
Parry, J. H. *The Spanish Seaborne Empire in America.* New York: Harcourt Brace and World, 1947.

Patterson, Thomas G., J. Garry Clifford, and Kenneth J. Hagan. *American Foreign Policy: A History.* Lexington, Mass.: Heath, 1977.

Paz, Octavio. *The Labyrinth of Solitude: Life and Thought in Mexico,* trans. Lysander Kemp. New York: Grove Press, 1961.

Pérez, Sonia M., and Deirdre Martínez. *State of Hispanic America: Toward a Latino Anti-Poverty Agenda.* Washington, D.C.: Policy Analysis Center of the National Council of La Raza, 1993.

Pérez de Barradas, José. *Los Mestizos de América.* Madrid: Espasa-Calpe, 1948.

Pescatello, Ann, ed. *Female and Male in Latin America.* Pittsburgh: University of Pittsburgh Press, 1973.

Petras, James, with Howard Brill. *Latin America: Bankers, Generals, and the Struggle for Social Justice.* Totowa, N.J.: Roman and Littlefield, 1986.

Pigafetta, Antonio. *First Voyage around the World* (together with Maximilianus Transylvanus, *De Moluccis Insulis*). Manila: Filipiniana Book Guild, 1969.

Pike, Frederick B. *The United States and Latin America: Myths and Stereotypes of Civilization and Nature.* Austin: University of Texas Press, 1992.

Plotkin, Mark J. *Tales of a Shaman's Apprentice: An Ethnobotanist Searches for New Medicines in the Amazon Rain Forest.* New York: Viking, 1993.

Powell, Philip Wayne. *Tree of Hate: Propaganda and Prejudices Affecting United States Relations with the Hispanic World.* New York: Basic Books, 1971.

Preston, David, ed. *Latin American Development: Geographic Perspectives.* Essex, England: Longman Scientific and Technical, 1987.

Price, Richard, ed. *Maroon Societies.* Baltimore: Johns Hopkins University Press, 1979.

Ramírez Berg, Charles. *Cinema of Solitude: A Critical Study of Mexican Film, 1967–1983.* Austin: University of Texas Press, 1992.

Ramirez Vazquez, Pedro. *The National Museum of Anthropology: Mexico, Art, Architecture, Archaeology, Anthropology.* New York: Abrams, 1968.

Randall, Laura. *A Comparative Economic History of Latin America, 1500–1914.* Vol. 1, *Mexico;* vol. 2, *Argentina;* vol. 3, *Brazil;* vol. 4, *Peru.* New York: Columbia University Institute of Latin American Studies, 1977.

Randall, Margaret. *Women in Cuba.* New York: Smyrna Press, 1981.

Randall, Stephen J., with Herman Konrad and Sheldon Silverman, eds. *North America without Borders? Integrating Canada, the United States and Mexico.* Calgary: University of Calgary Press, 1992.

Rawley, James A. *The Transatlantic Slave Trade: A History.* New York: Norton, 1981.

Reck, Gregory G. *In the Shadow of Tlaloc: Life in a Mexican Village.* Prospect Heights, Ill.: Waveland Press, 1978.

Redfield, Robert, and Alfonso Villa R. *Chan Kom: A Maya Village.* Washington, D.C.: Carnegie Institution of Washington, 1934.

Remini, Robert. *The Legacy of Andrew Jackson: Essays on Democracy, Indian Removal, and Slavery.* Baton Rouge: Louisiana State University Press, 1988.

Ricard, Robert. *The Spiritual Conquest of Mexico: An Essay on the Apostolate and the Evengelizing Methods of the Mendicant Orders in New Spain: 1523–1572.* Berkeley and Los Angeles: University of California Press, 1966.

Ritter, Archibald R. M., Maxwell A. Cameron, and David H. Pollock. *Latin America to the Year 2000: Reactivating Growth, Improving Equity, Sustaining Democracy.* New York: Praeger, 1992.

Rivera, Julius. *Latin America: A Sociocultural Interpretation.* New York: Irvington Publishers, 1978.

Rodríguez Monegal, Emir. *The Borzoi Anthology of Latin American Literature.* Vols. 1 and 2. New York: Knopf, 1984.
Rogin, Michael Paul. *Fathers and Children: Andrew Jackson and the Subjugation of the American Indian.* New York: Knopf, 1975.
Roosevelt, Anna Curtenius, and James G. E. Smith, eds. *The Ancestors: Native Artisans of the Americas.* New York: Museum of the American Indian, 1979.
Rosenberg, Mark B., A. Douglas Kincaid, and Kathleen Logan, eds. *Americas: An Anthology.* New York: Oxford University Press, 1992.
Sable, Martin H. *The Latin American Studies Directory.* Detroit: Blaine Ethridge Books, 1981.
Sánchez-Albornoz, Nicolás. *The Population of Latin America: A History,* trans. W. A. R. Richardson. Berkeley and Los Angeles: University of California Press, 1974.
Santagada, Osvaldo D., et al. *Las Sectas en América Latina.* Buenos Aires: Editorial Clarentiana, 1984.
Sayer, Chloë. *Arts and Crafts of Mexico.* San Francisco: Chronicle Books, 1990.
Schlesinger, Stephen, and Stephen Kinzer. *Bitter Fruit: The Untold Story of the American Coup in Guatemala.* Garden City, N.Y.: Doubleday, 1982.
Shehan, John. *Patterns of Development in Latin America: Poverty, Repression, and Economic Strategy.* Princeton, N.J.: Princeton University Press, 1987.
Shields, Jerry. *The Invisible Billionaire: Daniel Ludwig.* Boston: Houghton Mifflin, 1986.
Simmen, Edward, ed. *North of the Rio Grande: The Mexican-American Experience in Short Fiction.* New York: Penguin, 1992.
Simpson, Lesley Byrd. *The Encomienda in New Spain.* Berkeley and Los Angeles: University of California Press, 1950.
———. *Many Mexicos.* Berkeley and Los Angeles: University of California Press, 1959.
Skidmore, Thomas E., and Peter H. Smith. *Modern Latin America.* 3d ed. New York: Oxford University Press, 1992.
Smith, Peter H. ed. *Drug Policy in the Americas.* Boulder, Colo.: Westview Press, 1992.
Solberg, Carl E. *The Prairies and the Pampas: Agrarian Policy in Canada and Argentina, 1880–1930.* Stanford, Calif.: Stanford University Press, 1987.
Stallings, Barbara, and Robert Kaufman, eds. *Debt and Democracy in Latin America.* Boulder, Colo.: Westview Press, 1989.
Stavenhagen, Rodolfo, Ernesto Laclau, and Ruy Mauro Marini. *Tres Ensayos Sobre America Latina.* Barcelona: Cuadernos Anagrama, 1972.
Stein, Stanley J., and Barbara H. Stein. *The Colonial Heritage of Latin America: Essays on Economic Dependence in Perspective.* New York: Oxford University Press, 1970.
Stepan, Alfred, ed. *Americas: New Interpretive Essays.* New York: Oxford University Press, 1992.
———, ed. *Democratizing Brazil: Problems of Transition and Consolidation.* New York: Oxford University Press, 1989.
Stern, Steve J. *Peru's Indian Peoples and the Challenge of Spanish Conquest: Huamanga to 1640.* Madison: University of Wisconsin Press, 1982.
Street, James H., and Dilmus D. James, eds. *Technological Progress in Latin America: The Prospects for Overcoming Dependency.* Boulder, Colo.: Westview Press, 1979.
Strong, Simon. *Shining Path: Terror and Revolution in Peru.* New York: Random House, 1992.
Tate, Bill. *The Penitentes of the Sangre de Cristos: An American Tragedy.* Truchas, N.M.: Tate Gallery, 1967.
Tenenbaum, Barbara A., ed. *Encyclopedia of Latin American History and Culture.* 5 vols. New York: Scribner, 1996.

Thompson, Vincent Bakpetu. *The Making of the African Diaspora in the Americas, 1441–1900.* New York: Longman, 1987.

Thornton, Russell. *American Indian Holocaust and Survival: A Population History since 1492.* Norman: University of Oklahoma Press, 1987.

Thorp, Rosemary, ed. *Latin America in the 1930's: The Role of the Periphery in World Crisis.* New York: St. Martin's, 1984.

Thorup, Cathryn L., and contributors. *The United States and México: Face to Face with New Technology.* New Brunswick, N.J.: Transaction Books, 1987.

Townsend, Richard F., ed. *The Ancient Americas: Art from Sacred Landscapes.* Munich: Prestel Verlag and the Art Institute of Chicago, 1992.

Traba, Marta. *Art of Latin America: 1900–1980.* Baltimore: Johns Hopkins University Press and the Inter-American Development Bank, 1994.

Tuñón Pablos, Julia. *Mujeres en México: Una Historia Olvidada.* Mexico City: Planeta, 1987.

Tupper, H. Allen, Jr. *Columbia's War for Cuba.* New York: Bromfield and Co., 1898.

Tussie, Diana, ed. *Latin America in the World Economy.* New York: St. Martin's, 1983.

Tyler, Alice Felt. *Freedom's Ferment: Phases of American Social History to 1860.* Minneapolis: University of Minnesota Press, 1944.

United Nations. *El Desarrollo de America Latina en los Anos Ochenta.* Santiago, Chile: CEPAL, 1981.

———. *Five Studies on the Situation of Women in Latin America.* Santiago, Chile: United Nations, 1983.

———. Development Program. *Human Development Report, 1990.* New York: Oxford University Press, 1990.

———. UNESCO. *Introducción a la cultura africana en América Latina.* Brujas, Belgium: Imprenta Sainte-Catherine, Brujas, 1979.

United States Bureau of the Census. *1990 Census: General Population Characteristics.* Washington, D.C.: Commerce Department, 1991.

———. *1991 International Data Base.* Washington, D.C.: U.S. Government Printing Office, 1991.

———. *Statistical Abstract of the U.S., 1992, 112th ed.* Washington, D.C.: Commerce Department, 1992

United States Senate. *Covert Action in Chile, 1963–1973.* Staff Report of the Select Committee to Study Governmental Operations with Respect to Intelligence Activities. Washington, D.C., December 18, 1975.

Velásquez de la Cadena, Mariano. *New Revised Velásquez Spanish and English Dictionary.* Chicago: Follett, 1966.

Villaseñor, Victor. *Rain of Gold.* Houston: Arte Publico Press, 1991.

Wachtel, Nathan. *The Vision of the Vanquished: The Spanish Conquest of Peru through Indian Eyes.* New York: Harper and Row, 1977.

Wallace, Anthony F. C. *The Long, Bitter Trail: Andrew Jackson and the Indians.* New York: Hill and Wang, 1993.

Wearne, Phillip, with Peter Calvert. *The Maya of Guatemala.* London: Minority Rights Group Report No. 62, 1989.

Weatherford, Jack. *Indian Givers: How the Indians of the Americas Transformed the World.* New York: Fawcett Columbine, 1988.

Webber, Christof Anders. "Announced U.S., Assistance to Latin America, 1946–88: Who Gets It? How Much? And When?" In *Statistical Abstract of Latin America,* eds. James Wilkie, Enrique C. Ochoa, and David E. Lorey, 1081–1084. Los Angeles: UCLA Latin American Center Publications, 1990.

Weber, David J., and Jane M. Rausch, eds. *Where Cultures Meet: Frontiers in Latin American History.* Wilmington, Del.: Scholarly Resources, 1994.
Weyr, Thomas. *Hispanic U.S.A.: Breaking the Melting Pot.* New York: Harper and Row, 1988.
Wiarda, Howard, Jr. *Latin America at the Crossroads: Debt, Development, and the Future.* Boulder, Colo.: Westview Press and American Enterprise Institute, 1987.
———, ed. *The Continuing Struggle for Democracy in Latin America.* Boulder, Colo.: Westview Press, 1980.
———, ed. *Politics and Social Change in Latin America: Still a Distinct Tradition?* 3d ed. Boulder, Colo.: Westview Press, 1992.
Wilkie, James W., ed. *Statistical Abstract of Latin America.* Vol. 31. Los Angeles: UCLA Latin American Center Publications, 1995.
Wilkie, James W., Enrique C. Ochoa, and David E. Lorey, eds. *Statistical Abstract of Latin America.* Vol. 28. Los Angeles: UCLA Latin American Center Publications, 1990.
Willems, Emilio. *Latin American Culture: An Anthropological Synthesis.* New York: Harper and Row, 1975.
Williamson, René de Visme. *Culture and Policy: The United States and the Hispanic World.* Knoxville: University of Tennessee Press, 1949.
World Bank Atlas. Washington, D.C.: International Bank for Reconstruction and Development, 1995.
Worldmark Encyclopedia of the Nations. 5 vols., 7th ed. New York: Worldmark Press, 1988.
World Motor Vehicle Data, 1995. Washington, D.C.: American Automobile Manufacturers Association, 1995.

SOURCES USED: PERIODICALS

Althaus, Dudley. "The New Awakening: The New Faith, An Evangelical Earthquake." *Houston Chronicle,* October 4, 1992.
Andriance, Madeleine. "The Paradox of Institutionalization: The Roman Catholic Church in Chile and Brazil." *Sociological Analysis* 53, Suppl. (1992): S51–S63.
Bailey, Jessica M., and James H. Sood. "Banana Pricing Strategies for Exporting Companies." *Inter-American Economic Affairs* 39, no. 2 (Autumn 1985): 45–62.
Binswanger, Hans P. "Brazilian Policies That Encourage Deforestation in the Amazon." *World Development* 19, no. 7 (1991): 821–829.
Birdsall, Nancy, and Rebecca J. Foster Lowenthal. "Lessons from the East." *Institute of the Americas, Hemisphile: Perspectives on Political and Economic Trends in the Americas* 5, no. 4 (July–August 1994): 6–7.
Bitar, Sergio. "United States–Latin American Relations: Shifts in Economic Power and Implications for the Future." *Journal of Inter-American Studies* 26, no. 1 (January, 1984): 3–31.
Bodovitz, Kathy. "Hispanic America." *American Demographics* 13, no. 7 (July 1991): 15.
"A Brief History of the Mexican Economy." *Harvard Business Review* 72, no. 1 (1993): 38–39.
Burnett, Virginia Garrard. "Protestantism in Latin America." *Latin American Research Review* 27, no. 1 (Winter 1992): 218–231.
Cardoso, Fernando Henrique. "Freedom for the Have Nots." *UNESCO Courier,* November 1992, 21–25.
Castañeda, Jorge G. "Can NAFTA Change Mexico?" *Foreign Affairs* 20, no. 4 (September–October 1993): 66–80.
Center for International Education, U.S. Dept. of Education. *Title VI National Resource Centers.* Washington, D.C.: March 1993.

"A Chasm of Misery: Latin America's Rich and Poor Have Become Separate, Wary Societies." *Time,* November 6, 1989, 64–66.

Cloud, David S. "The History of the Deal [NAFTA]." *Congressional Quarterly Weekly Report,* November 20, 1993, 3180.

Coleman, John A. "Will Latin America Become Protestant?" *Commonweal,* January 25, 1991, 59–64.

Congressional Quarterly Weekly Report, "The Nuts and Bolts of NAFTA." November 20, 1993, 3178.

Constable, Pamela. "At War's End in El Salvador." *Current History* 92, no. 572 (March 1993): 106–111.

Conway, Patrick. "Debt and Adjustment." *Latin American Research Review* 27, no. 2 (1992): 151–225.

Cook, Guillermo. "The Evangelical Groundswell in Latin America." *Christian Century,* December 12, 1990, 1172–1180.

Correa, Carlos María. "Software Industry: An Opportunity for Latin America?" *World Development* 18, no. 11 (1990): 1588–1598.

Crew, Jan. "United We Stand! Joint Struggles of Native Americans and African Americans in the Columbian Era." *Monthly Review,* July–August 1992, 103–127.

DaMatta, Roberto. "Umbanda, Religion and Politics in Urban Brazil." *Journal of Social History* 25, no. 2 (Winter 1991): 389–407.

Dillin, John. "Foreign-Born Earn Higher Science Salaries." *Christian Science Monitor,* April 19, 1994, 3.

Duggan, Patrice. "Latin America's Overheated Debt Swap Market." *Forbes,* November 28, 1988, 38–42.

Erlich, R. "Phone Companies Fight for Burgeoning Latino Market." *Christian Science Monitor,* March 30, 1994, 8.

Frey, Bruno S., and Friedrich Scheider. "Competing Models of International Lending Activity." *Journal of Development Economics* 20, no. 2 (March 1986): 222–245.

Galeano, Eduardo. "Language, Lies and Latin Democracy." *Harper's,* February 1990, 19–23.

Gang, Ira, and James A. Lehman. "New Directions or Not: USAID in Latin America." *World Development* 18, no. 5 (1990): 723–732.

Girvan, Norman P., and Gillian Marcelle. "Overcoming Technological Dependency: The Case of Electric Arc (Jamaica) Ltd., A Small Firm in a Small Developing Country." *World Development* 18, no. 1 (1990): 91–107.

Goodman, Timothy, and Tom Ryan. "Latin America's Reformation." *American Enterprise* 2, no. 4 (July–August 1991): 40–48.

Guillermoprieto, Alma. "Losing the Future." *New Yorker,* April 4, 1994, 53–56.

Hakim, Peter, and Abraham Lowenthal. "Democracy on Trial: Politics in Latin America." *Current,* February 1992, 28–36.

Harrison, Lawrence E. "Latin American Democracy and the Market Are Not Enough." *World Affairs* 155, no. 4 (Spring 1993): 169–173.

Heller, Michele A. "Off the Air: Why Aren't Hispanics on the Networks?" *Hispanic,* August 1994, 30–34.

Hojunian, David E. "From Mexican Plantations to Chilean Mines: The Theoretical and Empirical Relevance of Enclave Theories in Contemporary Latin America." *Inter-American Economic Affairs* 39, no. 3 (Winter 1985): 27–53.

Inter-American Development Bank. *Development Policy: Newsletter on Policy Research of the Inter-American Development Bank* 1, no. 1 (March 1992): 6.

Kane, Joe. "Moi Goes to Washington," *New Yorker,* May 24, 1994, 74–81.

Krugman, Paul R. "Debt Relief Is Cheap." *Foreign Policy* 20, no. 4 (Fall 1990): 141–153.

"Latin Americans Keep Lots of Cash Abroad." *Wall Street Journal,* April 16, 1990, A9c.
"Latinos on the Rise." *The Futurist,* January–February 1993.
Lesser, Jeff. "Watching the Detectives: Four Views of Immigrant Life in Latin America [film review]." *Latin American Research Review* 27, no. 1 (1992): 231–244.
"Lessons Learned: Twenty-Eight Years of AID." *Agenda* 4, no. 9 (November 1981): 2–6.
Levine, Daniel H. "Popular Groups, Popular Culture, and Popular Religion." *Comparative Studies in Society and History* 32, no. 4 (October 1990): 718–765.
Lichter, S. Robert, and Daniel R. Amundson. "From Ricky Ricardo to . . . the Menendezes?" *Boston Globe,* September 11, 1994, 72.
Lowenthal, Abraham F. "Charting a New Course." *Institute of the Americas, Hemisphile: Perspectives on Political and Economic Trends in the Americas* 5, no. 4 (July–August 1994): 1–2+.
Lustig, Nora. "Economic Crisis, Adjustments and Living Standards in Mexico, 1982–1985." *World Development* 18, no. 10 (1990): 1325–1342.
MacPhee, Craig R., and M. K. Hassan. "Some Economic Determinants of Third World Professional Immigration to the United States, 1972–1987." *World Development* 18, no. 8 (1990): 1111–1118.
Maizels, Alfred, and Machiko K. Nissanke. "Motivation for Aid to Developing Countries." *World Development* 12, no. 9 (September 1984): 879–900.
Marcella, Gabriel. "The Latin American Military, Low Intensity Conflict, and Democracy." *Journal of Interamerican Studies and World Affairs* 32, no. 1 (Spring 1990): 45–83.
Martin, David, and David Lee. "Speaking in Latin Tongues: The Protestantization of Latin America." *National Review,* September 29, 1989, 30–36.
Michaels, James W. "The Fire Down South." *Forbes,* October 15, 1990, 8, 8–9.
Minard, Lawrence. "The New Missionaries." *Forbes,* May 14, 1990, 41–43.
Nairn, Alan. "Behind the Death Squads." *The Progressive,* May 1984, 21–29.
"The Other Crumbling Empire." *Economist,* February 10, 1990, 26.
Pastor, Manuel, Jr. "Capital Flight from Latin America." *World Development* 18, no. 1 (January 1990): 1–18.
Pastor, Manuel, Jr., and Eric Hilt. "Private Investment and Democracy in Latin America." *World Development* 155, no. 4 (April 1993): 169–173.
Pauly, David. "The New Spelling of Relief: Brady Unveils a Plan to Ease the Latin Debt Crisis." *Newsweek,* March 20, 1989, 32.
Pérez, Louis A., Jr. "Protestant Missionaries in Cuba: Archival Records, Manuscript Collections and Research Prospects." *Latin American Research Review* 27, no. 1 (1992): 105–120.
Portales, Alejandro. "Latin American Class Structures: Their Composition and Change during the Last Decades." *Labor* 20, no. 3 (1985): 7–39.
"Rep. Flood Had Secret Ties to Haiti While Pushing US Aid to Duvalier." *New York Times,* February 5, 1978, 1, 19.
Roberts, Paul Craig. "No Relief on Latin Debt without World Bank Reform." *Business Week,* March 6, 1989, 15.
Rosenberg, Tina. "Beyond Elections." *Foreign Policy,* Fall/91, n84, 72–92.
Rosenthal, Gert. "Some Thoughts on Poverty and Recession in Latin America." *Journal of Inter-American Studies and World Affairs* 31, nos. 1 and 2 (Spring–Summer 1989): 63–73.
Rother, Larry. "Liberal Wing of Haiti's Catholic Church Resists Military." *New York Times* (International) Sunday, July 24, 1994, 3.
Rowan, Hobart. "The Third World's Good News." *Washington Post National Weekly,* May 17, 1992, 5.

Ryser, Jeffrey. "Latin America's Protestants: A Potent New Force for Change." *Business Week,* June 18, 1990, 79–80.

Sherman, L. Roger, and Norman A. Bailey. "Putting Latin American Debt to Work: A Positive Role for the United States." *Journal of Latin American Studies and World Affairs* 31, no. 4 (Winter 1989): 1–21.

Smith, Peter H. "Crisis and Democracy in Latin America." *World Politics* 43, no. 4 (July 1991): 608–635.

"Some Latin American Nations' Actions Add to Risk of Holding Cash Accounts." *Wall Street Journal,* April 16, 1990, A9c.

Stafford, Tim. "The Hidden Fire." *Christianity Today,* May 14, 1990, 23–27.

"Step Up the Pace of Latin Debt Write-offs" (editorial). *Business Week,* March 13, 1989, 164.

Stewart-Gambino, Hannah W. "Umbanda: Religion and Politics in Urban Brazil." *Latin American Research Review* 24, no. 3 (Summer 1989): 187–200.

Stoll, David. "A Protestant Reformation in Latin America?" *Christian Century,* January 17, 1990, 44–49.

Stoltz Chinchilla, Norma. "Marxism, Feminism and the Struggle for Democracy in Latin America." *Gender and Society* 5, no. 3 (August 1991): 291–311.

Tapia, Andres. "Why Is Latin America Turning Protestant?" *Christianity Today,* April 6, 1992, 28–30.

Thiesenhusen, William C., and Jolyne Melmed-Sanjak. "Brazil's Agrarian Structure: Changes from 1970 through 1980." *World Development* 18, no. 3 (1990): 393–415.

"Tuned Out: TV Portrayals of Ethnic Groups." *Hispanic,* November 1994, 10.

"US to Seek Release of Businessman in Haiti to Hear His Testimony about Rep. Flood." *New York Times,* March 19, 1978, 27.

Vessuri, Hebe M. C. "O Inventamos o Erramos: The Power of Science in Latin America." *World Development* 18, no. 11 (1990): 1543–1553.

"The World after NAFTA, According to Paz." *New Yorker,* December 27, 1993, 57.

"World's Pay Scale." *Los Angeles Times,* October 1, 1991, H-3.

GLOSSARY

abrazo (ah-BRAH-zoh) An embrace, a psychological bonding.

Acción Democrática (AD) "Democratic Action," the political party that struggled to achieve Venezuelan democracy.

Agrarian Transformation The global transition from hunting and gathering to an agrarian ethic.

Aleijandinho (ah-lay-shawn-DEEN-yo) Colonial era Afro-Brazilian sculptor.

amigo (ah-MEE-go) A close friend.

asiento (ah-see-EN-toh) The colonial era imperial contract to import African slaves into Spanish American colonies.

audiencia (aw-dee-EN-see-a) Governing council appointed to advise viceroys and govern in their absence.

autos sacramentales (AW-tohs sah-crah-men-TAH-lays) Colonial era sacred plays, usually written by clerics for Indigens.

bandeirante (bahn-dey-RHAN-chay) Indigen bounty hunter and prospector who explored and extended Brazil's frontiers.

barrio (BAR-reo) Neighborhood, locality.

basismo (communidades de base) (bah-SEES-mo) Building block of theology of liberation; neighborhood mutual support group.

Batlle y Ordóñez, José Progressive criollo leader of Uruguay in the first decades of the twentieth century.

la boom The proliferation of quality Latin American writing during the late twentieth century.

botanica (boh-TAN-ee-kah) An eclectic spiritualist store associated with people of African Latin ancestry.

Bourbon dynasty Characteristically progressive Spanish dynasty that governed after 1701.

bracero (brah-SER-o) From brazo (arm); a menial laborer.

caballero (cah-bah-YEAH-roh) A gentleman; formerly a horseman.

cabildos de nación (kah-BILL-dohs day nah-see-OHN) Colonial era cultural societies formed by slaves and former slaves.

cacique (kah-SEE-kay) Native chief, political boss.

campesino (cam-peh-SEE-no) Fieldhand, rural worker.

casa de contratación (CAH-sah dey cohn-trah-tah-see-OHN) House of Trade; colonial Spanish bureaucracy supervising commerce.

casarse (cah-SAR-say) To marry; literally, to "enhouse."

castas (CAHS-tahs) Castes; term for nonwhites in colonial era.
caudillo (call-DEE-yoh) A political strongman, a personalist leader, a military chieftain.
ch'alla (CHA-yah) Earth mother ritual of Andean Indigens.
chinampas (chee-NAM-pahs) Indigen marshland island gardens in Mexico.
church of coercion One aspect of Latin American Catholicism.
church of compassion Another aspect of Latin American Catholicism.
cimarron (see-mah-ROHN) A Maroon, a runaway slave.
commercial transformation A societal ethic resulting from the evolution to ever wider economic intercourse.
compadre (com-PAH-drey) Godfather; plural means "godparents."
con los tuyos, con razón o sin ella (kohn los TU-yohs, kohn ra-ZONE oh sin AY-yah) "Loyalty to relatives, right or wrong."
la conquista (la-con-KEY-stah) The conquests of the Americas from 1492 to about 1560.
consulados (con-su-LAH-dohs) Colonial era merchant houses.
contras (COHN-tras) Counterrevolutionary mercenaries, funded by Ronald Reagan's administration, who opposed Nicaragua's governing Sandinistas.
conversos (con-VER-sos) Converts, colonial era Jews and Muslims who converted to Christianity, "new Christians."
corregidor de Indios (coh-rey-hee-DOR dey IN-dee-os) Local administrator of Indigen relations in colonial times.
costumbrismo (kos-toom-BREEZ-moh) In nineteenth-century art and literature, the quaint portrayal of everyday Latin Americans.
criollo (kree-OH-yos) Person born in the new world but of European ancestry and sharing European values and culture.
cross and sword Symbols of mutually supportive authority characterizing colonial era Spanish state and church.
cuartelazo (quar-teh-LAH-zoh) A barrack or military revolt.
cura (KOO-rah) Local parish priest.
curanderos/as (koo-rhan-DARE-ohs) Folk spiritualists, curers.
Darío, Rubén (1867–1916) Nicaraguan modernist poet.
debt-equity swap A financial deal in which ownership of Latin American property is exchanged for interest-bearing notes.
desaparedicos (day-sah-pah-ray-SEE-dohs) "The disappeared"; citizens kidnapped and killed by military governments.
descamisados (des-cah-mee-SAH-dohs) "Shirtless ones"; workers in Argentina who allied with Juan and Eva Perón.
día de muerte (DEE-a day MUER-tay) Day of the Dead, November 30, celebrates deceased family members, especially in Mexico.
dollar diplomacy Early-twentieth-century U.S. policy using debt manipulation to control Latin American governments.
dolor (dough-LORE) Pain, suffering (a symbol of dedication).
duende (DWEN-dey) A dwarfish, prankster spirit.
en buena guerra (en BWAY-nah GARE-rah) A "just" war; one that supposedly legitimized the taking of prisoners (or slaves).
encantado (en-can-TAH-doh) In Afro-Brazilian cults, a person possessed by spirits.
encomendero (en-coh-men-DARE-o) The holder of a grant known as an *encomienda.*
encomienda (en-koh-mee-EN-dah) An early colonial program of entrusting Indigen communities to Spanish colonists.

engage (en-GAH-hay) Colonial term for indentured Iberian servants contracted to work in the American colonies.
espíritus (es-PEE-ree-toos) Spirits.
European era In the Americas, the centuries following 1492.
evangélicos (ee-van-GEL-ee-cohs) Modern Protestant evangelists.
feitoria (fay-TOR-ria) "Factory," "plantation"; processing center for captured slaves on the west African coast.
Fuentes, Carlos Late-twentieth-century Mexican novelist; author of *The Death of Artemio Cruz.*
fuero (FWAY-roh) Legal, political, or social right or privilege; an exemption from normal civil law or duty.
García Márquez, Gabriel Late-twentieth-century Colombian novelist; author of *One Hundred Years of Solitude.*
Garcilaso de la Vega, Inca Born in 1536, son of an Inca princess and a Spanish captain; wrote from a mestizo perspective.
gauchismo (gawl-CHEES-moh) Popular nineteenth- and twentieth-century art and literary genre depicting gauchos.
gauchupine (ghow-choo-PEE-nay) "Spurred one"; colonial Mexican slang for the privileged, especially *peninsulares.*
gente decente (HEN-tay dee-SEN-tay) "Decent class" persons; those of European background and values.
golpe, golpe de estado (GOL-pey day es-TAH-doh) A blow to the state; a coup or overthrow of legitimate government.
greasers Early Hollywood genre depicting Latin Americans as dirty and ruthless.
guerrilla (gare-REE-yah) "Small war"; an insurrection, also a rebel.
hacendado (ah-sen-DAH-doh) The owner of a hacienda.
hacienda (also *la estancia,* known as the *fazenda* in Brazil) From late colonial times to the twentieth century, a landed estate with feudal-like social system.
Hapsburg dynasty Conservative rulers of Spain, 1516–1701.
hermandad (erh-mahn-DAHD) Brotherhood, military clan.
hidalgos (from *hijo de algo,* "son of somebody") Petty nobility.
el hombre por la lengua, la mujer por los piernas (el OHM-bray pour lah LEN-gua, lah moo-HAIR pour los PIERRE-nas) "The man for his speech, the woman for her legs"; a popular phrase expressing historic machismo.
human capital Technical expertise created by a society's expenditures on educating its citizens.
Humboldt, Alexander von Early-nineteenth-century naturalist who visited Spanish America and published his findings.
Iberian Person or thing from Europe's Iberian peninsula (Spain and Portugal).
Indian A person from India; a term mistakenly or deceptively applied to new world inhabitants in 1492.
The Indies A colonial term for Spain's American colonies.
Indigen A person descended from pre-Columbian Americans.
indigenismo (in-dee-hen-EES-mo) A movement to extol native cultures and peoples, strong in the early twentieth century.
industrial transformation Modes of thinking and doing resulting from the application of energy to productive efficiencies.
Inés de la Cruz, Sor Juana (Juana de Asbeje) Seventeenth-century Mexican poet.

informal economy Commerce and entrepreneurship beyond the bounds of legality and regulation.
inner world A supportive network of family and intimates.
ISI (import substitution industrialization) An economic policy seeking to replace imports with domestic production.
junta (HOON-tah) "Group"; in politics, a governing council.
Kahlo, Frida Early-twentieth-century Mexican painter.
ladino (lah-DEE-no) An Indigen who adopts European customs and values; sometimes synonoymous with mestizo.
Las Casas, Bartolome de Conquest era Dominican priest, historian, and Indigen advocate known as "Defender of the Indians."
latifundia Land use system characterized by ownership of large estates.
la leyenda blanca "White legend"; mythology of supposed Anglo-American superiority.
la leyenda negra The "black legend"; historic Anglo-American propaganda portraying hispanic society as inferior.
limpieza de sangre (lim-PAY-zah day SAN-grey) "Pure blood"; concept of impeccable Spanish and Catholic lineage.
lo mas barato (loh mahs ba-RAH-toh) The cheapest.
lost decade The 1980s, a period of economic depression in Latin America.
la lucha (lah LOU-cha) The "struggle"; gaining esteem by overcoming odds.
machismo (mah-CHEEZ-mo) Male strength, bravado, courage, or dominance.
macho (MAH-choh) Someone who practices machismo.
mae/pai-de-santo (my/pie day SAN-toh) Priestess and priest in Afro-Brazilian cult.
magical realism Late-twentieth-century literary style that exaggerates the common and makes the impossible seem natural.
mameluco (mah-may-LOO-koh) Brazilian term for mestizo.
marianismo (mah-ree-an-EES-mo) The cult of the Virgin Mary; characteristics related to the mother of Christ.
Martí, José Late-nineteenth-century Cuban poet and nationalist.
Martín Fierro (mar-TEEN FIER-oh) Mythic gaucho character of nineteenth-century writer José Hernández.
el mercado (el mer-CAH-doh) Market or marketplace.
mestizaje (MEZ-tee-ZAH-hey) Racial mixing that creates mestizos.
mestizo (mes-TEE-so) Of mixed European-Indigen background; a culture distinct from either parent group.
mi casa es su casa "My home is your home."
micro democracy Local level self-rule; "grass roots" movement.
minifundia Land-use system based on small plots.
modernism Late-nineteenth-century literary movement.
mordida (mor-DEE-dah) "The bite"; a bribe.
Mothers of the Disappeared Women dissidents who organized on behalf of *desaparecidos* in Argentina in the 1980s and 1990s.
mulatto (moo-LOT-o) Person of mixed African/European background.
multiplier effect What happens when investments repeatedly recirculate within an economy.
NAFTA The North American Free Trade Agreement among Canada, the U.S., and Mexico.
national era The period up to the present following the general achievement of political sovereignty after the 1820s.

National Security Doctrine Repressive U.S. policy in the 1960s and 1970s to oppose reform and revolution in Latin America.
native era In the Americas, the time of Indigen dominance; from 30,000 B.C.E. to the sixteenth century.
Neruda, Pablo Twentieth-century Chilean poet.
New Christians Spanish Muslims, but particularly Jews who converted to Catholicism in colonial times.
NGOs (nongovernmental organizations) Citizen volunteer groups.
el norte "The north"; popular Latin American term for the U.S.
nuestra América (noo-ES-trah ah-MARE-ee-ka) "Our America"; modernist term for Latin as opposed to Anglo America.
Obregón, Alvaro Mexican Revolution general and president who lessened the military role in politics.
orgullo (or-GOO-yoh) Pride, sometimes haughtiness.
orgulloso (or-gu-YO-so) Proud, haughty.
outer world The public and potentially threatening society beyond one's intimate circle of family and connections.
pacha mama The Andean term for earth mother.
palabra (pah-LAH-brah) "Word"; spoken or written speech, one's quality of expressiveness.
palenques (pah-LEN-kays) Colonial era communities of runaway slaves and Indigens hidden in remote forests or mountains.
patria chia (PAH-tria CHEE-ka) "Small fatherland"; loyalty to one's locality.
patrón (pah-TROHN) Patron or boss; owner.
patronato real (pah-troh-NAH-toh ray-AHL) "Royal patronage"; the right of Spanish monarchs to appoint Catholic bishops.
Paz, Octavio Twentieth-century Mexican poet and essayist.
peninsular (pay-nin-soo-LAR) Colonial era term for a person from Iberia; a member of the social elite.
personalismo (per-son-ahl-EES-moh) Personal charm or dynamism.
el pik (el PEEK) Late-winter strawberry picking in Mexico.
Platt Amendment Early-nineteenth-century U.S. policy to control Cuban politics, finances, and diplomacy.
Plattification The process of reducing Latin American governments to the will of Washington policy makers.
poder (poh-DARE) "Power"; "to be able to."
Posada, José Guadalupe Mexican caricaturist famous for depicting skeletons.
positivism Nineteenth-century philosophy; the idea that whites lead others toward material plenty and political stability.
Potosí Site of once rich silver mines.
PRI (Party of Revolutionary Institutions) Has dominated Mexican politics in the twentieth century.
quilombos (key-LOM-bohs) Colonial era communities formed by runaway slaves in Brazil.
la reconquista (la ray-cohn-KEY-stah) Recapture of Iberia from Islam by Christian forces between 711 and 1492.
reducción (ray-duke-see-OWN) "Reduction"; a "mission"; community of Christianized Indigens organized by Catholic clerics.
***repartimiento* (or *mita,* in the Andes)** The division of native workers among Spanish colonists.

Rivera, Diego Early-twentieth-century Mexican muralist.
Rodó, Enrique Early-twentieth-century Uruguayan essayist who wrote *Ariel y Calaban.*
Roosevelt Corollary President Theodore Roosevelt's statement that the U.S. should be the policeman of the hemisphere.
Rosas, Juan Manuel Early-nineteenth-century *caudillo* and dictator in Argentina.
Santa Anna, Antonio de Early-nineteenth-century Mexican *caudillo.*
Santiago (san-ti-AH-go) The warrior-monk patron saint of Spain.
sedentary societies Predominant social pattern of pre-Columbian America; permanent towns.
semisedentary societies Hunter-gathering societies, sometimes farming small and temporary plots.
se obedece, pero no se cumple (say o-bay-DAY-say PEAR-oh no say COHM-play) "One obeys but does not comply"; popular phrase meaning to fulfill the form but not the substance of obligation.
syncretism Blending of similar aspects of different religions.
Tamayo, Rufino Twentieth-century Mexican painter.
la tandona (lah tan-DOUGH-nah) "The rotation"; the dominant military brotherhood in El Salvador during the 1980s.
técnicos (TECH-nee-kohs) Late-twentieth-century political and economic leaders following North American type policies.
theology of liberation Radical Catholicism based on Marxist-Christian ideas; important in the late twentieth century.
la tierra (lah TIER-rah) Mystical concept of the land used extensively in Latin American arts and literature.
tierra caliente "Hot land"; tropical rain forest or desert.
tierra fria "Cold land"; polar or semi-polar conditions at high altitudes in the tropics or in southern South America.
tierra templada Temperate lands of mild climate found throughout Latin America.
"trickle down" economics Belief that investments eventually benefit the lowest wage earners in an economy.
"trickle up" economics Process by which profits accumulate in the top rather than bottom income groups of a society.
Velasco, José María Late-nineteenth-century Mexican painter.
viceroy "vice-king"; imperial representative in colonial times.
Virgin of Guadalupe The mestizo patron saint of Mexico.
zambos (ZAM-bohs) Colonial era blend of African and Indigen.

INDEX